Dave Ramsden was born in Bradford in  woodlice. He was class clown at school troop idiot in the Royal Engineers. He is country with an MA in Classical Civilisati teach history in an inner city secondary s ...inveterate diarist, who has raced sidecars and ridden amateur speedway and motorcycle trials, as well as travelling widely in the UK and Europe by motorcycle and bicycle.

Reviews for As the Crow Flies

'Dave Ramsden is at war with the modern world and half the people in it, but is he fighting a losing battle?'
Bertie Bassett, *Barnsley Whisperer*.

'Caution, may contain nuts, porridge, political vituperation, coarse language and crudités.'
Elsie Tofu, *Allergy Sufferers' Weekly*

'In his battle with the forces of evil Ramsden goes over the top many times. The message, or moral, is only strengthened by its endless repetition.'
Cornelius van de Plumber, *Commercial Vehicle Monthly*

'I can't believe this man's tenacity, he's like a rabbit with a bone – or is that a dog with a rabbit?'
Billy Dogood, *You and Your Environment*

'Porridge, perspiration, privation and polemics – Dave Ramsden's epic travel diary has it all.'
Dolly Coffin, *Trumpton Times*

'Ramsden's language is playful and at times pompous, his analogies are both crude and subtle. His references are erudite. There's something for everyone.'
Seetha Kanin, *What Dog?*

'Dave Ramsden has much to get off his chest. The bicycle is only a vehicle.'
Rajit Rajit-Rajit, *Fishing Times*

'Ramsden's stream of consciousness style is full of passion and poetry. One may not agree with his conclusions, but they are forcefully made.'
Lieutenant Colonel Quentin Hyphen-Snob, RAOB, CDM and bar, *Imperialism Today*

'He might be in the fields, but he's never on the fence. A Yorkshireman says what he means and means what he says. If in doubt, give it a clout.'
Christian Hypocrite, *Drystone Wallers' Weekly*

'The world as Dave Ramsden sees it - An antidote to that wanker Clarkson.'
Billy Whizz, *Fast Cars*

As the Crow Flies

2,500 miles on a homemade bicycle

David P Ramsden

To my friend Shamaila
All the best for the future

'...you can be one of those travellers who stay in motion... and never arrive or feel they ought to... the journey is the destination... travel was flight and pursuit in equal parts.'
Paul Theroux, *The Great Railway Bazaar*

'If I could only find the words I would write it all down. If I could only find a voice I would speak.'
Meatloaf, *Read 'em and weep*

The ABC of Cycling

The ABC of cycling
Is anathema to cars
I'll forsake all modern comforts
And sleep beneath the stars

I'll travel among nature
Of which men are a part
I'll meet all kinds of people
And quote them from the start

I'll enter every chapel
And smile at every child
I'll take my pen and make a note
Where morals are defiled

I will not fear the forests
Or creatures of the night
I'll revel in the darkness
And celebrate the light

In solitude or company
On tarmac or on track
I'll harbour inner fantasies
Of never going back

And when I meet inclemency
I'll shelter beneath trees
As sure as any man can be
I'm doing as I please

In the spring of 2019 I embarked on a bicycle tour of Britain to visit the places that came first under each letter in the index of my 1998 AA road atlas. I excluded any places that were on islands, unless there was a bridge. In the absence of anywhere beginning with X a random selection produced a second P. Set out on a map of the country they provided a good spread and a reasonably round trip route.

The destinations were Ab Kettleby (Leicestershire), Babbacombe (Devon), Caborne (Lincolnshire), Daccombe (Devon), Eagland Hill (Lancashire), Faccombe (Hampshire), Gabroc Hill (East Ayrshire), Habberley (Shropshire), Ibberton (Dorset), Jack in the Green (Devon), Kaber (Cumbria), Laceby (Lincolnshire), Mabe Burnthouse (Cornwall), Naast (Highlands), Oad Street (Kent), Packington (Leicestershire), Quabbs (Shropshire), Rachan Mill (Borders), Sabden (Lancashire), Tackley (Oxfordshire), Ubbeston Green (Suffolk), Valtos (Isle of Skye), Wackerfield (Durham), (X)Padanaram (Angus), Y Felinheli (Gwynedd), Zeal Monachorum (Devon).

To make the journey more interesting I undertook it on my favourite bike, which I made from scratch in 2014. The main frame is industrial steel box-section. The crank set is made using bits of old motorcycle handlebar. The forks are of a girder type seen on early motorcycles. For the trip I modified the bike to take a fourteen speed hub gear. It was fitted with big motorcycle handlebars and a sprung Brooks saddle. I made a rear carrier to take Ortleib waterproof bags.

I carried a small budget tent, air bed and sleeping bag, cooking equipment, spare clothes a few tools, an inner tube, spare pedal shafts for my home-made pedals, because I have snapped two in the past, and not much else. The plan was to wild camp or stay on campsites if I came across them. I don't use electronic cycling aids or a mobile phone and my only contact with home was by postcard.

I began the trip on Saturday 20th April and planned to be away for two months.

Day 1 - Huddersfield to Trough of Bowland (via Sabden)

(Yorkshire and Lancashire)

I was up early and at 7.30 set off on my home-made, army green, box section bicycle, equipped with fourteen speed Rohloff rear hub, via the Spen Greenway and main road to St George's Square, Huddersfield for a prearranged *grand départ* to my ABC of Britain tour. About thirty people came to see me off and there was lots of interest in my map, route, where I will stay, what I'll eat and how far I'll ride in a day, most of which I'd yet to discover.

Photographs were taken in front of the statue of Harold Wilson, and I said a last goodbye to Oades, who must have felt very strange. Along with the good wishes, I was presented with a bottle of beer and two packets of energy bars and I rode off at precisely ten o'clock to a big round of applause. Only after fifty yards did I realise I hadn't thanked everyone for coming, but it was too late, I was on my own.

I took the main road towards Halifax, including the long descent on the Elland bypass, and picked up the canal at Salterhebble Basin for the easy ride to Hebden Bridge. The sky was bright blue and a hot day was forecast. Even though it was less than eighteen hours since I was beside it the canal was beautiful – as was its continuation through woods and lanes to Hebden Bridge.

Before tackling the climb up through Heptonstall I sat in the park to begin Paul Theroux's *The Kingdom by the Sea*, about his early 1980s tour of Britain. The park was full of preparations for picnics and passing conversations in English and Punjabi. A boy balanced his bicycle on the front wheel as well as the back one.

Theroux pertinently refers to two books, the titles of which are *What went wrong?* and *Is Britain dying?* Which are fair questions. Then an old bloke called Malcolm came along. He was from Suffolk, visiting his daughter and knew all about cycling, camping and vicarious travel. He'd just bought an e-bike and we chatted for half an hour. He said I'd inspired him, presumably where dozens of travelogues and hundreds of cycling magazines hadn't. He must have been eighty.

The town was still awful – a traffic jam with shops – only more so as, being sunny, it was full of multi-coloured grockles.

I bought water at the Co-op (49p for two litres) and carried most of it up the hill, which wasn't too bad via the main road, rather than through the village, which I've seen before. It's mostly stone, old and expensive.

Sat on a stile at the top I had to shift for mother and daughter Claire and Pat from Bolton. Claire worked for a charity – a children's hospice. When they asked if I was doing a blog I said I was still stuck in the 1980s, which I shouldn't say because I'm not – I simply choose not to use a mobile phone. Pat said she was too. They were walking to Hardcastle Crags. They had no choice as the car park at the Crags had been full since nine o'clock.

Looking down into the popular beauty spot I could see pink humans lying on blankets listening to loud music. Obviously the internet doesn't entirely do it for them.

The scenery is a cliché and, unlike the road between Haworth and Oakworth yesterday, it isn't littered with pizza boxes and beer tins.

Over the moors many of the walls, most of which long since ceased to serve any useful purpose and are falling down, are built of stones that it would have taken several men to lift. Like many things they were once so important and now aren't.

It was past Widdop Reservoir before I saw anything deliberately dumped, and that was two sacks of waste bone and gristle. After that there were numerous piles of the cannabis root balls that are these days everywhere.

After turning by the WWII concrete lookout for Brierfield I sat in a big car park picnic area with the road I'd just travelled snaking over the hill opposite. Half a mile away at a farm dogs barked. A man shouted 'quiet' and they were. For a few seconds everything else was peaceful. Then three lads put music on their mobile phones, and cars passed every few minutes.

3

According to Theroux '"We're awful," say the English, "This country is hopeless. We're never prepared for anything. Nothing works properly." But being self-critical in this way was also a tactic for remaining ineffectual. It was surrender.'

A family were enjoying the view on the next bench. I went to talk to them using the view as an excuse (and regret not getting their names). They were from Burnley and regular visitors. After I'd told them what I was doing and they'd asked questions they wished me luck and told me to look after myself. They waved at me out of their car on the way down the hill.

I was determined not to go into Burnley and took a potluck right turn. My guesswork was soon confirmed by Tim and Sandra who were just leaving their home for a cycle ride.

Climbing out of Brierfield and looking back over the bypass the three most significant edifices were a massive empty mill, a mosque and an empty gas tank – what we used to call a gasometer.

And then, via Fence and Higham, two posh pubs and some very expensive houses I was in Sabden, the first of twenty six places I have decided to visit.

I walked up the hill out of Higham with Stu, who lives there. He said it was to be a degree warmer tomorrow and a degree warmer again on Monday, and it's been very hot today. He also said the land was very dry, 'not a drop of moisture in it,' and the reservoirs, though they filled up four weeks ago with a couple of day's heavy rain, were already rapidly emptying. The one he fished in having gone down by 2 ½ feet since the rains.

Sabden is a classic settlement in the bottom of a massive valley with a hill down to it so steep I daren't trust my brakes and had to walk. I went straight into Shippy's village store, where Louise Stevenson was behind the counter. Just as I wanted to tell her that I had arrived at my first stop she wanted to tell me she was a marathon runner, completing her first one at fifty seven. She wanted to know where I was from and where my next stop was, and said to call in on the way back. I told her I wouldn't be coming back this way, but said I'd send her a card.

I rested for a while by the war memorial - *'Pro Patria'* – in the garden of which there is also, coincidentally, a memorial to 'Nurse Stephenson,' who died in 1903, having 'lived for others.'

Almost everyone in Sabden said hello.

Paul Theroux says 'I do some pretty incredible things' is not an English expression (whereas it might emanate from an American). It might not be an expression, but it's a habit.

As I was packing up, Mateg from Slovakia asked me where the nearest pub was, and I was able to tell him it was just round the corner. He worked in Padiham and was out for a walk on his day off. Just round the corner I met four more young Slovakians and was able to tell them their friend had gone to the pub.

The hill out towards Clitheroe turned out to be just as steep as the way in, and longer, but soon opened out into well-walked moors with scattered rocks, parked cars and old quarry workings. Right on the top was Dawn Hilton. She was drawing a rock feature she tried to convince me represented a bow. Having been taught by aborigines in Australia she was an expert at spotting ancient stones and paths. Because I wasn't an expert the range of things she pointed out just looked like natural features to me. Dawn gave me a little leaflet that said on it 'Fantasies before Tolkien', and 'A rare insight to Lancashires (sic) finest prehistorical codes', and a section of a satellite picture with 'Clover,' 'Heart,' 'Dove' and 'Whitehawk' written on it. Obviously there are ancient remains – even prehistoric ones, but there's also the human tendency to impose imagery and meaning.

The summit was positively alpine and on the sweeping road down the only building is a grand pub that could be in those mountains. And next to it, above Clitheroe, is an all-weather ski slope 'not to be used without permission.'

I imagined Clitheroe to be a northern post-industrial wasteland, but to the romantic visitor it looked almost European, open and airy. Of course the Lidl store, which I rode straight into, helped, reminding me of travels in Germany. Outside I chatted to Derek Turner, a stout older fellow, who told me he had been a big cyclist in his time. He was still cycling locally, but considering an electric bike – not 34 amps, but 40.

I rode on through West Bradford, Grindleton and Sawley, thankfully all reasonably flat. The sun had gone down and the depression about where I would sleep was beginning to set in, with nothing really suitable or discrete.

Well out in the countryside there came like a vision Calder Farm Campsite. I couldn't raise anyone at the farmhouse so pitched by a fence where I could fasten up my bike, well away from the big tents and caravans with awnings.

While I put my tent up I chatted to Julie, who had come to photograph the gambolling lambs beyond the fence to which I had secured my bike. She too was a runner, who recently did Manchester to Liverpool, but has run a Scottish coast to coast.

As night fell I drank the warm San Miguel John had made me carry and made do with a cold meal.

The first day of my trip could not have been more perfect. I had bought sparkling water by mistake but as I had found a campsite and didn't have to wild camp it didn't matter.

Day 2 – Trough of Bowland to Dent

(Yorkshire and Cumbria)

I was cold and didn't sleep well. Hot days are no guarantee of warm nights in April.

I waited for the rising sun to warm me in the tent listening to crows, gulls, geese, all the smaller birds, cows mooing in the distance and horses chomping the grass beyond the fence. It came over the farmhouse big and yellow as I made my porridge. There were only streaks of light cloud in the broad blue sky.

The upmarket tea bags Oades packed for me say they'll make me feel new – and I do.

I forgot to mention that there was unfortunately in Clitheroe some tool riding round on a big quad in camouflage clothing flying a St George cross on a big whip pole. The first two people I saw entering the town were women in hijab, but whereas I see that as a positive thing he probably doesn't.

Within an hour I could hear the Easter traffic roaring along the A65, particularly the crotch rockets of the nouveau riche.

While I was packing up Rachael Clegg and her six year old son Reuben came to talk to me. She is an artist living in Manchester, but her parents live in this valley.

My stress free night's camping cost £10. The owners Peter and Clair have been on the farm for ten years, renting it for the first six and opening the campsite six years ago. Peter said he wanted to do what I was doing when he was a bit older. I told him not to leave it too late.

When I said the A59 was like a race track he said it was mad on their road – a glorified lane – 'with the motorbikes' – and sure enough not five minutes into the day's ride one sports bike blaated past me with a female passenger perched on an unsuitable pillion, her knees under her chin. Most of the sports bike owners ride solo, but some have a seemingly decorative female.
On a previous trip I wrote this;

Seven stone woman blues

I went into my dealer
But soon found all they had
Was a modern macho motorcycle
With a skinny buddy pad
I've got the seven stone woman blues

I've got a fancy foreign motorcycle
With a skinny buddy seat
But the seven stone woman
I have yet to meet
I've got the seven stone woman blues

On my skinny little buddy seat
Any normal woman would look quite out of place

I need a seven stone woman
With make-up on her face
I've got the seven stone woman blues

I don't want a woman
Like my sister or my aunt
My skinny little buddy seat
Won't take an elephant
I've got the seven stone woman blues

I need a skinny woman
To make my life complete
My skinny little buddy seat
Was made for the petite
I've got the seven stone woman blues

When I've lashed my cash around
On a fancy foreign bike
I don't see why I cannot have
The kind of bird I like
I've got the seven stone woman blues

There's a seven stone woman out there
But she's not heard the news
I've got a skinny buddy pillion
Only she can use
I've got the seven stone woman blues

She doesn't have to cogitate
Or comment on the news
I'll take her out on Sunday
So she can see the views
I've got the seven stone woman blues

She doesn't have to have a mind

Just decorate my seat
A schoolgirl Barbie lookalike
Would make my bike complete
I've got the seven stone woman blues

When it was quiet I could hear my left knee cap clicking every pedal stroke, but as it had done it for years I wasn't too worried.

Six more bikes roared past, then three, then five. Six brown horses stood in a line in a field like something Anthony Gormley might have created.

When I sat under a tree for my second breakfast it was like being a spectator at Brands Hatch with them all diving into the Settle turn and accelerating round the corner. Even as an ex-motorcyclist (never a 'sports' motorcyclist) I hated it. And then a group of them stopped on the corner and shouted at each other for fifteen minutes, right outside people's houses on Easter Sunday.

Then there were the camper vans, which are an entirely different thing. The only sensible person I saw was an old bloke on a utility bicycle.

Paul Theroux asks himself where and how to get the best view of the place; 'the problem was one of perspective... it was also a problem in tone – after all I [am] an alien.'

'The British... who had virtually invented the concept of funny foreigners had never regarded themselves as fair game...'

'But it was also a problem of itinerary. In a place that is criss-crossed with ant trails, a kingdom of bottlenecks and private property and high fences... A bicycle was out – too dangerous, too difficult – another stunt.'

Stunt it may have been – and several people asked if they could give to my charity in recognition of it (and if I'm doing a blog). I pointed them to the charity's website and BT Giving.

Leaving Wigglesworth the view was vast with one of the major peaks I don't know the name of in the hazy distance. The A65 pilgrimage to the Dales route wouldn't have even been visible in this landscape if there hadn't been an endless procession of vehicles along it.

Yesterday, as I started out, a crow sat on a wall and didn't flinch as I rode past. It was my crow, the one that follows me everywhere, like an eagle followed Napoleon. It once landed on my head near McDonald's in Huddersfield. During the morning there had been a dead crow in the ditch and I hoped it wasn't an omen. The woods were full of bluebells, the verges cowslips (I think). Rathmel had a reading room – a hangover from some bygone age.

Some cyclists exchange a cheery greeting. Others ignore you even if you speak first. Most have their heads down and their arses up and are going seven times faster than I am. At a comfort stop in the flat bottomed valley approaching Settle swallows strafed a field.

Crossing the main road a motorcyclist behind couldn't wait for me to execute my manoeuvre and had to do a body swerve to avoid knocking me off. Such are the perils.

I rode into Settle and straight out again, worried I might discover I needed a pot dog, an overpriced piece of wood with 'Home Sweet Home' painted on it or some traditional home cooked fayre.

I thought the B6479 would be OK, but it wasn't. It was busy and motorcycles continued to tear past me – some of them with ear splitting screams.

It was all a bit Mad Dogs and Englishmen riding on into the Dales. There was no shade and nowhere to sit, but who wants to sit next to the main road anyway?

Eventually I found a little rough turnoff and sat under a wall to watch the spectacle, the hillside opposite was being devastated by quarrying. A battery operated mountain biker came clattering down. There was no peace whatsoever. Then a truck and horse box, then a quad. I moved on, but not until another truck had bounced up in a cloud of dust and flying stones.

After Horton in Ribblesdale the country opens up into a vast range of low hills. Parts of it look like the Mongolian Steppe with walls, and it all will soon if we don't get any rain.

I'd almost decided to stay at Dent – even though it's out of my way and the campsite will be full for the Easter holiday.

Occasionally the traffic stops and there's only the bleating lambs and the distant sound of rich people killing things.

A gang of two-wheeled Darth Vaders stopped and remonstrated loudly with an innocent looking man in a beat up car and, while I leaned on a gate another angry motorcyclist made gestures at a driver who was impeding his relentless progress to nowhere. A motorcycle is nowadays no more a piece of practical transport than a jet ski. Motorcyclists used to wave at each other, but not anymore – it would be as sensible as waving at another man simply for having an ego.

A big hare ran across the field.

There weren't many trains on the Settle/Carlisle line because people don't need public transport on public holidays – and anyway it's more profitable to sell them cars. Consequently at Ribblehead the road was lined for hundreds of yards in each direction with four wheeled symbols of freedom, affluence and meritocracy, as people lined up to watch and photograph a train they wouldn't dream of being on go over the famous viaduct.

By mid-afternoon (I guess) I was seeing the same motorcyclists again as they came back from their posing in Hawes main street. I could never stand it when I was a 'biker' and now I'm a reformed one it fills me with horror.

I walked down the very steep hill towards Dentdale because if my bike had got going I wouldn't have been able to stop it, and then took the back road to the village, which was a mistake because it was hillier and longer and I'd had enough. I felt a bit of self-loathing for deliberately resorting to a campsite when I'd promised myself I'd rough it – but it's much easier to say than do.

I've stayed at the farm campsite many times in my motorcycling days and several times since. The owner was at the pub, where he is almost resident, and his wife was very ill. When she opened the top half of the farmhouse stable door when I went to pay an overpowering smell of animals emitted of the kind I've only ever once smelled so bad – in a house full of cats in Dewsbury when I was building. People go for breakfast in the farmhouse, but even if I wasn't vegan I couldn't possibly stomach it.

There's no shade except in my tent and it's so hot it's making my head hurt. People say it's lovely. It's not lovely, it's frightening – everyone knows Easter is supposed to be a washout. Last time I was in Dent a month earlier the streams were all full and the river was fit to burst its banks – now all the streams were dry and the river was a trickle.

As soon as I had decided upon my itinerary 'I had my justification for the trip – the journey had the right shape: it had logic; it had a beginning and an end.'

'I sometimes felt like the prince in the old story, who because he distrusts everything he has been told and everything he has read, disguises himself in old clothes and, with a bag slung over his back, hikes the muddy roads talking to everyone and looking closely at things.' I haven't talked to anyone or looked at anything today – it was mostly just a slog on a busy road and it was shit. I decided things will would have to change or it would become a punishment.

Conder Farm campsite is very basic and was not full after all. The upmarket one at the other end of the village was. It comes with the free endless duff-duff of footballs being booted, slamming car doors and yapping dogs. I'd had enough irritating noise for one day.

It transpired that the motorcyclist camped in the middle of the field knew me from years ago when I used to make an exhibition of myself at motorcycle rallies. He remembered me wearing a kilt and my homemade 1920s 'replica' flat-tank Norton. The cyclist next to him was from Bingley and knew all the climbs for miles around.

'The present contains the future' says Theroux. God help us. Of Britain he says there is 'a deterioration and decay that seems more futuristic than utopian cities of steel and glass.'

It cooled down as the sun set and I made my tea – chick peas and beans I'd carried from Settle for protein and bread I'd carried from Clitheroe. The chick peas were the healthy kind that are very hard and taste of nothing.

The cyclist said he'd gone to the farmhouse for breakfast this morning and it was only £3. I had to bite my tongue.

The toilets are a disgrace, as they've been for twenty years. The shower in the gent's doesn't work. A sign said men had to use the ladies shower, which I am sure would have pleased any ladies present no end. I won't bother them. There's a makeshift men's urinal under a tin roof that's also ancient. It stinks and flies were buzzing round it. You don't get much for £5, not even decency.

A cheeky bird (thrush size) kept coming right up to my tent. I didn't know what it was – which made me think of *What kind of fool am I?* - because everything reminds me of a pop song. What kind of fool am I? The kind who cycles all over the country on his own on a 23kg home-made bike when he could be at home being sixty two and sensible.

It came very cold quickly and when the sun set I turned in, determined not to get cold like last night. Sitting on the ground all the time is giving me backache. The sun (or dehydration) had given me a headache. The top of the tent was covered in little black flies attracted to its bright colour.

Everything has to be in its right place before it gets dark. Last night there was a light nearby, here there was nothing but the firmament above. And my pitch, like most of the site, was sloping.

Day 3 – Dent to Middleton in Teesdale (via Kaber)

(Yorkshire and Cumbria)

A better night's sleep though I heard the church clock strike three and four. In fact when it struck four I was outside relieving myself against the wall. Cockerels started at four, crows and the other birds a bit later. Sheep bleated all night.

At least when you stay on a campsite there's (usually) no dog shit. Everywhere else there is. And dog shit means slugs – sometimes hundreds of them. As soon as you waken you can see them silhouetted on the inside of the outer fly sheet, where they've crawled during the night. There'll be some of that to come.

The biker who knew me said it was a shame I'd lost my mojo. I haven't lost my mojo, I told him, I'm just not a biker any more.

I took my tent down and packed while the pan boiled for coffee and porridge, carried out minor ablutions and left, passing through Dent village with its cobbled street, its overblown sense of itself and exited over the ancient bridge.

Not far from Dent dormitory a posh car outside a posh house had a sticker 'Don't blame me, I voted remain.' There may be a message.

A lightweight cyclist called Ian pulled alongside me. His parents are from East Bierley and he was in training for 'the Fred Whitton' – some memorial endurance test. It's rare for lightweight 'racing' bike riders to exchange more than a greeting, as we are, in cycling terms, chalk and cheese. As we rode along he asked about the history of my bike – something else they don't usually do, being for the most part affluent snobs.

To the non-cyclist cycling can easily be categorised amorphous, but even a cursory investigation reveals it to encompass everything from teenage drug dealers through obsessive world tourers to hill conquering masochists.

And to emphasise this a tourer came the other way. He was 'bike packing.' This means no proper luggage (or mudguards) and fastening a lightweight tent and sleeping bag to the frame (requiring special equipment – and no doubt a special bike).

The river along the valley cuts through solid rock and runs over great slabs of it. Here and there are round pockets, where stones have bashed round for hundreds of years.

As I rode over Cowgill Bridge by the church of St John the Evangelist, I noted that it was repaired 'at the charge of the East Riding, A.D. 1702.'

I left the valley bottom to head up the very steep 'coal road' to Dent Station, which I tackled in twenty yard pushes, waiting for my heart rate to slow down between each one. A lightweight cyclist steamed past me like it was nothing and said, 'That's a pretty bicycle,' – not a phrase that's ever been used about it before. I only had time to say 'this is a bit extreme,' to which he replied 'it's a bit silly,' because he was posh.

The coal road had recently been resurfaced because the Tour de France, or something, had used it – and there's another thing. Everyone assumes because you use a bicycle you're interested in cycle racing. No one assumes someone going to the shops in their Fiesta is familiar with the doings of Nelson Piquet or Emerson Fitipaldi.

Looking down into the valley only the bottom two or three fields are cultivated, and then it's just grass for sheep. I have a feeling it wasn't always like this and that the walled fields much further up will have been needed to feed a much larger population living in the umpteen farmsteads, some of them, the higher up ones, now falling into dereliction, others taken over by yuppies who do their dirty work in the cities and live out here to avoid the consequences.

A caterpillar walked across the road, as lucky as I am that there are no cars. You notice things like that when you are walking, which I don't mind at all because it uses different muscles and gives your arse a rest.

Dent Station, at 1150 feet above sea level is the highest railway station in England. It is on the iconic Settle to Carlisle line that would have been axed decades ago if the bean counters had got their way – along with much of the rest of Britain's once great public transport infrastructure. A map from the 1940s shows Britain looking like a spider's web, with railways everywhere. Today many of them are long gone – along with the communities they served. The old Dent station building is now luxury holiday accommodation.

To my surprise a train came in and three walkers got off quietly. Then a party of loud Australians came and shattered the peace. One of them told me they were here for four weeks, staying in four different houses before cruising round the coast. When they'd gone off on the train the rest of their party of grey heads came and couldn't believe they'd left them. In between there was a lot of that irritating crunching that car drivers do in gravel car parks. I told the Australians that their friends had said, 'Bugger them we're off.'

As I continued up the hill a campervan driver with half his teeth missing stopped to tell me how hard the hill was, as if I didn't know.

At the top a commercial forest has been felled and replanted, the saplings among the stumps. There may be a metaphor or even a message in these woods – something to do with the recent climate protests – and it wasn't the top at all – that was a mile further on behind a false summit.

A beetle was crossing the road. A car came and killed it. I made that up, it's another metaphor, the beetle made it safely across.

It was windy at the top and I managed to ride the last mile up with it behind me. Naturally the views are stupendous, but there's only so many times you can say this. I had to dismount for part of the descent as well, it being too steep for my brakes.

The railway strikes a big arc and I rode under it at Garsdale, by which time I was hungry and had to eat a dry tortilla wrap because that was all I had besides dry oats (I could have boiled some water).

As I got to the bottom Ian I'd met earlier was coming up – he'd been round the hills via Hawes quicker than I could go over them. He was really in training.

There was a call box and I could have rung Oades, but it didn't accept coins, progress being what it is.

There is another splendid stone viaduct by the A684 and a three carriage train went over as I passed. The Australians might have been on it. Thankfully I wasn't on the A road long and a head wind turned into an oblique tail wind. A head wind blows my sun hat up and I am reluctant to apply filthy unguents to myself at the best of times and especially when I may not be able to wash them off.

Within half an hour I had entered and left Richmondshire and entered Cumbria.

The B6259 is a rollercoaster at first, with all too short descents and hard climbs, but then it descends generally for miles –

the first decent bit of cycling I've had since I left home. Unexpectedly I came upon Pendragon Castle and remembered photographing my homemade Matchless motorcycle outside it a decade ago.

Into Kirby Stephen – one more traffic jam with shops, very few selling anything anyone actually needs. I resupplied and rode straight out over the river, which was depleted and green at the edges. It was a lovely spot to eat my lunch, two hundred yards from the heaving main street, but there was no one there because there was nowhere to spend money.

I went back in afterward to buy postcards. Kirby Stephen is a bit 'Coast to Coast' themed, businesses having to latch onto whatever is fashionable, hence the ubiquitous 'dogs and bikers welcome' signs. Even the fish and chip shop is called Coast to Coast.

The road to Kaber was fairly easy as well. AC/DC blasted from a bungalow window, their original fans probably as old as me.

Passing through the chocolate box village of Winton I stopped for a drink at the *Bay Horse* because I could. The barmaid didn't listen to my order.

My ride through Winton
Was too hot for a scarf
I asked for a pint
And she gave me half

Winton Common (commons, today?) has a big ditch dug all round it. I strongly suspected that this was to stop people on their way to Appleby Horse Fair finding refuge. One is forced to ask what commons are for, and how it must feel to be part of a group no one wants. Actually I've been refused service in pubs because I was a biker – before it was fashionable and lucrative – and for being a socialist (The *Victoria*, Saltaire).

If I hadn't stopped to let a truck with a sheep trailer pass and waited for him to unload I wouldn't have met Tosh, a metal detectorist arriving in the field for an afternoon searching for treasure. He said he'd mostly found 'cow tubes', which turned out to be mastitis ointment containers, but he opened a little velvet lined box and showed me a stamped brooch that he thought might be Saxon or Roman. He told me that last summer someone found a Saxon hoard nearby. They sound pretty organised and he told me a Finds Liaison Officer assessed the origin of things they found.

I arrived at Kaber, my second destination, at around two o'clock (I'd no idea what time it was). It too is built around a common. The Primitive Methodist church was built in 1891 and is now a private home. The original schoolhouse was dedicated by Anthony Morland, 'Yeoman of Rookly' and rebuilt 'by the landowners of the township of Kaber' – all of which suggested a much larger population than there is now.

Camping was not allowed on the common (it never is) and a meeting was upcoming about Appleby Horse Fair with the police Gold Commander (and people who want the countryside all to themselves). The village crest includes a kangaroo – making a hat trick of my Australian asides. I have been told since that it is not unusual for British sheep farmers to spend sabbaticals in Australia.

I sent postcards to Oades and to Louise Stevenson in Sabden village store, before taking a lovely lane, and then the decidedly unlovely A685, into Brough and through without stopping – you've seen one faux market town main street and you've seen them all.

My cynicism earned me a big climb out, but an old milepost you wouldn't see from a car said it was 262 miles to London. The details of the other direction had been smashed off by iconoclasts, possibly. I've seen this before. Perhaps the distances were incorrect, but I can't see why this would matter – lots of things carved in stone, and seemingly carved in stone, are incorrect.

The A66, possibly the worst road in England, thundered along to my right.

The B road to Middleton in Teesdale looked like it was going to be a bastard from the outset – making my left kneecap feel as if it was going to fly off. Two lads went past on Panthers, making proper motorcycle noises. Panthers were made in my home town until production ceased in the 1960s. The factory was recently demolished to make way for a care home because looking after old people has replaced manufacturing as Britain's major 'industry.' Both riders were wearing 1950s gear.

Two miles out yet another ancient hillside was being destroyed by a quarry to satisfy our need for ever more roads. When I said to Dawn Hilton on Monday how awful it was what they'd done to the Australian Aborigines she said, 'They do it to everyone, they did it to the Welsh, they're doing it to us,' and she's right.

But at least it wasn't busy – I assumed everyone else had fucked off home so they could go to work tomorrow. Even Peter Fonda on his Honda and Denis Hopper on his chopper had gone back to Leeds to do something important in a suit, hanging up their badass uniform until Spring Bank. But I spoke too soon and forgot to allow for those would be racers and World Tourers heading back to Teeside.

There was a perfect bird skeleton on the verge and it looked like a miniature pterodactyl. A child recently told me that birds are dinosaurs.

Climbing ever upward the biggest landscape yet was behind me, with the road I'd travelled snaking down into the valley.

When I thought I'd done half the fourteen miles to Middleton I passed a milestone that said it was another ten. On the top there were black and white birds with orange beaks. And I was in County Durham, 'Land of the Prince Bishops.'

I was able to ride down all the hills because they weren't particularly steep, I could see where I was going, and the wind in my face was a better brake than anything I already had.

Selset Reservoir looked low – 'serving the people of Northumbria' (and corporate shareholders).

I didn't know what I was going to do when I landed in Middleton in Teesdale and even wondered about staying inside (the spirit is willing, but the flesh is weak), when on a road with nothing I came upon Mark and Helen's place. They bought the farm seven months ago and opened the campsite last year. Mark is a builder and has done the house up himself. The oldest part dates back to the twelfth century and the modern part from the 1630s. He said they'd found a witch's mark as well – though I don't know what one is (I don't know what a Saxon brooch looks like either). They also found the water, which comes from a bore hole, to be undrinkable, being contaminated with the oily deposits one sees around coalfields, and had to install a £5,000 purification plant. The area was mined extensively for lead and later, less so, for tin.

When Paul Theroux was writing his travelogue the tabloids were gloating about Thatcher's murder of hundreds of men on the *General Belgrano*. Today the papers report the killing by a suicide bomber of hundreds of people in a church. I didn't note where it was.

I could hear distant shooting – lots of it, but I didn't know whether it was toffs or Tommy Atkins, there are several military firing ranges round about.

Mark said they still call this area Yorkshire. After I'd passed the Durham sign I passed an old Yorkshire one. He said the diocese altered all the boundaries and sold off all their land in the area, including his farm, to pay a debt in London. He doesn't trust them and said he 'pays no more tithes' – he spends it. The Church as landlord must be fresh in many memories.

Paul Theroux thought that the Channel Tunnel was one of the most important engineering works of our century (He thought this before it was built, several attempts having failed). He said 'Britain's future might depend on it.'

Wing Commander Wraggett (he makes the names up) says '"We've got to learn to tighten our belts." His "we" meant everyone else of course.'

'But how could I take this trip with my mouth shut? On the days when I did not speak to anyone I felt I'd lost thirty pounds, and if I did not talk for two days in a row I had an alarming impression that I was about to vanish. Silence made me feel invisible.'

I had a long hot shower, but my clothes didn't seem to smell so I didn't change them. I only had pittas, peanut butter and porridge, so I ate pittas, peanut butter and porridge, spreading the peanut butter and eating the porridge with my Charles and Diana wedding tea caddy spoon. Then it was getting dark, so I went to sleep.

Day 4 – Middleton in Teesdale to Stanhope (via Wackerfield)

(into Durham)

The thing to do is not worry about how cold it is but get out of your bag and get going. I packed up as my pan boiled for coffee and put the tent down as it boiled for porridge – which is OK as long as it stays fine. When it's raining you have to boil the kettle in the tent porch and wish you were at home.

Helen brought her horse to the paddock before seven and told me she'd moved into the area from Newcastle with her parents. Her and Mark lived in the village for fourteen years before they bought this place, that already had a campsite. They have sixteen acres besides and her brothers keep sheep on them.

I didn't have to go into Middleton in Teesdale, part way down the chilly descent turning off through Mickleton towards my next destination.

I couldn't ride past Hayberries picnic area and stopped for a second brew – 'No Camping' (why?) 'Clean up after your dog' – some people hadn't – but that's normal. Dog shit is a sad fact of life like death and taxes. It's not like cycling with John or Geoff when they'll only stop if you make them, and only in John's case at an expensive café.

For a while the road was full of wagons bearing down on me from behind, especially up hill, changing down seven gears and getting angry. The animosity is palpable. If it's possible to pull in I do and they wave. I look straight at the driver to make him wave, but it's not always possible.

The landscape was the same, but different, craggier and more pine forests. There were four alpaca in a field, two white, one black, one brown. I sat in a ditch to write this and within minutes had big ants all over me.

A bit further on there was the lovely smell of pine from logging, whole hedges in blossom and a few daffodils left. A young woman came the other way on a racing bicycle with a cheery wave and no helmet, unusual in these Health and Safety obsessed days – as if the main problem for cyclists is actually an insufficiency of plastic hats. I'd only been on the road a minute this morning before a van overtook me dangerously into a blind bend.

A long rolling road took me all the way to Staindrop – much of it in high gears, a far cry from the endless first gear climbs of yesterday.

I treated myself to a café breakfast and met Michelle and Russell from Preston who had just opened a new ladies' clothes shop nearby. They were cruisers and talked about all the places they'd been, Madagascar, the Seychelles – that after we'd discussed the Hillsborough trial, which Russell thought had ended as it should because no malice was involved.

Also with John, an eighty two year old who had done eighteen years in the Royal Marines and thirty as a paramedic – and been personal protection to Ian Smith when he was president of Rhodesia, and various other dignitaries. He was also a cruiser and told how he'd been on one liner when it docked and two ladies had complained – they'd asked for an ocean view and were looking at containers. He said they were to tell the steward to tell the captain to move the ship fifty yards further along, immediately, because he wasn't having it – they'd paid good money and they deserved what they'd paid for. They asked him if he was something to do with the ship. He said he was Mr P&O and off they went. Michelle spoke for Russell and wished me a safe journey, saying how lovely it had been to meet me. John was talking to a man with an ostentatious gold cross round his neck. The breakfast was £8.

Approaching Wackerfield, after three days of sheep, it suddenly went all arable and I rode through vast fields of fragrant yellow rape seed. In the village, my third destination, there was plenty of whitewash and cropped verges and I chatted with Alf and Morris, 72 and 67, about not much other than that Wackerfield has seventeen houses and a Roman road nearby. They recommend Raby Castle, but I'm not doing castles, not at National Trust prices, I'm doing people. In fact I'm not doing old stuff. Doing old stuff is passé – unless it pertains to the present, which to a lot of minds it doesn't. 'The past is gone, what's important is the future,' they say, as they attempt to sweep the empire and all its enduring consequences under the carpet.

I'd guess the next place is about three days off.

While I was changing my map and putting some fresh air in my tyres Morris came round again in his Japanese truck on the way to look at his sheep and we talked for twenty minutes. He's lived in Wackerfield all his life and three generations of his family once lived in the only row of houses. He's had both his knees done and now finds it difficult to get over the gates, having to carry a little ladder and strategically place a concrete block. He's got a bicycle he uses sometimes to go round a-lambing, which he's now in the middle of. We could have chatted all day in an equal interchange, him as interested in me as I was in him, but he had lambs to deliver, like he always had. But do you know what? I don't think that today they'd do it if it wasn't for the subsidies – and therefore, in these free-market times, intervention is distorting entire production systems. Fair play to those who milk it to survive, but there are also the undeserving on landed estates, getting subsidies (and titles) for leaving land fallow.

Morris said he liked my bike, it was a credit to me and just showed what you can do if you put your mind to it.

When I mentioned noisy motorbikes, and how they nearly made you jump out of your skin, Morris brought up fighter planes, saying, 'You might be ploughing all day, listening to the stones going through, when all of a sudden one goes over and you think "what the fuck" and jump on the clutch.' I said at least he knew where his taxes were going. He said, 'They won't get many of them round here, nobody makes anything.' He said he doesn't have central heating and he doesn't want it. I concurred. I said I thought it made people soft. He said he never thought of going to the pub, but didn't mind a shandy occasionally at home. I said I was the opposite. I rarely drink at home, but don't mind a few 'shandies' in a pub.

My bike went much better with the tyres blown up, but I've lost one of the little nose protectors off my seeing glasses – first casualty of the trip.

When I was due for a rest a copy of the *Sun* was blowing in the verge. I saw Rod Liddle's name and picked it up to see what he was saying. He attacks the BBC for including rap music in the proms, the French government for discounting arson in the Notre Dame fire, David Lammy MP for being 'deranged,' young people for thinking diversity matters, scientists for talking crap and climate change protesters for being 'middle class Zombie tossers, armed with hipster beards, top knots, vegan shakes, lots of badges and stupid placards,' as well as 'well-bred polite narcissists, dim as a five watt bulb in an aircraft hangar' and 'morons with Waitrose snack packs.'

Rod Liddle has his doubts about climate change and says the misguided people who campaign against it should have a word with the Chinese or the Indians about pollution and the Africans about over population – just like the old Malthusian ostriches at my over-50s discussion group. It is disingenuous to blame the Chinese for pollution when we fill our houses with all the stuff they make, Britain has merely exported its pollution problem. On the way Liddle advocates more nuclear power and for the police to stop acting like social workers and batter a few demonstrators to teach the others a lesson. That's the *Sun*, read it and weep, or read it and then wang it out of your cab window into the countryside, closely followed by your Happy-go lucky meal box and your McShitty shake cup.

At Esperley a whole row of hundred year old slung-up cottages was being converted in a fake stone style and the builders' radio blared about the new Independent group of MPs who are determined to overturn the Brexit vote to who knows what dangerous consequence.

Cockfield common is dotted with the huts of pigeon fanciers. It's a whole new world the north east. How do they get away with it? A farmer in a pickup stopped and put four bags of rubbish and a toaster by the roadside, for it was green bin day, and the woman with arms full of tattoos in the Co-op let me off two pence. I made her laugh by asking a Morrison's worker what he was doing in there and calling him a traitor. I don't think he was quick-witted enough to produce a response, or a putdown that makes me look silly, as sometimes happens – like when I asked the 82 year old ex-Marine, ex-Paramedic who said he was from Whitechapel if he knew the original Ripper. This was before I knew he was an ex-Marine, an ex-paramedic and the Kray twins had been two years above him at school. I thought 'Lieutenant Colonel Hyphenated-Name,' but it turned out he was a sergeant and probably romancing, certainly romanticising Aden, Suez and the Mau Mau. I thought of John Newsinger's *The Blood Never Dried*, the antidote to old soldiers' rose tinted reminiscences.

I helped a woman to find the postie, to 'save her going into Bishop' and the buses are run by Sapphire and proclaim they 'make every day sparkle.' They are really run by Arriva, a global conglomerate. The women said the postie was going to come back to her house – she knew him. I'm not sure she was fully compos mentis, but it's all part of the service.

Mary had moved here from Newcastle too – and I don't blame her, it's a very special place. She said it was going to rain tomorrow. They all do. I made her name up because I forgot to ask it. That's what Paul Theroux does, but I don't want to make a habit of it. And having lightened the lives of various residents I made tracks.

Between the settlements on a long straight road Simpson's Fuels had an old coal truck for an authentic gatepost, but no bare breasted woman pushing it, or a four year old trapper opening the doors. During the Victorian era, when Britain was great, women and children worked underground to survive while their social betters got very rich. And then, when it was all going down the pan due to greed, wholesale ostentation and dissoluteness, they started a war to try to hold onto what they'd stolen, in which they attempted to convince miners, mill workers and ignorant farm labourers that they could have no greater love than to sacrifice their lives to maintain the current system. From Copley, for example, eight men died; T. Cross, N. Dent, S. Robinson, C.A. Dixon, C.H. Waters, E. Lowe, B. Sowerby and T. Rose. When they did it again twenty years later only J.P. Reed paid the ultimate price. Despite the increasingly cynical commemorations of past glories all of them are expendable collateral. Even in the middle of the village a whole family were shouting over the bleating of sheep.

Stuart Hodson was strimming the verge at Lane End. He's only been in his Victorian farm house for seven months, having lived in Leeds, Blackpool and Bolton. He already knew who was an incomer and who was old stock. He was an ex-Fylde cyclist and realistic about pollution.

In its heyday the next village, Woodland, had a population of 700. Since the mine and the railway line closed the population has shrunk to around 275.

Then I was out on the open moors again, with the wind behind me and only the occasional quarry truck or car passing, pedalling hard down one incline to crest the next. It was effing brilliant.

Eaglestone has a village reading room dedicated in 1887, a clock to 'the fallen' of WWII, and a new memorial to those who died in WWI. It features the now fashionable upturned rifle and tin hat motif, popularised by those who enlist the dead of the past to justify the wars of the present. The village green has a union flag and a flag of St George flying, just in case any advocates of multiculturalism pass through. The old school site was for sale with permission for three executive dwellings – make of that what you will.

I entered the North Pennines, which are an Area of Outstanding Natural Beauty and a UNESCO Global Geopark, but that didn't stop there being pizza boxes in the ditch and two sullen old sheep farmers going about in an old Daihatsu with a fucked exhaust.

And that's how it carried on – open moors, dead rabbits, shot gun cartridges, Greggs coffee cups, Red Bull tins, a following wind and very little traffic. Clearly other energy drinks are available.

The two old farmers came back. I smiled at them, they carried on looking glum. I started to see what I like to refer to as steadings, whether anyone else does or not. They are farms that look like cattle ranches and you see them a lot in Scotland.

Every time I got back in the saddle it felt better than the time before. When the ground dropped away to the left, as it often did, I felt like I was riding high, the king of the road. The Romans built their roads straight and higher than the landscape so that their soldiers marched by on the skyline. This was symbolic more than practical. Drawing straight lines across all that had gone before, as imperialists did across Africa and the Middle East, leaves the locals in no doubt about who is in charge. Churches are built on hills for the same reason.

I climbed steadily for an hour, past random jaw bones and the remains of sheep with plants growing through them. A quarry truck came down at a suicidal speed. A car coming up overtook me, causing a woman coming down to swerve. There was nothing else on the road. A Matchless and a Velocette passed me, little rabbits pricked up their ears and dived into their burrows.

And then at the top I left Teesdale for Weardale, putting on my windproof nylon gilet for the descent, during which I thought, 'If my brakes fail down here I'm dead,' and 'Why would anyone dump an old wardrobe there?'

At the bottom two men sat in cars with massive camera lenses sticking out of the windows and someone had left a little bag of dog shit on a wall. I leaned my bike on a black and white roadside bollard. It collapsed, just as it was designed to, and my bike fell over – to spring back when I took the load off it. The fur of a turgid dead rabbit ruffled in the wind and it stank of dead things.

Then I started to climb again.

There were feathers all over the verge and the creature that had been wearing them lay squashed. If you've never seen a bird hit hard by a car it's worth googling it. It's like a pillow fight in a posh school dorm. It has to be a white bird or pigeon. My feeling of disconnection was buttressed by a head of broccoli, still in its cellophane, placed carefully on a rock and, a bit further on, a fresh knuckle bone bigger than a man's fist next to two Kentucky boxes.

The road down into Stanhope was the steepest most winding ten percenter I've ever seen and I had to walk. After knocking on the door of a B&B to no response and being told at a pub that the advertised bunkhouse was now a storeroom I found refuge at the *Jolly Moorcock* (or something). The broad Irish landlord and the Scottish landlady were frazzled from the busy Easter weekend, closing early and not putting on food, which didn't bother me and probably won't have bothered the three bleary-eyed men power drinking shorts and talking about their footwear.

The landlord wanted my name in case the police came – 'It's part of our licence,' he said. I don't think he believed that I didn't have a mobile phone and put his palms up to placate me as he expressed respect for my privacy. I've never heard of such a thing – except of course I have and ignored it – freedom of movement, freedom of association, freedom of speech, freedom be bollocksed – it's all an illusion.

Today's cycling was over potentially inhospitable country. If I'd tackled it in bad weather I'd have had a good chance of getting hypothermia. I must remember that if a road looks on the map as if it crosses a barren wilderness it probably does – and there's another the same tomorrow, and many more to come. I was in my element, but recognised that being inside so early I'd blown the roughing it fantasy right out of the water. Stanhope is also on the Coast to Coast route and does a roaring trade because of it. Nowadays most people book their accommodation months in advance, or at least the day before on their smart phones. Those of us who take pot luck, as Paul Theroux did in 1983, are a dying breed, but that goes for many of the things I indulge in.

My bike is way down in the cellar, as safe as it's ever been.

The pub is actually called the *Bony Moorhen* and Zara and Tom, who've been here for a year, made me most welcome when I went down for a pint. When the two barflies left I was the only one in the place. Tom said it took him six months to learn that when there's no point in opening there's no point in opening. They've had pubs in Edinburgh, Spain, Germany and up the road. They've got property in Spain and the lot, and they are welcome to it. Tom told me that John, one of the recently departed, had all the friends he'd required to help him blow a two million pound inheritance. Now he was skint he was happy again and no one wanted to know him.

Tom said I should have a walk round the town, but if I didn't want to that was OK. Everything was 'no problem' and the professional sincerity wore a bit thin. They left me out a plate and cutlery so I could get food from a takeaway up the road. The trip was turning into a bit of an extravagance – and they hadn't told me how much I was paying for the room – which is my fault for not asking.

On top of the extreme cycling the two pints of cider took their toll. I couldn't see in the bathroom because the light was pathetic and it was done out in black plastic. The shower curtain had *Salle de bain* written all over it, along with the name of some hotel in Paris. I gave myself a once over with the smelly stuff provided, but didn't change my clothes because I didn't want to. I decided that when I'd had enough of them I was going to put my spare ones on and buy some more when I ran out, as if I was the man with the two millions who everybody loved.

On the wall of my room it said that in case of a fire 'The Fire Precautions Officer of (sic) his deputy on the affected floor will take charge of the evacuations and ensure that no one is left in this area.' Which is all very reassuring.

Then I went to the takeaway two doors up and bought the full mashing because I've embarked on a habit I can't possibly sustain. While waiting for my food I chatted to Marie from Sweden, whose husband is from Stanhope and they were visiting his family. She thought Stanhope was like Sweden, but with more pubs. I'd have to think about that, but didn't. Marie's husband was over the road having a quick pint.

My curry and starter were proper heart attack gear and there was loads of it – enough for two, but I was on my own, half a couple.

I didn't think any curry could be as good as one in Bradford, where a third of the population is of Asian heritage, but it was.

The cold tap in my room didn't work and obviously hadn't worked for some time. The cold tap in the bathroom fired water right across the room because the sink was so small, but all in all it was luxury – compared to the night before sleeping in a field.

After sating myself I read Paul Theroux by turning the bedside lamp on its side so some light came from the little bulb behind the thick shade. I found him stimulating, prophetic and eminently quotable, the ideal cycle tour company – though he's probably old hat by now, I thoroughly recommend him.

The lamp fell over and went out. I thought the bulb had gone, but it was one of those technology for its own sake things that came back on when I touched it.

Before I spoke to Marie from Sweden in the takeaway I had a look at *Men's Health*. It's a very thick magazine full of adverts with articles about the best beard to have and how to avoid having a shower after the gym by using certain products. I thought it must be comedy, or at least very tongue in cheek. You regularly hear these days that satire is dead. A spoof magazine couldn't be any stupider.

After dark, in the centre of this sizeable town, absolute silence reigned. In the countryside there never stops being noise, natural noise, but noise all the same. And then the church clock struck ten. I hadn't heard nine, or eight, or seven.

The backs of my legs are stinging with sunburn from too much going north. I'll get the fronts done when I come back down.

'I did nothing but make notes, scribbling from the moment I arrived in a hotel or guest house and often missing my dinner. I hated doing it. It was a burden. But if I had been in Afghanistan I would have kept a detailed diary. Why should I travel differently in Britain?'

Today I didn't make notes to transfer into my diary proper – I just wrote my diary by the side of the road, every mile or so, once I'd got enough stuff in my head I was going to forget something.

I forgot to mention that this pub has three of the uber-clichéd prints of anthropomorphised dogs hanging in the bar – the sort of art that should have been compulsorily burned in 1980 – dogs in hats smoking and drinking and, crappest of all, playing snooker. No one ever does a painting of what dogs really do – shit in every public park, path and playground, piss up every gatepost, bin and bus shelter and occasionally kill some unsuspecting child who has failed to notice that dogs are dirty and dangerous.

The clock struck eleven and I thought I'd better go to sleep, after I'd pissed in the sink and cleaned my teeth.

Tomorrow I must be more restrained in my expenditure, today has been ridiculous by any standards – but the cycling has been fantastic.

Day 5 – Stanhope to Haltwhistle
(Durham and Northumberland)

The next chime I heard was four, and then five – so I've forked out for a bed and not even taken advantage of it. I'm angry with myself for not looking for a campsite when there must be one when it's on the Coast to Coast route – and I've let them dictate my start time and wasted three hours cycling. On the other hand it's no bad thing that I've broken my self-imposed rule about not staying inside early on, all I have to do now is use B&B's in emergencies only.

I don't even want a full breakfast having gorged myself last night.

Zara said last night that Stanhope was like *Emmerdale*. I said I fell out with *Emmerdale* when Jack Sugden went off to Italy, came back a different bloke and his own mother didn't even notice. She said that was in the eighties – which is when I last watched soap operas.

Nor is it a bad thing that I can get a couple of hours reading in when I'm carrying two big books o'er hill and dale. Yesterday I could ride up all the hills. There's a world of difference between a long hill you can ride up and a steep hill you can't.

My piss smelled of onion bargees, the room smells of Lenor and I should have got my sleeping bag out to air. Ah well.

Paul Theroux meets on the train the Lucketts, who 'were off to wave plastic union jacks at a departing troopship.' (The *QEII,* bound for the Falklands). On the train door someone had scratched 'The Argentines are wankers – Bomb the barstards.' (sic) Rod Liddle would have been in his element, whipping up jingoism, the *Sun* printing union jacks lorry drivers could pin up in their cabs. Old men sending other people's sons off to kill and die. And so it is today. We've been through the wogs, coons, Hun, commies and Argies – now it's the ragheads, with all the racism and hatred that has caused, and 'our boys' can do no wrong – evidenced by the popularity of Help for Heroes and numerous other soldiers' charities. Now, as then, they are cannon fodder for capitalism and the best way to prevent the life destroying trauma they suffer is to oppose the wars they fight in and never to collapse into throwing that filthy flag over state sponsored murder. In war, as in football, it's better that Britain loses – every time it does it's one more nail in the coffin of its nauseating imperial delusion.

All Britain's history is tied up with the sea says Theroux, quoting Canetti. The Englishman's 'life at home is complementary to the life at sea: security and monotony are its essential characteristics.' An escape from monotony was how many would-be soldiers saw WWI, until their peers started returning maimed in mind and body, or not at all – and then they had to make them go. But mostly they still willingly went 'for king and country.' It does no good to call them fools – though fooled is what we are.

When the clock struck eight I got up, having wasted most of three hours cogitating and writing down the results. Though I got out the book I didn't copy out any of the poems for which I've been making notes for days.

I've read 92 pages of Paul Theroux, 'Brilliantly written,' says the *Daily Mail.* I wonder if the reviewer read it, considering it demolishes half of the shit it prints. It would be more appropriate if it said 'This man is a dangerous subversive, has no business undermining our proud pretences and should be sent back to the USA immediately, or clapped in irons.' Or perhaps that's just the way I'm

32

interpreting him. At any rate he offers serious challenge to our collective smugness.

I put the telly on for the time to hear that some company's profits are up (hurrah) and that two charities are warning that cuts to council budgets are causing increasing homelessness and rough sleeping.

The papers lead on Greta Thunberg's Westminster speech to climate protesters yesterday. She's pictured with Uncle Jeremy and Caroline Lucas. I had to turn the sound down – there's shit going on all around the world.

In the bathroom the toilet bowl isn't fastened down properly and you have to be careful when you raise one buttock to wipe your arse, lest you capsize completely.

And then, after a hearty breakfast (they'd done a vegan proud) and another dose of orange newsreaders on about alopecia, I was liberated from the clutches of a little fat Irishman with his fingers in too many pies. He said there could be as many as a dozen dogs in the beer garden. I said that kind of thing was not to my liking, he said he had no choice. I said if there was an alien invasion they'd have to put 'Martians Welcome' outside. When marginal groups become mainstream they have to be catered for on pain of losing precious business. No one, in the countryside at least, has thought of 'Muslims Welcome' with an alcohol free room set aside – but if they come in any number they will, while making jokes about suicide bombers behind their backs.

Climbing the seventeen percenter to freedom I could see down into the Stalag Luft static caravan park, from where they all come with their little pets to eat in pubs where the locals have special names for them.

Further up the houses clinging to the hillside were traditional and solid, as were the Range Rovers parked outside them, except that both had been hollowed out and stripped of their history as things of utility.

The homes on offer to and by those climbing the greasy pole were advertised by companies styling themselves 'Venture,' as in venture capitalism, and 'Lifestyle,' as in the accumulation of ever more stuff in an attempt to make yourself happy. Whoever told them they were meant to be happy, not to mention that getting stuff was the route to it?

A woman came past talking to a little dog like it could understand, carrying its shit in a little black bag. If the dog had the capability what would it think? There was an escape lane on the hill, it went down not up.

Unfortunately the emergency rations were expensive, the peanut butter was in a heavy glass jar and the pitta breads were white, but beggars can't be choosers.

Then suddenly all the moors were before me, with the 4x4s, the sun-bleached bones the fading beer tins and the banging quarry trucks. It wasn't long before I saw a dead sheep in the dry ditch, it's posture suggesting it had died a peaceful death, like a pensioner at Morecambe (see Alan Bennett's play). And then another looking skyward with its rib cage all open like a pensioner at Morecambe gutted of purpose.

There was a cold side wind and low cloud blew across the hills, making the future a mystery and the past a forgotten thing. I sat for a while on a roadside railing and looked out at a nothingness that makes me feel small and existence futile. 'One life, Live it,' say the Land Rover fraternity (as well as 'Ninety inches of pure pleasure' and 'My other toy has tits'). The railing was just the right height to have a shit from – like we used to do in the army (it's not like when we were young) – more comfortable than the wobbly bog in the pub. I can't believe it's only day five – I feel like I've been at it forever. I'm an outsider looking in (I can remember criticising Ted Simon for talking shit like this).

I was promised a tail wind, but it hasn't delivered – the wind is harder than the hills. I'm pedalling downhill.

While I was walking for a bit a young man in a car stopped and asked if I had issues. We all have issues. And I left Weardale. There was a standing stone, but I didn't know which manmade geographical construct I'd entered.

A massive quarry truck overtook me over a blind summit and made a fella coming the other way pull over and stop. I suppose I should be grateful he didn't pull back in and run over me with his back wheels.

Stopped to brew up just before Edmundbyers, which I discovered I could have got to by a shorter but even hillier route. Either I'm getting a cold or the poison from the Lenor doused duvet cover has got into my pipes.

Half an hour later I stopped to watch a cockfight in a field. With all the plumage, the strutting and the squaring up a Desmond Morris might call them the Hell's Angels of the animal kingdom. I'd call them bird brains.

In the top of a wall someone had stuck one of those little wooden remembrance crosses inscribed '1919 – 2018 – all who served, sacrificed and changed our world.' What balderdash. They weren't fighting to change the world they were fighting to keep it the same. The real commemoration should be of those in Russia and Germany who really did try to change the world and who the warring dynasties united to crush. If there was any real change it was due to ruling class fear. What there actually was after The War to End All Wars was an endless litany of broken promises.

Dropping into Blanchland I entered Northumberland 'England's Border County.' Blanchland looked like it was all owned by one man and the Lord Crewe Arms gave a clue – 'Vis unita fortior,' which roughly translates as 'everything you can see belongs to one bloke.'

I was relieved of £2.20 for a bottle of water and a bag of crisps, but console myself with the desire that the shop be here for future tourers. Peter and John, two working class mountain bikers, came in. They'd done a lot of touring by bicycle and on foot and we talked about the massive expense you can accrue touring if you don't rough it a bit. Also about the maniacs in cars who carelessly or deliberately try to run you off the road – they had been run off the road by two 4x4s on a green lane by someone who drove at speed straight at them, making them jump off their bikes to avoid being mown down. One shudders to think what would happen if you stood your ground against these bastards. I told them about the woman driving the horse box near Haworth last week who, with her own side of the road blocked by parked cars, drove straight towards four of us on our side shouting 'get on the fucking pavement.' Likewise one wonders what would have happened if we hadn't all cringed onto the verge.

Peter said Blanchard used to be a monastery, but that probably short cuts the process and by no means indicates it didn't belong to one man on dissolution – in fact it makes it more likely, as church lands and properties were divvied up between the sycophantic followers of the king.

This from Theroux is apt, 'The village had a monkish grey-stone appearance – there was once a Benedictine Monastery here – and the tithe barn and cottages all looked like they had been built by friars for the glory of God. In fact it was now a village of house-proud English people who, at great expense, had restored the place and planted roses.'

It was a 20% hill out and at the top I fancied that looking down over Derwent Water was a bit like looking down on Lake Constance.

There were a lot of privatised pine forests on the way to Hexham, which somehow makes it feel less lonely. And a dead snake in the road, the first I've ever seen in Britain.

Hexham was one of those places (aren't they all?) where you feel like a nuisance on a bicycle because the cars that are moving can't get past you due to all the stationary ones that clog the roads. It had charity shops, a tattooists and a massive police station. I bought a bottle of funny coloured pop full of e-numbers from a Middle Eastern bloke (there were Syrians on Hadrian's Wall eighteen hundred years ago) and left.

Like the cemeteries of old (even in ancient Rome) Hexham's was still out on the edge of town and hadn't been swallowed up by urban sprawl. I sat on the wall to drink some semi-luminous liquid while a dead fella was being disposed of, having served his useful purpose – like the Syrians on Hadrian's Wall.

It was nice. I tried to avoid all the smashed spirit bottles in the gutter. Commuters heading towards the A69, and even on the unclassified road after, desperate to see their precious families, overtook me far too close with abandon for I am, after all, only a member of the society that Thatcher said did not exist, by which I surmised it to be between five and six o'clock.

The birds were making their noise – a sure sign that it was becoming evening (even though a clock on some edifice said four) and I was knackered – another sure sign – but you do some of your best riding long after you should have stopped.

And so it was today. I followed the signed Hadrian's Wall cycle route all the way to Haltwhistle and camped among the jolly Coast to Coasters – except there were none because I camped just short of Haltwhistle on a static caravan park, the owner obviously wanting to get in on the act, but it was only £8, and 40p for the showers. I was the first camper this year and the cycle route took me through the Roman villa at Vindolanda, so I did see some very old stuff by accident, and it weaved me all over to avoid the A69 that I wouldn't have gone anywhere near had I been left to my own devices.

About seven miles out I met Bill and Mary, who were doing the Coast to Coast and making for Newborough tonight. They were done up like kippers, whereas I was in my shirt sleeves, so there's no wonder Mary was paggered. They also told me it was ten to five, so my body clock was a full two hours out due to my expensive insomnia last night. I don't know what the birds were up to. It is no doubt significant that I disregarded the best evidence of the time – a clock – in favour of dubious circumstantial evidence.

Zara asked me at breakfast this morning if I'd slept well – like you do when you charge people for the privilege of doing nothing on your property. I said, 'Not particularly – I heard the church clock at four and five,' but not, 'To tell you the truth I sleep better in my tent and I don't know why I gave you my money,' because that would have been impolite.

Bill and Mary also promised me an endless descent. They were lying, there was just as much up as down.

The nice camp site woman feigned some interest in my trip but didn't pursue the subject of my transport after she'd said it was sturdy.

As I was putting my tent up a train went past fifty feet away emblazoned with 'Fifty Years of the RAF' and a fighter plane motif. I don't know who paid for this normalisation of war message – surely not a private train company – although there's nothing wrong with keeping in with the government, who are, after all, 'The Committee for the Management of the Affairs of the Whole Bourgeoisie.'

The main A69 also runs at high level less than a hundred yards away, but I don't care – I've got peace of mind and earplugs.

I was cold so went for a nice hot shower. I put my 40p in the meter, but I must be stupid because I couldn't get any hot water to come out and I was buggered if I was going to get under cold. I went back to my tent and got into my sleeping bag for peanut butter, pittas and porridge. It might sound sad to some, but so might jetting off around the world to ogle poor people to others.

I'm amazed that all I've eaten since my full breakfast this morning, apart from my fruit, is one peanut butter sandwich and a bag of crisps. This is unheard of when I'm cycling and I put it down to my concerted attempt to stay off sugar, as advised by the doctor on the Steve Wright show, and therefore avoid peaks and troughs, highs and lows.

Theroux reports a woman who cooked rook pie in her pub, from birds shot as pests, receiving death threats. He says had she been a dog or a cat she could have counted on the support of the pet loving English public. To back this up (there are numerous examples) he quotes from the *Daily Telegraph* of 16th May 1972 (five days after I joined the army, aged fifteen) in which it is reported that a family in the Falls Road, whose daughters had been tortured and tarred and feathered by the IRA, had left their home, belongings and dog and gone into hiding. A woman on her own account and an animal charity rang the paper's correspondent to enquire about the welfare of the dog. This is nothing – hundreds of people will fret about pets out of doors and not give a second thought to people out of food, water or shelter. These are the people who speak soothingly to their Timmy on the greenway after they've just scowled at a cyclist for existing.

It tried to rain, but it didn't do much. It can do what it wants now I'm comfortably bivouacked – and it did. It could do with warming up a bit though.

I could read a bit later by wearing both pairs of glasses, readers and distance, at once, but eventually the light faded as the birds twittered and tweeted. There's nothing so soothing as gentle rain on a tent when you're snug inside.

The trains kept coming past, but the road went much quieter.

Day 6 – Haltwhistle to Langholm
(Northumberland and Dumfires and Galloway)

I was awake half the night again and discovered, due to the slope at the front of my tent, that I could have it fully open and lay on my back looking at the sky. I pulled my sleeping bag hood around me and a light breeze blew over my face. The sky was very dark grey with lots of little white dots. Light fluffy clouds moved across, followed by long wispy cloud. One of the little white dots moved swiftly across the sky, taking about ten seconds to move from the centre to my periphery.

I'd just nodded off when I was woken by a bright light and a roaring from the left. I jumped up in time to watch a long engineering train go slowly along the embankment, with bright headlights and lights in the cabs. Three or four twenty foot sections were grinding the rails and the whole thing was ablaze with sparks. It was a more spectacular light show than any fancy Blackpool tram.

When I'd settled down again a bird flew over silhouetted, tweeting as it went, and then another. I felt I'd discovered a whole new nocturnal world.

The sky gradually turned lighter and lighter grey and the little white dots disappeared. I turned on my side to face the encroaching dawn and took out my earplugs to listen to the chorus, and the occasional rumbling truck, its curtain sides flapping, the fans of a refrigeration unit whirring.

The little white dots disappeared until there was only one left above me – I swear this is true. (It was Ted Simon who went all mystical in *Jupiter's Travels* – anyone who gives their motorcycle a name is bound to lose the plot if they spend too much time on their own). I made some coffee. The engineering train went back with its headlights, but no grinding.

The pigeons start cooing later than the other birds, they wait until it's nearly fully light. They seem to like to live in dense fir trees when there's no railway bridge available and they're too far away to shit on Winston Churchill's head on behalf of us all.

There's nothing special about this campsite, in fact it's not really a campsite, but I'm facing away from the mobile homes and my stay has been very special.

I messed about doing nothing but savouring the experience for so long that I was cold and had to put my 'longs' on as well. Eventually I got packed up and going.

I didn't go into Haltwhistle because I didn't need to, preferring attempted suicide on the A69 in too many clothes instead. There was a cycle lane of sorts – it wasn't really a cycle lane and it was strewn with big dead birds who were still a smaller target than me.

Eventually there was a tunnel under, followed by a pedestrian path over the railway line and I sought refuge in the churchyard of St Cuthbert's, Greenhead for a second brew, even though I'd only been going half an hour.

Theroux reports on churches falling idle and being deconsecrated into carpet shops. He says the local Muslims always put in an offer, but are turned down as it wouldn't be right for Allah to be worshipped in St Cuthbert's. I don't get all this different God business. I thought they were all monotheists. There can only be one Supreme Being, like there could only be one Stalin. Anyway, if he went to Bradford, albeit thirty five years after he set down this fallacy, he'd find that worship of the Almighty continues in many a former bastion of the cult set up by the followers of the troublemaker from Roman occupied Nazareth.

'All I know is I'm not a Marxist,' said Marx long before his death, such were the sins committed in his name. I wonder what Jesus would have had to say about the Mediaeval Church or the contemporary Glory that is Rome – or that Onan probably has more followers 'and ought to have more' Steve would say. Steve despises religion and is always going on about overpopulation.

I keep saying, 'Come on, you're never going to get anywhere,' and I can hear Oades saying, 'You're not supposed to be getting anywhere, there's nowhere to get.'

The church wasn't open and though the graves were fairly old there was none of that skull and crossbones stuff that Durkheim goes on about. There never (hardly ever) is.

By Gilstead an old couple were out tending their sheep on a hillside, the women in a skirt and headscarf and waddling like overweight old women do. The man wasn't much better. How long can they keep that up before one of them has a heart attack in the top field and dies? And what will happen to the sheep? They'll be killed and eaten (after being disguised nicely in plastic and polystyrene) and their skins will be torn off and stacked stinking on pallets, like they are in an abattoir yard near Heckmondwike, to be bleached and sold as fluffy white rugs to customers at visitor attractions. 'Veganism is treating me as a person not a thing' says the well-funded campaign. Sheep aren't people and eating meat isn't nice. But veganism isn't the solution to the world's problems either. If only it was that simple.

Thirty good miles to Langholm. Nothing much to report except that I entered Cumbria, saw a Suma wagon from Elland, had my first rain and, at Penton Bridge, rode into Scotland. Whether I'll stay in it is another matter because the border is a forward slash.

From the top of the next hill I briefly saw the Solway Firth. The woods and the verge were full of bluebells, not Spanish ones but proper British ones. Then a sign said the road was closed. Some men laying cables, who didn't really know, said I'd get through. Roads are rarely actually closed to bicycles, but this one was. Thankfully there was a very rough diversion through a tree plantation up a steep, loose stone hill and I had to scramble up pushing my bike and all my belongings.

But I got round. As I re-joined the road a workman was stood at a cabin door, I said, 'Alright.' He ignored me. That was the first Scot I gave a chance to talk to me, unless he was Polish, which he could well have been.

I rode into Langholm, asked directions, and went straight to the campsite, just as it started to rain properly. It looks municipal and a notice said it was £6 per night for one or two people in a small tent. There was no one in attendance so I put my tent up where I thought I ought to and went to the big Co-op to buy nice things to eat.

When I got back the warden had arrived and on a whim I paid for two nights. It wasn't a particularly hard road today, but I found it hard going – hardly surprising, it was my eighth full days cycling (I went on a hard three day trip immediately before this one) so time to rest and feed myself up.

The campsite is attached to the rugby union ground and it's the 'sevens' tournament on Saturday, but I'll be gone – that is of course unless the weather's bad, because the next bit of the route is very exposed.

The warden said rain is forecast tonight and more on Saturday and that where I've put my tent floods. I'm worried about getting caught out on some of the exposed stretches in bad weather. It is, after all, only April.

I had a sausage sandwich, blackening my pan because I didn't have any oil, and then went back to the Co-op at the other end of town for the things I'd forgotten that were on the list I didn't take – tea, coffee and biscuits.

This was a bad idea because the sky was black and on the way back I got a good soaking. I have nowhere to dry anything. If I get wet and the sun, the wind or my body heat don't dry my clothes they don't get dry.

Langholm is on the A7, which is a busy road, but nothing like a busy road in England. It has a toll house at each end of the town, a little park by the river, a street full of shops that sell the things shops normally sell. This I noticed while riding through. Tomorrow I'll look at it properly and see if there's any surprises.

It wasn't late, but I took off my wet clothes and got into my bag to read while the rain pattered on the outside of my little tent and ate raw carrots so my arsehole doesn't heal up.

The feature of my tent I so enjoyed during last night also has its downside. Because the door has to be open you can't make a hot drink while it's raining or the rain comes right in on your bed.

Access to the campsite/rugby ground is by a Bailey bridge from the main road. Its wooden roadway is loose and as a car goes over, which one does every five minutes, it makes a noise like the world is ending – the biggest clap of thunder ever, times ten.

I thought the caravans that surround me were all empty, it being still out of season, but now I'm thinking they may house workers, like some budget township – the Scottish equivalent of US trailer parks for people who can't afford homes, or would rather spend their money on something else.

When I went out the noise was actually being made by old men getting ready for the rugby. They shouted at each other from one end of the place to the other. Relaxation for my £6 wasn't on offer.

But I did get the best, hottest shower I've had since I left home and dried myself on thirty seven of their blue paper towels.

It rained again as I was making the second course of my evening meal – I've done nothing but eat since I got here – and I had to eat it inside, risking spilling all over myself and my bed. Imagine thinking I could cycle miles on porridge and peanut butter.

And then back to my book: 'All travellers are optimists. Travel itself is a sort of optimism in action. I always went along thinking: it'll be alright, I'll be interested, I'll discover something. I won't break a leg or get robbed, and at the end of the day I'll find a nice old place to sleep. Everything is going to be fine, and even if it isn't it will be worthy of note.'

The man in the caravan next to me came back. He's definitely a worker, but he's OK. Campsites that have workers living on them can be a bit rough. He was interested in my trip and seemed to approve of the charity – though I don't think anyone would say to your face that they didn't.

One of the Scottish papers (sometimes just opportunist versions of the English ones) says Nicola Sturgeon wants a new independence referendum within the next two years.

There is a perception that Scotland is more progressive than England – and I could say here that a majority of Scots voted to stay in the EU, but that would be a fantastically crude yardstick, leavers and remainers cannot simply be equated with reactionaries and progressives, despite what many remainers would have us believe.

It is true that Scotland still has free higher education, for example, and for that they are to be congratulated, because the free market of everything is a global phenomenon which has to be actively resisted by governments. But Scottish councils of all colours have been no less enthusiastic in driving through cuts in services than their brothers below the border.

There is a strong element in the independence movement that want there to be a better, fairer Scotland – but that isn't automatic and will have to be fought for. Scotland has massive wealth disparity, much of the land is in the hands of great estates and in some places an almost baronial mentality persists.

I read until it was too dark and as soon as my head hit my blow-up pillow I was asleep.

Day 7 – Rest day, Langholm

I slept like a log, not stirring once in the night. Woken by the swooshing of the wagons on the wet road at what was probably a reasonable hour. My neighbour went off to work, the first to rattle the bridge.

As I walked to the facilities a man took pictures of the rugby field and others started arriving. One of the worst things about camping light is you have nothing to sit on and have to lie down in your tent. This means endlessly resting on your elbows and my left elbow isn't up to it since I tried to smash it to pieces nearly three years ago. The sun is out and the sky is blue, but it isn't yet warm enough to sit outside.

I forgot to mention that one of the contacts for the campsite, which isn't permanently staffed (or therefore secure), is called Aeneas – the legendary founder of Rome according to Virgil's made up myth designed to justify rampant Roman imperialism – at least the Romans didn't resort to intrinsic racial superiority and crude eugenics to bolster their imperial adventures, or cod us all with clashes of civilisation. It's a tired cliché, but when Gandhi was asked what he thought about western civilisation he said it would be a good idea. No country that routinely bombs the shit out of civilians while letting its own children go hungry and adults sleep on the streets can be called civilised.

Yesterday, having seen the old couple in the fields, I thought of my paternal grandmother, who I always called Nana, or Nan when I was older. She was born in 1901, the year Victoria died, and throughout her life, whether it existed in her time or not, she partook of a deeply ingrained collective memory of the workhouse, which she referred to as 'The Grubber.' Yesterday, while riding along, I made notes for a poem and I set them down here in the order in which they are in my notebook.

The Grubber

Life is not a picnic
And you must sink or swim
Whether going to the workhouse
Or going to the gym

If you wanted fairness
And no one's calling you
Don't hold your breath while waiting
You're not even in the queue

Whether spinning worsted
Or at Tankard's making rugs
Those who'd seen a better world
Saw it destroyed by thugs

In forty years of marriage
Not one bad word was said
And all around drew comfort
From the blameless life you led

You wore a Yorkshire hijab
As you walked to Whitehead's mill
You said you mustn't grumble
And lived by strength of will

You did most things together
There was no better half
For your ungrateful offspring
You killed the fatted calf

You laid your life down for me
Because you were my Nan
And now ten decades later
We're back where you began

Your husband had but three score years
And then your rock was gone
For two more long hard decades
You simply buggered on

And yet you voted Tory
And said you always would
So fattening up the bastards
Who spilled your brothers' blood

R.I.P. Lilian Ramsden, nee Atack

When I read it back, apart from the overt politics, it sounds like the sort of shit verse you might find in a birthday or Christmas card.

I strolled into town over the Bailey bridge, built by 78 Engineer Regiment in 1985. I used to build Bailey bridges with 38 Engineer Regiment and in training was instructed by a sergeant who warned us never to put our fingers in the pin holes unless we wanted to lose them, like he had.

There were signs for the 'sevens' along the roadside, which is what the old boys were hammering at last night. It was £10 to watch and £5 for concessions, £2 for parking (£3 for a pint, £2 for a burger etc.)

The first place on the way in is a café, where Bruce and Luke's coffee is 'hand crafted.' Then there are some luxury log cabins that look vaguely ridiculous with their TV aerials and Marley Modern roofs. I wonder how much the massed adjectives improve the sales of coffee and the letting of glorified sheds.

Where the through traffic has to slow down to 30mph a big sign says 'Slow down, here comes Langholm,' and so it does, proclaiming itself the birthplace of Hugh MacDiarmid. The big car park allows 'no overnight parking' (what possible harm could it do?), 'No camping' (likewise) and 'No cooking.' If I had a pound for every time I've brewed up in a car park it would pay for this trip – surely making tea doesn't constitute cooking.

It's a picturesque place, with a clean river and lots of public grass for dogs to shit on. There are what would now be called cottages across the river.

Thomas Telford is big – the road to Eskdalemuir is named for him, and there's a door hole on display that he made as an apprentice. But the only honorary freeman of Langholm is Neil Armstrong, the first man to walk on the moon. He could trace his ancestry through Ireland (possibly the less said about that the better) back to the Scottish borders.

And apart from the Butcher's, the Baker's and the tat shops that seems about it. I'd walked through Langholm's history in ten minutes. A good handful of shops were empty. Adverts in the community charity shop offered free hospital transport and free cat neutering.

Telford partially endowed the library, as did His Grace the Duke of Buccleuch. Hugh MacDiarmid's real name was CM Grieve and he was a 20th century international poet. Admiral Sir Pulteney Malcolm GCB, GCMG, 1768-1838 also appears to have come from Langholm, and who knows what adventures he had. Nevertheless it is just a through place on the way to somewhere else, the somewhere else we're all eager to get to.

There's a Springsteen tribute on at the Buccleuch Hall next week – everything happens at the Buccleuch Hall – so good of the Noble Duke to cast his crumbs among the forelock tugging folk – I'd have gone if I'd been here. 'Close your eyes and you believe it's The Boss,' said one reviewer.

I was robbed of 50p for a bent and faded postcard by a dour old woman who only wanted my money. I could have bought a model tank suitable for age 6+ if I wanted my child to grow up a little militarist.

And then I didn't know what to do with myself, so rather than a twee coffee shop I was forced into the *Crown* Hotel to spend money. It's ten hours till bedtime and I'm already bored. I'd have been better off cycling.

The book I bought for a donation from the tourist information office, because I haven't enough to carry, was given away free last year as part of Scottish Book Week because 'reading inspires creativity, increases employability, improves mental health and wellbeing and is one of the most effective ways for children to escape the poverty cycle' – an antidote to Tory policy then.

Though it's called *Rebel*, which I assume is a noun, rather than an imperative, its main aim is to encourage people to write, nevertheless; 'Everybody rebels. It's part of what makes us human to occasionally do things we know will provoke or fight against things we know are unjust. Rebellion incites opposition and change, allows us to find our own individual voices and inspires future generations to challenge convention and expectation.' Alternatively it might get you dragged off the street, and, if Rod Liddle had his way, battered by the cops for stating the obvious truth about climate change in the face of overwhelming vested interests.

There was no decaf, so I ordered proper coffee in the full knowledge that caffeine (and cider) keep me awake. The coffee was OK, the spoon was dirty, the place mats were slate, no doubt all the way from Wales, and the bar person sang when she wasn't on her phone. I asked if she was happy in her work. She said she was happy in her life – 'we only get one.'

I was the only person in there. Life went past the window in its car and the fan buzzed.

The first story was beautiful – about an eleven year old schoolgirl who stood up to a nun and was tacitly respected by her for it.

The staff member was on her phone going on about how some bloke wasn't doing right to his kids.

Thinking about the old couple on the farm again, the rough sleeping the charity warns of and about the charity I'm cycling for Paul Theroux says; 'Rural poverty always looked to me more bearable than the forms poverty took in a city. Poverty brought people low, and pushed them into the past. In the countryside this merely meant farming in a cruder way; poor city people had to go still further back and become scavengers in order to survive.'

He also says cities are full of indoor miseries that make him impatient. I can see why some people think Theroux is miserable – he's not one of the glass half full, look on the bright side brigade. He's not miserable, he's realistic – he can't look out of a train window

49

without thinking of gangrene because Britain is rotting from the inside out.

A man swore loudly several times from behind the scenes, loudly and unashamedly – all the men eff and blind here, all the old men at the rugby club did last night, openly and normally, 'I'll fucking this' and 'He fucking that,' but were nice with it.

I marched back to the campsite for my diary, regretting not having brought it in the first place. Copying up notes is tedious. There is no point in writing laying down when I can write in comfort in the library. It's tiny and has moved into one corner of Telford and Buccleuch's bequest. The librarian is also the postmaster – an outpost of some main office who had to keep ringing his dad for advice. Most, if not all, of the business was parcels.

But I was happy again – sitting in the library in a strange town is not one of the indoor miseries that make me impatient – they are the ones where I have to reluctantly part with money (cider is exempt) for things I don't want in order to keep out of the rain – robbed for wanting merely to be still, warm and dry.

There was a display of Muriel Spark's work – some dozen books – complete with obligatory Scottish flags. For all I know she may have considered herself an internationalist who thought countries were malevolent and malodourous constructs and borders lines drawn on maps by rich people. Anyway, I'd no idea she'd written so much. I enjoyed *The Prime of Miss Jean Brodie* and must look at more.

An old lass sat next to me and pointed out to her husband some of the juicier infringements of man against man (or woman) in the *Eskdale and Liddesdale Advertiser*, before saying, 'This fella's trying to study and there's me talking.' I said it was fine, I was only passing the time and took the opportunity to tell her my tale, but I learned nothing about her, not even her name, and the husband wanted to be off home so he could wonder what to do with himself.

Theroux could be writing of a thousand places from the Dales to Denbigh, taking in Haworth and Hebden Bridge, when he writes of 'the new class who moved in and gutted the houses, and then, after restoring the thatched roof and mullioned windows, hid a chromium kitchen in the inglenook that ran on microchips. Such people could make a place so picturesque it was uninhabitable.'

A man came in with a load of parcels. Within minutes he'd got on with the postmaster/librarian about food banks and how '*they* only care about the rich, *they* don't care about workers and the poor.' I joined in obliquely, and couldn't really tell if my opinion was required, but we covered independence, Brexit, the Tories (their name said with venom) and voting – and if we didn't agree about everything, which we did, there was scope for discussion. My sense that I was an interloper was reinforced when the man left without saying goodbye to me. However, being paranoid that people will think you are a twat is no reason not to talk to them – I played enough of the reticent inadequate when I was young.

Though it was raining they chucked me out of the library at two, being unable to staff it properly in these allegedly straightened times, and I had to decamp to the *Eskdale Hotel* across the road, where a lovely pint of Aspall's cider was reasonably priced, comparatively, but the price of the food was ridiculous, as were the verbose descriptions of the local attractions. Suffice to say Langholm is suitable for those wanting 'something more.' Actually, besides a campsite, it doesn't offer anything Cleckheaton hasn't got, unless you count a posh overpriced hotel, some famous sons, a connection with moonwalkers, beautiful scenery and a lot of swearing.

Men in the next room were talking loudly about rugby, about some winger being 'a killer' and the meeting up in such unfortunate circumstances – a funeral was advertised in the local shop – 'flowers from family only, charity donations in lieu to the surgery.'

'We're on the Wirral,' 'When I was in the RAF,' 'Catch me on the whiskey,' posh expats who stood in a long tradition of making it down south, in parliament, or as servants of the empire 'The Scots,' as if they are amorphous, were supposed to be oppressed by. Actually the shallow nationalist (as opposed to well-informed ones) always says he's oppressed by 'the English,' as if they too are amorphous. There was manly laughter, verbal back-slapping, shallow sincerity and tall tales. I'd rather someone told me to fuck off for being stupid, which is why I like working class pubs.

The menu disappeared so I couldn't order any food if I could afford it or the chef had any imagination – salmon swimming in a sauce of pointless adjectives, chicken marinated in nonsense. Posh people pay too much for stuff simply because they can.

These sixty and seventy year old men talk such empty vacuous shit their wives must be convinced they're married to idiots – you're either very angry with the system or you're part of the problem. Anyway the dead man must have been popular – no need for paid mourners or a pauper's grave. In death we are all equal – of course we are.

One woman was 'only' staying in a pub – so it was a basic twin room, 'but you only sleep in it.' There was women's and men's darts, so there was an atmosphere – but there was no rowdiness – thank God for that – better false decorum than honest, alcohol fuelled rowdiness.

Gin is popular and so is poncified tonic water to go with it – the elderflower tonic water is 'soft, subtle flavours of freshly hand-picked elderflower with a perfect balance of the tonic's natural quinine.' The Sicilian lemon tonic is 'made with only the finest Sicilian lemons, using the sfumatrice extraction method to produce a refreshing citrus taste.' And the ginger ale is 'made with a blend of three rare gingers to give an incredibly aromatic ginger ale.' And the name of JPR Williams was drop-kicked into the conversation in the other room.

A couple joined me in the side room (or rather they didn't join me). He was wearing a cardigan and an earring. She was reading about pointless celebrities in *Bella* magazine. He was endlessly at his phone showing her funny things. Posh people wouldn't be so crass. They were clearly working class people on holiday. But some of those next door were making a session of the funeral, and there's nothing wrong with that – though I'd rather talk about the availability of oil-based vehicle paints than rugby union, or even about the contents of *Bella*.

One pint led to another and eventually I discovered, by my own endeavours, that Norma and Davy were from Belfast exploring their roots in the Armstrong clan (uh-o). Davy was a motorway worker who'd travelled the land, Norma worked in a chemists. They were Loyalists and I was wading through eggshells in my cheap Go-Outdoors hiking boots, but we managed to cover Bloody Sunday, Brexit, Cromwell, families, relationships, monarchy and numerous other subjects without falling out. If I'd been as open with Republicans about my service with The Crown as I was with them I'd probably have been found dead out the back.

But anyway, my seemingly desperate day off buried in boredom turned out splendid and I walked to one end of the town for a tin of curry and back to the other end to my tent a proud man, safe in the knowledge that I could have been a career diplomat if only I weren't a socialist. I sashayed over the Bailey bridge like a pipe band drum major, swing my arms shoulder high 'chest in, arms straight, dig those heels in!' only hoping I didn't suffer a third degree burns night making my tea. 'Whadsome power the gift he gi us, to see ourselves as others see us.' 'Do you like Burns laddie? – Well get hold of this it's red hot.'

Monarchy was a dodgy area. They said they had pictures of the queen in their houses and always stood up for the National Anthem. I said I'd deliberately sit down for it. I said, 'You'll not be too fond of Cromwell then,' thinking that all the Irish hated him. They said he had it right. It never occurred to me that people thought wholesale massacre was a good idea – but of course they do – Yugoslavia, Rwanda, Bosnia, Germany *et al*. Just below the surface was the 'Never Surrender' spirit of Dr Ian Paisley.

On the subject of Bloody Sunday Norma and Davy acknowledged that Catholics had been demonstrating for their rights and had been illegitimately killed for it. But they didn't think soldiers should be put on trial for it because 'they had orders' (this, as everyone knows, is exactly what concentration camp guards said). In fact they think that things have now gone too far and that Catholics are favoured for fear of employers falling foul of the law, which is what reactionaries everywhere say when attempts are made to address the wrongs against an oppressed group. They hate political correctness, positive discrimination and the police 'having their hands tied,' 'acting like social workers,' etc.

Never mind that the alleged 'political correctness/positive discrimination' is designed to offset years of blatant privilege those now claiming injury have ignored or even enjoyed – five hundred years in the case of Indians and Africans, two hundred years in the case of Australian Aborigines and First Americans and two thousand years in the case of women. If women did ever get the upper hand, as some silly men claim they have (again as if they were amorphous) it would serve us right – just as it will serve the exploiters right when we take the lot off them and share it out properly.

A man went past in a big white van while I was warming up my curry and gave me a big wave. I gave him a big wave back, before he went over the bridge making a noise like Armageddon.

Safely to bed, fed and watered, a wiser happier man.

I'm a true bred Yorkshireman
My home is where my hat is
When I eat my curry
I eat it with chapattis

If they try to send them 'home' I'll be there to stop them – that's the beer talking.

There's a royal box scenario going on down the rugby field. The Duke of Buccleuch is probably coming to hobnob with the new money managing director of the Edinburgh Woollen Mill. There's hoardings for the latter all around the pitch. And so to bed. You've got to draw the line somewhere. Looks like rain. Goodnight bicycle. Goodnight John-boy.

Day 8 – Langholm to Peebles
(The Borders)

In the Borders
I slept well while I slept
But it wasn't a long sleep
Half awake, due to the fall of the dim light
And the noise of the river
I imagined I was camped in a ravine
Not on an acre of flat mown grass

It was hours before dawn
And I willed its coming
But it did not come
All one can do in the dark is think
I imagined I heard voices
And men were coming to kill me
I turned over the events of the day

An owl hooted
A flock of geese flew over
I fancied I heard
The church clock chime five
But that was impossible

It was also impossible to know
If the cars that passed
Were the last of the night
Or the first of the day

Then I heard crows, distant
And I knew that they knew
But they did not know
Because they were not crows
They were only creaking

Twice I looked out for the dawn
But there was only the false dawn
Of light pollution over Langholm
When I went outside to relieve myself
Into the night air, wantonly
The sky was like lead
And then I tried to sleep some more
But most of all I was desperate to write.

Political Football

Who builds these walls
We walk between
Is it man or is man kind
These walls that have no foundation
That can be taken down today
And built somewhere else tomorrow
Tarmac can be torn up
Mansfield can be man's field
Bradford a broad ford
Nottingham, forest
Newcastle, united

I very nearly got up and packed in the dark, thinking to go to the ablution block and wait for it to get light. As that was probably four hours off it's a good job I didn't. When I woke again it was fully light and raining. There's no point in a very early start – I can only cycle so many miles in a day.

Last night when I walked about the town half canned I looked at some of the display boards detailing Langholm's history. Like many places it once had at its heart a bustling railway station. The pathological short-sightedness of the men who wantonly destroyed this infrastructure, built on the hard labour of thousands of economically conscripted navvies, verges on a crime against humanity. And let it be recorded that they did not do it for communities, they did it against communities and for the motor industry. It was driven by the same logic that drove families off the land to replace them with sheep, and kidnapped Africans to work them to death in the Caribbean. Progress is an illusion while power lies in so few hands. We will not have progressed until it is wrested from their grasping grip and something other than profit is our guiding principle.

I feel like I have now to begin again and would rather bide here, in the library and the *Eskdale Hotel*.

I left Langholm to its bourgeois distractions – fifteen men and a bag of wind – and headed back into the hills, direction Eskdalemuir, weather fine but threatening.

After a steady climb the going was quite good. Four miles out I came upon an oval horse racing track in the perfect bowl of a valley bottom – all manicured and ready for the off.

I was apparently on a prehistoric trail – but you don't have to go back that far to discover what went wrong – the Levellers, like the miners, could have won.

At Bentpath I tried to use a payphone. They don't take coins anymore and the instructions for using a credit card, delivered by an American woman, were too complicated, and I needed the UK international dialling code, which I don't know because I'm already here.

The hamlet (it's hardly that) has a memorial to Thomas Telford that I've also photographed before as part of the Round Britain Rally. It will still be here next time I come, because it's part of our heritage, but the phone box won't be because it isn't. There's a note inside saying it's going to be taken away because it isn't used enough, in other words it isn't profitable – no longer can one arm of an industry subsidise another, any bit that doesn't make money must go, be it buses, trains or phone boxes. In fact the most evangelical of the neoliberals don't believe there is any point in providing any public health care or education and that 'the market' (peace be upon it) will decide who learns, what they learn, who lives and who dies.

57

I wondered if the railway had come through here, so a bit further on I asked two women walking Highland terriers in the middle of nowhere. The older one said not and told me where it did go. The younger one turned away because she needed to study something in the middle distance. Perhaps it's because I've had my clothes on for a week.

I should have brewed up at Bentpath and toasted Thomas Telford, who helped to make the modern world possible. I wonder if, like Einstein – horrified at the nuclear bomb – he would have said, 'I wish I'd been a watchmaker.'

Instead I drank delicately flavoured fruit tea on the edge of a brutalised commercial forest that had been made a temporary wasteland by logging. Already the two foot saplings were replacing the generation before. A big bird of prey screeched above.

It's also a 'Strategic Timber Transportation Route' so it was a good job it was Saturday.

There's not much at Eskdalemuir – about a dozen homes, a church and a cemetery with twice as many people in it as the village. One house had bunting, or prayer flags, and bells and I could smell dope.

Next comes the incongruous Samye Ling Tibetan Buddhist Centre, with its wedding cake tower and copper pinnacle, yin and yang flags and the Buddha sitting in the lake on a coiled snake. Given the prayer flags at houses a few miles either side of the centre Buddhism seems to have a bit of a stronghold in this valley. There are of course different kinds of Buddhism, as there are different kinds of Christianity and Islam. There's only one kind of Atheism (only in the spiritual sense – politically there are many kinds of atheism, from that of Marx to that of the clever fool Dawkins).

The road was as expected – long rideable climbs and descents, but the wind was against me much of the way and where I might have been bowling down hills I was pedalling. The day off has also failed to revive me in the way I hoped it would – and I found it all a bit of a slog.

Eventually I did get a good run, all the way down to the *Gordon Arms* Hotel on the A708. Nothing happened on the way apart from I ate a bag of Guatemalan-grown sugar snap peas and saw two big birds of prey. The scenery was as already reported. Straight across and back up again.

Same again – a long pull up a valley to the watershed and a good run down the other side to Traquair – 'Scotland's oldest inhabited house, restaurant, working brewery, maze, gift shop, big car park,' no thanks.

I thought I'd make it to Peebles today and I did, but just as I entered the outskirts, having got all the way with one light shower, the sky turned black and it dropped a big one. There was no shelter, but I waited until it eased a bit and rode on through standing water and rivers on the road. I didn't hold out much hope of finding anywhere to camp, but a site was clearly signed from the centre a mile outside. It was just the kind of campsite I hate – all the facilities, including a bar, but it didn't really matter because I was the only one on the camping field and the caravans and mobile homes were all a good way off. What did matter was that it was £20 – the same price for a backpacking tent as for a family of six. It was obvious that in season people piss each other off here because there were lots of signs asking them not to.

I couldn't be arsed riding back into town for food and decided to make do with what I had. Went for a shower when I'd got my tent up knowing from the sky it would be raining when I came out. It was, and carried on raining for the next two hours. 'Enjoy your evening,' the man on the desk said. Ta, I will. I strongly suspect he was unfulfilled and considered his whole life somewhat of a waste. I couldn't even make a cup of tea, let alone cook if I had anything to cook, so ate three dry tortilla wraps and drank cold water in my sleeping bag while the rain hammered on the tent.

It was nearly six when I arrived here – so at least eight hours cycling, probably nine, and well over fifty miles. Too tired to read and asleep while it was still fully light.

Day 9 – Peebles to Carnwath (via Rachan Mill)

(Borders and Lanarkshire)

Slept well – though it was raining every time I woke. Not raining and the normal bird noises in the morning, plus the irritating noise of someone's dog barking. Should be a good run today up the River Tweed through Stobo and Drumelzier to Rachan Mill, my fourth destination.

Almost all the way here I've been passing fields and moors full of sheep with lambs, hardly any cattle and hardly any arable. I don't understand who eats all the bloody things – 'woolly maggots' some people call them for their propensity to create a semi-barren monoculture.

Emerged to brilliant sunshine and scattering rabbits on an acre of empty camping pitches. Behind me in the valley mist hung over the river, but there are still clouds on the horizon – this is how yesterday started.

Only then did I realise I hadn't hung the official label on my tent so the groundsman could see I'd paid. I remembered when I first went to Glasgow and Danny McGowan described football referees as symbols of authority, and therefore enemies of the revolution.

I forced down the last of the porridge oats I've carried for 200 miles – recipe – oats, hot water, eat. A man told me the other day that after years of refusal he'd got into porridge as an alternative to cereal – it was alright if you put plenty of honey on it – durr.

I'm as stiff as a board and my digestive system is turbulent. 'It'll be the change of water,' my Nan would have said. It's hard work being an itinerant organism, we're meant to stay in one place like a fish in a pond. It's strange to consider that for hundreds of years most ordinary people never left their villages, and yet human beings had traversed the globe to get there.

There are four washing machines in the amenities block and two more similar blocks. Rosetta Campsite must be multi-million pound enterprise. There are signs up warning against unnecessary vandalism (necessary vandalism must be OK) on pain of eviction without notice. I wonder what kind of Stasi they have to enforce that rule.

The toilets in the big old stone building have a lovely echo – every plop resounding, which, being completely on my own I can enjoy to the full. One doesn't like to make a noise when there's someone in the next trap.

I was going to change my clothes, but they feel OK – so I'll get a bit longer out of them. For the first time since I set off my socks are properly dry (I've changed them once) because I put them, along with the flannel I use as a towel, on the radiator in the ablution block clearly marked 'do not cover.'

I don't know what Peebles has got to offer because I didn't look. On the way out I passed a B&B advertising secure motorcycle and bicycle parking that probably only cost twice as much as my wet night under Chinese nylon and a Co-op wagon overtook me too close going up the hill. On the back was a massive warning to pedestrians and cyclists to 'stay away from the vehicle as the driver may not be able to see you.'

Then Neitpath Castle, which is a rather impressive medieval tower house, like a normal house but stuck on top of a big tower – the equivalent of gated communities today – in case anyone gets the idea that the world is unfair and decides to act upon it.

The A72 towards Glasgow was a lovely level road and I was glad to be back on my wheels. A car coming the other way had COP for a registration – more despicable than all the Christian name crassness the selfish overpaid usually go in for – not the lord, but the lord's hired bully. Straight afterward CH415 overtook me, closely followed by LIB. Don't they know you can get stick on letters from B&Q and that for 30p each you could spell your name properly.

I left the main road to follow the Tweed upstream south west and saw something I haven't seen before – fifty little lambs running in a pack well away from their mothers – like kids on a school sports day. It is difficult to believe that lambs and sheep are the same animals. Put them in rows of ten and test them to destruction, that'll teach them to conform.

Then I saw my first dead badger. Norma from Belfast said badgers could be dangerous to campers (she's never been camping) – after I'd said there was nothing in this country that would eat you. That one won't.

A disused railway line ran right along the valley by the river. Stobo had a shut county library. The ancient cast iron finger post was lying smashed in the ditch.

A bit further on Stobo Castle and Health Spa, with its imperious gate top eagles, seemed to be doing good business – Rosetta mass campsite, Stobo exclusive health spa, you decide. Butlins or Barbados. A selection of top of the range 4x4s and a Jaguar entered. But I must stop being so prejudiced – these people are only spending their legally earned income. The question is – why is it legal?

In Stobo 'village' ostentation had spread like a disease and there were veritable palaces all along the valley. The first short climb made my thighs ache and I saw the first deciduous woodland there'd been for some time, much of it occupied by noisy crows. This is Britain, a nation (or rather country, 'nation' implies unity and common purpose) divided, not by Brexit but by wealth and privilege, just as it always has been. I was more surprised to see in what were effectively meadows in an alpine style the rotting stumps that showed it had once been a forest.

There were four bulls in a field so I told them to fuck off. Like Alan Bennett's dad did, only not in so many words, because they were at the other side of a fence.

And then I was in Rachan Mill. There was nothing there except perhaps a lesson in placing too much faith in destinations – certainly no mill of any kind, but four down and twenty two to go.

The next place was Broughton, where everyone seemed to be ninety. It was a few houses by the side of a busy road, but an old woman said they were staying here and wished me well. A whole troop of geriatrics spilled out of a building and got in their cars (some with personalised registrations). I suspected they were Christians hoping a Kia people carrier could squeeze through the eye of a needle. I imagined some kind of retreat where they could repent and pray for the world to be nice without upsetting the goose that lays the golden egg.

I found a bench in the sun, but the road was busy and it was no place to brew up. A Lycra clad lady went past, I said 'ey up.' She ignored me.

When I looked up the lane it was a little church – the Tory Party at prayer, or perhaps Tartan Tories. Anyway I celebrated reaching Rachan Mill on the bridge over the long gone railway with a mug of decaf and some peanut butter and pitta bread. Down below it was anyone for tennis and a woman laughed uproariously.

Sitting there on that wall, eating that pitta bread and peanut butter and drinking that coffee, between Peebles and Biggar, having got there by bicycle I find it difficult to believe it's all happening to me. Events have a kind of third person feeling, a sort of out of body experience, and riding along Leeds Road into Huddersfield seems like a dream, something from a different life.

A man went past ogling me with sports equipment sticking out of the back of his big van. He was moving the goalposts.

Up the road I stopped to let a flock of sheep pass from one field to another. 'Moving to pastures new,' I said. 'The grass is always greener on the other side,' replied the young farmer. That was the extent of our exchange, but I feel we had a kind of understanding.

And there were Spanish bluebells. Those Scots are in league with foreign flowers as well as foreign powers. On the opposite steep hillside a tractor dragged a Land Rover out of a muddy gate hole. It was a health and safety nightmare. More farmers are killed by overturning tractors than suicide.

I left the Borders and entered South Lanarkshire – 'Thriving on safe driving.' There were dozens of motorcycles, but so far not the screaming kamikazes of The Dales.

In Biggar I gave Sainsbury's some more money. It was ten to two (this was incorrect) and the centre reminded me of Thirsk. Most one street market towns remind me of Thirsk, or Ripon. I only had a brief exchange with a waddling dog walker about the state of the road and rode out on the B road for Carnwath. There's no point in carrying lots of food and water because it's only ten miles between settlements. Camping might be a different proposition and my bowels are still rotating.

Biggar has a lovely multi-level park with a ford, and above it a row of those stone detached dormer bungalows they only do in Scotland.

Entering Carnwath I crossed the path of some other long gone railway, between the abutments of a bridge that was built to last but didn't, such was the glory of Rome, by which time it was getting decidedly warm.

As if I was John Paul Getty or just a pillock I went straight into the *Roberston's Arms* Hotel and asked the fourteen year old bleached blond girl behind the bar how much a room would be if they had one. Like some sad stereotype she didn't know anything about rooms or how much they were and fetched a man who acted like he was *maître d'hôtel* at the Paris Hilton. I asked him how much a room was, though I probably couldn't afford it. He said it was fifty pounds. I couldn't afford it, but took it anyway – and it was only two o'clock, but I'm worn out I don't mind admitting.

Mr Professional asked when I wanted breakfast. I said eight would be fine, and then I told him I was vegan. He said, 'Poor you, you're right in the middle of farming country, you'll probably end up with grass.' I think he'll find, if he looks into it, that it's more than possible to sustain a healthy and enjoyable existence on non-animal products – and that farmers grow those too. Besides, I don't spend money to have judgement passed upon me. There's plenty of people who'll do that for nothing. He told me what time food was served. I told him I'd already eaten, which must have sounded ridiculous – I didn't know then that it was only two o'clock in the afternoon. Yesterday it was six when I thought it was four, today it was two when I thought it was five. Perhaps I need some proper rest. If I don't sleep properly tonight I'll never stay in another pub/hotel again as long as I live. And as for dinner – he doesn't know how much I'm enjoying my peanut butter and pittas in his pokey room with Agatha Christie's writing desk, followed by bourbon biscuits at 50p a packet. His food will be expensive and there's never enough for a cyclist anyway.

There's free Wi-Fi and he's only downstairs if I need anything. I probably need veggie burger and chips, but it might be illegal here – it is after all forty miles from the heart attack capital of Britain.

Paul Theroux is in Liverpool and meets a down and out woman. It's 1983 and she mentions the depression. 'We'll never get out of this one,' she says. It's just after the Toxteth riots and Theroux boldly rings the police headquarters and asks how many black police officers they have. He's told they have twelve 'coloured' officers – in a force of 4,600.

'And the "coloured" was interesting too. Policemen were "coloured," convicted criminals were "West Indian," purse snatchers were nig-nogs. But when a black runner came first in race against foreigners he was "English." If he came second he was "British." If he lost he was "coloured." If he cheated he was "West Indian."

Part of me wished I hadn't headed west and I'd gone straight north through the centre of Edinburgh on the grounds that it might be fun, when I knew all too well that it most certainly wouldn't be. Norma from Belfast said she loved Edinburgh. I don't. It's just one more big, stinking, car dominated city and, touristically speaking, just Blackpool for snobs

I was in bed for four, something I wouldn't even do at home without encouragement.

It's a beautiful day outside and my tent will be sweating away on the back of my bike. I couldn't very well bring it in to air because it was dripping wet when I put it away. If your tent is wet for too long it goes mouldy and that in turn gives you a bad chest.

I got out of bed to get showered and back in it again afterward, content to read. I've half-filled my note book and half emptied Paul Theroux's book, the latest bit about Wigan and the top down destruction of Orwell's bottom up observations. Soon I'll be on to his China trip, and the Highlands.

Actually I enjoyed a meal fit for a king of the road – a packet of cherry tomatoes, two pitta breads, two perfectly ripened bananas and too many bourbons.

Paul Theroux sees an England that is changing into a poorer more violent place – the implication being that the violence was physical and done by working class people, rather than social and done *to* them. This was four years into Thatcher's reign and only a year later her government, backed up by the boot boys in blue, were engaged in one of the greatest acts of social violence of the twentieth century – they were smashing the National Union of Mineworkers, for decades one of the bulwarks against the serried ranks of the ruling class. This opened the floodgates of neoliberalism and led directly to the cynicism and disenchantment that blights the country today – and all of it is predicated on the cowardice of our side. For all his Stalinist tendencies Arthur Scargill was right, and any honest appraisal must judge him totally vindicated. The responsibility for the defeat lies with NACODS, the TUC and the Labour Party, including 'The Welsh Firebrand' Neil Kinnock.

Day 10 – Carnwath to Kinross

(Lanarkshire into Perth and Kinross)
Thankfully I slept well – ten hours at £5 an hour – and didn't put the TV on. It would have intruded into my disconnection.

Part of me still thinks I should be going through Edinburgh, but the greater part doesn't. 'But if what people said was true, that it really was one of the [nicest] nastiest cities in the world, surely it would be worth spending some time in, for horror-interest.'

Looking back to Saturday afternoon and the conversation with Norma and Davy – Theroux has the same experience. 'Perhaps our conversation was typical. It took us forty five minutes to get to religion and another hour before Mehaffy volunteered that he was a Protestant. By then it would have been too late to quarrel about Irish politics. We were friends.'

He had not stated his religion. He had said in a challenging way, 'I'm British,' but that means the same thing as Protestant. And yet, this man he meets on a train says, 'We didn't have much money, and when we were short it was the Catholics that helped us out, not the Loyalists who were always running the Union Jack up the flagpole.' He was a scoutmaster who'd always had Catholic boys in his troop, with the priest's permission. The priest said, 'My only regret is that you're doing something I wish I was doing myself.' Local ecumenicalism and social interaction are good, and should be celebrated, but prejudice does not in the main emanate from within communities. It begins with a system that needs to divide in order to rule and a geopolitics based on ruthless economics. The divisions in Ireland are not accidental – they are deliberate – the product of a thought out policy, just as they were in Germany in the 1930s, India throughout the Raj, the former Yugoslavia in the 1990s, Israel throughout its existence. And so it goes on into the stigmatisation of Muslims today. Muslims can rush to help flood victims in Mytholmroyd, white people can show solidarity with refugees, progressives can oppose endless war, Bishops, Rabbis and Imams can meet, but the only real solution is class politics. Ordinary people in Northern Ireland, Catholic and Protestant, were, and are, both worse off precisely because they are divided.

But me, I'm going to go north, over the Forth Road Bridge and up into the Highlands to a place called Padanaram, which sounds like pandemonium (I can remember one or other of my parents saying, 'It's pandemonium in here,' when my siblings and I were noisy), and then up to Inverness and right across the country to a place called Naast, as in nasty, and then onto Skye to Valtos, and then down and by ferry to Glasgow, and then to Blackpool etc. – for weeks to come.

The bed was so good I didn't want to get out of it. I've also got attached to the clothes I've been wearing for ten days and see no reason to change them now – but I don't feel I can go down to breakfast stinking, where there might be a man in a kilt or a woman with brooches and her hair in a bun, and croissants.

There's still rumblings, and when I look at the chewing gum I've been consoling myself with it says 'excessive consumption may cause laxative effects.'

Obviously my breakfast was no problem for the person who was cooking it, as opposed to the prejudiced publican, but Radio 2 was on too loud, which was a bit disconcerting, apart from a country song, which sounded like The Dixie Chicks, but wasn't.

The waitress wasn't Scottish (lots of people in Scotland aren't Scottish), but I couldn't place her accent, possibly Dutch, but then why would a Dutch person want to leave her booming homeland?

The people on the other table were from Lancashire and attending a funeral. I initiated a conversation on the weather, but it didn't develop. In fact they wouldn't have even said good morning if I hadn't said it first.

Now all I have to do is cart these troublesome guts over open country and towards Livingstone and Broxburn and the Forth Road Bridge, where I don't expect there'll be much camping going on. A good relaxing stay and I'm glad of it.

I checked out bang on nine into a cold and misty morning – headed up the austere one-streeter, bought hot cross buns at the Co-op and straight back into open country, vying with timber and tarmac wagons on the A70, the sun already trying to break through and a good forecast. On a peripheral industrial estate the Chill Grill said 'Bikers or Cyclists Welcome' and people had dumped rubbish by the side of the road – or perhaps it was a council clean-up waiting for collection.

I took it easy on the thoughtfully provided, but glass strewn, pavement, which lasted almost all the way to the Auchengray turn off as the timber trucks thundered past. A sign said the road, part of my carefully considered route, was closed, but I decided to chance it.

'Journeys cannot be just measured in miles, but in recognition, acceptance and understanding. Each book, each film, each play and each life is a journey. The distraction is irrelevant.'

The route was only undulating and a whole host of wind turbines turned languidly, only adding to the air of relaxation, which is just as well because even on the minor hills the hearty breakfast lay heavy. Within an hour the sun was fully out and set for a scorcher.

A timber truck passed. On the back in big letters it said, 'Great life – No wife.' This western sentiment would be inconceivable to people in some parts of the world, where a man is not complete without a wife and children. And yet there must be unattached truckers in Kurdistan.

One fashionable farm had tulips on a dung heap, and an ancient cart pressed into service as a planter still displayed its lot number – no doubt the product of the auction sale at some ancient holding, and a family deceased or scattered to the four winds.

The road was closed for two men replacing telegraph poles and they didn't even look up when I passed, let alone say 'Can't you read?' or 'You were told the road was closed.'

A big goods train passed in the valley bottom carrying thirty containers, some emblazoned with the message that less CO_2 was produced by rail transportation. The whole scene was a symbol of what could be if it weren't for powerful lobbies and bent politicians. Greta Thunberg could have said, 'That's what you need to do – and get those trucks with their mad market philosophy away from our schools.' But will Greta Thunberg only be the latest Jose Bové or Lech Walesa – a flash in the pan to be subsumed into the swamp of establishment politics? It was a fine line, with a regular passenger service.

And I ask myself; why, and *how*, do people piss in pop bottles and wang them out of their cars when they could just get out and piss in the verge?

Woodfords was modest, with a long row of white cottages like something in the Hebrides, except there were trees distant. On that hill the mist did not clear and the veiled wind turbines only redistributed it. Noises above suggested I was on a flight path. A startled sheep seeing me coming tried to jump a fence it had no chance of clearing and made me cringe for its wellbeing. At the summit I entered West Lothian. A recently felled forest made me think of the devastation of WWI.

On the descent, with the slag heaps of the defunct Livingstone steel works just visible, I met Alasdair Anderson, a lightweight road cyclist from Edinburgh, with his roots in the midlands, returned to the land of his fathers. He recognised my Rohloff and told me the best way to avoid built up areas and busy roads. I was stopped at the time, or he probably wouldn't have. I must remember that. We managed to squeeze into the conversation Theroux, Bryson and Betjeman in relation to Slough, which he compared to Swindon as a place I didn't want to go.

Alasdair told me he'd done Land's End to John O'Groats in nine days on an organised trip – through big cities and the lot – which is madness.

Then a funny fella on a town bike went the other way and tried the weather trick on me. I should have stopped really. A Wildfowl and Wetlands man got out of his van and turned his back on me rather than speak. It is legend that people acknowledge each other once they are out of towns. It is also untrue.

As I descended into distribution centre sprawl I saw a woman driving a big Tarmac tipper. This is still a novelty.

And then, by luck, guesswork, the sun and the way the planes were coming in I navigated my way to the Forth Road Bridge. I knew it would be a bastard and it was. Among the endless 'schemes' and light industry there were pubs that styled themselves 'Village Pub' and 'Country Pub.' The scale of industrial park sprawl is breath-taking, as is the number of wagons going to and from them. I stood for a while right under the stupid planes to marvel and could clearly read what it said on them they were so low – 'Flybe,' for example, 'quicker than road or rail.' As Barry McGuire said fifty years ago *'We're on the eve of destruction.'*

> *And you tell me over and over and over again my friend,*
> *That you don't believe we're on the eve of destruction*

Newbridge, which has a pub built in 1683, has had to physically restrict the size of vehicle that can enter – or it would be one more HGV hell-hole. I said to an old woman stood at the bus stop, 'This is a right spot isn't it,' considering it myself a veritable hell on earth. She said, 'Aye it's lovely.' And another great big jet flew over about 100 feet above us, and then another. It has been said by someone famous that you don't need to go to an asylum to find insanity. A Martian, or even an objective observer, might ask, 'What the fuck are you people doing to yourselves?'

And then I hit the car showrooms – acres and acres of new child killing, community clogging symbols of our stupid self-destruction, with salesmen in shirts and ties smoking false fags just off the premises. None of them told me it was a dead end, but they laughed at me when I was coming back.

Kirkliston is no doubt an average place, it has a building on its high street built in 1682 and is blighted by the same through traffic as every other place in the land, but it looked lovely by comparison.

I stopped for a packet of pakora and ate them in the street. Two minutes later, over a field of yellow rapeseed, was the distinctive red Meccano of the Forth Rail Bridge.

I stopped at the viewing point to contemplate the three magnificent structures that span the Firth of Forth – the rail bridge, built a long time ago, the first road bridge, finished in 1964 and now open to only buses and bicycles and the new motorway bridge, opened either last year or the year before. The sky was blue, the water was blue and a train rattled over the bridge. I'd only gone and ridden my daft homemade bicycle all the way to the Forth Road Bridge.

Fourteen young Chinese people came, when they took pictures of each other, with the bridges in the background, they put two fingers up like Winston Churchill did. What does it mean? One of them got right up on a wall top that had a big drop at the other side. I was horrified. None of her party batted an eyelid. I spoke to their tour guide – they were all students in Britain. She lived in Glasgow. The bus had Chinese writing on it. Where would our universities be without the income from thousands of Chinese students doing Business Studies? – Probably catering for wider tastes, with the aim of creating rounded individuals rather than market obsessed automatons – that's where. And then she walked off to mess with her phone in peace. Actually she probably thought I was an old idiot because I failed to understand first time that they were all students here and that she understood perfectly well what I was asking and I didn't need me to do the actions of a plane flying.

Instead of the cacophony that once reigned on the bridge all was serene. Naturally there were signs for the Samaritans – who have 'teamed up' with the Tories to tackle internet sites that 'promote' suicide. It was 15.34 and 174 bicycles had crossed the bridge today.

While I was writing this two middle aged women came down a little path and my presence, right at the end of the bridge behind some bushes, frightened them and then had them in hysterics. I entered the Kingdom of Fife.

In Inverkeithing Sandy Wallace Cycles said 'Don't just think about getting fit – speak to the experts.' It had closed down. Across the road Ryan's Bike Surgery had closed down too.

From there I could switch off and follow cycle route one through the outskirts of Dunfermline towards Kinross. One 'scheme' was called Trondheim Parkway. I've been to Trondheim.

A nasty headwind got up and I passed the M90 commerce park, which housed both the Scottish Vintage Bus Museum and a mountain of thousands of tons of rags and carpets that had been there so long it was becoming a natural feature, with bushes growing out of it. While I was studying it a cyclist with panniers on rode past and ignored me.

Cycle route one took me off the B road and up a big hill (as they do) onto something called The Kingdom Cycle Route when it was getting towards time I was stopping.

Up and up and up it went, until Loch Leven and Kinross lay enticingly in the distance. The descent was alpine. It was a fantastic road even in the late afternoon when I'd had enough. It was a fantastic road *especially* in the late afternoon when I'd had enough. It made me grin. I resented the diversion at first, imagining that I had somewhere to go when I was already there.

Cycle route one takes a lap round Loch Leven, which wasn't to my liking, and was unlikely to produce accommodation, so I rode into the town and was tempted by the first B&B – it was twenty to seven, ten hours after I started cycling – but a man and his daughter came past and he told me there was a campsite a mile out, so I bought something nice for my tea instead.

Gallowhill campsite was a couple of miles further on the other side of the motorway (campsites for some reason are often near noisy main roads, or railways). I asked the man on reception if I could stay on his lovely campsite. He chuckled and said, 'Thanks for that, it is a lovely campsite.' But I thought he looked a bit shifty. I only gave him my surname and he called me Mr Ramsden nine times until it sounded like he was taking the piss. He also made a remark about my cowboy hat. It isn't a cowboy hat, it's a Tilley hat that can pass through an elephant without being harmed, or I'll get another one for free, as worn by the best explorers.

I followed his car up to a lovely field with a bench and table and the lot. There were the vans of workers, which some campsites do not allow, but they've got to stay somewhere if they follow Norman Tebbit's bicycle based dictum. 'I grew up in the '30s with an unemployed father. He didn't riot. He got on his bike and looked for work and he kept looking 'till he found it.'

The facilities are lovely. There's pictures on the walls, advice on local services and the notices are all polite, not orders from Herr Commandant as they were in Peebles. Incidentally the government has today announced that in an attempt to regain control of prisons it wants all governors to wear uniforms – presumably with knee-high boots and Herman Goering trousers. Critics say this will undermine prisoners' belief that governors can deal with their concerns and complaints impartially. The pitch was £9. Everything comes to he who waits. One of the best days so far overall.

There was even time for a bit of reading. Paul Theroux is in Northern Ireland during 'The Troubles' and details the horrors. He has little sympathy for, or possibly even understanding of, the philosophy behind the factions, implicitly suggesting they don't even have one, the violence having become violence for violence's sake. It didn't have to be like that. The British government didn't have to prop up

73

the sectarian state against the legitimate civil rights movement of the late sixties, like it always had done. It could have conceded that Catholics were human beings worthy of decent treatment. Instead it shot and beat them off the streets like dogs. What else would people do but turn on the occupiers and the collaborators? It's exactly what the French Resistance did and they are heroes.

The Scottish version of *The Times* today reports a rise in the number of people who oppose immigration – I wonder why. Scotland has always been very open towards incomers because the general trend is toward depopulation. (Actually some nationalists have always been against 'the English,' but that's a different matter).

Theroux, and he is not alone in this, has no notion that Ireland was colonised, settled and plundered with the same genocidal imperialist zeal as were Britain's numerous other possessions abroad, or that it has been partitioned, gerrymandered and policed ever since with the sole intent of propping up a sectarian planter state. Instead, like many others, he imposes a proclivity for violence upon 'the Irish,' thereby denying them the right to what is theirs – the right to rule their own country. In so doing he refuses to see that the nationalists' struggle is as legitimate as the Quit India Movement or the Anti-Apartheid struggle (as well as calls for Kurdish and Catalan homelands).

Socialists always support the right of oppressed nations to self-determination (through they reserve the right to criticise the methods used). War is a dirty business and the struggle in Ireland will continue, with all the horrors that that entails, until the British state finally quits one of its last imperial outposts. If 'the Irish' have become inured to violence it is because they have been brutalised for centuries. There is nothing innate about it – being creates consciousness, consciousness does not create being – in other words people think according to how they live – they do not live according to how they think.

Day 11 – Kinross to Forfar (via Padanaram)

(Perth and Kinross into Angus)

International Workers Day, deliberately downgraded by the Tories as part of their petty attacks on anything that smacks of working class solidarity [I'd gained a day somewhere].

Slept well with the M90 two fields away, thanks to earplugs. I don't see why I shouldn't get over the Tay Bridge today.

I emerged to a blanket grey sky and some frost on the grass – it's getting colder as I go north – and tried to convince myself that being cold was an attitude.

In his caravan nearby was John, a rough and ready wind turbine technician from Essex. He advocated being 'part of the change you want to see' and said Scotland had embraced wind power technology, but since the Tories cut subsidies much of his work was repairs and maintenance, rather than new installations. To those who don't like wind turbines because they are ugly (or even because their dog doesn't like them) he says, 'You won't be saying that when the polar ice cap's melted,' which might seem like short cutting the argument, but is exactly where we are.

We covered other stuff as well, from HS2, which he thought was the Tories' attempt to get a good infrastructure project to their name, to the rule on some campsites that no vans, and therefore workers, are allowed, which he considered understandable, and was waiting for a complaint. To some he'd be seen as a dumb worker, but he was no slouch politically or intellectually (clearly I set myself up as someone fit to judge).

I stopped on the bridge over the M90 to ponder at it. Alongside, potatoes were being planted and beyond that a green field had been turned over to a housing development. The cars and trucks roared past, oblivious.

I broke my never go back rule to return to Kinross to buy postcards. While I was writing one a woman from the garden centre came to talk to me. She was from Leeds and asked if I had a Facebook page (a Facebook page!) I referred her to my charity's website, hoping she could follow some link. How on earth did we exist before the internet?

The signs to new developments under construction read 'Weaver's Loan,' 'Lathro Meadows,' and 'Lathro Farm,' not 'Pretentious Park' and 'Crass Crescent.' I badly needed something salty and wasted £4 on crisps and a jar of marmite.

After Milanthort the turn off to Glenfarg was advertised as a cycle friendly road, an acknowledgement that all the others aren't. It isn't roads that are unfriendly, it's the drivers on them, and you still encounter aggressive dickheads on back roads.

The walls are made of big angular stones and the road passes through patches of arable, with cereals and rapeseed. There is the smell of the earth where potatoes are being planted, though there are still sheep about higher up.

At Duncreive a ratepayer (he told me, having paid for all the silly cycling sympathetic signs) came to tell me where I was going, getting out his 'more detailed map.' I telegraphed that I hate dogs, recoiling from his terrier and it stayed at a distance – not so the next out of control mutt with an owner determined not to let me enjoy a peaceful bench. The man didn't demonstrate resentment that I didn't appreciate his pet, but the woman did. The man even tried to control the woman's dog for her saying, 'He doesn't like dogs,' the implication being that I'm some sort of weirdo. It's not a question of not liking dogs, one could not like dogs from a distance, I just happen to think their filthy snouts shouldn't be in my food or sniffing at my bare legs.

The man was English. Two women who were walking past sounded posh. Exclusive properties abound.

I disobeyed the ratepayer and took the B road down 'through the glen.' He'd made it out to be a twisting rat run full of wagons, where I would almost certainly be killed. It was actually a delightful five mile descent through woods beside a rushing stream – though I salute the courage of the skip-wagon driver who overtook me across double white lines into a blind bend.

The A road was OK too. Into Abernathy, where bungalows are called 'Pitversie,' 'Earn View,' 'Tivoli' and 'Gairloch' and a brown sign pointed up School Wynd to 'Clootie McToot Traditional Dumplings,' by which time it was getting warm again.

I happened to disrobe by a sign pointing to McDuff's Cross, along a track used by Roman patrols, by McDuff when fleeing McBeth, by Queen Victoria and as a turnpike. It was designated, i.e. downgraded to, a pedestrian right of way in 1997.

The council had thoughtfully scraped a wide path beside the busy road – whatever next? – But it was only stone and too bumpy to ride on.

Then to my left was the flat, shining Tay, with its sandy banks, and I found a lucky five pence piece. (It may have been dry grass rather than sand, I was at some distance).

I left Perth and Kinross for Fife and Newburgh, which celebrated its 750th anniversary in 2016. I overheard a dog walker on the verge asking another, 'Have you got any pooh bags?'

The church clock struck twelve as I stopped for biscuits and pop in one more one street town with trucks and cars thundering through. I had a feeling that the unclassified 'coast' road that looks flat and waterside on the map would take me high over hills, and it did.

At the top I met 56 year old John Muir, silver haired and moustachioed, out of his van and surveying the scene. He did three years in the Black Watch, serving in Northern Ireland and still talking about it. Then he went AWOL for three years because, he said, back in Blighty everything they did was to impress the public and he wasn't into impressing the public. He's never settled since, had fifty eight different jobs and was eager to tell of the violence imprinted on his young mind – the SAS kicking the shit out of youths, the murder of innocents – and he knew, because he'd done fourteen years on the doors in Dundee, and a bit of boxing. We reeled off the places we'd both been, Crossmaglen, Balykinler, Strabane. John was of the opinion that the trouble would never flare up again in Ireland because everything was controlled by four men and they wouldn't allow it. His description made me think of Sicily and I said so. He said, 'Aye the world's a terrible place.' He also said thousands of tons of stone were once taken down the Tay, but not anymore. Now it's only the occasional timber boat and the channel is silting up.

Smart in his corporate pullover and slacks John Muir said he was moving to Elgin next month to be near his daughter, whose husband is in the RAF at Lossiemouth – and that his wife was 'no well.'

There are wrecks of buildings big and small along the foreshore, but mostly it's just crops right to the edge. A woodpecker tapped and got a response from further away. I've heard a lot of woodpeckers on this trip.

Just around the next bend I could see the Tay Bridge, as John Muir said I would. The trouble with talking to ex-soldiers about Northern Ireland is that many of them still believe they were on the right side, and, like soldiers in any war, their sanity depends upon them continuing to believe that. John went into the Junior Leaders at Folkstone when he was 16. I went into the Junior Leaders at Dover when I was 15, and for me, like him, that time has an increasing echo the older I get.

It is probably because my formative years were stolen by the state that I have never really settled, i.e. conformed to a two point four, semidetached existence, that I have two 'failed' marriages behind me, that I have to undertake these regular fact-finding missions, and why Oades, as ex-RAF, understands. But I no longer think I was on the right side in Ireland, and I have never been a bouncer in Dundee – I would never have considered myself hard enough. But if being a teacher taught me anything it was that if you put the right uniform on someone they'll start behaving like someone that should be inside it.

There are other ways to understand the world than to believe blindly what you are told by the self-interested state, to hate the people it tells you to hate and when necessary to kill them. But one doesn't usually come to an alternative understanding as a teenager, which is why the army runs a cadet service and sends recruiting staff into schools – because it is recruiting child soldiers like they do in the Congo. I was certainly a child when I joined.

Dundee looked romantic, almost dreamy, from miles away across the flat water – like somewhere that could be on the Med or the Adriatic.

Five tractors were in one field sewing potatoes and the air was heavy with the smell of turned earth. And then the smell of pine from stacked logs recently felled. The gorse is in flower, everything is tinder dry.

A dead deer was full of flies and stank – there was something rotten in the state of deerpark.

In the bus shelter at Bottomcraig there was a big mural of Gandhi – along with advice on the surgeries of the local MSP – 'Whatever you do will be insignificant,' the Gandhi quote said, 'but it is very important that you do it.' A woodpecker was right by me, but I couldn't see it.

Dundee still looks beautiful from right opposite, with its riverside frontage and gleaming white tower blocks.

I was sitting having some lunch by Wormit Boating Club when a man called Dixie came over and announced himself as ex-army 'served in Ulster – saw two of my mates die,' in the 1970s again, 'that was enough for me,' best time of his life. Likes to walk, walks miles every day, divorced sixteen years. 'Dixie' 'cos he was good at football, but the Dixie Dean that played for Celtic, not Everton. Goes in his local 'there's loads of squaddies in there.' I'll bet there is. Reels off all the places in Ireland he served because it's forty five years ago and he's still living it. I forgot to ask what mob he was in – he had a bus to catch.

Dixie said it says something for me that I'm riding round the country on my homemade bike. He didn't say what. To what extent these soldiers were Orange sympathisers consciously propping up an Orange state is impossible to say. I expect the occasional Catholic with no prospects took the queen's shilling as well. If they were like me they won't have had an inkling about the history of Ireland, but to a lesser extent the same religious sectarianism exits in Scotland and they may have imbibed it from an early age.

Cyclists cross the Tay Bridge on a central boardwalk afterthought and exit on the northern side via a lift to nothing under the end of the bridge. There are oil rigs moored and what looks like the hull of a big ship from the other side is actually a hideous building designed to look like that. But the first thing proper I saw was a bus with a full length banner poster 'proudly supporting the 3rd Battalion the Black Watch, the local regiment.'

I didn't like Dundee – cars went too fast and came too close. I left as quickly as possible east, along a four lane race track, expecting the next old bloke I saw to stop me to tell me he'd served in Ireland. It was pretty much like leaving the semi-derelict ports of Liverpool or Bristol, except the oil industry has postponed its death.

A scrap wagon did a stupid U turn and nearly caused a pile up. There were three beauticians, one advertising a toenail cutting service – presumably for the old and obese, but one never knows. A woman turned straight in front of me, but a little lad waved at me from the pavement. I asked him how it was going, he said 'guid.'

A sign pointed to the Scottish Veteran's Residences. It seems like the army is an institution round here. And I was lost. Ten minutes later I was back on track, passed the big Michelin factory, picked up the road to Kellas, cleared Dundee and entered Angus. It had only taken two hours and three years off my life. I could hear the birds between the speeding commuters. The headline on the local paper was 'Dundee Michelin workers feeding the needy.'

A transit pickup overtook me into a blind bend and then slammed on his brakes to turn right and stopped me dead.

Today, for the first time since I left home, I nearly came unstuck. It was a very long way to Forfar – further than I wanted to cycle, and I didn't even go directly there, having it in my head that I might avoid it. There was no sign for a campsite – it was obvious there wasn't going to be – and I toured the whole town looking for indoor accommodation. There was a hotel I knew I couldn't afford (or thole) and one B&B displaying a 'No Vacancies' sign and that was it.

Somewhat despondent I was forced at 7.15 to ride out of the town, past the headquarters of the local detachment of the Black Watch, and head for Kirriemuir, another nine miles away. I was getting desperate.

On the way I rode straight through Padanaram, my fourth destination, without stopping. There was nothing to see anyway – just a row of houses along the main road and some rendered boxes at right angles that wouldn't have looked out of place in Mixenden, a Halifax 'council' estate. Dotted all over are little groups of houses that seem to have been put up with no thought for their style or setting. But there is a good bus service between Forfar and Kirriemuir, even in the evening.

The first hotel in Kirriemuir, at eight o'clock, was a converted church and the woman told me over the intercom that she was full of a group of workmen. Then I spotted the big *Thrums Hotel*/pub down a street, which offered 'a taste of the glens' – and here I am. It's a double room and it's £55, but a very nice young woman fussed over me and my bike and I'm saved once more.

I must now admit, despite my big talk before I set off, that is simply do not want to fly camp in a field – though there's no certainty I won't have to before the trip's over, and in any case I've not seen anywhere suitable. It's nothing to be ashamed of because neither do 99.9% of the population – I just shouldn't have pretended to myself that I was going to.

It's been a mixed bag today. I've cycled too far and for too long. But once I'd had a shower, got into a nice big bed, eaten a tin of sweetcorn and a tin of beans cold and had a couple of cups of tea it was all OK again.

It's noisy here though – banging doors, revving cars, a rattling street grate – so it's earplugs again.

The hotel's welcome card tells me it dates back to the 1860s, when it was a temperance hotel. Paul Theroux reminds me of Morris in Wackerfield. A publican in Ireland tells him 'farmers don't stay up until all hours drinking. They work hard for their money, so they save it.' The bumf in the room tells me that Glamis Castle is nearby, as is a memorial to AC/DC lead singer Bon Scot, who was born in Kirriemuir.

And I am asked not to eat in my room and told that I can eat my own food in the dining room – not cold beans out of a tin surely, and not without buying beer.

I managed to finish Paul Theroux's section on Ireland, which he toured in the early 1980s talking to people – mostly Protestants it seems. It's not nice, it's not clean and there's certainly some gangsterism, but those who seek to reduce the whole conflict to gangsterism are refusing to acknowledge the underlying circumstances. 'Ulster' was a gangster state for forty years before the troubles – the gangsters were the Orange Order, it was only in the legitimate challenge to their hegemony that the media became interested and the problems appear to start, whereas they had existed for decades for Catholics, who had been denied work, housing, humanity and their dignity. The IRA gave Catholics back their dignity, just as war time resistance gave the French theirs, and there's no wonder they supported it. If things are all equal in Northern Ireland now, as Norma and Davy claim, then it worked. But I don't believe they are. And the fundamental problem remains – part of a sovereign country is under occupation by a foreign power. Britain got out of its other colonies and it should get out of Ireland.

Day 12 – Kirriemuir to Pitlochry
(Angus and Perth and Kinross)
I slept well – though hardly for long enough. In order to shorten the day I said I didn't want my breakfast till nine. There's no point in starting at seven if I'm going to have had enough by four. What I really need to do is 'waste' some time during the day. On the other hand the slower I go the longer I'll be out and the more I'll spend on my expensive B&B habit.

The weather forecast isn't too good for the rest of the week, which makes loitering outside difficult. The plan is always to sit and read for an hour, but it's easier to say than do. In a way I look forward to such as Blackpool, where I can rest for an hour in Wetherspoon's on the front without negotiating a city and spend only £1. Actually I could do the same in Macca D's and must bear that in mind.

An eighty seven year old man on the train to Oban tells Paul Theroux that the army wouldn't have him because he wore spectacles. Then he tells him how 'those poultices' in the House of Commons will eventually start the next war. There's shades of Harry Lesley Smith – old men who thought the world was getting better, only to realise in their dotage that the opposite is true.

And Theroux says something that I know myself to be true – 'Some travel is a fantasy of running away.' I wouldn't go as far as Theroux when he says 'In travel you meet people who try to lay hold of you, who take charge like parents, and criticise. Another of travel's pleasures was turning your back on them and leaving and never having to explain.'

Again I didn't want to get out of the nice warm bed and put on my smelly clothes – of which, if it gets any colder I don't have enough. When I put them on they were cold, damp and sticky. The room was cold too.

Besides two Germans, who had already eaten, I was the only one at breakfast, but the service was the slowest I have ever witnessed. It was a good job I had decided to slow down.

An old woman, who was either deaf or couldn't understand my accent, took ages to come and then spent ages rooting in the freezer for suitable components for my breakfast. Eventually she brought me an ancient packet of spicy falafel and asked if they would do.

The Germans left. The fake beams were all light oak, as was the floor, the tables IKEA. There were big mirrors and photographs of mountains. Through double doors with bevelled glass panels the next room had been done out like a library, with leather armchairs, except that the books, rather than being metaphorically wallpaper, were actually wallpaper. It would have been quite realistic did it not repeat every ten books.

When my breakfast came it had all been dipped in hot fat in the finest Glasgow tradition and nearly made me sick. It left a coating of fat in my mouth that the coffee wouldn't shift.

When I'd finished the cook came to speak to me, but only got as far as 'where are you going' and 'you don't go up that A9 do you?' before the Germans interrupted for their bill. There were extensive communication difficulties.

But the austere dining room, which had all the charm of a motorway services, was offset by the volubleness of the Mother Hen, who marched everywhere like she was in a long distance race. She was tour guide to the Teutons and couldn't work the credit card machine. In the end I had to give her cash and she nearly had me as jittery as she was – or was that the coffee?

As I left lots of old men in suits and pin badges were arriving in big cars with personalised registrations for a meeting. Probably the local lodge. One of them came back to ask about my trip in a friendly way. Then another – 'On holiday?' 'Where are you from?' to which I replied that I was from Bradford. 'I'm not being funny,' he said, 'but you won't see a lot of coloured people round here.' I had, women in hijab in Kinross and Peebles and two black building workers yesterday. I said I didn't make distinctions between people on account of their colour. He said, 'But there are an awful lot of them down there.' I said I hadn't noticed. He walked off saying, 'You're one of the best are ye?' And then I left before I got into an argument with a gang of old bigots.

In the Co-op I tried to find decent sustenance for the glens in a shop full of pop, crisps, chocolate, dog food and ready meals. The *Sun* says there is outrage at Marks and Spencer's decision to take animal fats out of all its sweets – it's P.C. gone mad.

Once I vacated the metropolis it was another beautiful bird singing morning – but decidedly coats on – avian calls mixed with the squeaking from my pedals, which I must one day do something about. Incidentally the clicking knees I thought I had turned out to be the ends of my long laces tapping on my boots every pedal stroke.

My crow appeared on a fence, at first pretending not to know me, but then she flew ahead to show me the way. And the way was good, for it was flat, and there were places where I could have slept for nothing, but only at a ten hour abstraction. There were sown potatoes, just sprouting cereals, blooming rape and low hills with gorse and sheep.

I rode through Kirkton of Kingoldrum, where there was possibly the most impressive domestic garden I've ever seen, with pergolas and statues and fountains. 'The Old Post Office' was a private house, 'The Old Barn' the residence of Buddhist sympathisers, pictures of that pot-bellied idol alongside the adverts for rhubarb. And then a small hill called for the removal of extraneous nylon and some regret for the deep fried falafel.

And so it went on through Dykends, Bellaty and Glenisla in its belittling vastness, my crow appearing occasionally on the fence to fly off as I passed to mark the next bit. There was little traffic, but a farmer coming the other way smiled, as much to himself as to me.

There were of course B&Bs up tracks, but middle-aged men busying themselves at roadside cottages did not look up, for to do so would be to deny their deliberate isolation – how wild an existence is it if a cyclist from Cleckheaton can casually ride past? This is after all a long established tourist trail – as the numerous thistle bearing brown signs demonstrate, guiding the way as they do to the alternative enterprise of crafts and coffees.

I fell, like the surrounding rain does, to the Loch of Lintrathen, where Carpenter Oak had in their yard the substantial wheeled and iron shod base of what looked like an ancient trebuchet, alongside great hunks of sawn oak perhaps destined for the restoration of ancient buildings whose walls had been built to withstand projectiles thrown from such instruments of war.

In the wood yard a man sang like Pavarotti and then almost yodelled. I felt like responding through the trees with the only few lines of opera I know from Verdi's *La Traviata*, but didn't have the courage to do so.

Hundreds of swifts were circling for flies and returning singly to their numerous burrows in the sandy bank of a former excavation.

A new post box stands at a junction, the old one still embedded at floor level in the base of an old milk churn collection point – unless perhaps the level of the road has been raised. The old one was Victorian, which isn't at all unusual.

There were some of those sheep that look like pigs – no neck, just heads at one end and arses at the other. And still there are Costa coffee cups in the verges. I simply cannot imagine what these people think as they cast them out of their cars into this Eden. The car makes people selfish. It is a cocoon, beyond the walls of which the world and its inhabitants are only virtual. It is like sitting in a drive-in watching a movie and dropping your pizza box out of the window for mere minions to remove. And by the way, the bloated four by four drivers in their expensive yellow sweaters returning to their bought and paid for tranquillity with down lighting and double glazing look miserable and resentful that anyone else is here. They are the terminally sick victims of an out of control afluenza epidemic. They do not like the cities on which their parasitic existence is predicated and yet they cannot exist without the industry there – I of course exclude the modest highland inhabitants in this analysis. And what of the self-made man? 'The source of all value is labour' – as their own guru Adam Smith asserted – and for the most part the self-made man does not exist. The self-made man does not maketh himself – he makes others into wage slaves to fund his luxury.

The Highland Adventure Centre advertises Team Building because there is no 'I' in team and you can't do enough for a good firm. The 'I' standing for individuality. It is the essence of military training to break the individual and re-forge him as part of a ruthless fighting unit. Applied to the workplace it destroys people (just as it does soldiers), making them appendages of the machine, mere collateral – human resources beside trucks and timber.

Modern post boxes do not contain a regal reference (not least because the Royal Mail is now privatised), but because the present monarch is coming to the end of her reign, as must we all, including the bourgeoisie. To my right not too distant was the vast Balmoral Estate that sustains her – along with the Privy Purse and various other pies.

I stopped in the picnic area at Kirkton of Glenisla and met Federico and Timon (of Holland, not Athens – Federico was Italian). They were literature students at Aberdeen on a five day walk with big old-fashioned army style rucksacks and we had a jolly exchange about the faux gypsy life, Scotland and education in general. It was Literature with Creative writing they were doing and they could follow many pathways. Timon needed sunblock for his red neck and I was able to oblige. It was their first walking trip and they went off with their adopted rough walking sticks.

The fairly recent introduction of the Right to Roam in Scotland seems to have resulted in the erection of strong fences and the proliferation of private property signs, but that could be just my imagination (Smokey Robinson) [It was the Temptations].

To avoid a bit of A road and because I am a glutton for punishment I dragged my 23kg bicycle and my 20kgs of gear over the flank of Meall Mor (550m a.s.l.) stopping to read a page or two of Theroux on the way. An empty salty snacks bag lay in the road. I suspected the occupants of the misfiring Peugeot that had overtaken me.

He talks to a post office worker and asks about the dog licence, which was then set at 37½p and cost four pounds to administer. 'Why don't they put it up to something realistic?' 'It would be unpopular,' says the clerk, 'No government would dare try it,' – just as they dare not impinge on the motorist's right to pollute. There were then six million dogs in Britain. Today there are eight million. Instead of putting the licence up and using the money to deal with the appalling unsanitary mess dogs cause they decided to abolish it. Only being soft on dogs could do more than tax cuts to get a government elected.

This is pheasant and grouse shooting terrain. I once heard a senior police officer on the wireless seriously assert that people who kill animals go on to commit murder. He didn't mean game shooters and foxhunters. He meant working class men who kill vermin cats because they shit in their flower beds and attack their pigeons.

At the top it was rocky and precipitous and an old cottage stood ankle deep in the waters of a more recent dam. Birds screeched, cackled, tweeted and quacked – all of them a mystery to me.

One massive pile stood empty and in serious disrepair, but generally I thought of *Deliverance*. There were cloven hoof prints in the verge, but they are only deer, of which I've seen several.

At an 'Ecocamp' one could bide in what looked like old railway guards' vans, but probably weren't. It's all downhill from there – and what a decent it is.

On the A road a sign warned of the possible presence of someone on a 1950s Triumph motorcycle with a dustbin fairing and a pudding basin helmet. A Shearing's 'Lochs and Castles' coach went past and two massive great green four propeller planes flew very low through the valley in some military hardware commemoration. Aren't these planes good? – They symbolise Britain's greatness and its heroic past. Yes, they kill people. That's their sole purpose. And we, like fools, celebrate them.

To the right of the B 950, beside a long flat road, the hills were once laboriously walled into small fields, but it doesn't matter anymore. A Lamborghini went past at speed and then three open topped old Triumphs came the other way looking like Thelma and Louise in miniature.

Just after I'd got on the 950 I was latched onto by a bicycle bore called Robbie Winkle (yes really) who insisted on riding with me nearly all the fifteen miles to Pitlochry. He was originally from Merseyside but has lived up here for twenty years. Though he was riding a lightweight bike in jeans he had all the jargon and he drove me like a bastard, first along the flat and then up a very long incline, all the while bringing me up to speed on all the climbs in Britain, his best time for this, that and the other and the doings of all his mates, while showing not the slightest interest in me or my mission. He was also a climate change denying conspiracy theorist and I imagined the tin foil he must be wearing under his helmet to keep out the voices. Robbie also sympathised with coach drivers who said they hated bicycles and went on about cyclists who run red lights. I don't go in for any of that self-loathing stuff – the roads are designed for cars and I don't drive a car. I have to make my own rules in order to survive. I ride the most environmentally friendly vehicle known to man that does no harm to the roads and keeps me fit, therefore saving the NHS money and I'm not going to be lectured at by some gas guzzling Neanderthal who thinks they're somehow superior.

Eventually Mr Winkle turned back and at least allowed me the final descent into Pitlochry, which is a shithole caricature of a proper place. I went to the Co-op for my tea, bought a postcard from a Sikh bloke so I could ask him where the campsite was and exited north ASAP. Pitlochry is the Hebden Bridge of the Highlands, the Tumbridge Wells of the Trossachs (it isn't in the Trossachs). It's Wetherspoon's meets Go Outdoors, without the charm or purpose of either. In season it's a seething anthill of alienated drones dressed in the latest breathable fabrics desperate to spend money – and every imaginable opportunity exists for them to do so. Pitlochry is the pits, it is possibly only exceeded in its empty pleasures by one place, and that is Aviemore. Tourism sucks. It sucked when it was done by train, it doubly sucks now it is done by car and it barfs off the Beaufort scale when it is done by plane. If travel really broadened the mind Pitlochry would not exist.

Faskally campsite, two miles safe distance from the hiking shops and the home cooked deep fried food pubs was all it should be and much, much more – a space age Soweto with knobs on – a reduplication in canvas and tin of the neighbourhoods people had left, little canvas Smethwicks and tin Pudseys jammed together, with a pub, a shop and a video shed in the centre. But that shouldn't bother me because the camping field is almost empty.

It started raining and I noticed that the cheap bitter lemon I bought the other day (I'm still using the bottle) was made by refresco on Citrus Grove in Kegworth, which conjures up a real romantic image. Then the two four prop planes went over again. I zipped up and began making my house as rain pattered on nylon, hoping they were wrong about the forecast.

As I was riding to the campsite, as safe as if I was already there, two deer ran across the road and Mr Small Prick overtook me in his Porsche.

Apropos the strong Scottish tradition of providing cannon fodder for the British state I wrote;

Gun for Hire

Why not have a son
What use is a daughter
Send him to the army
Like a lamb to slaughter
He will get good training
For some much needed role
In any case a sniper
Is better than the dole
We all must peg our noses
To earn our daily bread
Who's to care or worry
If it fucks him in the head
When he comes back damaged
A mental paraplegic
There's plenty who will sell him
His daily analgesic
Yes there's mothers out there plenty
Whose only lifelong plan
Was to nurture in their bosom
A mercenary man

Mr Winkle also told me it was the 1st May today, either I'm wrong or he is.

I'm having the time of my life and am glad to be in my little tent secure on a site. It was either nine or eleven pounds – I've forgotten which.

I faffed with my maps to my heart's content and am proposing to ride by the A9 all the way to Inverness in the belief that there is a cycle friendly alternative to it, though I decided this before I set off and my general direction is plotted in straight lines on umpteen separate sheets.

Again I should have got my sleeping bag out to air last night, though it probably wouldn't have dried in the cold room. One day the sun will come out and it won't be continually damp – though dampness even then is an everyday reality due to night-time condensation, which is worse on cold clear nights than warm wet ones.

I'm a para-SAS commando
Like back when men were men
In my little Wendy house
In some Scottish glen

The headline on one of the local papers was that a big local care home provider has gone bust. Maybe some venture capitalist can 'rescue' it, asset strip the land and flog the rest next year for a pound to someone who thinks they are going to make a mint and no more cares about old people than the man in the moon. Don't panic dear – it's only the free market. Keep calm and carry on the corruption.

In fact I faffed about for so long, without even taking my cycling gloves off, that I allowed myself to become cold and had to go get a hot shower, whether I wanted one or not, and I only had one yesterday.

Unfortunately I neglected to take anything with which to dry myself and had to use my T shirt, meaning I had to reapply the stinking one I've already worn for eight days. I cannot afford to use my third and final shirt because I will have nothing to sleep in when I get wet through, which may well be tomorrow, in which case I will surely die.

I was forced to eat my expensive organic vegetable balti cold from the tin and drink cold water because I cannot use my stove with the tent battened down against the rain, but it was still lovely and I am as snug as a bug in a rug.

And then I remembered I'd purloined just one small sachet of jam this morning, which made a nice jeely piece desert.

It was so dark I could only give Paul Theroux ten minutes. He reports in 1983 that a large aluminium smelter in Alness closed, with the loss of 900 jobs – better join the Black Watch then. He compares Scotland with Ireland, saying 'the fury of the terrorists was indistinguishable from the wilfulness of budget cutters and accountants,' which echoes Bruce Springsteen on the demise of the Ohio steel mills in his song *Johnstown* – 'Them big boys did what Hitler couldn't do.'

I'm afraid I gave my teeth a miss.

Robbie Winkle was also an ornithologist who said the swifts I'd seen were sand martins and a train spotter who went on about steam engines and Deltic diesels. He said his head was a radar and he could tell when danger was coming and that the area we were riding through was called Billionaire's Row because the heirs to Colman's Mustard lived there in a house painted yellow and Eric Clapton came to fish.

Day 13 – Pitlochry to Newtonmore
(Perth and Kinross into the Highlands)
I slept for three hours and then was as awake as someone who was very awake. The rain still poured and I had to carry out a difficult four stage tactical operation known as pissing in my pan. I was awake and bored, so engaged in some comfort food. I don't carry a torch and it is hard to make Marmite sandwiches in the dark, even when you've found your Charles and Diana spoon in your tiny tent among your larder, wardrobe and library.

Eventually I got back to sleep and woke for the second time when it was fully light, fine, and the birds were in full song.

I thought when I met the student walkers yesterday that Timon of Athens might have been an oligarch. His namesake thought he was a merchant. I think now he may have been a philosopher [He was a satirist].

When I emerged I found myself practically surrounded by two posh cars and four identical green tents twice the size of mine – so it was they whose giggling and door banging got through my earplugs last night.

There was much boot and door slamming while I breakfasted as they took every item of their belongings to their vehicles singly and sealed them inside, but it was dwarfed by the wagons going past on the road. My fellow campers systematically ignored me and within half an hour they were gone. Half an hour later so was I, discovering along the way that a spoonful of peanut butter makes porridge made with water a bit more palatable.

At the ablution block I had a long chat with campsite maintenance man Basil, a Zimbabwean of about seventy who had lived for a long time in South Africa and still called himself a Rhodesian, which speaks volumes, and had no time for black Africans – but then he's probably seen things I can only imagine. He tried to defend the British Empire on the grounds that it brought a lot of good things and credited its advocates with an innocence of what they were about – whereas actually philosophers and scientists were utilised to bolster imperialism and white supremacism *post facto*.

Basil was not a bad man. I'm glad I met him. He said he was glad he wouldn't be here to see Britain's eventual collapse. We covered travel, railways, the arms trade, the post-war boom and Britain's decline, among other things. He said politicians' intentions were good, but knew deep down that they usually aren't. He said, 'What can you do?' I said I was a revolutionary. He said some revolutionaries just shouted from the side-lines, and named a revolutionary in South Africa who'd got himself elected 'and then fucked everything up.' Of course he did – there was no revolution –

he only got himself elected, how was that going to change anything? If we could do anything fundamental with a vote they would never have given us one.

I forgot to fill my water bottles and couldn't clean my teeth because basil was painting the toilet door. He didn't rub it down first.

It's a long, long climb today.

Both problems were rectified at Kilikrankie Visitor Centre just up the road, where I could have put myself down for Scotland's biggest bungee jump. Just north of Kilikrankie a huge hillside is being slowly devoured – the hard rock to be crushed and used for the top dressing of roads.

And then it was Blair Athol. The Blair Athol Hotel has the flags of Britain, Scotland, the EU and the USA flying outside – the ex-imperialist, the would-be independent state, the bosses' club and the current superpower – all bases covered. Blair Athol was quiet today. Last time I passed through it I was appalled. It struck me as a perfect symbol of the stinking rotten anachronism that is Britain's class system. It was like a *Fast Show* parody of a Range Rover themed Hooray Henry hunting lodge, with men kitted out like century old throwbacks standing in the street with broken shotguns over their arms because they could.

Of course posh people would rather be shooting peasants. They despise the working class for its irreligiousness, its beer drinking and bawdiness, its apparent moral turpitude, its gallows humour, its honesty, its songs and most of all its solidarity. All the rich have is their stuffed shirt, stiff upper lip, stab in the back standards and their church door hypocrisy. Unfortunately for them they have had to let their precious pedigree be polluted by second generation scrap metal dealers, industrial spivs, jumped up policemen and the manufacturers of plastic windows, but they do their best to maintain their pompous, clench-buttocked self-importance in the full knowledge that the greater the degree to which you deny your roots the better you become at it. Done well it is Blair the international statesman, done badly it is Prescott the hypocritical thug.

I passed the Old Manse of Blair 'a boutique hotel.' I suspect no one I know has ever stayed in a boutique hotel, but some of them may have cleaned the shitpots. It flew the Scottish flag because, well, you have to – it's like the flag of St George has to be flown over a heart attack inducing truck drivers' food wagon. Except in the case of the flag of St George it means 'racists welcome here' along with all your other misdirected prejudices.

When I was with Robbie yesterday a Land Rover driver coming the other way had muddled 'One life – Live it' to 'One wife, livid.' Very droll.

And at Bruar stands one of the reasons – a clan museum perpetuating the notion that men who do the work have something in common with their exploiters purely on the basis that they have regularly been required to take up arms and die for them. The clan system is feudal, but it was dreamed up by Victorians. The war memorial celebrates the glorious record of the Highland regiments. There is nothing glorious about being dead or irretrievably disturbed. And beside all this pomp is the most hideously pretentious retail outlet known to man – where the terminally posh can buy the upmarket and marked up equivalent of a Tam O'Shanter and ginger wig available in a trashy gift shop in Edinburgh.

And then the climbing started. The Drumochter Summit cycle path climbs to 457m. A sign warns that weather conditions can be severe, even in summer, and that there's no food or shelter for 30km. When Oades and I were setting off down, last time we came this way, a man crested complaining as if it had been unmitigated torture, but much of it is quite gentle – no steeper than the average English greenway.

To the left the river cascades and thunders over rocks that are set on edge – part of some great fault, the railway is beyond that and the A9 is to the right.

I was tempted to rest on a flat rock over an idyllic falls, but more tempted to try to ride to Inverness, though I also knew it was impossible. There was still snow on one distant hill, and several others later, such abodes as there were are mostly now deserted.

95

Basil had said to me back on the campsite that it was obvious most freight should be on the railway. It is obvious even to a child, and yet it isn't. We are entitled to ask why.

I reached the Dalnacardoch Estate – through which the disused road that is now the cycle path used to pass, but I am not allowed to use it. It has returned to the ownership of one of the few people who own much of Scotland. I am relegated to a little path, and then to the verge of the current busy A9 – only to discover a bit further on that due to geography [geology?] the old road disappears under the new one. I'll let them off this once.

Out in the wilds I kept seeing black animals darting for cover. I thought they couldn't be black rabbits, but they were – and lots of them. I was always led to believe that if a foreign, i.e. coloured rabbit was released into the wild its fancy plumage would soon be bred out.

Towards the top it looked very much like rain in front and the *Royal Scotsman*, a diesel drawn train in vintage livery went past, it even had a viewing platform on the back like in Hollywood westerns. I officially entered the Highlands.

From there it wasn't much fun – the path was broken and bumpy, slowing me right down in fear of smashing my bike – it went up and down the embankment of the A9, ruining any sense of a descent, and a bitter wind got up and blew in my face.

At three o'clock I had to stop at the wooden hotel and café in Dalwinnie for chips and beans. While I waited for my food I shook and shivered and the rooms 'from £35' were tempting, but I'd still have this hard part to do tomorrow and the forecast for then isn't any better.

'This is Achfary,' Mr MacGusty tells Paul Theroux. 'The Duke of Westminster's estate,' says his wife. 'Does he farm here?' asks Theroux. 'Oh no, it's an estate. He keeps it for shooting and fishing. Prince Charles comes here in a helicopter sometimes, for the shooting.'

'The Duke owns a good bit of Sutherland,' says Mr MacGusty, 'It's an old way of life. It's very unfair in a way.'

'It was more of a shrug than a protest. But he was resigned. After all, we were talking about feudalism.' So much for the perception of a more progressive Scotland.

It wasn't a very nice place anyway – more of a truck stop. OK for a meal, but a bit shabby. Dalwinnie is a desperate and desolate cowboy town looking place.

It was a hard ride into Newtonmore – pedalling downhill into the wind – but I rode straight onto the farm campsite. I paid the old woman five pounds at the door of her bungalow. She asked where I'd come from today. I told her Pitlochry. She said I'd done well, that was 42 miles, and winked at me. I bet it's more than that on the cycle path, but I don't consider it a particularly great achievement, though half of it was uphill and the other half into the wind. It cost me as much again to get something for my tea at the garage. I suspect if I'd gone a bit further there'd have been shops.

It's ten degrees colder, so straight into my bag with my coat and hat on.

Inverness will still be a tall order tomorrow. It's further than the ride today and there's some equally high ground.

Theroux says the flummery of bagpipes and tartans and tribalistic blood and thunder was made into a highland cult by Sir Walter Scott. Most traditions are invented and the Highland Clan tradition is one of them – and yet when you tour round Scotland celebrations of the clans and clan museums are everywhere. In any case it was the very clan leaders the minions are supposed to worship who drove people off the good land in The Clearances. They weren't interested in people, they were interested in money and nothing much has changed. Some land was wanted for sheep, which is bad enough, but much simply became playgrounds for the rich or baronial estates – ownership for its own sake. Like everywhere else most Scots are good people, but it's nothing to do with their rulers who have been and remain as big a set of bastards as any.

I Only Watch the Documentaries

I like to put my feet up
When my shift is gone
I sit back in my armchair
And put the telly on
I'm ruthless with my viewing
I don't abandon hope
I just get my relaxation
In the bullshit world of soap
I'm just a silent witness
And don't need scorn or pity
I'm a vicarious paramedic
On board for Holby City
I watch it for the wildlife
And love the history channel
I like it served up bite sized
With David Starky's flannel
Those who call me goggle eyes
Really get my goat
But once I put my telly on
The whole world is remote

Basil asked me what I thought of Corbyn. I said he was the best thing that had happened to British politics. He said he was just a career politician, which is a) facile, and b) no different to any of the others. The weakness of this line was apparent even to him. It would have done no good to tell someone who still called himself a Rhodesian that Corbyn had been a consistent anti-racist and defender of the Palestinians. He probably thinks Zionists are as blameless as Boers and Afrikaners.

Some crofters were forced to scratch a living on bad land, all the while being able to see good land across the valley, from which their families had been evicted, lying idle – used only for grouse and stags to be shot by the vile rich. Thousands more emigrated, having been robbed of their heritage by people who simply did not care whether they lived or died.

The sky cleared. I'm going to be cold tonight. It isn't even warm in the toilets. For ten pounds you get warm tiled toilet blocks. For five pounds you get cold bare concrete blocks. But everything was immaculate – not like the farm site at Dent, the global standard for cheap campsite grottiness.

The railway line is about a hundred yards away and trains keep rumbling over a metal bridge.

I should have washed some clothes. In the laundry there's an ancient twin tub with wooden tongs like my Nan used, but in the evenings I can't be bothered to do anything.

I'm tired, cold and fed up and I wish I was in a nice warm room. I'm not looking forward to the night at all.

Day 14 – Newtonmore to Inverness
(The Highlands)

I was disturbed several times in the night by the cold, especially when I slid off my airbed and only had a thin layer of plastic between me and mother earth, and woke cold when it was fully light to trains, trucks and tractors with bouncing, banging trailers, as well as bird song and mooing. For some reason I thought first of the methane.

I lay wrapped up waiting for the sun to warm me and it did so but marginally. I had to will myself to get out and face the day. For once the tent wasn't soaking wet with condensation, which suggested it would be windy.

I opened the zip to an unpromising grey sky and prostrate, with my coat and hat on and still in my bag, I made coffee. The hills around have patches of left-over snow on them. I emptied my bladder and got back in my bag to make porridge. It's cold. Today I tried it with marmite. It was OK.

My socks were even dry.

To the intrepid traveller
When earth is hard and cold

It's well to act on impulse
Get up, go out, be bold

While I was putting my tent down the hills disappeared and it began to sleet and snow, putting a coating on the highest peaks. It soon passed, but there was clearly more to come – and much exposed road ahead. If I thought it might set in I would hole up somewhere, and I still might.

Newtonmore had everything a person could want including several big hotels – this is really tourist territory. It was a good roadside cycle path to Kingussie, but there were several more light blizzards. A female bus driver coming the other way waved to me in sympathy. The front of the bus was covered in snow. Within a mile my fingers were so cold I couldn't feel them, which, as any motorcyclist will tell you, can be painful as they get warm.

I stopped in Kingussie and bought overpriced and heavy rigger gloves, which weren't ideal, but were better than my fingerless ones. I was in Kingussie over forty years ago when I was in the army, building footbridges for the Forestry Commission. Since then the Forestry Commission has been privatised, and so has half the army, and the road signs have all gained Gaelic translations.

I considered the café only an hour into the day, but once I'd got the new gloves on it fined up and I kept going the eleven miles to Aviemore. I decided not to take the signed cycle path because I knew it would weave me all over. I also reasoned that if I was going to collapse from hypothermia it would be better to do it beside a road than on an isolated cycle path nobody else was stupid enough to be using.

Along the way there are numerous centres where the unimaginative with a Blackpool Pleasure Beach mentality, but more disposable income, can be spoon fed excitement. Alternatively the more sedentary and the semi-senile can be waited on hand and foot in hotels by young Poles and Lithuanians. I saw several other cyclists – most of them on lightweight machines, but one older woman on tour, all of them heading the other way with the wind behind them.

The sun came out, but a freezing head wind still blew. The road was fairly level, so the boil in the bag effect wasn't as bad as it could have been, but my shirts were still wet by the time I reached Aviemore. Just to remind me I was a nuisance cycling piece of shit a van overtook me far too close as I rode into town, for no reason other than he couldn't be bothered to wait two seconds.

The less said about Aviemore the better. Suffice to say it thinks it's in the Alps and it isn't. Nevertheless I had no choice but to patronise a surprisingly unpretentious café. I ate my beans on toast and then knocked my full cup of coffee over right across the table, thankfully away from me, which I put down to my over-exerted, unsatisfactory sleep, shivering state. The mothering waitress made me feel even more conspicuous by her calm understanding manner. The other waitress was a young Chinese woman. Actually in the café in my shop-soiled state I felt vaguely ridiculous, even though I was in one of the walking and outdoor activity centres of the world. Everyone else was smartly dressed and looked as if they'd arrived by car – though I did notice that regular service buses kept pulling up outside.

I followed the international cycle network signs out, believing it must now be a long downhill to Inverness, it being on the sea – how wrong could I be - and passed the preserved railway with an engine in British Rail livery – so much for that hiatus of progress.

Admittedly parts of the marked, partly purpose made, cycle route were interesting, even beautiful, but it was exactly the kind of path I'd feared this morning and I hated it. It wound me through estates of holiday bungalows, posh woodland mansions, over golf courses and bracken moors and through forests with the sole purpose of keeping the cyclist away from the road to save annoying drivers – no notion that he or she might want to get somewhere. Parts of it were rutted, others full of loose stones – as if I were some kind of mountain biker with nothing better to do than smash my bike for amusement, not someone with a fully loaded bike on tour.

And I've a terrible fear it's going to wind me in via Culloden, twenty miles east of where I need to be (an exaggeration). These paths, like everything else in this country are designed by and for car drivers, either the ones that don't want cyclists on the road or the ones that carry a bicycle five hundred miles on the back of a car to ride it fifteen miles on a track.

And then I realised I'd left my expensive, top quality, ex-army Gortex leggings ten miles ago outside the café in Aviemore. Given the conditions this is serious. I thought for four seconds about going back for them and then carried on.

It snowed like billy-o at Slochd Summit and was sticking. Five minutes earlier the road had been steaming in the sun. After that there was some seriously freezing downhill. The sun was back out again when I stopped for a warm outside Tomatin Distillery 'The softer side of the Highlands' – as opposed to the harsh side that I was enjoying.

On the way into Inverness – still another 28 miles – there was some of everything – thunder, hailstorms, rain, sleet, snow, slush and even some sun, and all the time the biting wind. I never expected to be riding through slush on this trip, I don't even remember when I last did it at home. And to think I was offering to come away in sandals to save the weight and washing of socks (not that I've any intention of washing any). Actually I was better off without my leggings – the showers were brief and my shorts got wet and dried again. If I'd had my waterproofs on I'd have been sweating and uncomfortable.

The cycle route did bring me by Culloden. Last time I was here I wrote;

Culloden

What should I feel
On this battlefield
Where my ancestors died
Should I feel sad
Or mad
Or pride

What should I feel
On this battlefield
Where my ancestors died
Should I have fears
Or tears
Or anger inside
What should I feel
On this field
Where many more come
To the sound of the drum
Than ever died
On either side
What should I feel
On this field of war
Why have I come
What is it for

What is for
This hallowed ground
This ditch and mound
With nothing to hide
And nothing to show
Where the more we learn
The less we know

Come to think with all the bystanders
The buses the badges the brochure
The same goes for Flanders

What is it for this battlefield
With the finds it can yield
With its tarmac and tea room and toilet
And the gawping grockles
With their dogs that despoil it

A mile out of the centre I did the most irresponsible (and yet responsible) thing I could possibly have done. I rode straight into the Travelodge and booked myself in for two nights rest and recuperation.

The nice East European receptionist was delighted to allow me to bring my bicycle into my room. I should think so too – someone had just checked in with a dog. I wonder if they set aside rooms that permanently stink of dogs or if they spread them out so we've all got an equal chance of enjoying the after effects. This particular dog had one of those funnels on its neck to stop it licking its arse, which was a start. Walking down the corridor it kept getting caught on the architraves.

I then tried to use £160 worth of water thawing myself out, which is impossible – it's like an all you can eat buffet – you can't come out on top unless you engage in some kind of dirty protest.

On the last descent I passed two big developments of stunning 4 and 5 bedroom luxury homes. For some reason I wasn't stunned – actually I was, but that was from riding a heavy bike fifty miles in atrocious weather, not at the erection of another batch of Barratt style executive egg boxes on a green field site on the edge of a major conurbation. There were slogans aplenty. One of them boasted 'bringing quality to life.' I wondered, in the absence of anything more sensible to consider, how it would be possible to make a subjective verbal abstraction live and breathe. I now realise it could also mean bringing a quality product to one's life – how clever. Out in the sticks a tranche of 'starter' homes were being built with priority given to those who live or work in the national park area. I find the phrase 'starter home' rather symptomatic of our sick society – as if anyone who bought one and stayed in it would be some sort of sad unaspiring failure.

More bigger better
Striving for the best
Must aspire to something
Or a cardiac arrest

It's a bit like the oft-whispered snipe in teaching, where anyone who wants to remain an ordinary classroom teacher and not move into management is accused of 'post blocking' – as if being good at what you do (or who you are) is no longer good enough – and so the rule that people are promoted to the level of their incompetence.

I have been beside the railway most of today, the same railway I slept next to last night. In the 1980s Paul Theroux talked to old people who said the railway in Fife had been a lifeline and the closure of lines in the 1960s and after was causing villages to die. No one but an old person would consider the railway a lifeline in that sense today. The railway had not been profitable, only useful. The railways in Britain are a joke – as is anyone who doesn't have or want a car.

Once warmed, and well aware that I looked like a cross between a tramp and the bloke with the eye patch who sang *Silvia's Mother*, I walked to Morrison's along a particularly unattractive dual carriageway. The receptionist said it was only five minutes' walk. I suspect she'd never walked it. It might have been a five minute drive. On the way I could have bought a carpet or a sofa, like you can on the way into any town in Britain, or stayed in one of seven other big hotels.

Morrison's stands in an area devoid of any history or cultural attraction. It was depressing and even more so to a worn out person on a very grey evening. Nothing is sadder than the truly monstrous. Inside I was horrified to discover it was 8.30 – I should have been asleep. I spent too much, but noticed that underpants are £10 for three pairs.

Walking back I caught up with an old bloke in shorts with legs like matchsticks and about fifty pounds on his back. His name was Richard and I asked him if he was going far. He just said, 'north,' and asked if I lived here. I said I was in the Travelodge, considering that I'd earned a rest after two hard days cycling from Pitlochry. 'In the snow,' he said. That's right. 'Into the wind,' he said. That's also right.

He said there was an inch of snow at Dalwinnie today. I came through there yesterday. He too needed a rest he said, because forty eight hours ago he was in Brazil. He'd obviously seen some action. I spoke to him because he looked like the kind of person most people would deliberately ignore – the weirdo on the bus, i.e. someone interesting. I wished him well and marched on with the sky threatening once more.

While I ate I put the TV on and was relieved to see it's still full of cheap comedy panel shows.

It appears that both Labour and the Tories have done badly in the local elections. We are perhaps on the cusp of the disintegration of the two party system and the rise 'from nowhere' of new parties, as has happened elsewhere, which in Britain is unthinkable. It is highly unlikely that any new party will be progressive. The best we can expect is a pro-EU party, the worst, fascists.

I am absolutely shattered, but given the luxury of light in the evening I didn't go to sleep till hours after I should have done.

In Stockton Paul Theroux meets a respectable man who says, 'It's the blacks see. We whites are the original inhabitants of this country, but they make all the laws in favour of the blacks. That's why it's all gone bad.' Margaret Thatcher wasn't black when she smashed the steelworkers and then the miners. Rupert Murdoch wasn't black when he smashed the print workers. Tony Blair wasn't black when he started privatising the NHS. David Cameron wasn't black when he imposed austerity, causing the decimation of everything from libraries to frontline children's services. The police didn't favour blacks when they shot Mark Duggan, Yassar Yaqub or a dozen other men in cold blood, or when they deliberately failed to investigate the murder of Stephen Lawrence. Once you start blaming people who don't fit your jaundiced view of ethnic perfection it's a slippery slope to the pogroms and the lynchings. It's happened before in many variants and Britain isn't exempt.

On *Have I got news for you* Greta Thunberg was shown with two opportunist politicians – the very people whose failures have made her campaign necessary, she was tiny beside them. Like all the BBC's irreverent satire based programs it is impartial. It ridicules the Tories and those who would oppose them alike, because they are made for liberals, who like to think of themselves as progressives, but are scared to death of Corbyn and his *Daily Mail* hyped threats to their comfy existence. This they have in common with the petit bourgeoisie – struggling self-employed sole traders, along with minor managers and lickspittle charge hands – who fear big business, but fear the organised working class more. Those who say the unions once held the country to ransom, not realising that if they really had Thatcher would have never succeeded.

Day 15 – Rest day, Inverness

Despite going to sleep much later I woke early as usual, feeling only marginally rested. The next few days (not today) are probably going to be the hardest – certainly the most exposed, and I could do with some better weather. I need to jettison everything I don't need (like flip-flops I should never have brought) and stock up with food.

Paul Theroux suggests that rail travel, especially rural rail travel, can seem like the height of civilisation. I agree – and buses too. When rail and bus travel started to decline we began to go backwards. Beeching, like Suez, was a nail in Britain's coffin. '...after a century's interruption of technology horses have possessed the [old railway] routes. I had seen this all over Britain, defunct viaducts, ruined railway bridges – and I thought of the lost hopes and all the wasted effort. Then, small dismantled England seemed simple and underdeveloped – and too mean to save herself – deceived by her own frugality.'

'I continued down the disused railway line, marvelling at the stupidity of it. They started by closing stations, then they cut the number of trains, then with few trains and a reduced service, they could prove that the line was losing money and not worth keeping: and then the line was closed for good and the tracks sold as scrap iron. And then it belonged to ramblers: it was where people took their dogs to shit.'

'It was a ghastly parody of hard times. In what had been the greatest railway country in the world, and the easiest and cheapest to traverse, the traveller was now told with perfect seriousness, "You can't get there from here."' It's a metaphor for anyone who ever thought the current system was ever designed to do anything but bolster the bank balances and property portfolios of a few greedy, selfish misanthropes.

In 1982 The Serpal Report had as one of its options slashing the rail network from 11,000 to less than 2,000 miles, leaving only a skeleton service. This option was greatly favoured by the powerful road lobby. Today, in a last ditch attempt to reverse the madness, a handful of stations on the still existing lines are being re-opened, but fast-sinking Britain will never be able to relay the tracks on its countless miles of glorified dog toilets.

A young woman says to Theroux, 'I wonder what's going to happen.' He wonders what she means and she says, 'I heard somewhere they're closing down whole towns in Canada.'

When I began to address the luggage situation I discovered that my coffee jar had come open in my pannier, covering everything in its foul sticky residue – that's two coffee related incidents in 24 hours.

Anonymously (this is the best part of it) I walked out of the Travelodge and down the same sad dual carriageway past the same sad retail outlets and the same sad shit food joints. I saw sad people looking out of the windows of sad buses. I was endlessly corralled by railings designed to make life easier for drivers and harder for pedestrians. The only people smiling were Colonel Sanders and the young people on a job advert who seemed to believe working in a fast food place was some kind of career.

On the way I crossed the railway. Beside it hundreds of mature trees have been chopped to the ground and bushes completely cleared. This is current Railtrack policy – to completely denude every cutting and verge of carbon sink and habitat, while school children plant pathetic saplings trying to save the planet.

A silly technology for the sake of it sign said 39 cyclists had used the path I was on today – alongside 39,000 who had travelled beside it in cars.

The big houses had their big cars outside. One big black Range Rover had GRO5SA for a registration, but I couldn't think of anything grosser.

The road leads straight into the belly of the multi-level car park of the Eastgate Shopping Centre, an Alhambra of bad taste – Tartan Tapas, Jammy Piece, Top Man, White stuff. It reminded me of a multi-level market I'd walked round in Rwanda, but with all the stuff Rwandans cannot get. There was nowhere to sit without spending money. Five minutes was enough to depress me.

There are lots of buses in Inverness, meaning it's a poor place. People have to be somehow transported from their run down estates to town for the latest thing that will improve their lives.

I went in Sports Direct because it was raining and ended up giving multi-millionaire Mike Ashley £17 for Chinese T shirts, socks and pants, having thrown my sweaty worn out ones in a bin on the way down.

Someone had sprayed on a wall 'Drop negative thought' but I couldn't. Everyone was in bright outdoor gear against the drab buildings. There were several back-packer hostels, pawn shops, and traditional Scottish pubs.

Eventually I found Wetherspoon's and was at home – Inverness or London you can rely on Wetherspoon's for cheap tea and coffee and endless refills.

In the next cubicle in the toilet someone was on the phone. I daren't begin until he'd hung up.

Eight loud men round a big table had all ordered generous full breakfasts. When they left not one of them had eaten it all, and half of them had hardly touched it. The food sat there like a symbol to any sane person that we are a destructive and wasteful species, until the next lot came in and ordered the same thing, *ad infinitum*. I opened my pasteurised soya milk carton and tipped the contents into the bin instead of into my tea – third beverage related incident in 24 hours.

I rushed the end of Paul Theroux's thorough indictment of Britain and gave it to the local hospice shop, posted my first full notebook home and bought bright yellow builder's waterproofs for £11.99 instead of proper walking ones for £29.99 and then back to Wetherspoon's for veggie burger and chips. Besides the post office my entire expenditure in Inverness town centre had gone to ultra-exploiting, British rags to riches, success story entrepreneurs Mike Ashley and Tim Martin – and of course to cheese stall to Supermarket Empire, Bradford hero Ken Morrison – if he's not a lord I'll want to know why. In every place I was served by teenagers. Retail is for young people because it's badly paying and they are cheap because the minimum wage, i.e. the minimum on which people are supposed to be able to live, doesn't apply to them.

Began reading Paul Theroux's *Riding the Iron Rooster – by train through China.*

A group of bikers and their long suffering wives came in with their loud-mouth, laughing at fuck-all alpha male leader – Highwaymen MCC. They were Irish and instead of being the teenagers Paul Theroux encounters in Brighton they were balding fifty year olds, with one of them nearer seventy. One of them had 'Ride or Die' on his back, another 'Belfast Harley Davidson.' There but for the grace of God go I. Have they no idea how ridiculous they are?

Theroux opens with a Chinese proverb and a quote from James Joyce – 'A peasant must stand for a long time on a hillside with his mouth open before a roast duck flies in,' and 'The movements which work revolutions in the world are born out of the dreams and visions of a peasant on a hillside.'

I have been like those bikers many times myself, probably even like the worst of them, but their raucous vulgarity irritated me – I drank up and left – the first time that my stay in Wetherspoon's has been spoiled. In fact the whole vulgar city irritated me. There were junkies, security men, drunks and dressed up people, besides the Go Outdoors, passing through types (I did not see one rough sleeper, which is unusual in any town), but most of all there was traffic queuing this way and that. And of course in a city full of people I spoke to no one.

And they queued solid on the dual carriageway as well, staring from the mobile goldfish bowls that are their freedom and their prison.

The rest of the afternoon I spent in my bought and paid for bed reading, drinking camomile tea, because it's the cheapest, and eating lovely juicy satsumas that were grown in Peru. They have been grown by some conglomerate and airfreighted to Britain, to be sold to a man in the Scottish Highlands, where it snows in April, who took them for granted and ate them as if they were nothing.

Theroux tells us about a man, who in response to attempts at conversation, said, 'Please don't ask. I don't have anything interesting to tell you, I've made a terrible mess of my life.' Theroux goes on to say that this was a sad memory because six months later the man killed himself. Perhaps if he'd talked more he might have found some purpose. It has today been realised that men need to talk, and numerous clubs and societies have been set up for them to do so. However it is debateable whether talking can ever be enough when problems are deep-seated and societal.

In an awful suburb of Paris Theroux is told that Samuel Beckett lived for years in one of the grotesque blocks of flats writing 'his stories and plays about the sheer pointlessness and utter misery of human existence' where people wait for Godot by watching television.

If anything I've made myself heavier today rather than lighter – with my new shirts and pants, a gas canister and big bags of porridge and raisins, but I've made a bit of space by getting rid of two books and my flip-flops. I took them out of my bag in Wetherspoon's when I was reordering my stuff, meaning to give them to the charity shop, but forgot them on the chair. They were still there when I went back, next to someone eating. They won't be the strangest thing that's ever been found in a pub.

Apparently Lech Walesa bragged that he'd never read a book in his life. Harold Wilson bragged he'd never read Marx. Alan Johnson bragged that he'd got no ideology. Being a philistine is no bar to being a politician.

Out of idle curiosity I put the TV on, but the remote control didn't work – it was a lucky escape, I could have been sucked in. Eventually the idleness bored me, just as it bores me at home. I have never been a sightseer, by which I mean going especially to look at things the brochures say I should. I'd rather walk round a cemetery or look at a country church. According to Theroux 'sightseeing is one of the more doubtful aspects of travel... one of the least rewarding things a traveller can do – primarily a distraction and seldom even an amusement. It has all the boredom and ritual of a pilgrimage and none of the spiritual benefits.'

Tomorrow I will be back on the road and I look forward to it. If I were asked the purpose of this trip I would say it has no purpose. The destinations are certainly not the purpose because they are random, and the purpose of raising money was only an afterthought. In fact if I carry on like I am doing I will spend more than I raise and could have stayed at home and given my own money to charity.

Theroux also finds educated Chinese people who think they should be able to read what they want, while believing that access to certain reading should be restricted for the masses. Naturally this leads to a reference to *Lady Chatterley's Lover*, 'a silly and unreadable book,' which a judge considered unsuitable reading for one's servants. This social and intellectual elitism has reasserted itself today in the notion that only ignorant people voted to leave the EU, the unquestioned orthodoxy being that the EU is intrinsically a good thing. The irony is that they have taken a good number of progressive proles along with them in this fantasy.

He also says that in old age Mao Zedong was senile 'and easily misled by Lin Biao, (*China's Trotsky*)' (my emphasis). He was told the first part readily by Chinese people, the bit in parenthesis is his own and it is sloppy. Stalin was never influenced by Trotsky in his dotage because Trotsky was dead and Stalin had had him killed. The name of

Stalin now means nothing to most people, but Trotsky is still the very devil to Labour Party hacks and tiresome tabloids. Stalinism means wheedling bureaucracy. Trotskyism means open, permanent revolution. There was no workers' revolution in China because there was no Trotsky.

And on that note it's time to sleep.

Day 16 – Inverness to Gairloch
(The Highlands)

And there was no Lenin either – and no party like the Bolsheviks. China's was a top-down revolution in which the working class (such as existed) played no active part. One may as well assert that John Prescott was Tony Blair's Trotsky, or that Stan Laurel was Oliver Hardy's. (There will be some who will like the Blair/Prescott analogy, but Prescott was a stooge who provided pseudo left cover for Blair's right wing policies, and he knows it. He has also said he should not have supported the invasion of Iraq.)

The forecast is for cold weather all week and for the wind from the north to continue – as I am now heading west it should be in my right ear.

I cannot believe it but I have managed to lose the piece of thick black plastic sheet 14 x 8 inches I use to stabilise my stove when I am camping. The only way this can have happened is in my rush to pack up before the rain came in Newtonmore. Bastard. That was an essential piece of kit. If I'm not careful I'm going to lose something really important, like my waterproofs.

Paul Theroux also retails the story about Chairman Mao, who, when asked what he thought about the French Revolution said it was too early to say. The only problem with this story is that it wasn't Chairman Mao and he wasn't talking about the French Revolution. Theroux has probably done much to promulgate the story. I think it was Chou en Lai and he thought he was being asked about events in Paris 1968 – but that could also be incorrect.

I'm angry about losing my stuff.

While I was outside oiling my chain I met Chuck and Leanne from Tennessee, who are on the last day of their UK tour taking in the Highlands and London, their first time in the UK. It was my bike that got the introduction and I recognised their southern drawl straight off.

After a bit of confusion through the near empty town centre I followed the River Ness to the Kessock Bridge over the Beauly Firth, past the remains of Cromwell's citadel. Once I cleared the town and was by the river among the industry and the docks and opposite colourful flats I liked it more because it was open, not oppressive like cities are. It was more like Whitby or Belgium.

The view under the bridge as I approached it was magnificent. There was even some sun on the gorse on the north bank. There was also rain coming from the direction I was going in. A brief icy shower approaching the bridge drove me into my new bright yellow waterproofs and I crossed with my hood up and all enwrapped. There were plenty of other cyclists about, but they didn't seem to be feeling the cold.

The ride along the north shore towards Muir of Ord was flat and picturesque. The sun made a brief appearance and I sat for a few minutes under a tree on the grassy foreshore with all my clothes on trying to pretend it wasn't freezing.

For miles it was single track road, but old people kept overtaking me in sensible cars, several with personalised registrations. I assumed they had all just left the static caravan park for a day of sightseeing and holiday treats. It turned out they were all making for the tiny church at Killearnan. There were fifty cars in the car park and I was in time to hear the first hymn being sung. The vicar was the Rev. Susan Cord. How we've advanced. It's not my religion, but I would imagine Christians worth their salt would consider it more appropriate to donate any cash they could afford to waste to the charity they profess to believe in, rather than spend it on the ostentatious misspelling of their name on their car. And yes, I am in fact suggesting that these people are hypocrites. But then aren't we all?

One church had a big banner outside 'Try praying.' Smug bastards. Try not voting Tory.

Despite the showers of the last few days when I passed a field being ploughed the soil was as dry as dust. The valley bottom is flat and wide with fields under cereals and rape. The hills are covered with gorse and sheep and the higher ones have a recent coating of snow. The road is pleasant and undulating.

In a yard I saw a mechanical device exercising five horses, pushing them round from behind. It looked vaguely cruel.

Marybank was decked out in SNP placards. No message, no promises, just placards with 'SNP' on them, as if everyone knows what they stand for. Their record in municipal office is not very glorious. Like the Liberal Democrats they are conservatives dressed up as radicals.

Once I got onto the A385 it was a hard slog into the wind and the awful road surface knocked me down two gears, though I did feel able to take off my nice new yellow trousers, which now contain most of the oil I put on my chain this morning. It also seems that I was wrong about this being the worst section for supplies – that was Thursday and Friday.

There's hardly a hill, but the wind ruins every minor descent, negating any possibility of using it to crest the next brow. It's bloody hard work. Cyclists are flying the other way with the wind behind them, even uphill.

Just onto the A832 towards Kyle of Lochalsh I stopped to talk to two lightweight cyclists. They were eating their sandwich and the woman said her feet were freezing. Five minutes later a dickhead with a big caravan overtook me so fast and close, and pulled in so sharp to avoid two vans coming the other way, that he nearly took my front wheel off. There was no one else on the road.

Then ROD went past in his Rolls Royce.

A deer ran across the road right in front of me, there were waves on Loch Luichart and I stopped to oil my pedals. They are home-made, run metal to metal and have been squeaking for days.

It made a remarkable difference and I should have done it days ago. I lost the top off my oil bottle in the grass, but that's no big deal.

I was wet through at Achnasheen and could easily have called it a day, but I decided to press on to Kinlochewe. The hotel was full, the bunkhouse was full and the campsite was full, which didn't matter because it only took caravans and campervans. 'Try Gairloch,' said the bloke in the hotel, 'it's only twenty minutes away.' It's actually nineteen hard miles and two hours away, but I knew there was a campsite there, having been to it years ago for a motorcycle rally.

I arrived at 6.30, having cycled for ten and a half hours, if not from the actual sea on both sides of the country, then at least from tidal lochs.

The young couple at the campsite were a bit 'cor blimey look at you' for me, especially over my bike. The woman charged me £9 (I'd just spent six in the shop on my tea) and said it was 71 miles from Inverness. I don't mind saying I'm quite pleased with myself that I can ride that far – but I didn't have a proper stop all the way, just snatching a bite to eat here and there stood by the road.

As far as Kinlochewe, after which there were some long climbs and descents, the roads were some of the most level so far, but they were spoiled by the relentless, debilitating, soul destroying headwind, which makes the distance even more impressive – I've worked ten times harder than I would have done had it been calm.

I am now within striking distance of my fifth destination and after it will be heading south for a while.

I made myself a most acceptable curry from a tin of vegetable soup, a tin of Pease pudding and some curry powder and ate it with tortilla wraps as if they were chapattis.

Disappointingly the showers were only warm.

It's rained nearly all the time since I got here.

The lesson of the day – don't panic, something will turn up.

Day 17 – Gairloch to Strathcarron (via Naast)

(The Highlands)

I was cold in the night and cold when I woke up. One day this cold spell will end. I woke to all the usual birdsong plus gulls, bleating lambs, a cockerel and the crashing of the waves on the shore.

Auchtercairn is set on the bay which is the western end of Gairloch. It is a lovely place with well-spaced white houses all around.

I had to force myself out of my bag. The sky was broken and it's even colder than it has been so far, with an icy wind, but for once it doesn't look like rain.

Everything I've got has got sticky coffee marks on it from the spillage in my pannier.

A couple opposite have two electric bicycles fastened to their camper van. Cycling is being colonised by the idle. It will have a detrimental effect on sales and production and eventually destroy the bicycle as a cheap, practical and healthy form of transport. Beijing used to run on the bicycle. It now runs on cars and electric bikes – all of which have to have their power generated somewhere. The bicycle is the solution to environmental destruction, the electric bicycle is not. Its batteries, copper windings and electrical systems all require precious resources extracted in war-torn countries with disregard for the long-term consequences. The electric bicycle is a marketing ploy like the electric car. Electric bicycles have got no more to do with cycling than electric wheelchairs have to do with walking.

Caravaners are walking dogs round the site to shit where other people sleep on the ground.

When I set off the sun was out on the beautiful bay, the tide was in, the sea was calm and clear. All around were low green hills topped with rocks and snowy peaks rose behind them in the distance. It was like a south sea island paradise but considerably colder.

It was a long climb out of Gairloch towards Poolewe and I was back into the wind. The rocks loomed, the roadside ferns unrolled and GUS went past in his Kia. He wants me to notice him. I noticed him. His money was well spent.

Six recent Red Bull cans lay at the roadside, otherwise it's a wilderness.

On top a small loch has islands like *Swallows and Amazons*. All is silent except for the birds (and the occasional car – and then a coach). The landscape is vast and varied, with a view from the descent over the end of Loch Maree.

Poolewe is also beautiful with the sun on it – a picturesque village round a wide road with a hotel, Spar shop and several B&Bs.

When I bear left onto the shore road beside the loch there's no sign for Naast, but if I get to Eversdale I know I've missed it. Along the way there are concrete bunkers looking out to sea and signs of historical peat digging, rejected now in favour of oil delivered by tankers. Lock Ewe, on which Naast sits, was a base for the Russian Arctic convoys in the Second World War. Around it were based Indian, Polish and Welsh soldiers, as well as WRNS, the RAF and Royal Engineers. The convoys, which sailed to Murmansk and Archangel, were described by Winston Churchill as 'the worst journey in the world' and 3,000 men lost their lives in the attempt to keep Britain's allegedly communist ally supplied.

I deeply resented riding to Naast because today was the day I looked forward to turning south and having this interminable wind behind me.

Naast is now about eight houses sitting high above the edge of the loch. As I entered the village a bin wagon came round the corner far too fast and I had to ride off the road to avoid being flattened. On the same single track road a minute later a man in sunglasses with a determined expression drove straight at me.

I turned round and rode into the sun for the first time in a fortnight.

So much had I anticipated being bowled along that I almost thought I was being, and had to make myself slow down. Coming out of Poolewe a woman in a car overtook me into a blind bend and made a woman coming the other way stop and blow her horn.

There are cars from Italy, Switzerland, Holland, France and Germany as well as campervans doing the fashionable 500 – always the man driving, the woman sat alert up front like a top gun co-pilot. The Highland 500 is a made up challenge like mine, but made up by someone else – that's what all the bikers are doing as well, ten at a time, mostly on BMWs popularised by TV adventurers. Many of the British cars are going far too fast because they are in a hurry to get nowhere. When they have to wait two seconds to overtake you they gun their engines childishly to remind you that you are an inconvenient nuisance. Some of them even get out of their cars to look at things or bicker. A car cut right in on me round a blind bend as a van came the other way. But the best ones are those that overtake you too close when there's no one else there. I hoped eventually they'd all get back on the motorway and relative peace would resume. Then the inevitable happened – a car overtaking me forced one coming the other way off the road. It rolled down the bank, killing both people inside. It didn't really, but it felt like it could at any minute, either that or I'd be forced down a bank, or into a wall, or run over.

There are cuckoos everywhere. I've kept hearing what I thought were they, but today I overhear it confirmed by an expert.

And what the fuck is a boutique guesthouse?

A massive area of gorse and heather has been burned, up and down the hillsides, right to the tops between the rocks. Actually green shoots were already showing through the ash.

I found the thirty-odd miles back to Kinlochewe tedious and tiresome – if there'd been a campsite I'd have stayed on it, but there isn't – only one of those Caravan and Campervan Club sites that are springing up all over and don't take tents. There isn't enough money in backpackers and cyclists. And it dawns on me that I have begun making the trip into a race. This is not a question of distance, but of having the right head on, not depressing yourself with biscuits as I had done. I decided to get a different head on.

Two young people with backpacks were trying to thumb a lift. They sounded French. No one stopped.

While I was sitting outside the village shop two different drivers went in and left their car engines running and a motorcyclist walked 200 yards from a B&B in his helmet and bought 12 cans of lager.

It is nine miles to Achnasheen and thirty five to Kyle of Lochalsh, which I hoped I would reach today.

There is a long climb out of Kinlochewe. To make it easier I started looking about, grinning at nothing and stopping regularly. There was a minor hailstorm, but I kept on grinning, even after the false summit. Making yourself grin is like doing the right thing irrespective of your motives.

At Achnasheen I turned for Kyle of Lochalsh and was following the railway again. A two carriage train rattled past on the primitive un-welded track and the noise echoed in the valley for five minutes after it had gone.

I saw the French couple again out in the barren wilderness, a dozen miles away from where I'd first seen them, walking back towards the Inverness road. And then a car overtook me really close for no earthly reason. There was no one else in sight.

I wouldn't like to be riding up the Glen Carron Pass I came down, it went on for miles. It obviously gets some hammer because the road surface was atrocious in places, with two, three and even four inch deep potholes, which begs the question of what they do with all the money they get from the tourists who use it – no wonder Scotland is desperate to stay in the EU, there are joint funding signs by every bit of reinstated road.

A car dealership demonstrator appears to have been rebranded a 'Customer Experience Vehicle.'

And then, like a fucking mug, I allowed some bald-headed chancer in a kilt with legs like two bottles of milk to rob me of £15 to camp on an old hen run opposite the Strathcarron Hotel, the bar of which was populated by four pissheads. There isn't a level bit of ground on it and I had to move once because the pegs wouldn't go in it was so stony. The collapsing chicken shed remained just as the last one had left it, the little ramp to the door still down. It isn't worth £5. In fact it isn't worth £2. If he thinks I'm going in his pub he's got another think coming. I wish I'd ridden the twenty miles to Kyle of

Lochalsh – I'd rather have paid £50 for something decent. He even had the brass neck, after I'd told him his camping was a bit dear, to ask if I wouldn't rather stay in in one of the shitty canvas 'pods' he's got on the same bit of scrub for £30. I've had a B&B for £35. And it smelled of dog shit, and there are wagons booming past all the time. I'm angry with myself. I paid £9 last night for a site that was manicured and had a new toilet block and £5 for one last week that was perfectly adequate. The only consolation is that it's rained since I got here and it wasn't £50. In fact for two pins I'd re-pack and let him keep the money. It's shit. I've got nothing proper to eat, not enough water and I've been scammed. He's making money out of me for providing nothing.

Note to self – send card to Strathcarron Hotel – 'Just a note to say your so-called campsite is the worst shit-hole I have ever stayed on and you are a fucking robber.'

Had a marmite sandwich and some raisins and got in my bag to read with the din of the road, railway and a farm/scrap yard going on.

I must have stopped far too early because the traffic is still banging past, and the convoys of motorbikes. Roll on the morning. Fuck, fuck, fuck.

It felt like four o'clock – though I knew it wasn't. I put my earplugs in and tried to sleep. When I woke the traffic had stopped, but it was still light.

Day 18 – Strathcarron to Broadford (via Valtos)

(The Highlands onto Skye)

Slept fitfully and woke up as it was getting light. The birdsong was good, including another cuckoo – and an owl in the night.

But to be frank my stay in the Highlands has not been very pleasant. The cycling is all on main roads full of selfish drivers. I've spoken to no one and I've been ripped off. I've always loved Scotland, but this time I'm looking forward to getting out of it.

And wearing a kilt behind the bar in a pub is dickish. I've always liked the kilts, the bagpipes and drums, thought it meant something – even said if I wasn't Yorkshire I'd have liked to have been Scottish – but I think I now see it for what it is, a stupid made-up gimmick. There must be thousands of Scots who reject the whole silly parody. The greatest thing against all the highland nonsense is that Prince Charles partakes of it. So when working class people dress up like highland dummies they are just aping the rich.

I couldn't undo the tent zip to get out and when I did the whole outside of the tent was covered in ice. I was off early without even a warm drink.

I foolishly assumed that the road down the southern shore of Loch Carron would be fairly level, which is why I thought I could have done it last night. Not a bit of it – it was a series of very sharp climbs and descents, most of which I had to walk, which is just as well because if it had been a long decline I'd have probably frozen to death.

Of course it was beautiful. The sun was shining on the houses on the other bank, but I was under cliffs or dense forest and there was no sun on me.

The roads were terrible – a half decent road will suddenly deteriorate into a potholed single track, like it used to do in Ireland before their boom. It began to remind me of Hungary or the Czech Republic.

This developed into a series of long, featureless, dispiriting, steep climbs, all of which I had to walk. There was nothing even to lean on, never mind sit down. I was wet through with sweat but my fingers were freezing.

Eventually it opened out into all its heather covered glory, but do you know what? I am bored of it. It has no humanity, no joy. I used to love Scotland, but now I am beginning to hate it.

At the first sign of sun I stopped against the Armco to let it warm me while the cars whizzed past. The wind is still bitter. It's a far cry from tootling round the Dales stopping for beans on toast and a shandy – like I was in the first week.

From there it was good cycling to Balmacara on Lock Alsh and I could see the Skye Bridge in the distance. The setting is idyllic, with picnic benches along the grassy front and the sun on the water, but it's freezing.

I bought onion bajis for my lunch and tonic water, which was cheaper than bottled water.

And it's all designed to be done by car. Not the slightest thought has gone into how the cyclist (or even pedestrian) might get to the Skye Bridge – you just simply hold up the traffic along the winding road, much of which has got double white lines. It's very intimidating and guilt inducing.

The bridge itself is a steep arch and I walked up. All the balustrading is aluminium, with great big electric welds. A more environmentally damaging material has yet to be found.

A van passed for a tour company – its logo 'Go beyond the guide books.'

On the other side the same as before, holding up the traffic, revving engines, dangerous overtaking, palpable contempt and lungs full of fumes.

Further on, by the aerodrome, someone had made big signs – 'Tax the poor so the rich can fly – How stupid do you think we are?' 'We need a school free of asbestos, not an airport.' 'We need a future, not an airport.' Quite, and likewise HS2.

And then, unfortunately, 'Flights for the rich or roads for us all.' A bench to eat my lunch on would have been nice.

It's all very twee – endless modern bungalows on big plots – car-owning, wi-fi connected crofters. The chapels are all boarded up, but they should have been rededicated to mammon – and the traffic is constant, with lots of big trucks. Broadfoot was tied in knots with traffic – it must be God-awful in peak season, as must the rest of the Highlands – it's bad enough now. And dozens of B&Bs, one styling itself 'ultra luxury.' Plus loads of craft shops and jewellers – people escaping the rat race to fleece tourists on Skye.

Among the false crofts in the populated areas of the highlands are the genuine war memorials. Alan Bennett has written that the thought of obtaining their own little smallholding sustained men through the First World War. In response I wrote;

Feet of Clay

This nation is a construct
Based on a rural past
What made all men appendage
Is ruthless to the last

In periodic spasms
That lead to petty fights
It needs the kind of soldier
Of which Robert Tressell writes

When called on by their country
To fight the common foe
The servant and the master
Must drop their tools and go

The cream of Britain's manhood
Fed on tea and margarine
Takes up the cloak of empire
And forsakes the fields of green

The best brains in the country
Are enlisted in the ranks
To beat rakes into rifles
And turn tractors into tanks

The warp and weft of workers
Keeps armaments at hand
To plough the fields and scatter
The good seed on the land

Either way their bodies
The wheels of profit oil

As they use themselves to fertilise
The goodness giving soil

But rather than with ploughshares
They turn the earth with bombs
And burn and bury soldiers
On Basra roads and Sommes

Rather than the harrow
They use a different blade
And DORA's in denial
A spade is not a spade

But on the fields of Flanders
Where high explosive reigns
As in the grime of mill and mine
The peasant mind remains

Between the calm and carnage
And cant from cultured throats
He can salvage his insanity
With thoughts of keeping goats

But the dream of rustic romance
Dies with them in the mud
Because there's always going to be
A maggot in the spud

The reward for human capital
Like cattle free to use
Is the granting of allotments
Beside some Somme or Meuse

They got their little plot of land
But not one they could till

And unlike the peasant farmer
They occupy it still

And yet now the wasted worker
With his fifty years of hurt
Has dreams of self sufficiency
On some shitty bit of dirt.

Eventually I had to sit on my waterproofs on the verge and risk the dog shit.

There were other cyclists battling the traffic, but all lightweight day riders. They pulled into a place advertising 'artisan, drum fired coffee,' whatever that is. I didn't. Though I wouldn't have minded a chat I'm not being fleeced by pretentiousness if I am by bare faced robbery.

When you stop on the verge the draught from the wagons nearly blows you over. There are loaded up estate cars from the Czech Republic and identikit BMW GS adventure riders from Switzerland.

While I was watching a bird of prey wheeling about over a plantation stood well back from the road two sports cars went past at 50mph.

There were coaches emblazoned 'The Hairy Coo says honk if you're Horny,' caravans and a convoy of safari Land Rovers. I've had more pleasant rides round the Bradford ring road. The scenery is sublime, but you daren't look at it because you're constantly worried about being forced off the road.

I had to physically cringe away from a Swiss van or it would have hit me. A Belgian overtook me approaching a plainly red light at road works and slammed on his brakes in front of me. It is positively dangerous. Anyone who thinks cycling on Skye could be fun should think again.

The pack of fancy coffee riders went past me again. I shouted, 'This road's shit,' just as a skip wagon nearly mowed them all down. I said it was horrible to the tail-ender. He said, 'It's lovely.' Then I watched a coach across an arm of the loch going up the hill behind them all at 4mph, the driver no doubt seething with hatred.

Just before Sconser (Sconsair) a load of Chinese people were out of their bus looking at cows. Both their guides had kilts on to make the experience authentic. That's what people want now (I'm told), not stuff, 'experiences.' Lacking the imagination to find these experiences themselves they subcontract to a firm all too willing to fleece them. No one asks the basics – like isn't a kilt a fucking stupid garment in a country globally renowned for its midges and sheep ticks – the latter of which carry a very serious disease?

The product from the salmon farms in the lochs is probably being airfreighted to where the bus full of gullible tourist's came from.

Another tour bus slogan – 'Don't just see, experience.' What does that mean? I once read that a slogan was meaningless if the opposite couldn't be true.

And so it went on – though the murderous traffic did slacken off a bit in the middle of the day. The fumes are giving me a sore throat.

I had to pedal all the way down the very long hill towards Portree or the wind would have stopped me.

I arrived at Portree, a place something like Robin Hood's Bay, at precisely two o'clock. Unsurprisingly it was full of people experiencing it who had not gone beyond the guide books. It was a minor road out, with less traffic, so the chances of being killed were reduced slightly.

I've seen a couple of proper manly campervans. They are army green, jacked up on big wheels and have jerry cans and shovels fastened to them in case the owner wants to go across the Hindu Kush (between the cappuccinos) after he's toured Skye. These vans are of course shop bought style, back to the roots retail.

Any dream I may have had of vacating this hackneyed paradise before nightfall was stymied by the fact that it was twelve miles of unmitigated torture to Valtos. I no longer cared about the scenery, not even the Old Man of Storr, or life itself. I just wanted the damn wind behind me – though the view across the Sound of Raasay is unmistakably stunning in a way that a five bedroom Barratt house isn't.

I don't want to go on about this, but among the other kamikaze driving a German coach overtook me far too close, a Czech one overtook me into a bend over double white lines, making two cars stop and a car overtook me on a straight road forcing one coming the other way to take to the grass verge at speed. But I've survived another day.

Day 19 – Broadford to Fort William
(The Highlands)

Slept well and woke before dawn cold. Went back to sleep and waited for the sun to come and warm me, which it duly did.

I rode far too far again yesterday, reaching Valtos, my 7th destination around five. I rode through Valtos to make sure it was just a collection of a dozen spread out houses, not a community. These names probably survive since the days of crofting.

I then took advantage of the wind and rode all the way back down to Broadford, arriving at the campsite at 8.30. The owner sucked through his teeth and said I was the last camper, and I was at that time.

It's more main roads today – there simply aren't the back roads to tack round like there are in England – the most one can hope for is a beside the road cycle path, but there's no escape from the noise and fumes from the traffic, or the constant fear of being knocked off.

I'm now heading south for two weeks at least.

Another bright, sunny but cold morning. There are eight other campers, seven are in cars, one is walking. The cheap socks I bought from millionaire Mike Ashley's emporium are very nice – much warmer than the ones I set off with, thinking it nearly summer.

Off at rush hour for the full experience (people have laughed at the notion of rush hour on Skye, but they haven't cycled there). Resupply at the Co-op. When I leaned my bike on a bench to write my postcard a wheezing old woman with a fag in her hand said, 'That's the bike park over there.' I wasn't parking, there was no one else there and if I had been parking I wouldn't have leaned my bike on a bench. Miserable old bastard.

Because the road doubles back on itself it was hard riding into the wind from the off. Of course the dangerous overtaking began straight away. It's probably only one in a hundred drivers, and all credit to those who take it for granted that other people have a right to exist, but some of those coming to the Highlands for an exciting experience should try riding a bicycle into a blind bend with a fuel tanker straddling the double white lines beside them.

I stopped to make coffee and crisp sandwiches on the loch-side picnic benches at Balmacara, trying to turn over a new leaf and take rests or wear myself out. If it had been warm I might have read a page of my book, but it wasn't.

It seems there is no escaping the demoralising wind. It was against me all the way down Loch Duich. I am noticing that quite a few of the cars that won't wait and overtake me too close are Volvos. Then I saw a camper van called 'Envy.' I used to work with a man who, when he was pleased with himself would say, 'Everyone wants to be like Tony.' They didn't, because they knew he was a tosser.

A couple of miles further on I came the closest I've ever been to seeing an articulated wagon plough into a car and caravan, he was overtaking me into a bend at the time and pulled in so sharp that his back wheels were all over the verge. They could have been all over me. I'm starting to think it's my fault for being here. If one of them runs me down it'll save me getting bowel cancer like Brian.

Near the top of Glen Shee, which was hard, I met a mountain biker out for the day. He said he'd ride in front of me for a bit to 'take the wind,' but I couldn't keep up and let him go.

At the top were Grant and Shelley, on holiday from South Africa and touring Scotland. Shelley was a petite and well-dressed. Grant was unshaven and dishevelled. Shelley said you couldn't do what I was doing in their country. Grant said, 'You'd get mugged.' He also said he didn't like Edinburgh Castle because it was a sausage factory. In fact, if I was in their country, where striking miners are still shot dead, I'd probably be black and too busy eking out a living or campaigning against corruption, inequality and injustice to be doing anything as frivolous as cycling round the country.

The wind, along with the icy rain that started and then got heavy also ruined the long flattish part. In fact it was awful and I hated every second of it. It was soul-destroying torment through miles of endless nothing – half way along which I realised I'd been riding with my pannier unfastened. Mercifully the rain had not penetrated my sleeping equipment or dry clothes or I would have been in a mess. It was the mountain biker who distracted me mid fuel stop. It's hard to keep in mind that the Highlands are somewhere you might want to be, and not the overblown, inhospitable, selfish tourist infested wasteland they look like. Next time an asylum seeker tells me they've suffered (they don't generally tell you they've suffered), I'll say, 'That's nothing mate, I've cycled in the Scottish Highlands.' And still the traffic roared past showing the same scant regard for me or the conditions, with the added bonus of filthy spray.

Only when I got to the A82 south did the wind give me some help, but not far along a coach overtook me through a load of water and soaked me. I didn't have my waterproof trousers on because I thought it would be just a shower, like it has been for a week. It's not good for the ego to be endlessly regarded by all and sundry as an unimportant speck of irrelevance. On my last cycle trip I met a man who told me his friend had been killed by a car while cycling. The driver didn't stop. When the police caught up with him he said he thought he'd hit a bird. Fair enough, bird, cyclist – what's the difference?

It was wet all the way to Invergarry – but after the wind the rain by itself seemed nothing – where, after some deliberation, I took the signed cycle route towards Fort William as it said it was twenty five miles, the same as the road. It was a lifesaver.

The first ten or so miles were on a forest track and it was hard going, but at least it was interesting. In the woods several solo walkers and one group had already pitched camp for the night, telling me it was getting late.

Then a good unclassified road took me past several tucked away millionaires and the half priced homes of slightly lesser beings. There were sign boards detailing the use of isolated beaches to practice for the Normandy landings. The last bit was on the Caledonian Canal 'towpath,' which had a good surface and I could go as fast as I liked, still with the wind behind me.

Approaching Fort William the path weaved me all over through a desperate looking estate – that'll be where the smelting plant workers live I thought (if it's still open) – to get me into town to be tempted by a B&B, but I knew where the campsite was and arrived at 8.20 (£10).

I asked the nice campsite man if there was a smelting plant and if it was still open. It is, and it employs 350 people. But he said it's now owned by Tata, whose boss he called 'a little bastard.' He said Nicola Sturgeon had been throwing money at it – 'You know what politicians are like,' on the promise of a new car wheel-making plant to employ 500 people, but no car wheel-making plant has come. He showed me the hydro-electric power plants up the hill, which he said were built in 1917 – 'a fantastic engineering achievement,' then said that Tata are asset strippers. The previous owners of the plant were Rio Tinto, which greases the palms of politicians from Australia to Mongolia and operates like a modern day East India Company in some places

Another mad marathon cycle ride I said I wasn't going to do, to the extent that I can't say when I'm asked where I've been.

He also said the new Forth Road Bridge won't last because it isn't built properly – he knew engineers who told him. And the old one got into its unusable state because the maintenance budget was cut.

Incidentally, this is what has gone in the furnace today to keep the ship sailing; a big bowl of porridge with dried fruit, four large white baps, two bags of crisps, nearly a full packet of digestive biscuits, five pitta breads, half a jar of peanut butter, three large apples and two raw peppers.

Day 20 – Fort William to Tyndrum

(The Highlands and Stirlingshire)

After only one open air piss in the night I awoke when it was fully light half rested as usual. Today is set to be the same – miles and miles of empty endless nothing – scenery that seen fleetingly from a car might impress, but on a bicycle passes very slowly – with Glencoe Pass thrown in. And yet part of me relishes the prospect – there is something satisfying about seeing a sign that says forty miles to somewhere in the middle of the afternoon and thinking, 'I can do that.'

The weather looks set to be the same too. There's a range of hills to my right that are entirely covered in snow – I take this to be the Ben Nevis range, which is high. If snow were added to the mix this trip would become positively dangerous, but surely not in May?

Putting wet socks on wasn't pleasant, but I didn't think there was much point in putting dry ones on – my boots are soaking and it's probably going to rain.

My front brake has been ineffective for a while so I fitted the spare pads I brought with me, only to discover that the cable was frayed to one strand.

Into the traffic jam that is Fort William (The Scottish Six Day Trial was in town) and bought and fitted a new cable easily - £9.98, approximately twice as much as it would have cost in my local bike shop, but the brake worked better than it's ever done with a bit of old motorcycle throttle cable.

And then it was full speed ahead down the busy A82, stopping to let trucks overtake etc. only today, it being fine, I could stop and brew up, which I did quite soon in a picnic area, and watch the campervans performing, the wife always out issuing instructions as they manoeuvre.

Back on the road all the verge is mashed for hundreds of yards where the wagons have left the carriageway – then there was a good roadside cycle path and I met Tim Sharp, who is doing munroes this week, but has cycled the North Sea Cycle Route to the top of Norway, which took three months. He told me the alternative ways I could have gone, all involving several expensive ferries.

When I pulled into a forest entrance to relieve myself, equipment reminiscent of the foot and mouth epidemic was in evidence – footbaths of disinfectant and advice to clean feet, tyres and animals. It is an attempt to stop the spread of phytophthora ranorum, which is killing larch trees.

The snow gates were open at the bottom of Glencoe Pass, the sun was out and I pressed on. The cycle path changes into a rutted forest path after Glencoe village, so it was back on the road for the ascent.

The motorcycle trial had a refuelling stop and a marked section a quarter of the way up the pass and a coach disgorged dozens of people photographing everything. I took it easy, stopping against the Armco several times. The driving was as usual, only today they got the chance to take liberties with dozens of trials riders' lives as well as the odd cyclist.

PAM went past in her Range Rover coupe – the ultimate symbol of a Thatcherite fuck you philosophy. Only in a country (that's all developed ones) that had been told there's no such thing as society could 4x4 sales be rising at the same time as car sales generally are falling.

The pass itself is not that steep – I did it all with no less than three gears to spare – its impressiveness is in the great piles of rock that loom over it. The footpath over the top – The West Highland Way – seemed to be just as busy, with long-distance walkers every hundred yards.

In a layby near the top was Mark with his BMW GS 1200 and all the trimmings. It obviously wasn't enough of a toy for him because he got out a drone and flew it to the top of one of the peaks to get pictures of the snow – the first time I've seen one in action. They'll be putting men on the moon next.

The summit, on Rannoch Moor, is 1,142 feet above sea level. I put my coat on for the descent. I was too warm and took it off again.

I entered Argyle and Bute.

There was another long climb after Bridge of Orchy and I entered Loch Lock Lomond and The Trossachs National Park, district of Stirling, which doesn't sound very far up Scotland at all.

The traffic thinned out considerably – so there was only the ones who deliberately drive too close to you when there's no one else on the road to contend with.

I was going to ride to Crianlarich, at one point imagining I'd get even further, but down the hill and straight into the Pinetrees Campsite at Tyndrum, £8. It was only ten to five and I was so pleased I spent a pound on a tin of new potatoes only worth fifty pence. It's a fantastic site – there's a little shelter for campers to cook in if it's raining, a full blown laundry, microwaves, kettles, even music in the toilets – everything you could want that the one I paid £20 for didn't have – even the showers were hot, which is rare. Some of these people must take lukewarm showers at home. I brewed up on a table and spread all my stuff out on it – such a change from doing everything on the ground. It being fine helps. A good day's cycling and a reasonable time to stop for a change – 47 or 48 miles I reckon from the map – not bad considering I changed my brake pads before I set off and then my brake cable.

Dunoon looks possible tomorrow, but there won't be a campsite once I get out of the tourist area. It's warmed up a lot today, but the campsite man says there'll be a frost tonight.

Forgot to mention that one of the royals has miraculously had a baby. One is amazed.

A man in China tells Paul Theroux, when he is asked if he minds people getting rich, 'In China, privilege is not bought with money. Power comes from the political sphere, not the financial sphere.' Pull the other one, it's got bells on. If that were true it would be like no other country on earth.

Between 1983 and 1986 China executed 10,000 people. In August 1983 thirty convicted criminals were executed in a sports stadium in front of 60,000 cheering people. Deng Xiaoping said, 'As a matter of fact, execution is the one indispensable means of education.'

Unfortunately someone's stupid dog is barking. And then another. I hate dogs. The Chinese execute people with a single shot to the nape of the neck.

Apparently there is a Chinese conundrum – 'If a place has a reputation for being beautiful, the Chinese flock to it, and its beauty is disfigured by the crowd.' It isn't just a Chinese problem.

'I fantasised that there were certain [places] in the world that could succeed only by becoming gross parodies of what they were – or of what people expected them to be.' Britain is full of places that are parodies of what they once were – Hebden Bridge, Haworth, Edinburgh, even London – in fact Britain is a parody of what it once was, with its real ale and its traditional fayre, authentic this and genuine that. You only need to attach one of these adjectives to things to make it obvious that they aren't.

Theroux is told the US has no cause to fear China – 'The Chinese are interested in only two things in the world – power and money. America has more power and money that anyone else. That is why the Chinese will always need the friendship of America.' This was 1983.

It was strange to make and eat my meal at the table instead of huddled in my bag against the cold.

Day 21 – Tyndrum to Greenock
(Stirlingshire to Greater Glasgow)
I woke once when it was light and then fell asleep again. I dreamed something had happened to me, let's say an injury sustained in heroic circumstances, rather than contracting gonorrhoea, and I had to have therapy that involved swimming in a certain body of water. Before I swam I had to eat a packet of small sweets – Parma violets and similar, there was a choice. On the second session I had to eat five packets. In the water this turned into wearing five different garments and I fell in love with the therapist, or rather she fell in love with me.

135

Obviously in the dream I wasn't a bald-headed 62 year old bloke with a month's beard growth who'd been wearing the same clothes for three weeks. There was also some flying, which I hate, on a plane with horses on board, some squeezing through small gaps, which is a regular feature of my dreams, and testing the water for cleanliness.

I slept well. Ear plugs are now *de rigueur*. There is the main road and a crunchy gravel path passes my tent between the caravans and the ablution block.

The surreal quality of the trip remains. I can understand how Ted Simon became mystical and how others have begun talking to their equipment. It is a strange thing to only have to sleep and cycle, sleep and cycle.

Last night a woman from a caravan asked me if I needed hot water, which, while being nice of her, is part of the assumption that sleeping in a tent is somehow to deprive and punish yourself. When it rains they say, 'It must have been horrible last night,' when it isn't at all – it's lovely and cosy. At the reception, when I asked the man could I camp he said, 'If you want,' meaning, 'if you really want to,' and threatened me with a frost. It's part of our inability, or unwillingness to grasp, or grapple with, what other people do, and goes all the way to why someone might want to be a sex offender or a terrorist. One of the semi-permanent caravans is surrounded by garden gnomes.

A very tame robin came to eat, or take away, flakes of porridge oats I put on the table for it. A couple walked past with three big Labradors, another man fawned over them. A lonely man who smokes, drinks and swears in long phone conversations is staying in one of the cabins with a dog and talks to it all the time.

In the toilets there is an electronic paper towel dispenser. You just put your hand under it and a towel comes out. Whatever pointless, energy sapping, because-we-can nonsense will we come up with next – self driving cars?

Some of the caravans have got all the comforts of home. And more comforts than our home.

A man drove past with a dog sat in the passenger seat looking about as if it was a person. A man at the washing up sinks told me it was 8.15. I said I'd slept in. He said, 'No harm in that, as long as you're not late for work.' I said I wouldn't be doing that, ever again. He said nor would he.

The music in the toilets was Bruce Springsteen's *Dancing in the Dark* and Chairman of the Board's *Give me just a little more time*.

When I got going there was a big dead, decomposing deer at the side of the road. What a waste! Some rich bloke could have shot that.

It was high gears and cold hands all the way down to Inverannan. I entered a Camping Management Zone, where wild camping is by permit only – so popular was the practice in the Loch Lomond area. Wild camping ceases to be wild once you need permission.

The Inverannan *Drovers Inn* has been providing hospitality for three centuries, but no longer looks as if a drover, if there had been such a thing for the last third of it, could afford it, although, on the outside at least, it looks remarkably unpretentious and has singularly failed to apply the destructive makeover required to make it look properly traditional.

At the massive *Ardlui Hotel* a bit further on walkers, bikers, cyclists and pets were welcome, presumably along with artists, racists, Belgians and brown people if they have money to spend.

The sun came out and I was feeling the pace a little. It might dry my socks, which have been wet for three days.

With little option I brewed up wrong side of the Armco on a bend that hung out over the loch, with the trucks making the 'bridge' bounce. If the cops had come they would have said it was dangerous and I could have said, 'What, more dangerous than cycling?'

It was one of those lovely twisting roads where, even when traffic is light, you can soon have a hundred angry and resentful motorists behind you, and with endless Armco only eighteen inches from your left leg there is nowhere to go to let them pass. Thankfully most of the gawpers were going north.

I pulled into one of the little loch-side glades where camping is not permitted. And you can see why. It was filthy – everything from cheap folding chairs to bin bags full of the remains of barbeques. The bluebottles were having a field day.

There was a speedboat on the loch and some tosser hovered about in a helicopter. There are no restrictions on being rich.

The much discussed right to camp where you want in Scotland does not exist and cannot exist. It is one of life's fallacies, promulgated by populist politicians who have no control over what private landlords do, and put about by people who have never tried.

The loch is plied by big cruise boats with a running commentary audible from the road. They finish their tour with the taped sound of bagpipes – ah, the skirl of the pipes. There's nowhere in the world like Scotland for overcooking it.

At the Tarbet crossroads I nearly overdosed on diesel fumes and then turned right onto the much less mainline car junkie A83.

'Cyclist chokes on digestive biscuit,' I thought as I cycled along eating – past the child recruitment centre for the Argyle and Sutherland Highlanders. They call them cadets, they're kids.

A sports car passed me. On its number plate was misspelled PLEBS, possibly proud to be nouveau riche. Army trucks overtook me regularly and a party of soldiers were doing team building exercises in a gorge.

There had to be a big long climb up to the Rest and be Thankful, which is mentioned on the Radio 2 traffic news regularly – that was the price for avoiding Glasgow. And I was wrong about the traffic.

The old road tracks the new one on the left, the glen twice desecrated by a species with unlimited access to tar and stone and an unlimited addiction to petrol and diesel.

I was flagging at Strachur on Loch Eyre and had gone right through the completely had enough barrier. For some reason I thought a family box of Indian starters with chilli sauce might sort me out. I ate them all at once at a picnic table in the drizzle.

From there it was a straight run into Dunoon. The only sniff of a campsite was a closed one. The hotel at Sandbank was closed too.

The only accommodation I could see in Dunoon was the big *Sheraton Hotel* and I daren't ask how much it was to stay, so I ended up in exactly the position I didn't want to be – getting the ferry to Gourock at tea time knowing there wouldn't be anywhere to stay there either.

The ferry is like a big bus, with about a hundred bus type seats in a single saloon, and the crossing took 25 minutes, with four bicycles on board stacked *ad hoc* at the rear. The ticket collector had modified a plastic pill container to catch the little circles of plastic and paper from the holes his tool made in people's tickets, because he probably has to vac the carpet in between sailings as well.

I was sure I'd crossed before on a vehicle ferry. I was sure I'd crossed by motorcycle, but I must have made that up.

I turned left out of the ferry port at Gourock and headed into and through the outskirts of Greenock, doubling back once looking for a B&B, but there was nothing. I had a feeling I knew the Travelodge was out on the Glasgow road so I headed that way and eventually came to the Premier Inn at about six o'clock. Thankfully the nice east European receptionist was able to provide me with a room – at £64. The computer system remembered me from some other visit – if not to this hotel then to another one. In for a penny, in for a pound I paid for breakfast as well.

I don't want to watch the news obsessively like I do at home (at home I listen, we've no TV), but did learn that school children are getting up to an hour less break time during the day than they once did, due to pressures to cram in more lessons – surprise, surprise – that's what introducing the market into education, by which I mean league tables and academy sponsorship, was bound to do – as well as stress kids and teachers. Soon there will be openly profit making schools for ordinary kids.

And then a fascinating program on the RNLI. They carried out a very dramatic rescue from a sinking trawler off Shetland, rescued a daredevil couple from the rotting superstructure of Weston-Super-Mare's derelict pier and, unbelievably, put to sea to rescue a dog that had fallen off the coastal path, thereby risking several men's lives for a silly pet – and they were happy to do it, being dog fetishists themselves. Then I put the telly off.

Before the news I'd watched Homer Simpson try to sell fracking to a suspicious public because he'd been 'promoted' to fracking publicity officer (or something), just one of those people who has to tell lies to the public for a job.

For my tea I had the same as I've had for the last two nights – peanut butter, marmite and curry powder flavoured pobs – only this time I added a bit of porridge oats because I only had two pitta breads. Some people will find this hard to believe, but it was lovely.

Tomorrow is Saturday and the 47th anniversary of my going in the army at 15.

I reckon I've done around fifty miles today.

Many Chinese people apparently believe that animals such as cats and dogs do not feel pain and that they are on earth to be trained, put to work, killed and eaten. Most British people act as if they believe the same thing, because they eat meat, but pretend they don't. The obsession with pets, particularly dogs and their welfare 'the British' have is complete hypocrisy.

I have a large room and leaning against one magnolia wall, under a typical hotel room picture of a flower, is my homemade bicycle. It is a fine machine and it has more work to do yet. I am glad it is in the room with me because I would be very upset if it was stolen. I would be even more upset if I lost my diary, because if my bicycle was stolen at least I could write about it. These are the thoughts the solo traveller has.

Chairman Mao spoke repeatedly about the evils of wastefulness. Paul Theroux regrets that the 'mania' for patching and repairing had begun to subside – people now liked things that were brand new, clothes were so cheap that no one had to waste time repairing them. Again this is not a particularly Chinese problem. When I was young everyone repaired their clothes. If we do not address it our modern throwaway society will be the death of us, but we are too busy with driverless cars and drowning dogs.

Crossing the Clyde was like re-entering civilisation. From now on I'll be able to choose what roads to ride instead of having only one choice, but I must make myself meander, rather than be tempted to rush down major roads.

I consider myself lucky to have survived my highland fling and have no desire to cycle those mad roads again.

Day 22 – Greenock to East Kilbride (via Gabroc Hill)

(Glasgow Area)

Woke at 6.30 to blue sky and bright sunshine outside, but I'm not rushing anywhere. Put the TV on for the time to a long report on the police's use of facial recognition technology. They say it is to help them arrest known criminals, but they have millions of images, gathered at football matches, demonstrations and randomly outside shopping centres. It is nothing but insidious, intrusive big brother, but I suspect there is very little we can do to stop it – even though people were protesting. All they'll do is get their faces on the system as trouble makers, as will those protesting against the third runway at Heathrow. One man, seeing the facial recognition system on trial in his local high street, covered his face up. He was given an on the spot £90 fine by police for disorderly behaviour. It is already an arrestable offence on a demo to cover your face up [actually the police still have to get a separate court order for each protest]. There are six million cameras in Britain, the highest people to camera ratio in the world. On average, wherever there are two people, a camera is watching them.

Labour has announced plans to abolish the slave wage that can be paid to young workers, bringing them in line with the national living wage for adults. The Federation of Small Exploiters has accused politicians of playing tit for tat with wage rules, but it makes a welcome change for them to be playing tit for tat with something so positive, rather than making ever more regressive taxation promises.

The Chinese laughed in Paul Theroux's face when he asked if he could visit a commune (for commune read community) – didn't he know that Deng Xiaoping had declared the commune experiment a failure? Didn't he know that everyone was now paddling his own canoe?

'It's all been broken up into "Geti Hu" – single family households, that is, every family for itself.' Far be it from me to make a comparison with Thatcher's destructive rhetoric, but this is the modern world – centrally funded social provision is a thing of the past, its days are numbered everywhere. Obviously people will resist its passing, but they will be met by repression, surveillance and brutality. We are entering a new phase of ultra-capitalist hegemony because the system is in crisis and profits must be secured at any cost.

The forecast is good from today. I'm only about a third of the way down the country and look forward to the rest of the trip.

In China in the 1980s people were robbing ancient graves and tombs to sell the antiques they contained. In Greece in 2017 people were digging up their undecomposed relatives because they couldn't afford the rent on the grave plots. The EU did this to them.

A regular visitor to China told Theroux she hated the changes and denied the suggestion that they were improvements – 'I hate the changes. Now all they want are trinkets and toys – colour TVs, cameras, watches, recorders, refrigerators, motorcycles. They're greedy, they're starting to be very crooked, they don't trust each other, they lie.' The old society had rules. The new one doesn't.

At breakfast (at which I pigged out) I sat with Donny from Spean Bridge, who was in Greenock to fit a crane to a boat. He said he didn't envy me cycling on the roads in the highlands – he's seen himself how overtaking cars made oncoming vehicles stop and go onto the verge, and that the only thing in Spean Bridge was the commando monument. I think it's actually to the founder of the commandoes.

When he'd gone I looked out of the window at the lovely view. Other people looked at their phones.

Greenock is one more piece of British history, a once thriving port that now isn't.

I resupplied at Morrison's and took the very steep B288 south, towards Bridge of Weir and Kilmalcolm, leaving the sea behind me for some time to come. Past the big brick-built Catholic church where a confirmation was about to take place, and through the outlying housing scheme, exchanging a few words with a bloke doing a bit of Saturday building work on the way. The estate of modern homes looked airy and pleasant, with plenty of green spaces and lovely views over the Clyde and to the hills beyond, but then it was glorious day and everything looks better with a bit of sun on it. A man walked past with a Doberman. It would take a lot of sun to make one of them look like anything other than a slavering pack animal with child killing potential.

At the top some big enterprise had been so comprehensively levelled that only the iron railings surrounding it gave any indication that it had once been important, perhaps even why these homes were built.

The last place was the cemetery, where we all must go, and the dead of Greenock have a lovely view, down over the football stadium, the new dockside flats, the retail parks and the empty quays, right across to Helensburgh and Dumbarton.

The view over humanity's doings was worth a hundred empty windblown glens. In the centre of Greenock is a tall significant tower but from up here it looks like a mere pencil stub. The whole sprawl looks like a model village on a table top, with the sea painted blue and the hills in shades of brown and green.

Near the top I met Bill MacIntee, who had walked from Port Glasgow and spent his time walking these hills or getting the bus with his pass if he felt like it. Bill could remember when, after the war, whole fleets came into Greenock. He pointed out the distant hills and the best places for the views, then we both carried on doing our own thing.

At the entrance to Caledonian Water Alliance premises a sign said 'Nothing we do at Caledonian Water Alliance premises is so important we can't take the time to do it safely.' It makes you think of the cavalier attitude to safety taken by employers through most of Britain's industrial history. Even when I was young it was a given that three men a week died in the British building industry, and in their heyday thousands of men died in British coal mines.

Having said that this sacrifice of life for profits was nothing compared to the First World War when millions of human sacrifices went to the altar of free trade.

The farmland I plunged down into was something new, with cattle line a beam advancing over the grass, and the almost ever-present cuckoo in a wood.

In a field a big sign said 'Christ died for our sins', like it might do in the southern states of the USA.

If there was one constant yesterday it was the verges full of bluebells – I wasn't sure I knew the difference, but today I've seen artificially planted ones, and their much fleshier greenery gives them away as Spanish.

With the exception of one or two sharp climbs, from which I could see the snowy peaks I passed two days ago, it was rolling farmland and light traffic all the way.

The lambs get bigger and fatter as I go south, becoming more serious in their demeanour in readiness for their short life as sheep. Gone are the wedded bliss campervans and the macho man tours of adventure motorcyclists, though if anything this area is more rewarding and much more varied than the highlands. It is a Garden of Eden in comparison to that wilderness – the problem is that it is not vast and wild enough to induce the primeval spirit of man conquering the untrammelled earth on long strips of tarmac to restore the twentieth century disconnection that is manifest in modern man's inability to build his own shed. Instead he tries to reconnect himself through ever more of the very technology that caused his separation, measuring endlessly his average speed, his altitude, his heart rate and his experiences per pound spent, instead of taking a blade of grass from the verge and blowing through it to make a noise like a constipated seagull. It is not challenge or endurance enough. This landscape is merely pleasant, hardly more of an adventure than sitting in a pub beer garden in Haworth and speculating about Kate Bush.

I saw a big rock in a field so I went to investigate. It is the Clochoderick Stone 'a fine example of a glacial erratic composed of rock different from that below the soil on which it rests.' It has been there since the ice age 18,000 years ago. Various legends are attached to it – that it was a place where the druids dispensed justice, also that it marks the burial place of Rydderick Hael, monarch of Strathclyde, whose crushing victory over paganism resulted in the conversion of the country to Christianity. On the information board someone had tried to scratch out the word Christianity, as if by doing so they could erode two thousand years of history and its good and bad aspects. I spread-eagled myself on the stone to commune with the past, actually with the people of the past, as many more must have done before me, and nearly went arse over tit getting back over the stile, narrowly avoiding falling four feet onto my face.

I sat on the old bridge at Howood in Renfrewshire and ate oranges from Morocco and apples from New Zealand, writing with a BIC pen made in France in a note book probably made in China, but sold to me by a company based in Bradford. The bridge had carved on it names from long ago – one I noticed from 1954, two years before I was born, when the world looked full of promise.

Through Uplawmoor and by back roads, not really sure where I was going, in Ayrshire, whose motto is 'Forward Together,' as in Avanti! Which I believe was the motto of the Italian fascists, and Vorwarts, which was a revolutionary newspaper. *Nihil sub soli nova est.*

A woman told me I'd almost feel as if I was going through the yard of one farm 'with buildings both sides, dogs and that' and she was right, I did, and a jack Russell deserving of a kick in the teeth snapped at my ankles. A young man lurked in the dark recesses of a big shed.

I was lovely cycling and I felt as if I was a cock-stride away from my next destination, but then I went wrong and was forced to ask a man with a big brown dog, thinking he'd know about where he lived. Naturally he resorted to his mobile phone – they won't even look at my map – while the stupid thing barked at me. I wanted to shoot it dead, especially when he said to it, 'Go on, you have a sniff at the bike' (and my leg).

A bit further on a walker kindly distracted two snarling dogs while I cycled by.

Eventually, by many contortions I found Gabroc Hill, my 8th destination. It consists in two farms and nothing else. Next stop Blackpool.

As I made my way north to get round the unpopulated area centred on the Laird's Seat the snow covered peaks of the highlands were once again in front of me and a distant plane went up at a sharp angle from Glasgow airport.

I didn't really want to tack east through Neilston, Newton Mearns and East Kilbride because I knew the roads would be full of rush-hour fruitcakes, but then I remembered it was Saturday and there would only be leisure time fruitcakes. And it was five o'clock with no prospect of anywhere to stay.

I called in at what looked like an Asda supermarket. It was actually an Asda 'plus' and entire undercover high street, with dozens of shops and all the leading chains. And it was buzzing at six o'clock on a Saturday evening. Shopping is the new something or other and we're pissing in the wind trying to save small businesses on the real high street – if they survive they'll be reduced to petty traders catering for an impoverished proletariat on the margins of society, like they are in developing countries. The drive to the mall is the future for everyone else.

After picking my way through the above-mentioned places, asking directions several times in the absence of signage, a Travelodge or Premier Inn became inevitable, and I at last found a Premier Inn in East Kilbride at 7.15. Alessia on reception was funny and nice, but there was nothing she could do about the fact that it was £82. She said she used to do things like I'm doing – she was only about twenty four – and gave me a disabled room on the ground floor so I could easily get my bike in.

I got the telly on in time for the top Saturday night entertainment of celebrity *Pointless*. As an aside, following a question about Jesse Owens, the bespectacled expert behind the expert's desk revealed that Jesse Owens had said he wasn't actually snubbed by Hitler, as reported, but by the US president FDR, 'which speaks volumes.'

Instant mash and beans for tea – good hotel room fodder – having sustained myself all day on fruit after the full breakfast.

Some frustration today in skirting greater Glasgow and not being able to find my destination straight away – but a different ball game altogether to the A roads in the Highlands, mostly very good cycling roads and scenery.

Unbelievably *Pointless* was followed by another pointless quiz with flashing lights and star struck greedy contestants. I put it off.

In 1984 Paul Theroux is of the opinion that China is virtually a failing state and that the army are in the wings watching the corruption – the implication being that there might be a coup. I have forgotten when the Tiananmen Square events took place, but don't remember any suggestion that the army might be disloyal to the regime.

I carried two litres of bottled water for the last ten miles of the ride today, though I don't know where I thought I might camp out to use it – what I passed through were endless new housing schemes and featureless dual carriageways. The water cost me 17p and is still on my bike. The plan tomorrow is to head east to the M74 and follow south the B road that runs beside it. If I can get an early Sunday start I might risk the A road south to Strathaven. I have Gretna in my sights.

Theroux is also told that Chinese people in their thirties who had grown up in the Cultural Revolution were the most selfish. We had to wait for the nineties for our yuppie 'greed is good' culture to take off. And he tells students that everyone has anxiety dreams –

like having to take an exam they are not prepared for – I know I do. I still dream I'm at Glasgow Uni and I haven't been doing the work and will have to drop out, and it's twenty years since I was there.

I can't be tired if a can sit about reading. I don't even ache much. In fact I couldn't sleep for fretting about how much I'm spending or where the next campsite is likely to be – doing sums about how much it will cost if a stay inside every night. Oades is realistic and she did sums on that basis beforehand. When I tell her I can build a bicycle from scratch for nothing she tells me it will cost a thousand pounds, and it does. I've stayed inside six nights out of twenty-two, which is nearly one in three. One in seven would be more reasonable, but I am still disinclined to wild camp, though I will if I have to, Alessia on reception last night said that the right to camp anywhere in Scotland was really a non-starter. You can do it, but you have to be very determined, and I'm not. And I feel softer because of this unwillingness, less of an outdoor type, less of a man.

I'm not bothered about the cost in the abstract because I'm having a good time and it's as good a thing as any to spend the bit of a windfall I got from the teachers' pension on.

I was awake in the night – a waste of my money spent on the hotel – and read.

On the short excursion into the Dales we had before I came on this trip John was taking the mickey out of Oades and I for using the word *lollygagging*, to mean hanging about wasting time, as if we'd made it up, but Paul Theroux uses it.

Day 23 – East Kilbride to Longtown
(Back into England)
Eventually the birds started and it began getting light. I got up before five.

The sun and the wind have made my earlobes dry and my lips dry and cracking.

Paul Theroux visits the remains of a once great city in the outlying Uighur region of China – 'It is very thrilling for an American to consider such a place, because we don't yet have anything that qualifies – only ghost towns and fairly insignificant small cities, but nothing like the monumental corpses of once-great cities that are known in the rest of the world. Probably American optimism arises from the fact that we don't have any devastated cities. There is something wearying and demoralising about a lost city, but it can give you a healthy disregard for real estate.'

It depends upon your definition of devastated, but I imagine Detroit would now qualify on some grounds.

I'd had my porridge and was back on the road by six, taking the deserted A road to Strathaven (Stra'ven). There was quite a frost in the fields, but the sky was blue and the sun was up.

At Strathaven there was a diversion sign for the B7086 to Kirkmuirhill, but I ignored it (there never was anything to indicate why it existed). When I stopped on the bridge over the river to brew up the lack of traffic had me worried, but eventually some came past. The stones the bridge is made from are six foot long, about eighteen inches square in section and must weight two tons each, and yet they are cut remarkably accurately. No one will ever build a bridge like that again, and yet they did it with the simplest of tools.

It took a long time for the sun to provide any warmth, but there was no wind – tens, if not hundreds of wind turbines stood motionless – flawed technology people who don't like them near them say. They'd rather have a coal fired power station near someone else.

On the back road to Lesmahagow I passed 'Dogchester – a luxury home for pets.' Meanwhile people sleep in the streets and attempt to cross the English Channel in rubber boats. There are whole aisles of dog food in supermarkets while people in and out of work are forced to use food banks.

The paper shop in Lesmahagow didn't have a postcard, or anything else much. The woman said 'Ye could'ne get ane frae here anywa,' which I took to mean that postcards of such a unattractive backwater might not be particularly fast sellers.

From there it was marked cycle route 74 all the way to Carlisle. I left on the broadest, smoothest continental style cycle path

I've seen this side of the channel. It was so wide you could have imagined it being used by thousands of commuting cyclists heading to a soviet tractor factory, rather than a few locals and the odd End to Ender.

Parts of it are one lane of the old A74 and the route flirts with the new M74 all the way down. At Coalburn a lovely picnic bench was provided so I brewed up in the sun. Unsurprisingly Coalburn used to be a mining area. The last pit closed in 1968.

A dog walker came and let his dog sniff my legs. He said, 'She'll nae bother ye pal,' but 'she' was bothering me because I don't want his, or anyone else's dog anywhere near me, a possibility which dog owners seem absolutely oblivious of, having convinced themselves that a semi-domesticated slavering pack animal is a member of their family with equal rights to a human being.

Evidence of an even older road is all over. The newest old road then does a big climb and has a terrible bone shaking surface. The verge is littered with bottles of piss and other rubbish, including builders' waste and old tyres.

The M74 stretches like a wide French boulevard straight over summits, whereas the old road tracks the land, man has at last achieved his pyric victory over the earth.

I bumped into Jim and Stephanie Reader, who live in Portugal, but were on route from Dover to the Orkneys and in their fifth week, staying like me on campsites and in Travelodges. I told them to be careful in the Highlands. They were perhaps a bit older than me and Stephanie said she walked up hills. So do I if I feel like it.

Then local cyclists Douglas and Ricky Burns caught me up and we rode together for a couple of miles, talking bikes, tours and Glasgow University, where Douglas's wife and daughter had been. Ricky told me to send him an e-mail to let him know how I'd got on. Douglas said he and Ricky were members of the oldest cycling club in the country and a medal had been found that was given to someone in seventeen fifty some. Then he corrected himself. The bicycle wasn't invented until the mid-nineteenth century.

I called in at Abington services to let them rob me for a packet of Hobnobs, but couldn't thole overpriced water as well, so will have to make do with one bottle. At last I found a postcard to send Oades.

Just after Crawford, below a bridge on the old road, is a little chained off area about thirty feet in diameter. Within it are the graves of the men killed building the railway, which follows the road. It isn't believed any of them were employers, financial backers or MPs.

Eventually it warmed up and brought out small white butterflies with orange wing tips that fluttered around each other like crazy lovers. The terrain is hilly, with heather and pine forests, a modest version of the highlands. First the motorway and the railway are on one side and then the other. An Eddie Stobbart truck proclaimed it was delivering sustainable distribution. This is greenwash: practically nothing we currently do is sustainable, certainly not carting loads of stuff we don't need up and down the motorway in diesel powered trucks.

Into Dumfries and Galloway, my last county in Scotland.

While I was having a sandwich another of the numerous middle-aged men called David pulled in on a flash titanium road bike. He told me he'd treated himself to it for his fiftieth birthday, and what he'd had for breakfast, where he was going, how I should have a bit of weight at the front, how he'd done the end to end in ten days and how they knew him in Abington café. I'm always suspicious of people who say the owners of businesses know them – as if they give a fuck who they are while they're taking their money. All they care about is getting as much out of you as they can – that's business. The friendliness is a marketing strategy. When I said my next place was near Blackpool he said, 'Morecambe?' And he referred to my bike as being made from square bar – as in the oft heard 'man beaten with iron bar,' meaning hollow steel tube.

Quite a south-westerly got up, which was a bit of a pisser, but only to be expected. It is after all the direction of the prevailing wind and it could be against me for the next fortnight.

The marked route carried on in a similar vein, fairly level, following the M74 on the B road past Moffat, Lockerbie and

Eclefechan until the last bit, when it sent me up a hill and via country lanes coming into Gretna from the west. I called at the Co-op for supplies and then, re-entering England, rode the two and a half miles to High Gaitle campsite (£8) on the advice of a man in Gretna, but where I've been before.

It's a lovely flat, open site. I'm the only camper and pitched next to a table to spread my stuff out. It's an immense relief to get on a site and know you can stop and are safe for the night. It's the same feeling in a hotel, but there it's tempered by the fact that you have been robbed.

At a guess I'd say I've done between eighty and ninety miles today. I threw away all my Scottish maps, though it was tempting to keep them for posterity. I even washed my shorts and shirt and hung them from a tree to dry on a very pleasant evening. For the first time since I set off I was able to sit comfortably outside until the sun went down – and I saw the first grass being cut for hay/haylage I've seen this year on the way into Gretna.

When I first came to Gretna thirty years ago it was a backwater, with only one obvious claim to fame. Now it's got a massive retail park, a big Co-op and an ever-expanding Barratt and Persimmon periphery.

Day 24 – Longtown to Kendal
(Cumbria)
I woke as the sun came up in another blue sky – freezing. It is marvellous how a sleeping bag can feel big and fluffy at night but a tissue of nothing in the morning.

The clothes I'd washed were crisp and dry by the radiator in the utility block and I warmed my arse by the same means.

Yesterday from the road I saw two men sitting in a back garden having a beer and got my first small pang of homesickness. It's easy to think the trip's nearly over because I'm heading south, when in fact it's hardly begun. I look forward to riding the sea front at Blackpool, and along the south coast.

I cycled into Longtown on the pavement of the A7 to avoid the wagons, over the broad Esk, which flows over great slabs of red stone. The town is pleasant enough, based on a broad crossroads with a seemingly thriving main street of 'traditional' looking shops. The houses look traditional too, with through passages to rear yards, but who knows what they may once have looked like – perhaps not with the brightly painted facades they have now – but it's all blighted by endless wagons rumbling through – timber trucks in particular. All this timber should be on the railways, along with most of the other stuff that's carted up and down the motorways, some of it several times.

I spotted the sign for cycle route 7 and, though no destination was indicated, I thought it must head south and followed it past the war memorial onto the back roads, past the red stone St Michael and all Angels and acres of seedlings covered in polythene.

It was marvellous for ten minutes until I followed an ambiguous sign down a bumpy track, convinced myself it was wrong, took the alternative, and ended up back on the A7 two miles from where I'd left it and still eight miles from Carlisle – this is the nature of our National Cycle Network.

It was noisy, dangerous and intimidating. Once more I was forced into the gutter to ride through grates, potholes and long stretches of broken surface.

No one in their right mind would believe that a rutted and overgrown farm track could form part of a serious cycle infrastructure – bearing in mind that hundreds of cyclists use these routes as the basis for a long trip – and if they must be, then a reassuring sign wouldn't go amiss. But never mind, we'll soon have HS2 and a new runway at Heathrow.

The thundering racket alone makes relaxation impossible – in fact it is stress unlimited. In the occasional brief seconds when there isn't a truck or a convoy of car junkies bearing down on me I can hear the birds sing. It's bloody awful. This is not a holiday.

It hardly eased on the urban run into Carlisle after the motorway junction, where the show house on the new sprawling edge of town Lego estate was called 'The Boston.' I say urban – it was actually a sprawling jungle of car dealerships, retail outlets and fast food shit holes.

I avoided the queuing traffic on the near empty pavement. I don't wait in lines of stinking stationary motor vehicles, if I wanted to do that I'd buy one.

Straight into Morrison's café for a second breakfast only ten miles into the day. It had fake pine tables and coloured teapots on shelves – all the height of civilisation. It's just a pity they aren't collectively owned.

But it could be worse. I could be on a plane shitting myself on the way to somewhere I don't really want to go. Paul Theroux gives a marvellous account of his experience on an internal flight in China – as far as I'm concerned they are all awful. If we had been meant to fly evolution would have given us wings.

Leaving Paul Theroux tackling China I went to tackle Carlisle.

Which to be honest I enjoyed. The broad pavements were divided between bicycles and pedestrians, the sun was out and I'd calmed down in the salubrious and relaxing surroundings of Morrison's delightful café.

A church with a wayside pulpit said 'Your life will either shed light or cast a shadow.' It was next to the Tory club, which looks as if it was built in the sixties when everyone else was thinking of progress. Next to that is Co-op Funeral Care – life, death and conservatism. Britain keeps ticking along.

The big houses and cast iron fenced communal gardens reminded me of Edinburgh (or London).

On the way out the big solid, square, red stone *Railway Inn* was long boarded up – soon no doubt to be demolished.

And Carlisle had everything else – Halfords, B&M, Carpetrite, Sofa World, Uncle Tom Cobbly and all. Every time you revisit a familiar place there's more of these monstrous sheds surrounded by tarmac than last time you came.

One local monument commemorates the men who 'fell' in the Great War, thereby sanitising the horror and celebrating the noble enterprise in the same sentence.

Having lollygagged on a grand scale I thought I'd better crack on. I want to be in Wales this week.

The landscape is green and lush (the council is Eden District) and the A6 performs a similar role to the road I followed yesterday in that it shadows the M6. It's a bit busier and has more peaks and troughs, but it's wider and better surfaced.

A bike packer went the other way loaded up to the gunnels, but determined against all reason and for the sake of fashion not to have panniers, or mudguards.

I've seen a palm oil company and a fuel oil company advertising themselves as green. Johnson Fuels has a slogan, 'Energy delivered by people' – as opposed to cats or guinea pigs presumably.

Instead of dead deer on the road I'm now seeing badgers and hedgehogs. Paul Theroux goes on (i.e. moralises) about the Chinese driving species to extinction, but we're in danger of doing the same to the hedgehog.

A fighter plane went past. It's easy to blame the Chinese – it can't be our fault, but they're polluting because we're consuming.

It's hot and some crops are a foot high. A young farmer crossed the road to the farmhouse sneezing. He probably has hay fever (all the fields were cut). His wife will be making him a traditional ploughman's lunch. They're even making hay on the verges, where it must be full of diesel, rubber and brake pad particles – as must my lungs.

All around a mad scramble is taking place to cut acres and acres of grass with millions of pounds worth of equipment. It's going to be hot and fine. Farmers aren't stupid.

It seemed a long way to Penrith, another traffic jam with shops, where I bought postcards in bulk and stupidly spent money on tasty fripperies and water in a garage when there was a B&M bargains nearly next door. In the past we've done anything but buy water because it's a crime to be selling it. At the garage a man asked

155

me about my bike. I said I'd made it. He said, 'Is there anything special about it?' I should have said, 'Yes, when I am on it I can enter different time zones like Doctor Who.'

I left through Clifton, where the last battle on British soil took place – unless you count Peterloo, Orgreave and Wapping – or numerous other places where the class war has been waged.

Three blokes went past on Harley Davidsons (I've seen hundreds of them), all with their feet in that silly wide and forward position. It made me think of three old men on mobility scooters. Earlier I saw a man in in a flashy sports car, registration TOY – prick.

Past the massive premises of AW Jenkinson Forest Products. Their wagons have been passing me for a fortnight, some of them safely (they were a constant even down into Devon and Cornwal).

And then bugger me if I didn't see the result of another combat – Car one, deer nil.

When I stopped for fuel I watched a sheep repeatedly butt away a little runt of a lamb that wasn't its own, and yet humans have employed wet nurses.

Virgin West Coast express trains go past first on the right and then on the left. But no freight. That's all on the M6 beside it in some kind of sick mockery. A stone gatepost is covered in lichens that take a hundred years to grow.

In Shap village, when I stopped to post a journal home, Malcolm in the post office noticed I had a Rohloff hub. He didn't notice it was a homemade bike. The postmaster, obviously starved of excitement, had to come out and look as well.

Half the vans on the road now have yellow stickers on the back telling cyclists how to ride – mostly the aggressive 'cyclists stay back.' These stickers first appeared on wagons due to the danger to cyclists from them turning left, mainly in London, where a good number have been killed. But in a country where most cycle provision takes the form of a pathetic white line on the road that consigns cyclists to the gutter, telling then to 'stay back' is meaningless. What the stickers actually signify is frustration, anti-bicycle prejudice and jealousy that nothing, but nothing, stops a cyclist making progress. Cycling is progress, hampering cyclists or cycling is reactionary.

Shap summit is 1,400 feet above sea level and 'wintry conditions can be dangerous.' As beside many a Scottish trunk road the old single track Shap road lies to the left and the M6, bifurcated at this point, is way over in the distance, the landscape sliced like a wedding cake. A military helicopter flew over.

A lad went past on a 1974 Honda. A Japanese motorcycle of that vintage is a rare thing. Its registration was 43N. The CB250 G5 I bought new in that year was KCP 39N.

As with Glencoe the hill isn't that hard, it's the scenery that's impressive. There used to be a phone box on top, but that's long gone. Instead of a phone everyone could use there was a man in a car making a call from a phone only he could use. I wonder if there's more money in that.

A stone memorial pays tribute 'to the drivers and crews of vehicles that made possible the social and commercial links between north and south on this old and difficult route over Shap Fell.' Remembered too are those who built and maintained the road and 'the generations of local people who gave freely of food and shelter to stranded travellers in bad weather.' The memorial was unveiled in 1994.

An old lad called Rob, out on his son-in-law's electric mountain bike, caught up and stopped me to effuse about my bike. He said it was like a Clelland and wanted to know all about the welding, the crank and the brakes. But first he concurred with my 'I still hate Thatcher' badge, the first to do so in three weeks, saying she was directly responsible for every bit of bitterness, greed, discourtesy and selfishness in this country today.

When I look up Cleland at home I discover Rob wasn't wrong. Clelands were rugged forerunners of today's mountain bikes designed by Geoff Apps. The company was forced out of business by a creditor in 1984.

A couple of miles out of Kendal a couple were sat in their swimming costumes in deckchairs in a layby by the side of the main road sunbathing, obviously wanting asthma and lung disease as well as skin cancer.

The descent into Kendal was fab, and at the bottom I rode straight onto the lovely Caravan and Camping Club site – non-members welcome.

Roma was on reception and her husband, Stan, who is from Knott End, where I hope to be soon, both very formal in polo shirts with name badges, showed me to my pitch. It was right by four great iron tank turret looking things on the hill top. Stan said they were inspection covers for the water main that fed Manchester – the stuff you learn – and they, and presumably what is under them, were made by J Blakeborough and Sons, Valve Makers, in Brighouse, who are possibly now defunct. (Blakeborough Valves was founded in 1828 and in the 1960s employed 1,300 people on a fifteen acre site. In 1926 the company made the biggest ever water regulating valve. As with many a famous British company the name survives only because someone has paid to use it spuriously.)

It was only five minutes to the massive Morrison's on the edge of Kendal out of town shopping experience village, so I went and spent too much on my tea again – sugar snap peas from Guatemala, baby corn from India.

One of the big camper vans on site is called Apache and has a motif of a big chief, a squaw and a wolf on the side. There's a sign outside the toilets that says 'No Dogs' because they have to be told. The Caravan and Camping Club calls itself the friendly club, but everyone looks miserable and those that walk past don't let on unless you make them. Perhaps there's a policy or protocol I don't know about. Perhaps it's my badge.

It's a beautiful site, It's been a beautiful day and excellent riding. Obviously there were some frustrations, but I've already forgotten about them because when I stop the morning seems days ago. Every day is its own adventure.

Of China, and of course of nowhere else, Paul Theroux says, 'Sightseeing is perfect for a dictatorship. China is surely not anything else, politically speaking. The tourist visits, sees the sights, and when they've seen it it's time to go. The non-sightseer lingers, ignores the museums, asks awkward questions, fills people with alarm and despondency and has to be deported. Also, typically, the non-sightseer is not a big spender and in his or her unregulated way is quite a dangerous person to have around.'

Personally I seem to get into political discussion within ten seconds of meeting people, and I did during my brief stay in China as well.

'It was no good saying a particular place was hideous or pointless. It was the ritual of visiting, the outing that mattered.'

Interestingly a sign at a Neolithic site Theroux visits reads 'People in this primitive society with low productivity couldn't understand the structure of the human body, living and dying and many phenomena of nature, so they began to have an initial religious idea.' In this one sentence is encompassed the hammer blow – God did not make man – man made God. It is perhaps possible that in an ostensibly God-fearing country such as the USA such a devastating sentiment would be unacceptable at a state run public monument, which only demonstrates that the right to freedom of expression is relative and complex – an authoritarian dictatorship can acknowledge that God is bollocks, but a liberal democracy can't.

My fellow 'campers' – there are one or two other campers here, but none in small tents – are all old. Of course they are – all the young people who can afford a campervan are at work – and they carry piles of washing up round in coloured plastic bowls. It's always the men who wash up.

'Encouraging people to live in big cities and tall buildings made it easier to control their lives... robbed them of any interest and made them plainer and reminded people they were merely screws in a vast machine.'

I could have washed all my clothes on this lovely site this evening, but I didn't. Instead I just read my book and stayed stinking.

I was sticky in bed and wished I'd showered. After it was fully dark I was woken by respectable people on acres of quiet campsite having a dog conversation by my tent. Posh campers returned from their pub meals making people carrier noises – chugging diesels across soft grass. Dog walkers shone their lighthouse beam torches about unnecessarily and I could still hear the whine of wagons on the motorway through my earplugs.

Day 25 – Kendal to Lytham St Anne's (via Eagland Hill)

(Cumbria and Lancashire)

A very sticky and unsatisfactory night's sleep. Wearing the same clothes for days when it is cold is a different proposition to wearing them when it's warm.

Got up at the first sign of dawn. Considered washing all my clothes and sleeping bag liner. But it would have cost £4.50. I didn't have the right money, or a full load. So stuck to the original admittedly wasteful plan. Got a shower with a tiny piece of soap, put on clean T shirt and pants and threw the old ones away.

It is a marvellous thing to witness the day begin. Over my porridge and coffee, in a field, overlooking green hills, with birds calling and crows crowing, I lapsed into one of those 'Is this really happening to me?' moments.

Caravans and campervans really are ridiculous. They are all about possession, self-expression, self-reliance and individualism. They are conspicuous and ostentatious – the traveller writ large, rather than the traveller discrete. One could just as easily tour the country by rail and stay in little huts in lovely places like this, thereby saving millions of gallons of fuel and tons of steel, aluminium and plastic production, but where would be the profit in that? Where would be the right to self-expression and independence that masks the reality of stifling capitalist conformity? By buying into the dream of self-propelled travel you buy into the system that makes it desirable and necessary.

I was back on the road as the sun came up after being talked at by a campervan man 'not a motor home, a campervan, just big enough for me and the wife.' He'd had a Morgan for forty two years and had replaced all the nut and bolts with stainless – 'they're all nuts and bolts, Morgans' – except for those in the steering, which have to be high tensile.

Some people have done all sorts with their lives, but now they sit outside campervans on campsites, prior to sitting in conservatories in care homes, waiting to die.

I rode out past the NHS building, which is interestingly called Enterprise House.

There's no point in saying that Kendal is sprawling out into the fields with stunning traditional hyperbole because everywhere is. It matters not that there is a great big empty factory in the middle of town that is going to be made into exciting retail units when it could be made into flats.

There weren't many people out in Kendal so early, but half of those who were out were swinging little bags of dog shit like tasteful talismans.

The main industry in Oxenholme seems to be ripping commuters off for parking their cars near the station. If you used one of them over five days it would cost £40 a week – slightly more than an asylum seeker gets to live on. I should have asked one of those walking to the station where they worked - Carlisle? Lancaster? Possibly even Manchester. They are lucky to have a railway station, we haven't, and Cleckheaton used to have two. Railways aren't the solution to everything, but they are part of the solution to some of the biggest problems facing us – pollution, climate destruction and overreliance on the private car – they need nationalising, heavily subsidising and massively expanding. No other option makes any sense. Hybrid and electric cars are a con designed to protect the economy, not save the environment.

Second breakfast at St John the Baptist at Old Hutton. Adverts on the notice board for welding, child minding, yoga and Holy Communion, against stealing bits from the church, of three nice smiling local Police Community Support officers and details of those in charge of safeguarding, which the Church has eventually had to accept responsibility for, given the scale of the scandal that has engulfed it.

They are still interring people in the graveyard and there's plenty of room for more.

I plumped for the B road via Kirby Lonsdale (which is a bit too close to home for comfort). It looks flat on the map, but it isn't. Again all the shady verges are full of bluebells.

Pedigree Holsteins were being weaned in their own little pens, each with a little plastic hut – as if being dependent upon fertiliser and diesel wasn't enough for farming. They had been taken from their protectors in a way that would make a meat eating dog owner distraught.

From the top of the hills the landscape is massive. The Highlands have got nothing to offer that Cumbria and the Dales don't have in spades. And at least the Dales and this part of Cumbria have a network of roads the cyclist is likely to survive.

There was a good steep descent into Kirby Lonsdale. Half way down a sign said 'Think Horse,' the second part of the slogan was missing – 'Think Posh Twat.'

I didn't need anything in the aspic set centre so kept right on into Lancashire for Carnforth, which is also famous and trite, through the picturesque and relatively unspoiled village of Whittington on a nice flat road. A grand old place was being done up at Arkholme for some scrap man or plastic window seller and a dozen new fake village houses had been built in a little obvious cul-de-sac.

Besides that along the road there are some very old properties and Storrs Hall, which is surrounded by a fancy wall. At the gate the visitor has to ring a bell and wait for security – because the occupants are frightened. Hopefully one day not too distant they'll need to be.

Like a fool I followed the marked Lancashire Cycle Route instead of trusting my own judgement and at the first junction there was a sign that took me right down into Cressingham, where I didn't need to go. Here the hawthorn was just blossoming.

Back at the top of the hill a bearded farmer was herding a dozen escaped sheep along the road, shouting at them, for my benefit I thought. Suddenly one of them dropped down dead, so dead that after trying to kick some life back into it he had to haul it up onto his quad.

After that there was some climbing. Up on the top there was a Thoroughbred Retraining Centre – I suppose they re-educate race horses so they can be sold for general riding – otherwise they'd be dog food. Would that so much money could be found for ex-soldiers.

From Caton the Millennium Cycle Path goes under the impressive Lune Aqueduct and straight into Lancaster (and on to Morecambe). From there without much difficulty and help from two mamils (middle aged men in Lycra) through town and onto the Lancaster Canal, never thinking that I could have got on at the aqueduct.

I sat on a bench for a minute to recover. Someone had burned the bin to the ground, it was ankle deep in cigarette butts, stank of piss and on the back of the bench someone had written in big letters 'Space travel is fake.'

Ten minutes further on I came across Neil, a big grey curly haired old bloke with a little pug and a coke sitting at a table outside a canal-side pub. He stopped me to ask about my bike. I don't generally do dog owners, but we went through all the motorcycles we've had. He said he fancied a big new BMW, but I managed to talk him out of that. Like most new stuff they are whizz-bang, form over substance, over technical, throwaway rubbish. As motorcycles they are top-heavy, half plastic, macho man Christmas trees. Like many another company BMW, which used to make good, solid, made to last motorcycles, is now only interested in making money by selling garish trinkets to people it considers idiots who can't tell quality from crap.

Neil said he came from near Blackpool, but he didn't like to admit it 'because it's a shithole.' He then told me a second-hand homophobic story about a gay bar there and I moved on.

The towpath degenerated to gravel and then in turn to a bumpy rut, a very bumpy rut and grass – and I asked myself (again) why I ever think it will be easier to cycle by the canal – the perfect cycle network, only needing a bit of investment. Never mind, we'll soon have HS2 and a new runway at Heathrow.

A bit further on I met John on a lightweight bike, doing the end to end in bits, his wife meeting him along the way, and today hoping to get to Penrith, which for me would be impossible, but with no gear to carry he might do it – if he got off the canal.

It was jarring, tiring and slow and eight miles took a long time, but it got me to Garstang from where it was only three miles on back roads to Eagland Hill in the parish of Pilling, my ninth destination. It is a mile long with a dozen houses and farms.

A big black Rolls Royce passed me, registered 97 KAY. It was probably famous comedian Peter Kay. And then KAZ in a big open topped car. The headline on one of the papers said the UK is heading for US levels of inequality – where thousands of working people live on trailer parks. The rest lead on the suicide of someone who bared all on the *Jeremy Kyle Show.*

And after all that there was no water and the ferry wasn't running. A man sat watching said he'd never seen the river so low and he was seventy four.

I had to ride the ten miles all the way round on the most awful busy and bumpy road possible at school leaving time, hassled by drivers and driven into the gutter. At one point there was queuing traffic on both sides.

Eventually I got to the seafront at Fleetwood and cycled straight along it to St Anne's and the Lindum Hotel, where we've stayed before – despite promising myself for days that I would savour Blackpool promenade. They had a room at £65, which I took because I had intended to all along. It was a good time to ride down the front – very low dog infestation. In fact Blackpool seemed virtually empty. The tower is 125 years old this year.

While I was in reception a clever dick came out of the hotel bar and asked if I'd been walking. When I said I was cycling he said,

'That's not normal cycling clothes.' I told him I wasn't normal, which he found highly amusing. I heard him telling his mates at least twice.

Strangely, though I was knackered from cycling, I was able to walk to the shopping centre, after I'd been across the road to the pictures to find there was nothing worth watching. I thought about Wetherspoon's, but fancied a curry. There was nowhere, so I bought food and a big bottle of cheap cider to consume in my room. On the TV an advert for proper man-size Jeeps says we're all born 4x4, if only we'd realise – a sentiment they've obviously pinched from the religious, who'd like to believe we all believe in God if only we'd realise. The telly was crap, but I watched it anyway – wildebeest migration and *You've Been Framed*.

Day 26 – Lytham St Anne's to Southport
(Lancashire and Merseyside)
I didn't quite finish the two litres of cider last night.

Put the TV on for the time. A man in a suit and a woman in a dress fronted the BBC's coverage. A woman in a mini dress with long blond hair and bare thighs came on to tell us about England's victory over Pakistan in the cricket – which is only right and proper, because we taught them how to play. The government continues to crow about low unemployment figures and rising wages – the *Independent* draws attention to the other side of the story – that poverty is at an all-time high. The BBC rightfully asks just how well paid and permanent these miracle jobs are.

Today is set to be even hotter.

Cross party talks about Brexit are still deadlocked and Donald Trump is to visit Britain to bolster his ego by demonstrating that he can do whatever he wants whether millions of people want him to do it or not.

It appears that 'Care Deserts' are forming – areas of the country where no care homes are available for the frail and elderly as the privatised system breaks down.

The telly is addictive. I ended up watching a man breaking the record for how many needles he could stick in his head – nearly 3,000.

The Chinese too have graveyards by their railways – most of them were built in the nineteen sixties and seventies with a combination of forced labour and patriotic fervour. Chinese railway workers are in a union, but it doesn't challenge the system [says Paul Theroux – as if British unions do]. Britain's rail unions used to be part of the Triple Alliance of powerful unions – and they still resist attacks, but along with their brothers in the pits and steelworks, which have been likewise decimated, their power is much diminished – but only in theory, because they could stop the country at a stroke if their leaders weren't really an essential conduit for the preservation of the status quo.

It is going to be hard not to allow the next few days to become stressful – the road into and out of Preston can be difficult, as can crossing the Wirral, and the off-road route round into Wales can be hard to find. But it's no good complaining about the Highlands with its certainties and then complaining about built up Britain with so many choices.

In the absence of instructions at breakfast I sat in someone else's place and was moved to a table in a big dining room on my own looking at the wall. I felt as if I was being punished while the holiday coach parties chatted about their terminal conditions in the other room.

The breakfast was as disgusting as I expected it to be, the hotel hanging onto the tradition of deep frying slices of bread and serving raw halves of unripe tomatoes, but I filled up on cereals and toast and jam and was outside by nine.

A nice woman, in her thirties probably, opened the door to allow me to get my bike out of the typically filthy unseen area and filled my water bottles without me asking – she had only been at the hotel three weeks. She hadn't yet mastered the time worn polite contempt of the woman with the limp in charge of the dining room, who has always been there, or the polite but formal East European waitress. Mohamed who let me in last night has only been here a month.

I rode out past the ornamental lake garden, constructed 1909-18 'The whole scene' of which 'has a charming enchanted ambience.' A bit like the Lindum Hotel.

A lot of people in the hotel were Scots. A lot of people in Scotland, particularly in the Highlands are English. It's all about going *somewhere*.

The dog walkers were out in force, along with arm swinging walkers with baseball caps having seemingly one sided conversations with people at the end of their telephones.

There is quite a breeze against me and I must take it easy and not resist it or it will get me down. I overtook people who were talking about mental health and hotels that aren't fancy. Across the water I can see Southport. I can see why people retire to Lytham St Anne's (St Anne's or Lytham – it's difficult to know which you are in) the whole place has the air of a sheltered community.

I had a good chat with council worker James Murray from Paisley, who was picking up litter round the sea front picnic tables. He'd been 'down here' thirty eight years and I took him for one of those career council workers. But until recently he was working on the extensive sea defence/promenade refurbishment, and had been laid off till the next phase. He'd always worked in construction, but had three years off when a load that fell from a crane and could have killed him only crushed his leg.

James has family all over Britain, including Yorkshire, and has no desire to go back to Scotland, though he described the views from the hills above Paisley with great fondness. He was fifty five and could see the finish line, the light at the end of the tunnel, but not yet the tunnel at the end of the light.

A woman in a therapist's uniform stepped out of a gate with a big blue ball and we nearly collided.

Lytham celebrates its War Weekend in August and the poster features three smiling WAAFS in too much lipstick. They're called the Bluebird Belles because that's what the war was all about – big bands, bosomy WAAFS and the Dunkirk Spirit. If only we could relive it. Well we can – up and down Britain every weekend of the summer. A country that looks back positively on one of the most horrific episodes of recent European history must be well up shit creek. Steam fairs, preserved railways, castles, caricatured and cobbled villages and war weekends – wasn't Britain brilliant? It's all John Bull Nigel Farage nonsense – people still fighting the Hun instead of fighting their exploiters. It's not difficult to find otherwise reasonable people parroting the line that 'the Germans' are still trying to take over Europe. In fact one Scouse comedian, who has rightfully disappeared, made a career of it. It was people like the young Ben Elton and Alexi Sayle (though he'd hate being in the same sentence) who had to break the stupid mould and refocus the anger on Thatcher and her acolytes. But those two long ago disappeared up their own arseholes and Thatcher into the fiery flames. We should have lined the street to turn our backs on the cortege or even blocked its progress to tip her out of the box and string her up for what she did to Barnsley miners, Bobby Sands and the crew of the *Belgrano*. Were there a grave the passing traveller could piss on it – as I believe Byron advocated they did on Castlereagh's, who also had a deep hatred of the common people. When Castlereagh cut his own throat William Cobbett wrote 'People of England rejoice! Castlereagh is dead.' We should similarly rejoice at the passing of Thatcher. Instead we allow septuagenarians and charlatans in suits to prolong the myth that there was no alternative because the unions were holding the country to ransom. In a class war only one side can be winning – and currently it's not us. If Scousers can't see who the enemy is I don't know who can – they've had it harder than many. At least they boycott the *Sun* following its scurrilous reporting of the Hillsborough disaster. The police too were typically mendacious in attempting to cover their own backs. The main critics of the regime today are guilty conscience liberals, who can see that things have gone too far, and fascists

Kylie's coming to town and so are Rod Stewart and Michael Ball. It's all happening in Lytham.

The first hint of a hill made my thighs throb – it was only a ramp to the sea front.

The cycle route wound me pointlessly through built-last-week, faux regency suburbia, where Greek nymphs pour water from garden centre jugs, and then took away the signs, leaving me to find my way back to the main Preston road a hundred yards away from where I'd left it.

A pleasant roadside cycle path took me through Warton and Freckleton – the road wasn't too busy so the endless swooshing of rubber on tarmac was bearable.

I went into a Tesco Express for jam and bananas, vowing to try to curb my spending. Bruce Hornsby was on the radio – 'Some things will never change, that's just the way it is.' There were placards in gardens against fracking.

In Freckleton the carved name of the mill that used to employ everybody was set ironically into the brick wall surrounding the exclusive detached houses that have replaced it.

Urgent silage cutting was taking place everywhere – two tractors in a field, two cutters on each, taking a twenty foot swathe – to be covered till winter and fed to the cows I'd seen in barns, stinking and up to their ankles in their own shit.

The fire brigade were messing about with pumps and rubber boats at Preston Marina. I told one of them I'd seen the RAC training to do their job and one day they'd privatise them like everyone else. He just shrugged his shoulders.

The Preston Guild Wheel, a marvellous use of funds, takes the cyclist right into the city, but a big dog ran straight in front of me, making me brake hard to a standstill. Its ineffective owner said nothing, and neither did I. What's the point?

It would have taken me right out again too, but I decided to go to the art gallery to look at *Why War* (1938) by Charles Spencelayh. The naivety of the question speaks volumes about the poverty of politics. Armaments are the most profitable industry on earth, working people are expendable, and war is the inevitable consequence of a system built on ruthless competition.

I asked the attendant, Sidiq, a third generation British Indian, i.e. as British as me, if he knew what the painting in the background of *Why War* was – it was clearly of some hero having his kismet moment – he said everything in the painting was significant and about war – I knew this, it was a basic lesson we taught to year nine kids – the bust of Napoleon, the gas mask, the front page of the paper. I also thought the toby jug at the top of the picture and the pig were relevant.

Sidiq, who'd just been given a permanent contract at the gallery, was very keen to talk about South Africa, where he and his relatives had spent four months, and his new perfume business. He said he thought it was people from Mozambique and somewhere else that were causing the problems in South Africa now – all the white people had gone to Australia. As he was of Indian extract and of a business bent he probably thinks Muslims are causing the problems in the Middle East and not rapacious imperialist thieves, but I didn't press him on that. He probably also thought I was obsessed by racism and would say, like many do, that he'd never had a problem. I didn't say I'd been an active anti-racist for 27 years or that I thought it was as bad now as it had ever been – more pervasive, more deep-seated and more mainstream.

While I was inside someone stole my water bottle, nothing else, just my water bottle. It was only an old pop bottle.

On the way there I asked directions from two women. One of them said, 'Turn left at Ann Summers.' I said I always turned left at Ann Summers. She said, 'Don't we all.'

On the high street a man had a big easel with colour prints on it of 'the six most hated men ever to live.' Included were Jimmy Savile and Mao Zedong – hardly in the same league. I don't know what he was up to. I think I'd have gone for Thatcher, Blair, Bush (either), Cheney, Kissinger, Franco and Pinochet, but I could be persuaded otherwise. There are dozens to choose from.

Outside the Corn Exchange there is a big memorial to four workers shot by the military in the general strike of 1842. Several thousand workers were protesting against wage cuts and for the 'charter' of democratic rights. There was also a plaque to all those killed and injured at work and the slogan 'Remember the dead. Fight for the living.'

Cycle route 62 towards Southport took me through housing estates. A man in his stocking feet was out in the street in the sunshine berating a woman at the top of his voice about how unfair she was being to him. I bet she wasn't.

With a few hiccoughs the signed route took me away from Preston by the side of the headquarters of the Lancashire Constabulary. In the overall picture the pigs are significant.

A Christian Biker went past, big cross on his back. Now there's a funny thing – someone riding probably the most egocentric, self-promoting symbol of customised capitalist individuality propounding a religion of modesty, charity and community, or the polar opposite of sacrifice, sack cloth and ashes. As if Jesus would have been seen dead on a Harley Davidson chopper when he deliberately rode a donkey to prove his humility. 'What would Jesus do?' is clearly not a question some Christians ask themselves.

All the streets of Much Hoole are named after the constituent parts of the medieval manor it overlays. It was very hot and I could hear fighter planes high above. They are proud to make them round here.

The cycle route began to bore me with its pointless mileage creating meanders, so I took to the main road, where there had once been a six and seven foot wide path. In places it was now reduced to eighteen inches due to many years accumulated dirt, debris, encroaching bushes and austerity.

Powered by perfectly ripe bananas and blue pop it looked as if it would take me all the way to Southport. On the whole it looked as if one could safely drive the last dozen miles into Southport in a Sinclair C5.

But at four o'clock, with Southport and the perennial problem of accommodation looming I came across Leisure Lakes Country Park at Mere Brow with a little brown sign showing a wigwam, the sign that means they take tents. I knew it would be expensive and noisy. I also knew there'd be nothing else.

The warden was entertaining in her back garden and complained I was making her work on her day off (so, according to the sign, it must be Wednesday).

It was £15, but it wasn't £65, which it would have been if I'd kept going. Last time Oades and I cycled through Southport we ended up in the Travelodge.

There are Scouse accents (there would be), loose dogs, electric scooters and swearing. A young man, shirtless and full of badly done tattoos is walking round in circles waving his arms around and swearing into his mobile phone like a TV Scouse stereotype – 'my bird' this and 'my bird' that.

I'm not leaving my tent except to get washed and all I've got to eat is porridge, jam and tortilla wraps – so porridge, jam and tortilla wraps it is.

Even the small children, Jason and Kylie, have ridiculous Scouse accents and their mothers eff and blind at them – ten minutes later tattooed man was still 'my bird'ing it, and half an hour after that. All power to the proletariat.

And there isn't a level bit of grass anywhere, and people have had campfires all over, and there's jet skis blarting about on the lake. It's like one of those parched sites in German forests that are full of ants.

At least now I can enjoy the front at Southport, Formby and Crosby without worrying about where I'm going to stay. I can worry about that on the Wirral.

Telephone man and the woman I took to be his 'bird' were OK when they came to talk to me. 'Respect,' they said, and 'Aren't you brave,' when I told them what I was up to. They asked me how old I was and were amazed that I was 62, 'Good on yer mate,' no doubt because if I was from their neck of the woods and my age I'd have a good chance of being bronchial, obese, on sticks, twelve pints a day or a mobility scooter. To carry on the theme he had a big cross tattooed on his back with 'Judge Me' written underneath it. I couldn't read what it said over it, but I suspect it may be something like 'May the Lord.' It sounds a bit like the motto of a licentious libertine.

Scousers seem incapable of communicating with each other except by shouting and one of them appears to be steadily destroying the woods with a battery powered chainsaw.

Deck of Cards

Life is what you make it
And clichés such as these
Unless your hands have swallows
And you're dealt a pair of threes

Life is what you make it
The starting sheet is clean
If it was that simple
We'd all be Philip Green

Life is what you make it
As politicians know
They make it for themselves each day
And for all those below

Life is what you make it
As Richard Branson proves
He hardly harms a lily
As up the pole he moves

But if you come from Toxteth
Or Bristol Temple Meads
You may disprove the fallacy
This crock of bullshit feeds

Life is what you make it
So climb the hill of beans
It may be in your ethos
To survive by any means

One man in a million
Can wear the champion's cap
But that's all it takes to justify
The there by merit crap

Life is what you make it
That's the commonplace
But some of those who say it
Were clearly dealt the ace

I must have now done nearly half the trip. On Saturday I will
have used up half the time I tentatively allotted.

Paul Theroux reports how the Chinese use cormorants to
catch fish. They are restrained by strings and a band is put around
their necks to stop them swallowing what they catch. When the
fisherman has all he needs the band is removed and the cormorant is
allowed to satisfy itself. It is the extraction of surplus value in a
nutshell, except that the human worker appears to be free. Were the
cormorant capable it would no doubt console itself with axioms
about a fair day's work for a fair day's pay, believing that its master
had 'created' the work in the first place. And, to prolong the
metaphor, it would probably vote for him in an allegedly free and fair
election in which he and his fellow robbers were the only candidates,
believing all cormorants suspicious of the process to be rabble
rousers, agitators and outside infiltrators.

And one of the mothers nearby calls her child a 'fucking liar'
as a matter of course.

Last night I drank two litres of cheap cider. Today I have drunk
two litres of blue bubble-gum flavoured pop. I wonder which was
best for me.

The showers were fine and I was able to use one of the little
bottles of soap I took from the hotel this morning – and fill it up for
next time from their hand wash dispenser – and to think I was going
to invest in a bar of soap.

Then loud music started. Some of it wasn't to my taste, but let them have their pleasures. I've got ear plugs and I'm on holiday. Actually the adverts between the songs were more annoying and no one wants or needs them.

It appears that the voyeuristic and exploitative *Jeremy Kyle Show*, which makes ordinary people's problems into excruciating 'entertainment,' is to be axed – 'now is the right time,' says ITV after it's all gone wrong and they've driven someone to suicide.

The cormorants could cost the Chinese fisherman up to £1,000 – a handsome investment comparable to installing a new piece of machinery in a factory, or, less socially usefully, employing a highly paid banker or solicitor for a day.

Theroux deliberately goes out to eat forbidden food – that is endangered animals – and then feels disgusted with himself. 'This sort of eating was the recreation of people who were rich and spoiled.' It is of no consequence to the underprivileged that the ultra-privileged feel guilty about their excess. It butters no parsnips. And, as it is impossible for them to refrain from their addictions, they will have to be forcibly deprived of them.

'A revolution is not a dinner party, or writing an essay, or painting a picture, or doing embroidery. It cannot be so refined, so leisurely and gentle, so temperate, kind, courteous and magnanimous. A revolution is an insurrection, an act of violence by which one class overthrows another.'

It makes little difference that the man who said this turned out to be a despotic autocrat. However, it may be possible, in certain circumstances, for revolutionaries to be kind, courteous and magnanimous. In any case a country that held to the Divine Right, still claims the support of the Supreme Being (ELIZABETH DEI GRA REG FID DEF), has perpetrated horrors on a global scale and utilises an archaic institution to prop up an unquestioned economic monolith should not be too sanctimonious about other people's despots, many of whom it tacitly supports.

Smooth Radio played Labi Siffre's *Something Inside So Strong*, which is a call to action.

For his disgusting meal Paul Theroux pays the cost of two of the best bicycles in China – a form of transport most Chinese could only dream of.

For my tea I had marmite and curry powder flavoured porridge, followed by tortilla wraps with blackcurrant jam. I couldn't have been more satisfied if I'd had smoked salmon and caviar.

When a boy of about five couldn't throw a Frisbee his dad told him he was gay. Then the children got tired and moody and had to be smacked.

In the evening the jet skis were rivalled by someone on a Moto-cross bike.

I thought I might chance sleeping in just my underwear for the first time in three weeks – as opposed to my tracksuit bottoms and fleece against the cold.

A problem has occurred. I cashed in my ablution block key as they won't be up early enough for me to get my deposit back in the morning. Now I'll have to wait till it's dark for a piss.

Paul Theroux describes Mao, among other things, as 'rebellious in a youthful way.' Maybe he was, but it is also what they say about Corbyn. In his case it is meant to be dismissive. He is regarded as a fool because at his age he ought to know better. It is OK to be idealistic when you are young, but when you are old you ought to be either pretending to yourself that the world is fine, or accepting that it's shit and pretending that nothing can be done about it.

This is one of the noisiest places I've camped (and the second most expensive) and I've camped next to major roads and railway lines.

Day 27 – Southport to Prestatyn

(Merseyside into Wales)

I was right about the warmer night, though there was a full moon throughout. The early morning noise was provided by geese on the lake.

Waking up in a tent and looking after myself is immeasurably preferable to waking up in a B&B and, were there sites available, I would be happy to do it all the time.

Up and off early. The cycle path was positively continental until a mile short of Southport, when it reverted back to a narrow and overgrown footpath. There were two more campsites on the way. None of the three were signposted from the cycle path we've entered on before – hence the resort to the Travelodge.

Coming into Southport it's impossible not to notice that the buses are run by the same global conglomerate that runs them at home. How much better is that than municipally run services that subsidise the rates? You used to know you'd gone somewhere because the buses were a different colour – not any more. That's the trouble with communism. It would make us all the same – we'd all have to buy our stuff from the community co-operative instead of Tesco, IKEA and Carpetright.

I passed Cockle Dicks Lane. Who would not chortle at such quaintness?

Straight to the front for the full experience. There was dog shit, a fake paddle steamer and the smallest pub in Britain. The tide was out.

Southport was receding
It had to have a punt
It did what Winston Churchill did
And opened another front

Down by the manicured acres of sandy nothing you could eat in the same chain restaurants as you can in your own home town. There are car parks aplenty and all the other amusements one would expect at the seaside, like crazy golf, the ghost train, trying to get skin cancer and binge drinking, as well as a Mexican tavern and a fake fort.

As quick as it had begun it was over, certainly nothing to get excited about, and I had to ride back in on the third promenade for supplies – carrots and bread, £1.55.

In a campaign entitled 'Betrayal of our Heroes' the *Daily Express* blares 'New law to stop hounding of our heroes.' This is no doubt part of its crusade against soldiers who overstep the mark being made to answer for their actions on the grounds that once you put on a British army uniform you are above the law and answerable to no one. This attitude is, after all, what made Britain great.

The cycle route out is safe if dull and I was soon beside endless commuters heading like drones for the metropolis, one person per car, in an obvious display of insane illogicality. At every junction there were queues, but some of them still had their top down determined to pretend they were enjoying the freedom of the open road like it shows in the adverts.

There's an RAF station coming into Formby with a fighter plane for us to admire – as if it were a benign piece of engineering with no consequences.

The cycle path became very good – aside from the roar of traffic and the invisible fumes.

It doesn't last though, and I'm soon reduced to a narrow, badly maintained, overgrown footpath with the traffic going past at fifty miles an hour, and a strong head wind got up.

Approaching Crosby an illuminated sign said 'Air Quality – current pollution levels low.' That will have been because it was windy – the shit is being blown somewhere else.

Into Crosby, Shirley Williams' old constituency. She was one of the last gang of social democratic frauds to leave the Labour Party when it looked like it might actually become social democratic. Their allegedly centre ground party was eventually a flop, demonstrating that right wingers like them need a pseudo workers' party peg on which to hang their pro-capitalist hats. Whether the same will be true this time remains to be seen. The sensible centrists this time seem bent only on overturning the Brexit vote, thereby betraying millions of workers who elect people like them – just like social democrats do every time there's a war.

Sick of roaring traffic I followed the signed cycle route for Bootle. Typically it wound me through loads of places I didn't want to go, as if I'd got nothing else to do, and then the signs disappeared. Then, as I often do in cities, I navigated my way south by the sun, hoping I knew what time it was. Everyone seemed to be wearing slippers and on the phone and I badly needed a piss.

Eventually I got onto one of the main depressing, congested, semi-derelict drags and availed myself of Sainsbury's facilities. From there I could see the top of one of the cathedrals.

Incredibly, new luxury apartments were being built beside six lanes of traffic. There was tarmac, concrete and railings everywhere and the whole lot was full of banging, roaring racing trucks and thousands of cars. It was a horrible, dirty, stinking car dominated nightmare.

And there are a lot of fucked-up people about too. It could well be the fumes that are doing it. Living for generations beside this mess can't have done people any good.

Eventually I was in the centre of the great imperial city and rode between the Three Graces to the ferry terminal and booked myself on the next crossing at noon.

Outside I met slow talking Larry Wolfinger from Oklahoma, in the UK for twelve days doing London and the Lake District etc. He was a cyclist who did some self-contained touring and was amazed I'd only got one gear 'up front.' I don't think he understood I'd got fourteen inside the back hub.

People were queuing up to photograph the bronzes of The Beatles and there's a shop dedicated to them that's part of the terminal. No one was interested in Edward VIII with a pigeon shitting on his head. A city that once had everything going for it is reduced to relying on four here today, gone tomorrow pop stars.

The ferry goes down the river first so we can look at all the derelict docks and scrapyards. Naturally there's a commentary and *Ferry across the Mersey* is played. It's all rather nauseating.

For most of the way to Queensferry there was an alternative to actually being on the road – I simply couldn't be bothered with the weaving circuitous cycle path that takes all day to get nowhere – and I followed the road all the way there, though where it was a footpath it was invariably overgrown and reduced in width by accumulated weeds and dirt. We can't keep our paths clean, but coming into Queensferry a massive great formerly green field site was being developed. It looked like either a new road or a retail park, both of which we clearly need.

The big *Queensferry Hotel* by the bridge was long closed and boarded up and a 155 acre site was on offer for development opposite it. Perhaps they should build a hotel.

Queensferry, Shotton and Connah's Quay all run together like one big high street. It was school coming out time so naturally they were all gridlocked. I rode on the pavement politely, until a sign asking me not to made me feel guilty. Some pavements we are told to ride on, some we are told not to ride on. And I'm in Wales, but you wouldn't know because the same company is running the buses. Didn't they tell us that deregulation would mean choice? 'Choice' is an empty meaningless mantra designed to obscure the giving away of services to parasites and thieves. You wouldn't know you were in another country, except you would because everything is written in two languages – one that has developed organically, the other which was deliberately suppressed and has been largely reinvented – 'tacsi,' 'golff,' 'cafi.' I'm not saying the Welsh shouldn't do it, and I recognise that speaking their own language is a symbol of their resistance to oppression, but it's a bit like me insisting on speaking Saxon or classical Latin. Or is it? It becomes a bit of a mockery really because a bus stop is obviously a bus stop, a taxi a taxi, a golf course a golf course and a café a café no matter how many languages you write on it.

I sat in the church yard of St Mark's to recover. It's probably going to be a B&B – that's if I can find one. This coast is very alive and very dead at the same time – with shut pubs and hotels one after the other.

In a flash I was in Flint. With a bottle of water for 17p I pressed on for Prestatyn. Coming out of Flint, Asda and Sainsbury's are next door to each other. That's the logic of capitalism – two big supermarkets next door to each other selling the same stuff, with two supply chains and everything else duplicated. The choice is beans from one or beans from the other. Choice is the mantra, but it's a false choice, not even a choice between a kick in the head and a kick up the arse.

I was shouted at by a knob head in the passenger seat of a car – the first one of the trip, or at least the first one I could be sure about. One expects this kind of thing. I wasn't even on the road, but on the footpath going in the opposite direction.

I've ridden this way before – the choice is a mad road or a bumpy pavement, but the wind was behind me and I made good time. The cycle route offered to send me away from the coast up into the hills to make it easier for car drivers and harder for me, but I wasn't having it today. There's no such thing as a practical cycle route in Britain – only ones that are half as long again, and with more hills than going by the main road.

On the basis that something always comes up something came up – a campsite just outside Prestatyn at about 5.30 (£10), near the main road, but otherwise very quiet. I shall be very comfortable. For the first time this week there are clouds in the sky.

Paul Theroux has, on the face of it good, but actually facile advice for anyone who might not be able to decide whether to be frustrated and slow on cycle routes or risk death and be deafened on the road. Don't let either get you down. 'It is wrong to see a country in a bad mood: you begin to blame the country for your mood and to draw the wrong conclusions.' The north coast of Wales is in a mess, and no amount of positive thinking is going to alter that fact. My mood is neither here nor there – I know shit when I see it. How can that not depress me? Subjective and individualistic mind over matter solutions are no solution to collective ills, they amount to living a pretence in a fantasy world. It is what Buddhists and Jehovah's Witnesses do and it is what miring us in empty and stultifying materialism is meant to do.

Nothing since I left Scotland has been as bad as I thought it would be, not negotiating Liverpool, not crossing the Wirral, not finding accommodation last night or this – on both I expected to end up paying too much for a B&B.

I've slogged it all day on main roads again today. It isn't fun, just a mad race – the opposite of what I said I was going to do.

In the evening someone started up with a motocross bike. I was fed up, or perhaps just tired, put my earplugs in and tried to sleep.

Day 28 – Prestatyn to near Caernarfon (via Y Felinheli)

(Denbighshire and Gwynedd)

And I slept all night.

I am under some flight path, I know not which, but there are planes every few minutes, bleating sheep and ducks as well as the normal chorus. A much more cloudy and overcast day.

Almost immediately after I'd opened my tent to look at the weather it began raining.

It was a cold meal last night – bland Indian starters in bread and a cold breakfast this morning – jam and bread. I have enjoyed most of a Morrison's sunflower and pumpkin seed loaf in the last twenty four hours, and a full jar of jam in forty eight, but I am not doing biscuits and chocolate bars like some people do.

It didn't rain much at first.

I notice when I emerge that I am not actually on the touring field, which is through another gate and expansive, but on the edge of a field for the permanent caravans. I wondered why there were no other tents. There are two over there, including one belonging to a strange woman with a dog, who, when I backed away from it last night, called me sir, mockingly I thought. She then took it into the toilets with her, which is why there needs to be a sign. It is difficult not to come to the conclusion that some dog owners are idiots. At least by camping here I didn't leave myself open to her forcing herself upon me as if I was some common spirit under canvas, which I am not.

The dog had on one of those pathetic but fashionable harnesses through which the owner can exercise no control. On it was written 'Please ask to pet me' the assumption being that everyone wants to.

'Britain is a nation of dog lovers.' No it isn't – it's a nation of dog fetishists, people who are ambivalent and dog haters, and I, along with many other people I know, are in the latter camp. In some countries calling someone a dog is an insult. In this one it gets you two good meals a day and a seat on the settee to lick your balls.

I sheltered in the campsite games room for a minute or two. Rather than having a Ping-Pong table where campers could enjoy an undercover workout it had four one-armed bandits (or modern equivalent), one ice hockey table, two shitty gift machines and two unhealthy sweet dispensers. All were running twenty four hours and several of them played music. It was like Kylie, *duelling banjos* and the music from two toddler's TV programs all playing at once. What must the electric cost? But they must make a profit.

I set off in the rain and immediately onto cycle route five, which took me by marshes, a golf course, the promenade and the wide main road footpath to Rhyl. I didn't need to go into Prestatyn as I had four slices of jam and bread, two full water bottles and a ten pound note, but I thought I'd better have a look at Rhyl, rather than ride straight past, because my auntie Nellie, who wasn't really my auntie, used to come here every year and swore by it. But that was fifty years ago and Rhyl now looks pretty much like all the other faded seaside places, with hotels along the front, garish amusements, medieval and pirate nonsense and closed slot machine arcades. I imagined it also to be like New Jersey for some reason (the reason is Bruce Springsteen).

My auntie Nellie was best friends with my Nan and great aunt Edith, who were very close sisters. Auntie Nellie made up a trio, though my Nan sometimes referred to her as 'mutton dressed up as lamb.' Auntie Nellie lived in a tiny old house on Parrat Row, Laisterdyke, Bradford, which is still there, but like my Nan and real auntie she moved into pebble dashed modernity on Holmewood council estate as many of the old back-to-backs were demolished and Rachman was replaced by the council rent man, only to return with a vengeance in the twenty-first century. Though auntie Nellie took her turn in providing Sunday teas for my siblings and I after my parents split up I have no recollection of what happened to her after I went in the army and my mother and siblings moved away.

Anyway, that was Rhyl.

I suspect there wasn't any of that Welsh going on when auntie Nellie came here – or great big lumps of cast aluminium forming the handrail round the Old River and harbour.

It was a bit dismal and if there'd been a Morrison's I'd have gone in it for a second breakfast, despite my endless promises to myself. It was only about eight o'clock.

There wasn't a Morrison's but there was an ASDA and I thought 'fuck it, it's time to lollygag.'

The café was only a prepared sandwich counter and there were no beans and no self-service coffee machine I could keep getting refills from. I waited ten minutes for a deaf or daft old woman to turn up and the best I could get was a bit more jam and bread – and not even nice bread, cheap white bread. 'ASDA – save money, live better' ASDA radio kept saying, between the adverts for packets of hash browns, pies and chocolate cakes. She was nice though and nudged me like she was my nana as she tried to dispense some jam from a jar onto my plate, making a mess of the job.

The papers are saying that Theresa May has been finally forced out by her own backbenchers and that Boris Johnson is the front runner to take over the Tory party and the prime ministership. The front runner is rarely the eventual winner, but with Boris at the helm it would seem to make any election clearly a choice between leave and remain – because remain is the position Labour will finally take – irrespective of the fact that it means dismissing the majority vote of seventeen and a half million people. Shitting on the working class on behalf of the bosses – that's what they're there for, Corbyn notwithstanding.

Having wasted the best part of an hour I moved on.

The tide was in for the ride along the coastal defences to Colwyn Bay – though the rain spoiled it a bit. Along the way I passed the North Wales Canine Hydrotherapy Centre. Yesterday I passed several dog specialist facility providers, including trainers. I'm not an expert, and nor do I want to be, but I imagine the first stage in training a dog would be to put a choke chain on it and resist treating it as if it is a person.

There were big black sea birds stretching their wings on the groin posts, which for all I knew could have been cormorants, but probably weren't. What I could more easily recognise were the regular piles of dog shit and the abundant snails that feast on it, which I kept crushing beneath my tyres to hang like sticky snot off the end of my mudguards. My bike and equipment are also covered in sand, which I hate, especially on my chain. I had to leave the cycle path at one point because it was buried in sand, but further on a little road sweeper was keeping it clear. And I think my left had crank bearing is failing.

Coming into Colwyn Bay I took conscious boyish pleasure in the waves bashing on the rocks and spray shooting onto the promenade. The place was almost deserted for the twice daily show. It was 10.30. Where the beach begins a council worker was putting up big flags prohibiting dogs for obvious reasons, the tide having cleansed the beach of their ubiquitous fouling.

At Ross on Sea I stopped to take my waterproofs off again as the cycle route leaves the front for Conwy. Off shore there are hundreds of wind turbines in ranks. I could complain about the contrived route, but it was peaceful and scenic and brought me straight into town past the castle and the railway bridge that is in keeping with it.

Walking through Conwy, having failed to find a shop that wasn't going to rob me, I realised what it was that had fallen off my bike three hours earlier. It was the front adjusting screw of my Brooks saddle. I have been sitting on the rails for some time as the leather has stretched, but now the front is floating about all over.

Sat by the harbour having my sandwich I met William, a first generation British Jamaican from Crewe. He had achieved Junior Sergeant Major in Royal Ordinance Corps boy service and gone on to serve in the Gulf with a parachute battalion – though he failed P Company on his ten mile run. When he said he was junior company sergeant major I thought straight away 'was that tokenism?' and I could have said it, but didn't because it would have been to suggest he didn't get it on merit. I did ask if he had had the piss taken out of him in adult service for being a junior sergeant major. He said he had, but he could handle things. We all can – right up to the point where we can't. Besides bikes and the army we spoke about the *Windrush* scandal. His eldest brother is 59 and was born in Jamaica. 'Is your life in there?' asked William, pointing to my panniers – and I suppose it is. He said he was jealous. Why are people jealous, or at least why do they say they are jealous of me not having a mobile phone, a TV or a car and of me cycling around stinking and yet carry on living as they do?

Back on the cycle path west over the dunes the dogs were everywhere. One women was trying to control five, all of them loose. As I rode past, consciously saying nothing, she sarcastically said, 'You're welcome,' as if I should be somehow grateful for being able to use the cycle path while her dogs were on it. They expect you to thank them when they've made you stop while they fuck about theatrically as if they've never seen a bicycle before. I said, 'For what,' thereby reinforcing the mutual contempt.

And I've inadvertently bought toothpaste that is supposed to whiten your teeth. It was no doubt cheap because it was discredited on the telly last week.

After Conwy the main road, the railway and the cycle path are like the three strands of a plait twisting about one another.

While I was effecting a temporary repair to my seat four old women came and completely took over the picnic table I was at without so much as a by your leave. They weren't impolite, but I would have asked. And then one of them did ask where I was heading. Another loose dog came and sniffed round the old women's picnic. I think it was a Chihuahua – one of that kind of inbred little runt anyway. Only one of them laughed when I said, 'That's big for a rat.'

Within half an hour I'd met a miserable dog owner, four selfish old women and a lovely black ex-soldier.

Half a mile further on I rode straight over the silly extending lead stretching between a man at one side of the path and his dog at the other – it was so thin I simply did not see it. The man was on the telephone and smoking a joint.

The path is plastered with signs asking owners not to let their dogs foul it on penalty of a fine. As an incentive to decency this is not entirely working.

The construction of the cycle path around the coast required some elaborate bridges and walkways. At one point it is between the two lanes of traffic on a gantry below a steep hill of scree that is as elaborately walled and reinforced as the Hanging Gardens of Babylon. One minute I was at sea level, the next hundreds of feet above it.

The whole path has the familiar cycle path odour – possibly because they've recently cut the grass and flung the putrefying piles to atoms. Even on the high gantries there are piles of shit.

Approaching Bangor the route takes to a high lane with views across the northern entrance of the Menai Straight to Beaumaris on Anglesey. Further on the road was closed and being completely re-laid, wider and better. An alternative was signed for cycle route 5, but I can't believe the half mile of rough stoned track across fields was put down only for a few cyclists.

Just beyond it I met John an old lad originally from Manchester, but living in South Wales. He was presumably on his annual treat, four days in a hotel in Llanrug and cycle route 5 in stages. I told him he'd probably have to push up the loose stone diversion, whereas I managed to ride down it. John complained about being pointlessly sent up the hill when there was a perfectly good path by the side of the main road. I'm not sure there is. He told me how to pronounce the name of my next destination, Y Felinheli, but I couldn't repeat what he said.

And then the sun came out for the first time today.

I put it to the test. John was right, there was a path, but the first part of it was so dangerously narrowed by years of encroaching leaf mould, nettles and bushes that the oncoming traffic was inches away. I knew I was getting near town when my biggest hazard became people walking towards me while looking at their phones.

I slipped round the bottom of Bangor – with all the other traffic as it happened – and out past Curry's/PC World, Carpetright, TK Max, Pets at home, Costa, Next and B&Q. It was like coming out of Bradford on Canal Road at rush hour. There was everything the passive consumer could possibly want. I was even accidentally funnelled into one of the massive car parks and couldn't find my way out, which might be a metaphor.

After a short bit of main road to the turn off I rode along the main street of my tenth destination, Y Felinheli. For a change it was quite a big place. The main road used to go right through the centre but it now it bypasses it. Like many places it has been deprived of its congestion and custom to be superseded by multinationals on the main road. I didn't see anyone that seemed as if they might want to talk to me, in fact I couldn't see anyone at all, so I carried on out of the other end, heading for one of two campsites shown on my proposed route, aware that campsites shown on maps are usually not nice – but then every campsite I've been to so far has been empty.

I deliberately noted that the shiny strait was very picturesque in the sunshine because I thought I ought to.

The unclassified road to Bethel was a rat run, but that's OK, because work was already underway to replace it with a nice big new one, because as everyone knows, building more roads creates more traffic, and therefore more profit.

The Rhyd y Galen Caravan and Camping Club site wasn't hard to find, but the warden was a funny young guy with a trendy old bloke's name who pretended he wasn't the man I was looking for, and then did sums in his head to work out he needed £16 off me –

the second most expensive site on the trip – and he put me on what is a most acceptable pitch, but outside the barrier. It's actually the late arrivals field. He must think I'm going to have a party, or that I smell, which I do.

Tomorrow's hills look inviting under a now blue sky. It's almost like a return to the highlands and I look forward to it.

Would a train ride for pleasure be too extravagant – or a trip up Snowden?

There's a camper van in the corner. It belongs to Dave and Jen from Bridgewater who are walking the coast of Britain in bits. They've done all the way round from Suffolk to Bridgewater and are now on this bit. Dave had an Isle of Man TT hat on, but I didn't mention motorbikes.

The warden said you pronounce Y Felinheli as it looks - which is meaningless because it probably doesn't look the same to a Welsh speaker as it does to me.

People don't say it so much now, but I wonder if the term 'mousey,' as in mousey hair, has anything to do with the Chinese 'mao zi', meaning light hair (literally old hair). It's as likely as bungalow or Pyjamas to have entered the language through Britain's imperial rampages around the world.

Paul Theroux is insistent that the Chinese are only interested in foreigners in order to pick their brains. He backs up this claim with the words of Feny Gulfen, a nineteenth century Chinese philosopher, 'A few barbarians should be employed,' he said, and Chinese people should learn from them so that they can teach others. 'We should use the instruments of the barbarians, but not adopt the ways of the barbarians. We should use them so that we can repel them. A foreign expert is a barbarian with a skill to impart. They are in China to be used, and when they are no longer useful, to be sent home.' What this means for business and foreign relations today it is not my place to say, but The Donald is not making things any easier.

A good hot shower followed by curried porridge oats with chick peas and peanuts, with dried mixed fruit for pudding – more appetising, filling and nutritious than any of the specially prepared hiking food you can buy if you've too much money and are easily taken in by advertising.

Same shirt and pants back on. I'm wearing them to destruction, with one clean set in reserve.

I feel very chilled (to use a term I hate) and relaxed. Bar a few bits on the main road it's been good cycling today.

'Muslims have been in China for well over a thousand years and yet they are still regarded as strange and inscrutable and backward, and politically suspect.' So much for the integration self-appointed protectors of our precious British culture demand. Though I suspect a Muslim has never been Home Secretary or mayor of a major city in China. Since Paul Theroux wrote Muslims have been further oppressed in China – put in camps and denied their rights. I wonder if anything like that could ever happen in Britain. Human history is not a one way street. People who think Britain is too advanced and sensible and democratic to resort to pogroms, given the right government, are fooling themselves.

The warden, even though he is young, doesn't go anywhere on the site unless he goes on a noisy quad, even in the evening, when people might be sleeping.

Day 29 – near Caernarfon to Bala

(Gwynedd)

A perfect night's sleep, not cold and not too warm. I woke just as it was beginning to get light and the TV was on in the warden's caravan – as it had been at midnight. Went back to sleep and woke again when it was fully light, birds singing, trucks going past on the road. It's all to play for.

A broken sky with some heavy cloud, buttercups and daisies around my tent that I didn't notice last night.

To the anti-American rant of a deranged Chinaman on a train Paul Theroux responds, 'I hear you comrade, but I don't understand,' which he says is a stock phrase for stonewalling someone.

Someone else's homesickness makes him ask himself where he'd like to be, and he decides right there on a train in China doing what he's doing. 'Perhaps it was a simple choice – of being at home or elsewhere – surely this was elsewhere?' Home is good and it can be made interesting, but travel is always interesting – even if it is sometimes excruciating, like Rwanda was for me. Being on the road with nothing but what you need is lightening. The lightness allows you to rise above the trees and see the jungle for what it is. Today I am heading back into the hills and looking forward to it. But by buying in bulk yesterday while there was chance I have made myself heavy.

As I passed the warden's caravan the TV was still on. There were two empty wine bottles and the remains of a takeaway on the table. Now there's a happy man.

I soon came to a sign that said the Pass of Llanberis was closed this very day from 09.00 to 12.15, being Saturday I can only imagine it is for some sporting event. I decided to press on. This is my general rule at road closed signs.

As I cycled beside the twisting road, overlooking the lake, in the warm early sunshine, with the whole mountain shrouded in mystery, I could have been in a foreign country (not to mention the dual language signage). This was going to be a good day.

I saw quite a few classic sports cars with rally plates affixed, the pass being one of their proving grounds – the Blackpool tower of the sports car fraternity.

I could have ridden straight by Llanberis on the bypass, instead I rode straight through it. It has all the pretensions of a Swiss mountain village and none of the charm. There were even some old mining trucks to remind people what used to sustain it before the tourist dollar did – although I believe it was a mecca in Victorian times. There were Welsh and EU flags up the same pole above placards for Plaid Cymru – confused nationalists who fought to be free of one empire only to place faith in another.

The road was closed for a triathlon, but a man head to foot in fluorescent yellow told me that on a bike I'd be fine, as long as I was aware of the runners (it turned out to be cyclists). Having had my awareness of the obvious raised I proceeded. There was much traffic beside me going in to Llanberis and none coming out. It was silent. In

191

front of me was a great grey wall of a hillside tiered and faced by decades of slate extraction.

At the bottom of the pass proper I approached another pair of fluorescent clad jobsworths with a barrier at the same time as a peloton of head down arse up cyclists. They weren't for letting us through, but were prevailed upon.

The peloton soon disappeared and fifty yards further on I was applauded by a group of lads. I said, 'Fuck me, am I going to have to put up with this all the way up?' but was drowned out by their cheering and banging on pans. Those spectators walking up also joined in the piss-taking.

Soon the riders started passing me on their five grand plastic bikes – men and women. A few of the men tried a bit of comedy, a few of the women a greeting, but mostly they just grunted.

Twenty minutes up I sat on a wall for a sandwich and the first rider came down at great speed. It had taken that long to find somewhere to sit. The road is fortified on both sides – we aren't supposed to stray from the straight and narrow.

Actually once the cyclists started coming down *en masse* and overtaking each other my presence *was* a danger and I could see why they'd shut the road. One rider descending at great speed shouted at people walking to get off the road.

The form seems to be to shout, 'come on, keep it up, you're doing well,' or some other platitude. But I find it incredibly insincere, especially as I've no idea whether they're doing well or not – though I can tell one that's coming down with no regard for his own safety because the red mist has descended and he wants to win. That's what sport is about – proving how good you are by showing how crap other people are. It's the opposite of collective endeavour reflecting the very essence of capitalist individualism. Throwing a collective blanket over this individualism is a way of bolstering the nation's place in the world. It's why Baron de Coubertin re-founded the Olympics and why for years Russia or the US won most of the medals. I don't know who does now, probably China, but if it's more shared out it only demonstrates that the world order is collapsing.

I don't want to blow my own trumpet but when I set off again I could catch some of them and could even have overtaken, but didn't think it right for ultra-sports people to be overtaken by an old bloke on a 23kg bike with all his camping gear. One woman started a conversation, saying she'd done it last year and was doing it again with her daughters, and then, probably in frustration with herself, asked me not to ride close behind her as it was 'driving her nuts.' I didn't think I was too close, but was horrified and dropped right back (she wished me good luck on the way back down). The rest of the way up I stayed well behind the only woman I saw who was pushing and I never dropped below fourth gear. The fast ones were very fast. The slow ones were very slow.

The descent to the Bedgelert road is steep and at the junction confused motorists caused a traffic jam because they don't have a map and a road closure throws them into panic. One of the marshals remarked to another that there were a lot of females in the race, which I suppose is marginally better than saying there were a lot of ladies. I have discovered that the more progressive of my sisters prefer to be referred to as women, or, as the un-PC cartoonists of *Viz* had it – 'Wimin'.

The surrounding foot paths over the hills were like ant trails with multi-coloured walkers in specialist gear. The road was lined with parked cars and disgorging vans for a mile – and no wonder – the view down the valley from the long steep descent toward Bedgelert is picture postcard perfect.

In the next place cars were parked on every available bit of ground as if Elvis or the pope were coming.

The Royal Goat Hotel in Bedgelert said dogs were welcome, which is disgusting, and the car park was reserved for the MG car club's luncheon. Apparently goats stink too, but I've never got close enough to one to find out. I have noticed this morning though a couple of diesel cars that stink as if they've been round the clock twice and are worn out, like taxis often do.

The Samworth Church Academy minibus said on it 'Be the best you can be,' which doesn't strike me as a Christian sentiment. It strikes me as a capitalist one, but then I would say that, because I naively thought Christianity was about love and charity for others, not egocentric self-promotion.

I brewed up on a bridge over a gurgling stream on the very quiet A4085 and spent as long, but not as much, as I would have done in a café. Nourishment today is peanuts, dried mixed fruit and brown sauce sandwiches. When I get started on the dried fruit and the nuts I can't stop because a) I have to feed the machine and b) because I'm a greedy bastard and always have been.

The bridge, with its flat wall top was the perfect place to stop and rest awhile and I was glad I had waited for it, rather than just loitering stood up in some gate hole.

As well as the relaxing, good for the spirit gurgling I heard the tooting whistle of the nearby Blaenau Ffestiniog preserved narrow gauge railway. Those passing in their cars heard neither, though I was deprived of Joanna Lumley or Brian Blessed telling me to go straight on for two miles before turning left onto the B4391. If I'd had a radio I'd have listened to *Popmaster* and I quite miss Steve Wright in the afternoon, but on balance I'm better off without one.

As the day progressed groups of motorcyclists emerged to do their Saturday man-thing – though in this area they're more Geraint Jones than Giacomo Agostini. And in this way I wasted most of an hour of my allotted time.

Further on a lone house had placards 'Vote to leave the EU, Free us from the scam.' Within half a mile I had passed a lovely old gatehouse and two very interesting towers, and then took the B4410, which I expected to be hilly after hours of downhill and flat – no one should get off that lightly. I was right. If a minor road joins together two major ones there are only two things that can happen; it will either go up and then down again or down and then up again, but the surface was still pristine and there was virtually no other traffic save a VW camper quaintly called NEL and another called FUD.

Walking up hills the load makes it feel as if someone is behind you holding onto the rear carrier trying to pull you back. I removed another layer of nylon – two is my minimum, one to soak up the sweat, one to stop sunburn – though Mike Ashley's cheap T shirts don't do a very good job of soaking up sweat – unless it's the sweat of the people who make them in China.

For a while specially planted and self-germinating oak seedlings dominated the side, and then, entering Rhyd, I got a brief glimpse of the sea far off to my right. Earlier on a couple had passed me bike packing, forsaking mudguards and panniers for fashion. Now a couple went the other way touring on Brompton folders. The woman let out a gleeful scream, pleased to see another of her kind. If only one could stop and talk to them all and get beyond the details of their trip – there might be social workers, soft furnishers or submariners among them.

Things started to look like other things and the *Oakley Arms* Hotel at the junction with the A487 looked remarkably like a place I'd stopped in Scotland. The Oakley motto was NON TIMEO SED CAVEO, which I translate as 'I am not afraid, but I am alert.' I am afraid I showed off by asking a completely innocent woman what she thought it meant because I wanted to tell her what I thought it meant – and this after bringing her up to speed on what I knew about the MG event. She kept saying, 'Thanks for that.' I was in fact 'mansplaining,' that is giving a woman the benefit of my knowledge whether she needed it or not.

Some wankers in a wanker's car blew their horn at me, but it's better than having half a carton of juice thrown at you, which has happened before.

Another climb, another county. The dam of what I take to be Tan-y- Grislau Reservoir is hundreds of feet above to my left below a pyramidal peak.

A Lotus car had to do a braking swerve to avoid me because he was hugging the racing line on a blind left hander. Mynwent Cemetery had many recent graves, almost as if there had been some disaster (I thought of Aberfan) and many others with simple wooden crosses. I couldn't say if it was due to piety, poverty or a pre-permanent memorial, but the local mason must be busy.

Eight men went past on motorcycles, mostly the pseudo trail type. There are women on their own motorcycles. They are usually petite, and never on big trail bikes.

Climbing again out of Festiniog the dam is still there and below it communities cling to the hillsides in a clichéd way. One could get the impression that here Welsh is the *lingua franca* because the very hills, the slate mines, the squat stone dwellings in sheltered nooks, the sheep and the twisted hawthorns are Welsh – why would the language be that of an alien place where regimentation and red buses rule? This country is rugged and untamed – it obviously needs a language that consists only in consonants. Even the attractions seem understated without the kilted kitsch fanfare they have in Scotland. The so-called Welsh national dress, that only seems to apply to women, is also bollocks and they seem to have more sense than to prostitute it for a quick buck. Wales has been robbed and raped and its people oppressed by the imperial British, whereas Scotland has never been, and yet the Welsh are subtle in their resistance, whereas the trade in tartan tat in Scotland is brash and unseemly. And the Highlands, like Cornwall, which I have yet to enjoy, are a busted flush.

I saw a road snaking off to my left for miles over high hills. It looked Hardknott and Wrynosed and I thought 'surely I can't be going over there.' And I wasn't, but part of me wished I was.

My road levelled off and stayed mostly two lane. The walls may have been slate not sandstone, but they were crumbling just like they are in Yorkshire. And there are the same abandoned hovels of no use to self-made men with money to burn, due to lack of access.

Near the summit (it wasn't near the summit at all), thanks to the Rees-Jeffreys road fund 'W.R.J. 1872-1954 – for your enjoyment of this view' I can look down on a Welsh Cirque de Navacelle and a tumbling falls. There's a little fenced off area below the plaque, accessible by steps, where one could picnic, or even at a push camp, but it's unkempt and could be made much more of – any sort of enterprise of the kind you see at the top of the Alps wouldn't work because the road is practically empty. Alun Gethin made his mark in

'08, Owain in '09 and Karen in 2015. None of them thought to draw a big penis or make any kind of statement except that they were here because they had to be somewhere. To really make your mark you have to write your name bigger than the attraction itself – like Churchill or Hitler.

On a Saturday in mid-May the B4391 was a fantastic road to be on. There were no jelly mould joyriders and nothing to spend money on, though it's worth more than Blackpool's Pepsi Max. Other times of the year are available and I couldn't say what it might be like then – though I suspect until someone builds a theme park, a Costa, a Macca D's, a traditional home cooked food pub and several dozen tat shops and renames it the Pass of the Philistines it may be OK for some time to come.

Every time I thought I was going downhill fast I wasn't, until eventually I was. There's no more water in the streams and the ground is just as dry as in Scotland. And even then it wasn't over, but still had its ups and downs. Not for the first time my thighs throbbed. There were so few people about I began to think Martians had landed or there was a big football match on.

Then there was the A road to Bala below. Even that did not seem to impose upon the majestic landscape. The Welsh have every right to be proud.

Up I went again, and here an old road to the right was only a half healed scar. It could no more disguise itself as a farm track than the five tiered disused slate quarry on the hillside.

Five two-wheeled man-toys passed, two of their riders standing out like sore thumbs in full urban camouflage.

A bit further on I was bonking again and had to stop in a layby that stank of piss and was consequently full of flies. Bonking is what racing cyclists do when they've run out of energy. It's a sort of delirious fainting feeling. They get over it by squirting sugar and chemical jelly down their necks while moving and throwing the wrapper in the verge, but a brown sauce sandwich or half a packet of biscuits does the same trick. About twenty Porsches went past.

Under the waters of Elyn Celyn, which the A4122 half encircles, is the former Quaker farmstead of Hafod Fadog, and from this valley came many of the Quakers who emigrated to Pennsylvania, having been subject to persecution and pogroms.

Four miles out of Bala I plopped straight into the Tyn Cornel Campsite, £8. It seems that anyone who charges more than a tenner to pitch a small tent is an opportunist thief.

I never intended to ride further than Bala today because the road east into England is without sizeable settlements and I didn't want to get caught out. In any case, though it's been the best day's cycling yet, it's been hard and I'd had enough.

The young woman in reception was mightily impressed that I'd ridden all the way from Caernarfon today – about 50 or 60 miles I reckon – but then she probably doesn't know what a good day's cycling is.

I fancied a new recipe tonight – garden peas and tomato puree in my porridge, but that will have to wait. Instead I paid £1 for tin of beans from the very limited onsite shop – limited in that if you wanted anything other than cereals or chocolate to eat it was beans. And it was a pound shop – everything was a pound, whether it was worth it or not.

I'm in the bottom field, where there are seven encampments including mine. There are five fires on the go, each patrician playing his own little Prometheus and earning prestige through the distribution of meat hunted in cellophane from Sainsbury's. Tomorrow the tribe will move on to new hunting grounds in their people carrier with their proud provider at the wheel.

Sometimes at home, for comedy effect, I say 'I am man, I make fire.' Oades thinks it's hilarious (actually she thinks I am an old fool, and not just for this, or rather she thinks I am incorrigible, which is the impression I try to create).

Try as I might, by making endless cups of tea, I could not run out the second gas bottle I brought from home. They take ages to properly empty and are no good in the morning when they are cold. It is necessary, therefore, to always have two on the go.

And then it began to spit, while it would have been satisfying, my luck being in again, it didn't rain properly.

I cannot think of Bala without thinking of the pointless story my RS Head of Department when I was teaching insisted on boring the kids with, about a young girl who walked barefoot to Bala to buy a bible. They probably just wondered why she didn't go to Bala in the family's car, or better still buy a bible, if she really needed one, on Amazon.

This is hard. I'm ready to sleep at the end of the day after finishing my notes, messing with my maps and reading a bit, but it's fun – there's something satisfying about being dog-tired at the end of the day. You feel like you've earned your rest.

I waited for it to rain properly until I walked the five hundred yards to fill my water bottles.

That's me inside now. I don't care what it does. I'll only come out for a piss twice and if it's raining heavily I'll piss I my pan.

Porridge with baked beans was most acceptable. One begins to realise how people survived on one main staple – by not treating it narrowly and using some imagination.

Despite my enormous input I am crapping much less than I do at home. I must be efficiently converting mass into miles.

Paul Theroux has no trouble finding a Chinese man who has no sympathy with protesting students. He wouldn't have any difficulty finding a British one either. 'The government is paying for their education,' says the man, 'and what do the students do? They demonstrate against the government... if they demonstrate they should be removed.' To start with the government, whether it is in China, Britain or Botswana, doesn't pay for anything – it funds such services as it provides, after it has spent most of its available capital on arms, the military and the police, to secure itself against the enemy without and within, from taxation. We, the people, pay for education, or at least we did until 'the government' decided it was a marketable commodity rather than a means of intellectually and socially enriching the nation. Now the students pay for it themselves. Students have as much right to protest as anyone else (which is virtually no right in China) – where would we be without the likes of Greta Thunberg, Tariq Ali and Peter Hain? And Chinese students in the UK have more right than most because they pay twice as much, being milked like cash cows by a sector that can never be profitable so long as it seeks to provide a broad curriculum. In my experience the countless thousands of Chinese students in the UK, the vast majority of them doing Business Studies, don't engage politically, let alone protest, but they should – as should every other right-thinking person bearing witness to the systematic funnelling of wealth, all of which is created by workers, upward into the bank accounts of a tiny parasitic minority. They should also be protesting against war, homelessness, police murder, corruption, nepotism, arms spending, nuclear power, racism and fracking. Unfortunately they're not, at least not in great enough number, and until they do the slide will continue. Working people never got anything because enlightened governments gave it to them, they got things because they demanded them with menace – and as proof of that we have words from the horse's mouth in the honourable personage of Quintin Hogg, later Lord Hailsham – 'We must give them social reform or they will give us social revolution.'

It is no surprise that the Chinese man who thought students shouldn't protest was also a supporter of the death penalty. I suspect one might find some correlation here too – and possibly various other backward sentiments that could be ticked off a list. But that's enough of that.

The only bad thing about reading and writing in my tiny tent is that it is uncomfortable leaning on my left elbow because it is full of metal – ignore this if I have begun repeating myself.

The inevitable consequence of the marketisation of higher education has been the marginalisation of arts subjects, the collapse of course provision and the narrowing of the remit to the needs of bosses. Concurrently there has been a seismic mushrooming in the rise of business studies and economics courses, where students have their heads filled with discredited free market nonsense by academic ostriches who refuse to acknowledge fundamental trends in capitalism because they undermine the comfortable orthodoxy – to the extent that a minority of students have demanded that they be told the truth.

I cite in exemplum my own *alma mater*. The Classics department at the University of Glasgow, where I was privileged to study, for decades occupied a prestigious wing of the ancient building. For generations the sons, and occasionally the daughters, of the well-to-do were inculcated with the notion that Cicero, the sycophantic reactionary, was the archetypal statesman and Caesar the progressive revolutionary was an upstart usurper. The hallowed halls have now suffered a worse fate – they have been taken over by Business Studies. Business Studies is not an academic subject – it is capitalist propaganda. That young working class people are volunteering *en masse* for this indoctrination is the academic equivalent of the stampede to enlist in 1914. It is a tragedy of such proportions that Aeschylus himself could have written a play about it.

The people who are driving the changes in education are not innocents trying best to manage an unwieldy system, as they would claim – they have a deeply held ideological agenda. It is to smash every vestige of the gains made in the 1960s. The politics of that decade, determined not in parliament, but on the streets and in workplaces, had a lasting effect on the whole education system and the establishment hates it. That was a period of progress and this is a period of reaction. They are busy doing the same thing to schools as they have done in universities and they will continue to do it as long as we let them.

We paid for students to be educated because it is the right thing to do. Making young people pay for their education in the UK is a retrograde step. It is the sign of a greedy ruling class who'd rather have tax cuts than see properly funded public services, a jealous ruling class, who think privileges like education should be paid for, a frightened ruling class who don't want to see the working class educated at all and a neoliberal ruling class who think any vestige of human existence should be available for them to make money from.

Blair's facile mantra of 'Education, Education, Education' turns out to have been cleverer than we thought. It has produced a whole army of young people marinated (marionetted) in the pro-capitalist dogma of consumer choice, whose only philosophy is that we are what we buy, who actually believe that being able to buy mange tout in February is a kind of democracy. And worse still millions have decided that the thieves' kitchen of the EU is their saviour. But all is not lost and the recent upsurge in youthful activism, in particular around issues of the environment, which will provide a better education than years in the classroom, could prove to be the start of their undoing. The rot has to stop somewhere.

Day 30 – Bala to Clun

(Wales into Shropshire)

I was awake half the night. And once I got the above diatribe, polemic, call it what you will, in my head there was no way I was going back to sleep. I waited hours for it to get light so I could vent it and now, as it gets properly light, it's raining steadily and I'm fucked.

This is what I dread most, and it dawns on me that if I am not careful I will exit Wales today without having had a single conversation with a Welsh person. There's nothing to prevent me staying here until it fines up, but that isn't what I want to do. This is Wales and it's meant to be wet. I'm lucky I've got this far without a good soaking (and that I had a piss while it was fine). The campsite will empty today when the weekend warriors go home.

The thing to do as always is just get going, but cycling along the seafront in waterproofs is one thing, cycling over big hills in them is quite another.

The problem remains the same as yesterday. It's forty miles to anywhere sizeable and I had no plans to go there. My best bet is to head for Welshpool, where at least there'll be shops and hopefully accommodation.

And with that I got up. What's the worst thing that can happen? This isn't the outback after all. But when I put my head out it was truly miserable.

The coffee I bought in Conwy isn't decaf – no wonder I've been buoyant these last few days, and unable to sleep last night after having it at lunchtime.

Apropos youthful activism – Several years ago there was a serious upsurge of student struggle, and we pinned our hopes on it only for it to subside through lack of leadership. And we pin our hopes on this one. The Chinese had their Cultural Revolution in which the intelligentsia were made scapegoats, but actually there is always a cultural revolution going on. In a deeply divided class society culture, of which education is a part, is no less a battlefield than other areas of life.

Even with my procrastinating I was off before most people got up – and I don't know what the fuss was about – there was blue sky appearing.

The enforced hardtack has had undesirable consequences. My spent fuel rod took some squeezing out this morning and in the past this has led to Chalfont St Giles. It must be rectified forthwith.

Outside, well inside, the bogs I met Ian from Camborne in Cornwall. He was impressed by my transport and said he wasn't an engineer 'not to that standard,' but had made gates that could keep a bull in and his own trailer. That's all the skill needed to make a basic bicycle – and the confidence to have a go.

Ian was touring in a camper van with his disabled son and offered me a tow if I wanted it, but I think it was a joke.

I had no recollection of crossing a bridge over the river into the site, couldn't remember which way to turn on the main road and had to guess. I wasn't sure I was going the right way (except it was downhill), until I came upon an Irish Tricolour in a layby that I knew I hadn't seen before. It was beside a monument to 1,800 Irishmen who were interned here after the Dublin Easter Rising in 1916. The British had lived up to their reputation as the inventors of the concentration camp. The inmates, as most political prisoners do now, not least the Palestinians, but Trotsky and others, devoted their time to educating themselves.

The prisoners were brought here by train, just like the Jews. The railway has now gone, but the occupation of Ireland continues. I had no idea any of this happened, even though I have read about the Easter Rising and quite a bit about Irish history in general.

I need not have worried about supplies because the Spar shop in Bala had everything I needed and more. The *Daily Mail* reveals, as is its wont, that one of Jeremy Corbyn's 'closest allies' is a former spy for the Czechs. He can't do right for doing wrong. If he's not best friends with traitors he's failing to prostrate himself before hereditary monarchy or wearing the wrong clothes. Anyone would think he was a threat, not some bearded, jam making old social democrat. 'Give me men about me that are fat, sleek headed men who sleep o'nights. Yon Corbyn has a lean and hungry look, such men are dangerous.'

Outside I met Eric, born and bred in Bala, a former forestry worker and now well-fucked at sixty nine (only seven years older than me). He had limited mobility, a bad back, a shuffling gait and difficult to understand speech. I wouldn't be surprised if he'd had some kind of stroke. Again it was my bike, like a dropped handkerchief to a regency dandy, which gained me the introduction. We concurred that the bloke who said hard work never killed anyone was lying. His mate walked past limping – 'He's as fucked as me,' said Eric. Eric was still driving. Not far I suspect.

And then Mavis approached me in a sort of sly way. She has a backpacker's hostel in town, saw me cycling last night and hoped, for purely altruistic reasons that I was heading there. She was a bit of a funny woman who came at you sideways as if she had been damaged in some way.

Bala has all the tourist trappings and a statue of a famous son who has in his hand a piece of paper. It looks like Chamberlain, but it's not him. It's a bloke called Ellis, who no doubt did good works – though as his curriculum vitae was adumbrated in Welsh I remain in ignorance of what they were.

It occurred to me, idly, that Mavis might not be the kind of hostel keeper who had my best interests at heart. When I offered her my hand she gave me her little fingers and said 'gently.'

A lovely flat road took me to the bottom of a hill. The sun came out and there were two more campsites on the way as I left.

Why are half derelict crofts romantic? It wasn't fucking romantic living in them. And for that matter why is Ironbridge romantic when in its heyday it was a Hades ruled by Vulcan. In fact why do we romanticise any history when most of it was bloody hard for the majority of people? Because too much history is about rich people, that's why. The French wore powdered wigs, the Romans ate lying down, the Victorians covered their table legs (the Scots wore kilts). No they fucking didn't – they grovelled about on the ground trying to survive on oats, turnips, the corn dole and margarine and bread.

An old bull had big bollocks that hung on sinews a foot long. Hence the comfortable trousers.

The question is, do sheep have any thoughts at all on the pile of bones in the corner of the field that was their cousin, or rabbits when they see their siblings squashed on the road, like some of us do when we see the body of a little boy washed up on a beach?

The B4391 was a right royal roller coaster, and on a Sunday morning at least it was practically all mine. Only the Costa, KFC and MacDonald's cups suggested it led, like all roads, to Rome.

No one passed until I was having a piss and then everyone and his dad were on their way to church.

While I was eating my fruit sixteen Porches went past from as far away as Switzerland, Belgium and Germany. They were taking part in the Snowdonia Rally. They kept coming and I stopped counting. Good for them I say. On the left the sky looked like lead.

The Morgan lot had also had their breakfast and were out and about. It turned out that I'd picked a steep and winding route that is popular with posh car drivers. It was a long hard road. It's a good job I didn't rashly change my shirt, but it was worth it for a road even better than yesterday's top of the list.   The scenery was spectacular and made me think of *The Big Valley* with Barbara Stanwick, or Montana, which is probably nothing like Wales.

Later on the bikers were out. I only saw one with a woman partaking of this most macho of pursuits. She was pillion and petite.

The road crossed two county boundaries. The one at the top took me into Powys, Montgomeryshire. Someone had put a sticker on the sign 'Bollocks to Brexit - It's not a done deal.' These are people who believe in democracy as long as the vote goes their way.

I've already used all the words that could describe the descent and the views from it many times, and none of them could do it justice. Suffice to say I'm glad I fixed my brakes or I'd have entered Llangynod at a hundred miles an hour.

The pub says it's been there since 1751 – just in time to sell beer to the men who were digging stuff out of the surrounding hills.

There wasn't much there – certainly not a retail outlet that might sell me a postcard. There was however a big ugly static caravan park for people who have to own the bits of the countryside they like. There was also by it the smell of dog shit. And a campsite – there's loads of them till you want one.

I thought I might have to climb again, but the river was going my way, which is always a good sign.

I did my post office business in Pen-y-bont-fawr. They were speaking Welsh in the shop – even the kids. But in the street outside the two people I heard were English. The pub is called the *Railway Inn*. There's no railway, just loads of traffic. The scenery is now a typical rural patchwork. The bluebells are still there, some hawthorn is still in blossom and there are verges full of what we used to call Stepmother's Blessing.

There are splitter's chapels everywhere. The slur against the left made by those cheeky and posh *Monty Python* boys could equally be made against Welsh non-conformism – or non-conformism in general – as detailed in Ken Follett's *Fall of Giants*. It got very hot. Chorley Wood bread is death to energetic cycling. It lies heavy on the gut like the mass produced for the plebs over-yeasted dough it is.

There was more climbing through Pen-y-Garmedd to the B4380.

Signs kept encouraging me to go to Lake Vyrnwy. I did not want to go to Lake Vyrnwy. It supplies much of Liverpool's water. When they weren't covering up their table legs the Victorians built great waterworks. 'We' have sold them to multinationals and now their purpose is not to provide clean water but shareholder dividends.

Coming into Llanfyllin a man reminded me, in case I'd forgotten, that car drivers can be right wankers.

The Llanfyllin Workhouse is now an underfunded cultural centre that is trying to raise money to maintain its master's house. It had a bunk house and an Abba tribute were coming. A poster for the history centre depicted a high-collared master wagging his finger at two girls. They were both spotless and blemish free, but looked suitably admonished for daring to be poor. Big black MF clouds loomed.

Over the lynchgate at Bwlch-y-cibau church it said, 'Passed from life unto death their works do follow them' and 'Watch, pray, heaviness may endure for a night but joy cometh in the morning.' And someone was commemorated who'd 'given his life for another' in Somaliland. Now, what would a Welsh bloke be doing in Somaliland – good works no doubt.

So called lodges on holiday parks start at sixty grand (so do Range Rovers). If the minimum wage was £8 an hour, which it isn't, it would take someone on it four years to *earn* the cost of such a lodge. There are millions of people on the minimum wage – is there any wonder people are bitter? Twenty or thirty years ago many of the same jobs paid decent money.

I was worn out by Welshpool, but decided to press on for Clun and the youth hostel on A roads, which weren't too busy at Sunday tea time. Cars passed with 'Stop Brexit' stickers in them, as if stopping Brexit will stop the general rot.

There was some good downhill and I prayed there wouldn't be a big climb in the last few miles, but there was. I walked up it exhausted. There followed a steep descent and I found Clun Youth Hostel without too much trouble. It was closed, locked up, empty.

Both pubs were full and a man at the bar of one said, 'Don't go to Clun Farm.' Another man asked why. The first said with venom, 'He's a twat.' The young man behind the bar apologised for the customer. I can't imagine that I look like the kind of person that might be offended by swearing, or the honest expression of an opinion. I went to Clun Farm. It looked expensive. There was no response. I was, to coin a phrase, as sick as a parrot. I roamed the village. There was nothing else. Having resigned myself to asking someone for some water and camping in the hostel grounds I asked two women walking small dogs on the outskirts of the village if they knew anyone who did B&B. 'Me at a push.' Said one of them. Bingo. Her home was just nearby, her name's Maureen. She's a bit of a fuss-pot, I've to use her bathroom etc. and it's £35. She said I can stay three nights, which was the plan I hatched on the way, to visit two destinations from here. She does B&B, but, being on her own, normally only takes women. I don't know what I must look like with my beard and Tilley hat, but people don't seem to mind talking to me and they tend to shun anyone who looks like a weirdo.

Maureen has lived a long time in Spain, but her partner died suddenly there and she came back to the UK. I heard her neighbour telling his neighbour, or someone visiting, that he'd been brought up on the farm at the top of the hill and hadn't been far. I have, quite far enough for now. The only problem is I stink, and though I can put my clean underwear and socks on it will leave me with all dirty stuff. I've no clean top shirt or shorts and my tracksuit bottoms and fleece are minging and covered in feathers from sleeping in them. I'm going to have to sit and talk to Maureen, but that will be OK, and I can hardly make one of my porridge concoctions for tea.

After I'd got showered and messed with my maps unnecessarily at the kitchen table – it's like being at a friend's place – and Maureen had faffed with her evening meal, she let me warm my own food and I did have mixed beans in porridge. I'm into the porridge thing in a big way and I'll do it at home. Savoury porridge, mmm.

While I was eating the dog was busy round my bare legs, which I hate, but I can hardly say anything when I've been taken in off the street. The dog is Spanish and is spoken to in Spanish. I don't think a dog can have a nationality considering nations themselves are human constructs that have no basis in objective reality. That's a good philosophical question 'Do nations actually exist?' an ideal counter to all the bullshit about British values. Does a Spanish dog have different values to a British dog? – Of course not – then why should a British and Spanish human being be any different. (Dogs don't have values).

In the evening John came round. He's a farm labourer who used to work on Maureen and her partner's smallholding, but he's now become a fixture, like a surrogate son. He's probably thirty five and lives in a shed. Maureen doesn't think he can read and write, but he's quite personable and no slouch conversationally. He likes the Eurovision Song Contest, so we talked about that. He says Britain came last because none of the other EU countries voted for its entry. John comes for his meals and for *Country File* and other TV programs. Maureen tells him off for using the wrong plates, picking his nose and not speaking grammatically correctly because she was a language teacher. She's lonely, he's a nuisance. It's symbiotic. He's heartbroken apparently because a woman half his age, whom he had no chance with, rejected him. He's scruffy, smelly and hardly has any teeth. John was left the small family farm. He doesn't work it and has allowed the farmhouse and buildings to fall into disrepair. He's unfashionable, unkempt, wears something like a weightlifter's belt and his hair sticks up all over.

It was a godsend meeting Maureen and her friend in the road. It's going to cost £105 to stay three nights, but I need a rest and it would cost, or in fact has cost, nearly that to stay in a Travelodge for one night. I'm looking forward to the rest and hope I can get a bus. If I can't I'll cycle back up the road without my gear the day after tomorrow.

Maureen is a fussing old woman, but has a heart of gold, not just for taking me in but for the way she is with John. We talked about asylum seekers too. Apparently thirty have been rescued from the Channel today. This 'problem' is getting bigger and it's only a matter of time before someone dies. I don't suppose the government wants such blood on its hands. It could cause another Alan Kurdi moment.

I'm also told that Theresa May's Brexit deal has failed to get through the commons again today.

We talked about Radio 4 and *The Archers* and Jeremy Hardy and Paddy O'Connell. She tells me the bloke next door shot himself in the house and that someone else has got a Thai wife. They can't believe the youth hostel is shut.

It's always been the anonymity of Travelodges that I've liked – the not having to deal with people – but at last, in my sixties, I can deal with most things.

I made my excuses at 9.30. In bed I tried to read, but was falling asleep because it's past my bedtime. They were still talking about nothing and put the TV on after I'd gone upstairs. I caught snippets of speculation on the Euro elections before I put my earplugs in. One of the papers today advocates Nigel Farage being put in charge of Brexit. It was the Tories losing votes to Farage's UKIP that partly led them to calling their foolish referendum in the first place. Farage was the unacceptable face of the pint quaffing, fag smoking little Englander, but he now looks rather mild (and pathetic) beside his openly racist successor Gerard Batten.

Earlier Maureen had said that Brexit was a disaster and she was worried about the economy. I didn't know if she meant the vote to leave or the process of leaving (or not). I said I was worried about the privatisation of hospitals and schools. This was met with the normal mix of mild surprise and disinterest. The Tories have managed to get people to think entirely in the terms of their problems and not ours. It's their economy. It's about their profits, profits that are made at our expense.

I'm starting to miss silly things like riding through horrible Cooper Bridge into Huddersfield.

I'm back in England now, but so close to the border I might yet re-enter Wales.

I couldn't say how old Maureen is, perhaps seventy, but she limps, is waiting for an operation and isn't a well woman generally. She does teas in her back garden at a table under a gazebo with lovely views across the valley 'for something to do.' 'What could I do instead?' She asked. 'I could knit, but I don't want to knit. I could clean the house, but it's already clean.' But she doesn't tell anyone about it so hardly anyone comes – only occasional passing walkers. Maureen has recently obtained a degree in Spanish and has advertised as a private teacher. She has only had a few takers, who drop it after a few weeks. It's quite hard work talking to her because she misunderstands what you say and five minutes later has forgotten what you said.

There's an electric blanket on the bed, which Maureen said I might need. It's May and I haven't used an electric blanket for twenty years, since before our house was properly insulated. The suggestion brings back memories of my Nan trying to cook me as a child.

Day 31 – Habberley and Quabbs

(Shropshire)

Slept well and woke as it was getting light. I feel dehydrated – I would have drank much more after a hard day's cycling, with sweat pouring out of me at times, than was on offer here. I must help myself to water today. I think I have decided to cycle to my two local destinations, rather than walk or get the bus – even the closest is probably a ten mile round trip and would hardly be a rest if I walked it. The other will be more like a fifty mile round trip, but it will be luxury to do them without all my heavy gear. Otherwise the plan is to finish Theroux on China and find another book to keep me company.

China has marriage laws 'as simple and straightforward as a driver's manual.' A man cannot divorce his wife if she is pregnant or immediately after the birth of a child. A woman can divorce her husband whenever she wants. And yet, in our advanced and democratic country people have to jump through all sorts of hoops.

China once eradicated venereal disease, but due to tourism, when Theroux was writing in the 1980s, the clinics had reopened. The penalty for engaging in prostitution was a bullet in the neck. Maureen told me that one of her neighbours was on his second Thai wife. The first one 'took him to the cleaners.' I said I had not heard of any man who had a Thai wife speak of her with any respect, and what I saw of US, European and Australian expats in Mongolia with their Mongolian wives didn't impress me. But this is not true – there was a man in the MZ Club who had a Thai wife he had met by chance rather than getting her on eBay. My opinion on white men with Thai wives is largely founded on a bus driver we spoke to at length in Devon and a man at a motorcycle rally, both of whom were arseholes – the latter proudly describing his Thai wife as having the body of a fourteen year old.

It's a good job it's warm in Maureen's because I've only got a T shirt to wear that doesn't stink.

I read for a while and then when I thought it was about time (we had arranged breakfast at 8.30) I got up. It was only seven, so I came back upstairs to read some more. But Maureen got up and went to the bathroom so I went downstairs. I don't want to be sitting about here. I want to be off on the road. Staying here for two days is an unnecessary interruption. It made me think of coitus interuptus. It's too much contact. The contacts should be fleeting and leave you wanting more information, wishing you'd asked a few more questions. Despite my late-in-life almost overcoming of my absolute avoidance of possibly embarrassing situations that once marred my life I'm still not 100% comfortable with this situation. I say this as I sit at Maureen's kitchen table.

At seven o'clock in the morning I'm already bored and waiting for something to happen. It's a lovely day outside. This three day stop feels like a betrayal of my purpose, whatever that is. I wish I'd gone straight to my eleventh destination or stopped somewhere else for one night. I've made a mistake – but surely the rest will do me good. It's spoiled the trip, taken away the urgency, the impetus. It will take me several days to get back into it and then in no time it will be over. It's a bit like the mid-point in our ride to Turkey that we aborted in Croatia when Oades dropped the bombshell that she didn't want to go on. It's not of that magnitude, because I am going on, but it feels like it. I don't need a three day rest – if I was tired I could have just had a few short days, or made myself slow down (which is easier said than done).

One doesn't think of it, but the Germans had established quite a foothold in China in the late nineteenth and early twentieth centuries – building railways, breweries and grand governor's mansions and other building in the German style, most of which were smashed up during the Cultural Revolution. They were doing fine and dandy until they were disabused of their imperial ambitions by the First World War and their conquests were divvied up among the other thieves – the Congo to Belgium for example. The Americans too have made their presence felt – with and without permission, China is far from the closed and uninvaded country it is sometimes believed to be. The British of course fought a war to encourage opium addiction.

> The US couldn't tolerate
> (It being there to use)
> The thought of losing China
> When it wasn't theirs to lose

The other thing is that in the kitchen I am bombarded with the news via the BBC and I don't want it in such large doses. I had been making do with looking at the newspaper headlines in supermarkets and shops.

Donald Trump has threatened to destroy Iran if it threatens US interests. He says it will be the end of the country.

Two Tory campaigns have been launched today. One is called 'One Nation,' the other 'Blue Collar Conservatism.' The nation is fundamentally divided on class lines and anyone who says otherwise is a liar. Any blue collar worker who votes Tory is a fool.

Nick Robinson took to task an actress who has said that Britain is 'safe and *seemingly* democratic.' She stood by her assertion and said she was worried about the future. The best that can be said about our system is that it is a representative democracy in which those elected do not even pretend to represent us and their selection is not democratic. The worst that can be said is that we live under an unjust, unfair unelected plutocracy. The actress didn't say this. She said she was worried. We should all be worried because when we decide we've had enough of this gang of self-aggrandising crooks and decide to do something about it things will get very nasty, and it won't be our side wielding the weapons. They have got a lot to lose and they won't give it up easily.

Maureen's 'voluntary work' is in the village shop in another village. She says the prices in the Spar shop in Clun make you weep. The only other shop, she said, was the butcher's, which closed recently, but when I went for a look around there was quite an extensive hardware shop. I don't expect the prices in her village shop are anything to write home about either. Village shops are a nonsense nowadays – not least because there's no such thing as villages any more in the sense of self-contained communities, demonstrated not least by the fact that places that were once just called so-and-so are now called So-and-so *village* on their proudly erected new signs. Most of them are just dormitories, where exploiters and overpaid administrators of a shit system have priced everyone else out of the market. It would make more sense to make a local shop into a Range Rover dealership.

As I rolled along the lanes I decided to rectify my *faux pas* by visiting both places I needed to today and getting back on the road tomorrow. So much for the bus and the train and the mountain railway and all the other side amusements I thought I might have on this bicycle based marathon. A big bird of prey soared above against the blue sky.

At breakfast Maureen couldn't find the jam and discovered a little pot of it in the cupboard that she had put out for some previous guest and had turned to tar. Thankfully she found the jar and gave me some fresh. It was like being at your half senile grandmother's house.

We discussed Travelodges versus B&Bs with regard to anonymity and social interaction. She said the Travelodge in Portsmouth was now £90 a night even if you booked ahead. I didn't ask why she needed to go to Portsmouth, but it dawned on me later on that it's for the ferry to Santander.

There were gunshots last night and there are again this morning. I don't think Shropshire has the same attraction for posh folk who need to murder things that Scotland does – probably just a farmer or gamekeeper, though I have seen pheasants, or grouse – I don't know the difference.

Maureen made breakfast in her towelling robe. It had grubby cuffs from when she'd done it before. The crockery wasn't particularly clean. There were spider's webs in the corners and the bathroom was stacked out with her potions and unguents.

Maureen said she'd heard of Quabbs, when I knew in my heart it didn't really exist, because people always like to pretend they know their area. After an hour of fruitless riding about I asked a walker. He was no help either. I had to turn back. It was dispiriting and I had to admit I was physically and spiritually exhausted and on a pointless mission bagging places of no interest whatever for the sake of it. My plans to visit both places today are kyboshed before they begin. I haven't the energy to be bothered.

So I did what I'm supposed to have been doing all along, and what I'm supposed to be doing today. I sat on a wall in the sunshine and read my book. 'To right a wrong it is necessary to exceed proper limits, and the wrong cannot be righted without the proper limits being exceeded.'

A Chinese man tells Theroux; 'To put it bluntly, it was necessary to bring about a brief reign of terror.' He's talking about the Cultural Revolution, but leaving aside the rights and wrongs of that particular period, it has been and will be necessary to bring about a brief reign of terror to right the wrongs in the world, and 'Going too far has a revolutionary significance.' One hopes the capitalists can be made to see sense. If they cannot they will have to be dealt with in other ways.

A man who sounded Spanish came out of an isolated house and asked me if I was OK. I told him I was looking for Quabbs. He said he wasn't from round here. He had on his nose the biggest blackheads I have ever seen. Does he not look in the mirror? They would not have remained on my nose for long.

My little oranges were from Spain as well, and I added another fifty miles to their travels yesterday.

Christians from all over also colonised China with their Big White God and built grand churches everywhere. Whole towns in China look German, or they did in the 1980s. If the German parts still exist after forty years of mad expansion they will have the relevance of Little Germany in Bradford.

When I'd calmed down I set off for attempt number two, the overall scheme for today having probably reverted to plan A. The frustration I feel is at not being able to tick things off and move on. It's a coach trip mentality and I need to stop it. I went back and took the turn I should have taken in the first place and walked my bike up a long steep hollow road, thankful it was much lighter with only the day's needs on it.

I did consider leaving my bike at the bottom and walking up, but it might have been stolen and, despite my theoretical bus plans, the job was to go to all the places with my bike.

A postie came down in his van. He confirmed that Quabbs was 'up there somewhere.'

I tried to walk up the hill in short bursts – out of necessity, and to retain an element of freshness in my last clean shirt. But it was no use. The sun shone and the flies buzzed.

After half an hour's climbing I was on top of one of the highest hills around, wet through and none the wiser. Hundreds of feet below I could see the house from which Senor Blackhead had emerged to check on my wellbeing.

In the end I decided that I was wasting my life and, though I cannot honestly say I have been to Quabbs, I can say I have been in the vicinity. After wasting three hours of my life searching for it it made no sense to carry on.

I came back down from the mountain by a different route, the one I'd gone up being so steep and rough I would have worn my brakes out at least, and possibly fallen off and lay unconscious on a road used by one person a month. It would be nice to say 'and then I found it.' So I will. And then I found it. If the postie doesn't know where Quabbs is what chance have I got?

Back in Clun, after a pot-holed, potentially bike smashing descent, the sun was at its zenith and it would have been madness to set off to Habberley. I set off to Habberley.

I should not have done what I did yesterday. Not ridden all the way to Clun. Not planned for two days off, as if I was on some sort of holiday and not passed one of my destinations. I should have stopped for the night in Welshpool. I now have to retrace my steps and I hate going back.

I rode into Bishops Castle hungry and spent too much on my lunch. I had my picnic in the churchyard and then stared into space for a bit. It was two o'clock when I set off to ride even further away from my accommodation on the day when I was supposed to be resting.

Maureen said there was probably only a bus to Bishops Castle once a week. People who wouldn't be seen dead on a bus always think the service is worse than it is – that's their reason for not using it. Consequently it gets worse and they are proved right.

It was a long descent down the Hope Valley to Minsterley and a long, hard, steep climb and descent to Habberley. There was no indication I was there, so I asked a man and his son in their drive. They were Dave and Ben Winter, who asked me all about the trip, which makes it a bit more worthwhile because I was beginning to hate it. Dave asked me about my bike and when I said I'd made it he said I was a bit left field. I nearly said I was a bit left wing as well. My 'I still Hate Thatcher' badge was away from him, but as he was loading a posh car outside a posh house and he'd said I was left field for making a bicycle, suggesting he was something superfluous in the city, I kept my trap shut. I am a man, I make things *cum his manibus*. That is why I have opposing thumbs and the capability for conceptualisation. At least I found the place and spoke to someone. Dave asked if there was a giving site he could look up. When I got home I discovered that Dave and Ben were the only people to sponsor me having spoken to me during the ride.

Maureen said Habberley was lovely. To my jaundiced eyes it looked like a soulless enclave of the affluent from which people who actually do the work in the world have been socially cleansed.

I didn't find the ride back up the Hope Valley the slog I expected it to be. Not far after that I leaned on a gate to read a few pages.

Confucius said, 'The asking of questions is in itself the correct rite.' I once heard Arthur Scargill say the same thing; 'Question everything.' Unfortunately, we don't.

My broken saddle is, after thirty one days, beginning to hurt me because I am sitting directly on the steel rails, rather than on the leather that should be stretched above them.

There was some good downhill after that, and one big walking climb three miles out. Five miles out I got a right good soaking and was still wet through when I got back to my billet at 6.30. John was there again, having his tea made for him – another joint of meat. No wonder people get ill. John's beat up Range Rover, which he calls 'the van' was right outside the gate. When I got back I had to ask him to move it so I could get my bike in. He didn't really want to and said the last time that happened the cyclist just lifted his bike over. There was hardly room to walk by it, never mind carry a heavy bike. The laziness of his parking was reinforced by the fact that the Range Rover was full of stuff – the back piled to the ceiling, the passenger seat and foot well also full, with a loaf of white sliced bread sitting on top.

I went to my room to read that 'travel is personal. Even if I went travelling with you, your trip would not be mine. Our accounts of the journey would be different. If you spoke about Mao, I would contradict you.'

Maureen sent John home while I was at my ablutions because he had left his dog alone for eleven hours. Last night he stayed until midnight and, according to her, they're like teenagers discussing lost love, though I don't believe that. She complains all the time about his smell etc., but he's actually the only company she gets, certainly in the evening.

I turned in at nine, getting the impression that Maureen had expected a conversation. When I said I was going to bed after looking at my maps on the kitchen table while Maureen was watching something Spanish on TV, she said, 'It's a bit early.' And 'will you want a drink later.' Which is the sort of thing your partner might ask, rather than a B&B hostess, but the house is so small you have to pass through the sitting room to get upstairs. Some might say the situation was a bit creepy – if the roles had been reversed it certainly would have been. But Maureen is just a lonely old woman – like lots of other lonely old women.

In bed I tried to read, but couldn't keep my eyes open. I've done fifty miles on my rest day, but I'm moving on tomorrow.

There were three campsites on the way back from Habberley I could have stayed on if I'd done things in the right order, but then I'd have ended up pushing up that hill this morning with all my gear on – and actually the steep hill into Habberley – so perhaps things have worked out for the best.

When I told Maureen I'd been to Habberley she said it was only up the road. It's fifteen or twenty miles up the road and the same back, which is further than most people cycle in their lives, and I'd already done a dozen or so miles looking for the other place. I'm not saying I didn't enjoy it, or pride myself in the achievement, but riding that big heavy bike in the sun and rain up and down these hills is hard.

Day 32 – Clun to Nr Bromyard

(Shropshire and Herefordshire)
Slept without interruption and woke at 4.30. There was no reason why I should have woken at that time apart from my own body clock – and I always do.

After widespread demonstrations in China Deng Xiao Ping told the visiting American Secretary of State that the recent trouble had been caused by 'a leadership crisis.' It was a euphemism for a power struggle. 'It is now over.' He said, and added cryptically, 'but it may continue for a while in the minds of the Chinese people.'

There are so many new political parties being formed in the UK, with both the major ones in crisis and the third one openly promising to overturn a democratic vote, and sections of the people are so wound up, that anything could happen.

At six o'clock, wide awake, or as near to wide awake as I'm going to be, given my exertions, two and a half hours before the appointed time for breakfast, I was thinking that if I was in my tent I'd be packing up and ready to go by now.

It's bright and sunny outside – the best part of the day (but not the time when I do most miles, that tends to be the afternoon, or even the early evening). I hate this hanging about. That's another thing about Travelodges – you can get up and go at five if you want.

Having lost his minders Paul Theroux wanders China unrestrained and discovers there are other long nosed foreigners doing the same. 'Were they writing books about China?' – 'Probably. Everyone seems to be doing that. The only satisfaction was that any travel book revealed more about the traveller than it did about the country.'

I am coming to the end of my book and had a fleeting thought about what I'd like to read next. I thought of Trotsky's *Their Morals and Ours*, which I've had for years, but never fully read, or his *Problems of Everyday Life*, likewise, but they're on a shelf at home and I know that if I was there they'd be the last things I'd read. Or maybe I'd pick one of them up and read a few pages before putting it back on the shelf for another decade.

I prefer travel books nowadays but it wasn't always like this. I have read Trotsky's autobiography, as well as his *History of the Russian Revolution*, which runs to eight hundred pages, and, without wishing to brag, *War and Peace*. And during a trip like this when there are few pressures, I could probably read them or similar books again.

220

For two pins I'd get up and go, but that wouldn't be right, precisely because being taken on trust into someone's home implies a relationship very different from that with the waged staff at a hotel. Of course there are vastly different types of B&B and some are effectively hotels, but this one isn't. This is personal.

I suddenly became very tired, couldn't focus on my book, and could hardly be bothered to lift my arms.

I went back to sleep for an hour – something I never do – and dreamed I was so tired I was staggering in the street and swinging round lampposts. Then that I was working on a building site. On the next site a bricklayer was keeping a roll of plasterer's scrim cloth on top of his head. It was sunny. I went to the shops in the electric wheelchair of a man that is always at party conference and it went so fast that it was like the on-board footage of one of those madmen going round the Paris ring road on a motorcycle. The joystick was delicate and I swerved at speed, narrowly avoiding buildings. But of course I didn't hit anything because that would have been like hitting the ground in a dream about falling. Eventually I brought the chair under control, its speed reducing like a car under full braking, just in time for the steps back down to the building site.

I was woken by Maureen moving about and farting in the bathroom, probably trying to pass all that meat. I once read, or heard, that meat eaters have six pounds of undigested meat in their guts at any one time.

What on earth was I still doing in bed dreaming at 7.30 on a sunny day when I was supposed to be on a mile munching marathon? Knighton, Leominster, Bromyard, Stow on the Wold – it's all set out.

The Tory leadership campaign is well underway, with one of the candidates offering tax cuts in a country that is already unable to fund vital public services.

Over breakfast Maureen asked me all the same questions about my trip again. She told me how ten years ago her husband Rod had dropped dead on the forecourt of a Spanish filling station, leaving her to deal with a farm, houses in two countries, an ex-wife and a family who blamed her for everything. She told me how she was a war baby who had been conceived out of wedlock and taken into care, to be cast out at sixteen into the world to find her own way. How she'd gone on a secretarial course, one of the few options open. How lonely, isolated and friendless she was in Clun. How she felt as if she was on a precipice and didn't know which way to jump. About her ill health, her two cancer operations, and how she'd never travelled less that she had in the last two years. She was talking about jacking it in, upping sticks and moving – as if she was thirty or forty and such a thing were possible.

She put butter on my toast when I'd said twenty times I was vegan. I gave her seventy pounds. She wished me a safe journey and I left Clun up a series of very steep and very long hills, hills that would seem nothing in a car, but are mountains to someone pushing a loaded bicycle. And this is the problem – only effort expended leads to appreciation – everything else is a stage on the way to dissolution (or dissoluteness). I was sweating like a pig within minutes, but there was little traffic, the sun was out, the birds were singing, the verges were full of wild flowers and the scenery was magnificent.

At an isolated house half way up one hill six dogs bounced at a gate barking and snarling at me. I wanted to shoot them all dead. They made me grind my teeth. What business did they have to be imposing on my reverie?

Nicki Lauda, the archetypal brave sportsman has died. One death is a tragedy, a million is a statistic.

It took me an hour to do the first mile and a half and two minutes to do the second – into New Invention, then up again. Of the four buildings one was once a blacksmith's shop, one the *Stags Head* and one a Methodist chapel. The origin of the hamlet's name is lost, but one clearly bollocks explanation is that a local blacksmith discovered a way of fitting horseshoes backwards to confuse the enemy in times of war.

There's no wonder this border was full of castles and those beyond it resisted invaders – though the Welsh were no laggards when it came to fighting for the British Empire – as *Zulu, Fall of Giants* and *Goodbye to All That* show. The hills are beautiful, but I long for Leveller times.

[Editor's note – The capital letter suggests that the author is alluding to the Levellers, the Bolsheviks of the English Revolution, who nearly four centuries ago advocated a progressive politics that, did we have it today, would mean death to the present system, and entailed such as free and fair elections, annual parliaments and instant recall of MPs that did not represent us.]

It was only about seven miles to Knighton and it was just waking up as I arrived through the back door past a big fenced railway yard. It was one of the first places I'd been for a few days that actually still had a railway line to it.

I bought a long M8 bolt and some nuts from the builders' merchants (26p) and fixed my seat by the cenotaph. The place was full of mountain bikers, mostly middle aged men, though some women went to the shops to get them coffee. I brewed my own with the soya milk Maureen had sent me off with and after fixing my seat had a leisurely half hour. I don't think I've paid for coffee since Aviemore. The sun was so hot the pages of my book curled and my clothes smelled like fresh laundry being ironed.

One of the women helped me with directions too. The men weren't interested as they were in their little clique. The biggest hotel in town is closed and for sale.

It was only when I'd drunk two strong cups of coffee that I remembered it wasn't decaf – I could already feel myself getting jittery. I couldn't even write properly and thought I'd better put the rush to good use up the hill.

My mended seat is a hundred times better. I can now ride up hills I would have walked as my weight isn't directly on my arse bones. I am delighted with myself. I can fix my seat because I am left field. Generally people who make and fix things all day are just ignorant mekaniks, the mob, in the eyes of our betters.

A youngish woman in a top of the range Range Rover waited for me to ride up a hill before pulling out, giving me a big smile and a wave. They are blissfully unaware, or they pretend not to know, that they steal food from the mouths of the starving. Or they subscribe to the ridiculous notion that people being poor has got nothing to do with them being rich. They've 'got on' unaided, except for inheritance, the aspiration ethic, the educational opportunities, the tax funded infrastructure and the pseudo democracy that endlessly favours them, why shouldn't everyone else?

During the Cultural Revolution Chinese people with bourgeois or liberal tendencies were 'reformed through labour.' *Arbeiter mach frei, Labor Omnia vincit*, hard work never hurt anyone – the slogans of people who never did any, and despise people who do.

Paul Theroux finds a man who'll drive him to Tibet. It'll take five days he's told. In the car he asks what the music is. 'The driver says nothing, but his pal said, "Beethoven, symphony number two." "Isn't it six, the Pastoral?" Mr Li laughed. His laugh simply meant wrong! "The Pastoral goes dum-dum-dee-dee-dum. No this isn't number two. I know two, five, six, seven and nine. This isn't a symphony, it's an overture."' So much for 'the knowledge.'

The Norton manor Estate provides 'park homes of distinction' and a Monteverdi concert was upcoming. The audience will no doubt be full of taxi drivers. It is well known that immediately after the Russian Revolution the arts thrived and working people flocked to the opera to see what they had been missing. It is only under a deliberately divided system that we need to be force-fed a diet of inane drivel packaged as popular culture – Carmen or Jeremy Kyle, Mozart or mudslinging. Culture or cockfighting. I could go on.

In Presteigne a school has one of those walls of poppies to commemorate long dead but opportunistically disinterred men who thought they were fighting for decency and democracy. The memorial hall has two of the trendy black silhouettes. 'Remembrance' can rightly be referred to as an industry, and a deeply political one at that.

It also had a brand new cycle path all the way through. There's something 'the fallen' could celebrate. If they hadn't been blown to pieces in their prime they might have celebrated the Health

Service, only to see it start to be dismantled in their dotage – whether or not they'd waved flags and voted Tory throughout their lives or had illusions in Labour.

A man went the other way on a proper Triumph Bonneville – produced during the death throes of the British motorcycle industry. Fewer and fewer of these bikes are on the road, being worth more than they ever were and in the hands of collectors as investments – use value converted to capital or collateral. Invest in old motorcycles, gold or property their independent financial advisor might say. Utility motorcycles that retailed for seventeen guineas in 1919 are now worth thirty grand through Bonham's or some other price jacking auction house.

And then I met Mike, out for the first time on the lightweight racing bike he'd 'built' (i.e. assembled) while recovering from a foot operation. We had a lot in common. He's had lots of motorcycles, including MZs and was knowledgeable without being a bullshitter. We went through Norton 16H, BSA M20/21 and the rip off price of bicycle parts. We'd both packed in motorcycling around the same time and were both glad we had. Then he turned back and I carried on.

My bike has developed a squeak on the right hand crank down stroke – a bit like a loose cotter pin – but I don't have cotter pins. All noises mean something. There should be no sound from a well-maintained and efficient bicycle except the freewheel and the tyres on tarmac. It was hot.

I passed a house where a man had made a virtue of industrial salvage in a Fred Dibnah style – now so much scrap – the relics of an industrial age when metal bashing was something we didn't leave to the Chinese while pretending we'd got our emissions down. Only this morning some Tory claimed this government had done more than any for the environment. On this logic Margaret Thatcher was the best environmentalist ever. She destroyed the steel workers, and then the miners, in favour of coal being dug up in South America by children.

225

A bit further on someone had simply piled four scrap cars in the edge of a wood. It looked like hillbilly country and I thought about Chuck and Leanne I'd met in Inverness. Leanne had a way of opening one eye really wide to express shrewdness or incredulity. She was Patrick Moore and Roseanne Barr, only hopefully without either of those two's racism.

Discover Parks Country Holiday Park in Sobdon was called Pearl Lake. What could be more Chinese than that? It sounded like it should be suffixed by 'prawns' and import sea food to satisfy western diets by destroying Bangladesh.

A man on a Harley Davidson Sportster asked me the way to the airfield. For some reason motorcyclists like to take pictures of their bikes next to planes, especially war planes. I sat on a bench sponsored by Sun Valley Poultry, which also sounds Chinese.

On the village green were a millstone, some kind of press and a freshly erected memorial to 'the fallen.' I wouldn't be surprised to discover that parish and local councils had been actively encouraged to set up these cross-class commemorations, like they were in the 1920s, in an attempt to restore the *concordia ordinarum*.

The Sportster rider can't have had much business at the airfield – it is even possible he was doing the Round Britain Rally, often a solo rather than a pack exercise. He gave me a big wave as he went past. What a jolly world it is away from the mean city.

I took a deep breath before lifting the lid on the bin, knowing exactly what I'd discover. There are two things you'll find wherever you go – dog shit and yuppies.

A man had called his bungalow *Yar-it-be*, another 'No Parking or Turning.'

There started to be a lot of wagons and the road surface bore witness in two great grooves. It isn't much fun being in a groove. The quiet roads are probably over. There was a nice looking campsite that didn't call itself a holiday park, but it was far too early to stop for someone who'd barely done twenty miles. If I've seen one Old Toll House I've seen twenty.

I was astonished by four big four propeller planes flying over in close line astern at fairly high altitude and wouldn't have seen them if I hadn't been stopped. Whatever could they have been up to? It was like something from the blitz, when we all had a common purpose and pretended the division between exploiter and exploited did not exist.

Two more common as shit assembled in Milwaukee, Taiwanese made, American freedom machines rumbled past. These were proper Harleys, not Sportster 'girls" bikes.

And then there was a memorial to 'an obstinate, bloody and decisive battle' fought during the War of the Roses, which comedians and silly men in northern pubs caricature as a battle between Yorkshire and Lancashire, a nonsense that is perpetuated by the populist media and dragged out at the slightest provocation – northern rivalry being an excellent tool of divide and rule, manifest in the whingeing by people like Andy Burnham that this or that post-industrial northern shit-hole gets more of the crumbs from the table of the money laundering southern metropolis - when it was actually between two royal houses for the succession, and therefore had as much relevance for the majority of the population as membership or not of the EU has today. When you are being scammed by the rich it doesn't matter which gang of them it happens to be.

There are a lot of Tudor style timber framed houses round here – and a firm selling 'bespoke oak structures' to the select wine quaffing class. It's middle England on steroids. The best of them might vote Liberal Democrat, the worst for Farage. Between the Tudor, the mock Tudor and *The Beeches* it's all a bit bungaloid – *Normandie*, *Dunvegan*, *Paxmead*, *Braemar* and *The Hollies*. One of them was even called *Tudor House*. It was no more Tudor than my cock's a sausage.

But I'll say one thing for it – it's as flat as a pancake.

And then I came back to the War of the Roses memorial an hour after I'd last passed it the first time. How the fuck did that happen? 'The slaughter was great on both sides and many Welsh persons of the first distinction were taken prisoner.'

227

I sought the assistance of a man with only one ear and not many more teeth who was trying to re-attach his car exhaust at the roadside. He put me right. It was ambiguous signage again. And the ear? Had he sent it to his lover or lost it to cancer by not wearing a hat? My ears are all split and peeling.

The sky looked like something over the wheat fields of the mid-west – only it was rapeseed not wheat.

Most of the front pages of the papers show Nigel John Bull Farage splathered in milky jizz while on a glad-handing walkabout. It serves the pipsqueak patriot right. I bought seventeen pence worth of water at Morrison's, just in case I have to kip out.

Then I skirted south of Leominster centre. When I asked an old woman on a fifty year old Raleigh for directions it threw her all into confusion and all her shopping fell off her rear carrier because she was trying to hold it on with one of those integral spring clips that were never any good for holding anything apart from a pair of rubberised canvas over trousers.

I'd no sooner got onto the Bromyard road when there was a sign for a campsite, which would have made me a very lucky man, but it had clearly been closed for some time, which didn't make me unlucky, just not lucky yet.

While riding along I composed;

Fair Game
Cycling on the A roads
Leaves no shred of doubt
That when car contacts creature
Its guts will all fly out
If it wears a fur coat
Has feathers skin or scales
Spread along the roadside
Will be its red entrails
If one of those bastards
Makes brief contact with me
The tarmac will be tainted

With what I had for tea
I may not die of cancer
Of my rectal thoroughfare
But lose it on an S bend
Exposed to country air
Surely I'm not destined
When Rodin's kiss is felt
To be pounded into leather
Like some long-dead rabbits pelt
There is no moral message
In this enquiring verse
I just ask is colon cancer
Or being road kill worse?

I saw what looked like a campsite on top of a hill. But it was chicken sheds. It was another few miles before I rode down a farm lane on the advice of a sign on the main road. A nice man at the first house told me to go further, his snarling dogs thankfully behind a fence. A nice woman at the second house said the same. She was holding the ugliest baby I've ever seen.

The farm was at the bottom and a woman crouching by a little pond told me who to speak to. The woman of the place was dressed up, about to go for dinner, was late, and said 'not tonight.' So I begged and she relented. It's one of the nicest sites I've stayed on, and it wants to be, because due to 'things' (I don't know what things) not being properly functioning she only charged me half the price, which was £12. She let me off with eleven. Twelve isn't half of eighteen, and neither is eleven. Life couldn't get any more perfect (unless it was five). I don't know what extras I could have enjoyed had the full service been available, but I didn't notice a sauna or billiard room. Incidentally, Maureen thought food was available on campsites. She must have been thinking of Butlins. The other day I saw a site advertising camping pods and glamping services. What the F are glamping services? Like having sex is engaging with someone else's genitals camping is carrying your tent, putting it up and sleeping in it. Like cycling is riding a bike, not carrying it about on the back of your car. Anything else is going to the movies, or maybe to the park, for a seat on the same old bench (Chi-lites, *Have you seen her*, 1972)

As I turned in the gate two more alienated lone wolfs from the Stereotypes MC went past with their Nazi insignia and throbbing penis extensions.

Within ten minutes my little house was up and I was comfortable and safe for another evening. The sun was still out, the clouds were still fluffy and white and the crows were making a right racket. I haven't seen my crow today, but she'll be around somewhere.

My tent is a bit smelly from being rolled up wet for two days, but so is the bloke who's getting in it. When I said to the woman that showing me to my pitch had got her a bit of exercise before her meal she said she got plenty of that because she had two dogs (she said what make they were, but I didn't care enough to take note). I have never seen anyone walking with a dog in a way that could be described as getting exercise. They usually stop every ten feet to let the dirty bastards sniff at another dog's piss on some piece of publicly funded street furniture, or shit on the pavement before smearing it on with one of those little bags they then throw in a hedge.

I am incredibly happy. There's no point in being homesick or missing Oades (who, truth be known, I've almost forgotten exists) because I've got a job to do. Feeling homesick is for those who already know they are wandering aimlessly.

A little girl went past on a bicycle wearing a chrome plated crash helmet. She never glanced my way (don't talk to the strange man). Who on earth discovered they could chrome plate plastic? Is it really chrome? So many questions. So the young woman like a fishing gnome by the pond must have been the baby sitter.

This is idyllic.

And then three Guinea fowl walked past like Wilson, Keppel and Betty. I'm the only person on the site (this has happened a lot). I can go to sleep when I like and leave at five if I want to.

Tonight's recipe – Camping Curry: feeds a greedy cyclist
I cup porridge oats
I slice pumpkin seed rye bread
I teaspoon mild curry powder
I vegetable Oxo
I squirt tomato puree
I pitta bread

In a bowl pour boiling water onto the porridge oats, curry powder, Oxo and tomato puree. Stir vigorously. Crumble and stir in the rye bread. Eat with pitta bread as if in an expensive restaurant. While feeling self-satisfied do not spill full mug of tea in sloping tent so it runs under own arse or it will soak shorts and knickers. If this happens reapply dirty pants and hang tea soaked wet clothes on bicycle so they will be even wetter in the morning and/or a bird will have shit on them.

'West of Xining, and through the whole of Qinghai and the whole of Tibet, there is only one vegetable (barley) and only one kind of meat (yak). As might be supposed, faced with only two ingredients, the people of this region have learned how to cook them in a number of different ways.' (Editor's note - The author may be accused of disingenuousness here. The text continues; 'But that is no more than a gesture. The taste is unvarying. It is the taste of yak.' Later Paul Theroux, who the author is quoting, says, 'The yak is a lovely longhaired animal, like a cow on its way to the opera.')

On the back of Paul Theroux's book Ludovic Kennedy says; '...one marvels at the degree of self-punishment.' One assumes that Ludovic Kennedy regarded anything less than five star luxury and accompanying obsequiousness as self-punishment. What Paul Theroux experiences is adventure, purpose and the confirmation of the human spirit. To not struggle in some field is to be the superfluous man detailed by endless Russian authors and no doubt some British ones I have yet to read.

The facilities were OK, but a bit grubby – but as I was told they weren't ready that is to be expected.

While I was filling my water bottle the woman came back from her meal and asked me if I was OK. She let her dog out and it ran after me for petting, and no doubt pissing on my tent so it could stink for the rest of the trip. I told it to fuck off and it did.

In the toilet cubicle there was a lovely reproduced poster of potato planting. Men and women placed seed potatoes a foot's length apart in a furrow and a Nuffield tractor followed them with a front-mounted coverer. It was a scene of pastoral idealism and no one finished the day with a bad back or the week on a pittance.

Theroux refers to himself as a barbarian in China, as I sometimes refer to myself as a *gora* in Bradford, and called myself a *mzungu* in Rwanda. At home I am a middle-aged white man, and therefore the cause of many problems. It is good to recognise what it is that you are, and indeed what it is that you are not – a member of the master race for example.

I read for an hour in the fading light with both pairs of glasses on, and that was another day all used up. And then the laughing guinea fowl started up, which set the crows off anew, and then a grouse (or pheasant). I'm camped in the middle of a fucking madhouse aviary. I put my earplugs in before the owls started. If there isn't bird shit on my pants in the morning I'm a Chinaman.

I have probably never been so flatulent in my life. I can't imagine what could have caused it.

I now need a Sports Direct. I don't see why another issue of millionaire Mike Ashley's cheap underclobber shouldn't get me most of the way round this terminally faded jewel.

Today I have pissed about across four counties – that's the way to do it.

Day 33 – Nr Bromyard towards Stow
(Herefordshire and Gloucestershire)
Not for the first time I waited and waited and waited for it to get light. It's amazing how you can convince yourself it's getting light when it

isn't at all. If I had a torch I could read. I was reduced to using my lighter to make notes until it burned my thumb.

It was a cold night and everything was damp with condensation. At the first sign of light I took out my futile earplugs to listen to the clucking, quacking, tweeting and hooting. There was also an irritating whole valley barkathon, distant lonely truckers, a high altitude roar and eventually early commuters.

After I put my earplugs in last night I didn't hear the birds. But could I bollocks sleep. When I did drop off I was woken by a bad dream, the details of which I can't remember. That'll be the Spar Rich Roast. I vowed to scatter it to the wind like the remains of a roast rich relative.

When I was young and we thought homophobia was funny we called anyone who had an airbed a puff. Now air beds are *de rigueur* and not having one is rigor mortis. A bloke did actually die in his tent at a winter motorcycle rally I attended – but that was possibly alcohol induced. That was the same rally at which I saw bikers openly flaunting EDL patches and recognised for myself the reactionary potential of ex-servicemen – and it was in the dark walking back to my tent horrified that I fell in the river. On building sites we ridiculed any bricklayer who even thought about wearing gloves, and Nivea for Men was a long time in the future. The sand on bricks wears away the skin on a bricklayer's left finger tips, assuming he is right-handed, until very painful holes are created. It was not uncommon to see bricklayers with blue or red insulation tape round their finger ends to protect the painful sores. In one story Sherlock Holmes identifies the perpetrator of some crime as a bricklayer because he has no proper fingerprints. The only possible flaw in Conan-Doyle's cleverness is that the bricklayer would either have to be ambidextrous or handled something with his non-main hand, i.e. not with the one in which he held his trowel.

When I put my head out it was almost fully light, but there was still a very bright moon. I guess it was four or half past. A hundred crows were circling above. I made fruit tea still in my bag with my coat on. I'm interested in the crows, but the crows aren't interested in me. They've got their own affairs to deal with. I can see why the crow has its place in ritual – they can be quite intimidating. I'm thinking of Hitchcock and Morris dancing, but the image I've got is from a school text book of a man draped in black with a big beak full of flower petals to ward off the plague.

The owners of the site are called Tim and Karen. When I came out of the toilet block the man I took to be Tim was in a chicken coop on his hands and knees looking out through the netting. He asked me if I'd turned off the light.

I had to set off minus one cycling glove – the latest thing I've lost.

The road was quiet but for the occasional thundering truck and early commuter, but I can sense that mad, inconsiderate driving is coming back.

Bromyard Scaffolding's trucks have big St George crosses on the front. It's always one of my considerations when I want a scaffold putting up – whether the scaffolders are patriotic, or racist, enough. Without wishing to tarnish a whole trade I think we can assume that the majority of scaffolders probably are. I was once told that scaffolders and fairground people are one and the same, but that was in the day when they wore sheepskin coats with the sleeves cut off, not harnesses and fluorescent romper suits. It's health and safety/P.C. gone mad.

Bredenbury Court is an exclusive wedding venue. Who does it exclude?

I didn't have to go into Bromyard, being diverted round to the Ledbury road. On the signpost was a placard for the Brexit Party. Their slogan is 'Change politics for good' and it's utter nonsense, just like the rest of them. People have spent their whole lives trying to change politics through parliament. Corbyn is one of them. They are pissing in the wind. People don't change parliament, parliament changes people. For the most part it makes them into arrogant, self-important elitists who think they run the country. In a proper democracy the member of the main assembly would be the least important person, someone that could be replaced at any time. The people who elected him or her would be sovereign and the representative would be mandated. That would be democratic. What we have is nothing of the kind. Usually the more the word is used the less the reality exists.

The road surface on the B2414 was terrible, deep potholes, broken surface and bad patching, but the traffic wasn't too heavy so I wasn't generally forced through the holes risking smashing my back and my bike. You have to pick your way through it on a bicycle. Car drivers just drive over everything. They won't read the road, or they're going too fast to, and they've no idea, or don't care, how other road users are dealing with it.

All I could find to sit on to brew up after my usual first ten miles of so was a massive tyre restricting the entrance to a big commercial orchard, but it was surprisingly comfortable. In fact, with a little table in the middle, it would make excellent, durable outdoor seating for people to sit round in a circle.

Further on a tractor was ploughing and the earth looked red and rich, but not very moist. A proud patriot was flying a union flag. He had decorated the pole and fence with a string of poppies, as is the fashion. They were made from the bottoms of red plastic pop bottles. So it was a simple statement; 'I support our boys against the alien hordes,' rather than a willingness to give to the Haigh Fund.

There was a deep thirty foot long crack in the road at one point that a cyclist's wheels would have gone right into. This is the sort of thing that could get you killed if you were forced into it by dangerous overtaking.

I went into Ledbury at 9.30 because I needed fruit and a new book. The woman on the till in Tesco's was way over the top with her 'my dear', 'my lovely' and 'young man.' In the animal welfare shop I chose John Lanchester's *The Debt to Pleasure* for 75p. I hope it goes to badgers and not dogs. Ledbury is one of those long shopping street market towns, with a very old timber framed market building.

I bought gas, a notebook and postcards and stamps to keep my public informed and sat and read for half an hour, as I promised myself I would at the start. The postcards were 20p or six for a pound.

Usually they are 35p and I've been charged 50p. The church notice board had adverts for baptism and the food bank. Ledbury is at the heart of England. At the heart of England is a food bank.

Out towards Tewkesbury. Houses became thatched. Castles had deer parks. The road had a better surface, mostly, there were still some shockers, and was virtually empty.

I found an old penny in the gutter, which must have been where I was looking, on the steep climb to Hollybush. It's badly bent, but I can make out it's 1962. That's all I can make out, but I know it also says that Elizabeth II is queen because God wants her to be. He must have wanted Charles I to be king as well – so that was one in the eye for God. What if we decide we don't want Elizabeth to be queen – what's God going to do then? Actually it wasn't Cromwell that got rid of Charles. It was God, because he's omnipotent. He wanted Stalin and Hitler to kill millions of people. He wanted Korea and Vietnam and the Somme and Dresden. They all happened, so they must have been what God wanted. If he didn't he'd have stopped them. What – 'free will,' isn't that a cop out?

I had my lunch on a grassy common just in Worcestershire and scattered the coffee that's been keeping me awake. Two young women came past on horses. One of them was skittish. Its rider said, 'Go on, it's only a man having his dinner.' She can't have been posh or she'd have said I was having my lunch. I've never been on a horse in my life, but I'm convinced that talking softly to them makes them worse. Cannon (the horse breaker up our road) wouldn't do that. He'd dig his knees in and say 'ger on.'

The bridge under the mad motorway appears to have nooses hanging from it.

Severn Trent Water have got their own slogan. It's a good one; 'Health and Safety is no accident.' Double meaning. That's a good thing in a slogan. 'Brexit means Brexit' – that's not really a good slogan because it's a meaningless truism.

The papers today say the Tories have thrown out May's fifth re-hash-with-no-substance of the deal she negotiated with Europe months ago. And that's going to be her legacy – 'no, no and five times no.' the next bastard won't do any better either, unless they're prepared to properly split their party.

They won't vote for May's deal because, a) It isn't leaving, and b) It isn't staying in. It's a fudge that pleases no one.

I crossed the big lazy Severn and into Tewkesbury. I first came here over forty five years ago when I was in the army. As I looked at nothing then I won't be able to say if it's changed – though it almost certainly has.

Tewkesbury's oldest pub is a big timber-framed no doubt grade 1 listed building. It's shut because no one wants it. The main street on the way in is a mixture of the very old, the fairly old and the ugly slab-square modern. The latter is a big BUPA dentists. Enough said.

There are some ugly flats overhanging the shops in a hideous parody of Tudor streets where people used to empty their chamber pots out of the windows, allegedly. The street is still full of shit, but it's coming out of the queue of cars – and people are sitting outside Costa and doing their shopping breathing it all in like we're some kind of rational beings.

Obese people walk past wearing crosses, seemingly unable to respect the body they believe God gave them. Young men with tattooed necks and tracksuits swagger. There are traffic islands up the middle to stop drivers overtaking up the main street, because they would. They are also referred to as 'pedestrian refuges.' There is no refuge – Recently pedestrians who wanted to avoid breathing in the stinking fumes of passing vehicles were advised to walk as far away from the road as possible and not to cross half-way to where the fumes were worst, but wait until they could get all the way in one go. The pathetic nature of this advice says all that needs to be said about the overwhelming focus on mitigating the symptoms of pollution and climate change while doing absolutely zero to avoid it. When I first heard it I thought of *Protect and Survive*, the government pamphlet in the 1980s that seriously advised the public to shelter under their kitchen table from a nuclear explosion. The cops came through heading for some emergency and the traffic couldn't get out of their way because of the deliberate narrowing of the thoroughfare. There were charity shops and pound shops and a Bangladeshi restaurant. I could have murdered a curry.

I don't need to write about any more towns because I've written about this one and they're all the fucking same – choking with fumes and full of enticements to spend on stuff you don't need.

After I'd cleared the mad retail jungle that under capitalism stands in for a community – 'We must save our high street,' Why? Because petty traders are the backbone of stability and conservatism, that's why. It's got nothing to do with community and everything to do with profit and politics. There are a thousand different ways we could create communities if we really wanted to – they don't have to depend upon us patronising petty traders who probably vote Tory anyway.

There was a wide cycle path all the way to my B road, so I didn't have to mess with the pumped-up sociopaths in their prize possessions, their badges of honour, their symbols of success. As Thatcher said – anyone who is still using the bus at thirty five is a failure – and like a lot of Thatcher's class war nonsense we fell for it. She told us the trade unions, the only bodies that represent us, were holding the country to ransom – we believed her and let her and her coterie of thugs smash them. She told the Argentineans were our enemies. We believed her and let paratroopers and marines go and bayonet teenage conscripts in their trenches for some shitty islands. The only person that pulled the wool over our eyes more than Thatcher was Blair, whom she said, along with New Labour (i.e. old conservatism) was her biggest achievement.

There was a nice Premier Inn, but it was only two o'clock and I rode on.

We don't buy what we want to buy, we buy what we are told we need. They spend billions telling us we need it. No one actually has free will – we are influenced by all sorts of things. It's actually no good moralising with people about using cars and consuming like the planet is infinite, but they aren't going to stop selling the stuff to us because their system depends on mad consumption. Without mad consumption there's no capitalism, it's finished, fucked, over, finite. If it carries on we're all fucked.

They're not going to stop so we're going to have to make them. The longer we bury our heads in the sand and pretend that's not the case, fool ourselves that MPs really represent us and that we only have to vote the right ones in, the worse it's going to get. There'll be more floods, more droughts, mass migration, wars over water and food supplies, social breakdown, the collapse of public services.

Getting rid of them by force sounds a big thing, but doing nothing is probably worse.

And then, all of a sudden there's a tank proudly on display at a junction outside the Ashchurch Defence Equipment and Support place. That's what they need to keep their system secure. Arms is a massively subsidised and profitable industry, and they fool us into making it all so they can line their own pockets and get our sons to kill other working class people who are our enemies because they live somewhere else under their own shit system and its robbing rulers. The whole lot stinks.

Ashchurch is a massive place, bigger than any factory or complex making anything else, bigger than a small town in fact. None of it is economically viable, even in real capitalist terms. None of it is socially useful and it's all paid for by us.

There were civilian workers inside the high security fence. One had a Tilley hat on like mine and put his thumb up to me 'On the basis of a hat?' I thought, or an army green bike maybe.

One of the first fields I had time to look at still showed signs of medieval strip farming – five hundred years ago.

This morning I was on an A road with no one on it. This afternoon I'm on an A road and then a B road full of banging stinking trucks, with one behind me all the time and nowhere to go to get out of their way, and aggressive, engine-revving car drivers whose attitude says 'get out of my way you scum.'

There's going to be a lot more of this now I'm entering the south of England, where there's no such thing as a road that's not busy. The only alternative is the unclassified roads, which, because they take you over hills and into valleys and often aren't signed, would take four times as long and wouldn't be feasible in the time I can afford to stay out.

As I stood in a field gateway fifteen yards from the road I could feel the ground shake as the wagons went past. If that's sensible, given what we know, I don't know what would constitute stupid. There's no way you can relax and it isn't remotely enjoyable. It just becomes a job of work you have to get done.

Ye Olde Hobnails Inn on the B 4077, 'a country inn and restaurant,' claims to have been there since 1743. Has it bollocks. The sign saying they wanted staff had fallen into the dirt and it was shut – 'a fantastic business opportunity' for someone.

I was thinking all this and how I hated it when a lovely Caravan and Camping Club site appeared right by the side of the road. So I pulled in. It was three o'clock - the sensible time to stop. It was £9, but I had to spend another £5 on food because for the first time on the trip I'd no food at all on board, planning to get to Stow, which was obviously mad – and another six quid doing all my washing while I sat about in my bright yellow waterproofs and red nylon sleeveless gilet sweating like a pig and looking ridiculous with everyone else in shorts outside posh caravans. It's still cheaper and less wasteful than buying new clothes and should keep me going two more weeks.

Looking at the overview map and how much I've done I think I can afford to slow down a bit.

My glove turned up. I gave the heavy work gloves I bought in Scotland to the campsite man.

I had a rationalisation and cast a load of bags and packets I don't need out. I need to stop trying to carry wet stuff, sauce, peanut butter etc. in jars and make it into sandwiches before I go to save weight.

I took it for granted that I was going to type all this up. Now I don't know if I can be bothered even to write it, though I'll regret it if I don't. I reckon to live in the moment, but spend all my time writing about the past.

It didn't take many pages for me to realise that I cannot do John Lanchester's book. It is entirely about gourmet eating, something I have no interest in whatever because I am a simple eater – simple foods, tasty and plenty of it. I can't abide pissed about with food that there isn't enough of. Food isn't art, it's fuel. Only the rich and the wasteful can piss about eating artistic creations that leave them unnourished. If they did any work they'd know you have to pile it in.

Camping and Caravan Club sites are always clean and tidy, mown and manicured by friendly, uniformed and sometimes even name-tagged staff, and they are as reasonably priced as anywhere else. The cheapest sites are usually farms. The most expensive ones are the ones that aspire to be holiday parks and specialise in noisy children, cabaret bars and car door banging contests. This site has a big sitting room with leather armchairs, which is rather offset by the fact that it also contains a miniature bowling alley and a TV.

At seven o'clock I put my earplugs in and went to sleep.

Day 34 – Toddington to Bletchinton
(Gloucestershire and Oxfordshire)
It was fully light when I woke happy, calm, rested and positive, ready for another relaxing day's cycling in the countryside and through the occasional pretty village. A cock was crowing, bedsides the pigeons and small birds.

I emerged straight away into the chilly dampness under a blue sky with wispy clouds and the slash of a jet plane's trail straight across it.

In the toilet I waited for Justin Timberlake to finish to learn it was 5.30. When I got back to the tent I realised there'd been a splashback on my nice clean shorts.

An older woman came out of one of the big caravans and waved to me (beside it was a big black 4x4). She had a big black poodle that bounced all over, jumping in the air and doing turns like a pit pony released for the summer break. She did all she could to make it walk beside her, to make it conform to what she wanted it to be, rather than an animal in its own right with all the unconscious joy for life immature animals have. And I thought 'how pointless.' The big black poodle is complimented by a big white one – a kind of his and hers.

Overpriced, over processed, sugar laden Granola is nice (though not quite vegan). No wonder people reject less processed and healthier alternatives for it. They also reject cheap cereals for the branded ones – the only difference being that the branded ones contain more sugar. The same is true of biscuits.

The wagons were already thundering past.

For two pins I'd throw my waterproof trousers away. I haven't put them on the last few times it's rained – not even in Scotland, when it rained nearly all day. My shorts dry quickly and if it's torrential I can take shelter or overnight refuge.

The only food I'm setting off with today is a big bag of prepared sandwiches - peanut butter, brown sauce and tomato puree. Everything else I've used up.

Sitting here I can think 'fuck the traffic – just let it wait,' but within minutes I know it will be stressful and dangerous.

Despite all the wagons there are rabbits all over the site. The wildlife has to put up with the din and pollution and go on raising its young just like we do.

I was on the road before seven, straight into the sun. The road was smooth the terrain level and the traffic not too bad. Past a pair of yellow stone gatehouses, a mansion in the same stuff and into Toddington, where the village hall was a polling station. It must be the Euro elections that were never going to happen and which, when I left home seemed months away. Harold Wilson said a week is a long time in politics and he was right, but a month is nothing on the road.

An estate of 3,4 and 5 bedroom 'Cotswold country homes' were under construction in imitation yellow stone on a greenfield site. The houses aren't just built, like normal people's homes, but 'crafted,' by bricklayers and joiners who swear, drink and abuse their partners.

A few frontages had multiple doors and a rendered finish. They contained the token pokey homes the council had demanded as a condition of granting planning permission. On this occasion it seemed the contractor had not managed to wriggle out of its commitment to include some affordable properties.

There were big old signs saying that the riding of horses on the footpath was unlawful under section 72 of the 1835 Highways Act and a maximum fine of £10 could be incurred. Only in the Cotswolds could such a sign be necessary.

There were direction signs for two other estates of yellow executive four and five bedroom boxes under construction and a newly built one called The Laurels on the way out. The Cotswolds seems like the place to be if you've got the mentality and the wherewithal of a yeoman Tory.

Just beyond I crossed one more short stretch of preserved railway – infrastructure reduced to tourist attraction. Had it really been preserved it could have got the yuppies who live here to their dull desks wherever and brought in the servants who walk their dogs, look after their children and clean their toilets.

Further on yet, at the turn off to Stanway, was a First World War memorial like none I have ever seen. Depicted in life-size bronze, on a tall yellow stone column, was a slim youthful warrior in armour slaying a dragon. This pseudo archaic and intensely patriotic monument must be one of the greatest distortions of the conflict anywhere. It coincides entirely with the myth of a noble endeavour current politicians and revisionist historians are trying to create. The First World War was brutal, mechanised, industrial scale slaughter, a fight for the right of the strongest to rob the world. It had nothing to do with morality, nobility or defence of the homeland. The message of this misplaced George and Dragon image is that Germany was intrinsically evil and Britain intrinsically good. It is a negation of the lives of all the German men who believed exactly the opposite because that is what they had been told to believe. No serious historian believes anything other about the First World War than that both sides were equally to blame, that both sides knew it was coming and that both sides consciously and systematically armed themselves to the teeth to fight it, whatever the human cost.

Straight after that there was a long steep hill to teach me a lesson for my treachery. Like others who dare to question I had been sent to the salt mines.

Some people love the Cotswolds. I hate them. They are the seat and wellspring of the stinking hypocrisy on which Britain is founded – and the seat of the third generation millionaire, who married the daughter of a millionaire, our erstwhile Prime Minister, David Cameron, whose political faux pas has probably done nothing to damage his career – if rolling in money can be described as a career.

I despise the people living in these yellow stone mansions with their eighty grand Range Rovers, while other people are trying to survive on the minimum wage, sleeping on the streets and resorting to food banks. Any system that allows these two extremes to exist is a crime against humanity and needs to be smashed to the earth and burned – for goodness and solidarity to rise from the ashes.

Meanwhile...

A Land Rover over took me belching blue smoke. A mini hovered so long right behind me that I had to lean on the verge to let it pass. The driver revved his engine fit to make the valves bounce to show me, unaware of the tiny little valve stems in his three times exported throwaway engine.

These are the kind of people who consider me 'left field' (what is that anyway) for making my own bicycle because all they know how to make is money.

If you've smashed the once great infrastructure of a country in the interests of the car, oil and road transport lobby then you can't destroy an environment by building crass homes on it, or service the needs of the inhabitants without wagons that smash the roads to pieces. What is obviously necessary then is to starve councils of the funds to repair them so you can give tax cuts to the people who vote for you.

And soon it was banging tipper after banging tipper – dozens of them.

When Andy Wing built his own house he put four hundred tons of prime quarried hard core into the soft earth and probably another two hundred tons of materials above it. That's just for one house that required no new streets or roads to be built.

As there were quarries nearby, extracting from the bowels of the earth the yellow stone they smash to make its imitation, the road was full of dust and the passing wagons raised a dust storm like one on the Mongolian Steppe. I felt as if my mouth had been stuffed with Ginsberg's clay as theirs had been stuffed with silver. Some of them were carrying soil, dug out of fields to be replaced by tarmac and foundations. There is a Chinese proverb about the stupidity of a man who tried to move mountains.

And none of it is necessary because we could easily build sustainable homes from local materials, served by public transport. Housing ladder aspiration is an illness. It breeds in the affluent a mad desire to live in the style of the old aristocracy they ape, when one family controlled whole counties (as they still do), and no one seriously pretended that Britain was a democracy. It is simply not sustainable for the entire Tory voting executive class successive governments have systematically created to live like lords of the manor. As well as stealing food from the starving they are leading us all to destruction. I believe it was Kant, who in his Categorical Imperative called on people to act only in a way in which it would be possible for all to act.

There were hoardings for a point to point at Chipping Camden and a business called Architectural Heritage, where people who have fuck all to do with the countryside, and the taste of a nouveau riche rag and bone man, can buy fluted colonnades, armless statues and amphora in the attempt to make their homes look like the villas of the most obscene of the Romans.

And only then, at the top of the hill, did I officially enter the Cotswold District. The poor bastards at the other side aren't even within this hallowed handmade Eden built in brick, stone and privilege.

While there's an epidemic of diabetes in Bradford the disease here is affluenza. 'The poor will always be with us' – indeed, as long as the rich are. The money so badly needed in Bradford and Burnley is here in the Cotswolds.

One big yellow mansion was being built smack in the middle of open green fields. How the fuck do you get permission for that (other than by greasing someone's palm)?

I daren't even think about how much a pint might be in one of the pubs that don't know where to put their apostrophes.

A jazz evening was upcoming and I do believe it featured three black men. I wonder if they serve them in the local hostelries or they have special shed out back – for generally speaking the Cotswolds are an ethnic ghetto where people don't easily integrate. They stick to their own customs and don't speak proper English.

I was inspired to sing Woody Guthrie's *This Land is My Land* as I rode through fields of rape, well-maintained stone walls and manicured verges. Cotswold Council must have money to burn, whereas Bradford is cutting front line children's services. Get me out of here, I'm not a celebrity. Struggling hill farmers it isn't. Here the earth is bountiful and the subsidies generous.

After the quarries and the farm where the topsoil was being tipped the wagons stopped and it was fairly pleasant into Stow.

One mansion was under renovation, its great gateposts protected by plywood boards against the clumsy proles, they being the very symbol of the heights the new owners have reached – 'through these gates all is mine, and you shall not enter. Ring the bell and my man will come.'

Moving On
Feudalism didn't die in 1642
The old is with us in the new
The barons simply changed their masks
And kept the spoils like robbers do

Like lions in a gilded cage
These leopards cannot change their spots
Their carriage crass and manor vain
Are bought on tithes from the have nots

And what of those who want reform
Who will the deck chairs rearranged
Who promise all by one small cross
They come and go and nothing's changed

When the meek inherit all we'll do away
With needless blandishments like these
And what of those who robbed us then
We may just hang them off the trees

A sports car overtook me far too close and immediately afterward a car skidded to a halt inches behind me, the driver having decided at the last second not to overtake straight at the car coming the other way.

I could have ridden straight past Stow, but as I'm now taking my time and enjoying myself I thought I'd give it a look – and anyway I was in need of reading material. It is a historic market town, which is a widespread and not very original claim, the centre built around the old market cross. A plaque also details the slaughter of two hundred royalists in the square after Civil War Battle of Stow in 1646.

I sat on the steps of the cross inviting attention. Two clearly Chinese people came to take photos. I asked where they were from. They said Australia, and nothing else. It was ancient stuff they were interested in, not people.

Then, while I was eating my brown sauce sandwich, I talked to Carl and Sabina from Seattle, who'd been down south and into Wales, but didn't have time for Scotland.

I bought Helen Dunmore's *The Lie* (an apt title), because the First World War is my default reading, and Kenneth O Morgan's *A*

247

Very Short Introduction to the 20th Century for a pound each at the charity shop. Morgan says the First World War was 'in all senses a profoundly imperial war for empire as well as king and country.' The 'king and country' bit is tacked on cynically. The country wasn't under threat and the monarch was an irrelevance - in fact he was related to the monarchs of Germany and half of the rest of Europe and would have been just as royal and just as safe under German hegemony.

Because the main traffic didn't go through the middle of it the square was a peaceful place, but its deliberately maintained state was debased by hundreds of parked cars.

I rode out on the A road with a roaring tanker up my arse and took the B road towards Chipping Norton, the set of which David Cameron is apparently a member – a bit like the Bloomsbury Set, but talentless.

It was a beautiful road that passed yellow mansions on which no further comment is necessary, and chocolate box villages such as Bledington and Foscote, where I thought of calling in the polling station and asking what the turnout was like – Tories and toffs always vote because it is vitally in their interest to do so. They have not decided 'they are all the same' because for them they aren't. To them Labour is still socialist and Corbyn is the devil.

And here there are some relatively modest houses, and even a school. It's not the back to backs of Huddersfield, it's not even Bingley or Steeton, but it's not vulgar and pretentious either.

But generally it's a different world, a parallel universe even. There'll be no camping round here – they won't encourage that kind of proletarian activity. Even keeping a campsite would be below some of those who hang onto the notion that physical work is vulgar. The mob will be able to come here to work, but return to its hovels in the cities by sundown, because in the dark they may get up to things – like a bit of mindless disappropriation.

Without any irony the next village was called Churchill. A plasterer came out of a cottage with his trowel and hand board. I said 'bish, bosh,' but he was too young to remember Harry Enfield's sketch that did so much to seal in the public mind the belief that builders were making a fortune. There's modernisation of properties all over as pre-Thatcher 'greed is good' old folk die and the incoming rich rip out their homes. The village had an ornamental fountain bigger than anything I've seen outside a city. There's always been concentrated wealth here.

'Profound tensions that shook the United Kingdom are juxtaposed against equally deep forces of stability, cohesion and a sense of historic identity,' says the editor of Morgan's history. 'On the eve of world war [one]... Britain seemed to present a classic picture of a civilised liberal democracy on the verge of dissolution.' And yet weeks later a 'mood of united purpose gripped the nation.' Aside from the fact that this is not entirely true it demonstrates the timeless benefit that war, or the identification of an external enemy, has for struggling ruling classes. They all do it – from the US which wheeled on Muslims when the Soviet threat subsided, to the Mullahs in Iran who launched a war with Iraq to quell a progressive revolution.

The consensus regarding the justice of the war was 'very far from universal.' And it took the TUC to outdo the government in their patriotism, as usual supporting their member's right to die for the bosses. It also took Lloyd George 'the most left wing member of Asquith's government' to make a speech justifying the war. It was Kuwaiti babies, weapons of mass destruction, women's rights or any of the other bollocks justification Britain's rulers have put forward for war, it was 'poor little Belgium' – one of the most ruthless imperialist powers on the planet. Ruling class cynicism of course knows no bounds.

It continued to be a quiet road because only a few rich twats live there. The population density is about the same as the Australian outback, not counting the aborigines (in Australia the aborigines don't count, and never have).

I don't know what I expected of Chipping Norton, but from a mile out it looks like a red and yellow scab spreading across a green landscape. A man went past in a flash car with ROSITER for a number plate. We should die of envy – for that is what we subscribe to – 'the politics of envy.' We really want what they've got for ourselves. On this basis they justify their greed, consoling themselves that anyone else would do the same because it's human nature. Only by pretending hundreds of thousands of years of human existence did not happen can capitalist priorities be judged eternal, and only in the arrogant and misplaced belief that societies are static can anyone assume they will go on forever. Capitalism must end. Our future depends upon it.

Chipping Norton is not only the province of Cameron and his clones – it is also a normal place, with normal houses and normal people. The first election placard I saw said 'Vote Labour,' as did the second, the third, the fourth, the fifth and the sixth. These placards weren't fastened to lampposts, the result of some surreptitious blitz by two zealots. They were proudly displayed in people's front gardens. And though I only skirted the town I didn't see a placard for any other political party. There were flats, modest homes, a big, modern comprehensive school and several care homes.

I remember thinking the same thing about Witney, which David Cameron actually 'represented' – along with 'why do people keep voting for that posh idiot?' but my impressions of Witney were always going to be prejudiced by a girl of that name I tried to teach, on whom the best Swiss finishing school would have been wasted.

I then set off to tack my way to Tackley on an unclassified road, where the tar was tacky and my tyres were bursting little bubbles of it, between big open fields with a view for miles across the A44. It was brilliant, what I should have been doing all the time, not slogging on main roads with the traffic. Besides the soft bursting of the tar bubbles there was only the birds and a light plane far above. It was the distilled essence of the trip – of what it should be.

Even in the countryside there were black cabs driven by Asian men. These will be out of Oxford, which I could visit with its 'dreamy spires,' but I'd rather not.

Poppies are beginning to appear in the verge and there are fields full of buttercups. I could hear small arms fire to my left. If I remember rightly Bicester is a centre of shooting excellence.

I went through a place called Gagging Well, and while I was thinking how Theroux comments on the quaintness of English place names (though other places must have the same, especially Welsh – Tom said Pen-y-bont meant home or field at the end of the bridge) another cyclist came alongside and scared the shit out of me. He asked where I was heading so he could tell me how far it was and then rode on.

A man walking was using a 1937 pattern army large pack for a rucksack. Doesn't he know that modern fabrics and styles are available and that using perfectly serviceable eighty year old equipment is no way to keep the economy going? I might have told him so, but he had a dog.

There isn't a barn, a stable or a peasant cottage round here that can't be extended into a mansion – and everything available is being.

In The Bartons, a village, I saw a small, shy window poster for the Liberal Democrats, 'Stop Brexit.' Even that slogan is better than the pathetic, decades old 'Winning Here.' They don't deserve the kiss of life after their shameless support for the Tories as a means to taste apparent power.

Stopped at a garage for cheap pop – resisted any overpriced treats. The papers have photos of Theresa May red-eyed, Thatcher style, in her car. Some say she's 'holed up in Downing Street.' Andrea Ledsom has quit and the Tories are expected to be wiped out in the Euro elections.

Just after I'd crossed the A4260 I heard a police car brake hard behind me – it wasn't an emergency, he stopped at the next lights, and then an RAC van overtook me far too close. One would expect that both these people had been taught how to drive with respect for other people.

At Rousham I cycled past the long wall that separated some stately pile, which looks as if it is still in private hands, from the ugly world beyond.

It was a very bumpy unclassified road to Tackley. Nevertheless a concrete wagon came the other way at fifty. I could see its double rear axles twisting individually through the potholes. It showered me in loose stone and created a cloud of dust. Long sections of the hawthorn hedge were covered in the densest spider's webs I've ever seen.

Tackley, my thirteenth destination, is much like many other 'villages' up and down the land – a core of old houses where simple folk used to live, an inner periphery of twentieth century utility houses, pebbledashed semis, bungalows etc, and an outer ring of big yuppie houses built in the traditional material. Sometimes you can see the gentrification and the just-caught tradition in the same building, where a brick built house has a nice stone extension. Yellow signs pointed to new housing developments and a church, whose clock said it was 3.15 – time to stop.

But I still sat on a bench to eat my sandwich in the sun. Good job I did, because a nice old lad called Dave Bowerman came along and admired my bike. His granddad had raced on the continent and he'd done a few time trials. His granddad had a re-badged German bike from after the war 'when there was a bit of anti-German feeling.' I can remember anti-German feeling among older men when I was young, and anti-Japanese too. Now the old boys don't mind riding in a Volkswagen or a Nissan.

He was also an ex-motorcyclist who'd done a lot of trials on Ossas and Montessas right up to the Gas-Gas period. He knew all about grass track and dropped in some of the names from when I was obsessed with grass track and speedway. And not only that – he told me where the camp site was (actually I'd already ringed it on my map), and more importantly a short cut to get there. So far today has been one of the best.

At the church there was an exhibition – 'Tackley: from prehistoric times to the present' – I didn't have time for that, but I bet there wasn't any social speculation about prehistoric societies that didn't believe in survival of the fittest and winner takes all.

Dave said I was to take a broken road by a big old farm built in an Adam style. I don't know Adam style from Adam and I couldn't see the building through the trees that were surrounding it. But I saw the broken road and the massive Vodaphone satellite dishes that were hiding down there, which was why the road was broken – it was like Jodrell bank and they don't want people near this now vital piece of infrastructure.

Over the canal and past the *Rock of Gibraltar* pub, which, unlike the Rock, is for sale, one more exciting housing development, a bit of close overtaking, some abuse from a car passenger and I was there – a big manicured and beautiful farm campsite at Bletchington, £10 – and £3 for my tea and breakfast. I am surely the luckiest man alive.

I said to the woman on reception when I plonked my tins on the counter that I ought to soon get something fresh or something would happen to me. She said she didn't know – she'd been watching something on TV that said tins were fine.

It was baking hot, but there was shade or sun on my perfectly flat pitch, as I liked.

The question now is whether to detour to Ramsden, my namesake village, or head straight south. The next place I need to visit is Faccombe, south of Newbury.

And, talking of Churchill, Blenheim Palace, country seat of the self-promoting old warmonger, is just down the road. 'The Dardanelles Campaign... did immense harm to Churchill's reputation as a natural politician, from which he took years to recover.' He should never have recovered. He should have been put on trial for a 'colossal exercise in military mismanagement that wasted hundreds if not thousands of lives.'

There was a bench round the corner in an empty play area. I began my new book. '*The Lie* lays bare... the invisible wounds of a global catastrophe.' *The Independent*. '... physical death is only one way in which war destroys utterly.' *The Herald*.

'If any question why we died
Tell them because our fathers lied'
Rudyard Kipling

On page three there's a sentiment that could have come from The Diggers. 'Why shouldn't she have her bit of land, when there's others that own half the country?' And then there's an industrial accident that leaves a boy orphaned and a victorious soldier that comes back to live in a tin and canvas shack for his pains.

There was a Dodge V8 'Magnum' 'Genuine Spirit' pick-up truck parked nearby. It was part of a camping rig that also involved another part as big as an articulated wagon trailer called a 'Rockwood Signature Ultra-light'. It didn't look ultralight to me. It looked as if the macho man who owned it thought he was the top turn in an international circus.

I'm happy and tired and happy to be tired. I didn't know how many miles I've done today and I can't even remember where I started.

Not only were the leaders of organised labour more than willing to send their members off to be killed for the bosses in 1914 the leaders of organised religion were too. It does no good to say Germany started it. If the trade union leaders and the churches in Britain *and Germany* had refused to back it there is good evidence that their members and congregations would have backed them and the war could not have happened. This is why we can never trust the trade union leaders, the Labour Party or the Church. When it comes to war (and many other things) they'll quickly fall in line and back the establishment to the hilt. All three have played progressive roles at certain times, but all three are fundamentally conservative organisations. Afterward the Church will return to its sermons about peace as if it was some great accident that could never happen again.

One of the reasons the war didn't go on longer is because the working class weren't prepared to let it and the main reason for that was revolution in Russia. The Russian Revolution was the biggest anti-war movement ever and quite possibly the only one that succeeded.

Though World War One poets have portrayed the conflict as one of pointless slaughter, which is what it was, they do not appear to have reflected the mood at home, where mass enthusiasm for the war bordered on the cultish. A hundred years after the war to end all

254

wars we are in danger again of cultish behaviour with regard to the military, as governments add new days to the calendar, tabloids defend soldiers' every action, no matter how gross it is, and Help for Heroes and other soldiers' charities attain the status of institutions. It is not heroic to go abroad and kill people any more than it is to work in an abattoir or a nuclear power station. It is a job, sometimes entered into voluntarily, sometimes under threat of prison, hard labour or social opprobrium (the latter during WWI not least from some female suffragists).

This is a big flat site and all the staff ride round on little tractors, especially when showing people to their places. What on earth would be wrong with a bicycle?

As often happens I am nearly under an airport flight path and close to a busy railway line.

I made one of my big sandwiches I've been carrying into pobs and had it with tinned new potatoes. It did the job most adequately. It was still warm, I guess it was about six, and it made me sweat again. I thought 'I could murder a biscuit' and then remembered I'd got a few digestives left. A tin of beans and a tin of mushrooms I saved for breakfast – along with another sandwich. There were still some left that would see me through the morning at least.

I waved to a bald headed man with a big belly, a big man truck, a big caravan, an overweight wife and two overweight, giggling teenage daughters, who was using a power tool to wind down the legs of his Clubman 'Lunar'. He put his thumb up to me. On the road of course he would have cursed me, and quite possibly I him.

As I was sat in the entrance to my tent out of the sun the giggling girls probably thought I was something like a ridiculous hermit.

'There is an insidious tendency to lapse into a passive and lethargic attitude, against which officers of all ranks have to be on their guard, and the fostering of the offensive spirit, under such unfavourable circumstances, calls for incessant attention.'

In the photographs of men queuing up to volunteer in 1914 many of them look thin and weasel like. Many of them were rejected because they simply weren't fit enough – this was how the country had looked after the men it now expected to fight for it (Given the figures on child poverty the same may possibly be true today). Some recruiters turned a blind eye and took anyone, even though they were obviously either mentally or physically unfit for war service abroad. Today army recruiters on commission in the US still help possible recruits to mask and lie about conditions that would otherwise bar them from service. To encourage the mad volunteering (one of a soldier's maxims is 'never volunteer') the government printed moralising propaganda posters, such as the one where an innocent child asks his 'draft dodging' coward of a father what he did in the war. Very few thought that 'I fought against it with every fibre of my body son, I encouraged others not to go and they put me in jail for it' to be an acceptable response, though it is undoubtedly the right one.

When the war was over many of its heroes were reduced to selling matches or dusters in the street – just as todays 'heroes' end up propping up bars and sleeping on the streets. Ex-soldiers' charities exist because they are needed. The government's rhetoric has got nothing to do with looking after soldiers and everything to do with justifying the wars they fight in.

Five very long necked geese flew over low, they may have even been swans. They weren't making a noise, though I didn't think swans flew together.

'For unto everyone that hath shall be given, and he shall have abundance: but from him that hath not shall be taken away even that which he hath.'

The planes roar and the geese call, the caravan owners faff, but I've had enough. It's been a good day.

Day 35 – Nr Tackley to Newbury
(Oxfordshire and Berkshire)
Asleep before the sun went fully down and up before it rose. I opened the tent in time to see seven white doves land on the path. The crows are noisy here also, along with the geese.

I always make sure I have at least three mugs of tea before I set off (I've stopped the coffee altogether). Getting plenty of fluids is one of my obsessions. It's easy to become dehydrated cycling up and down hill in the sun. If I think there'll be shops I carry a litre of water, if not two.

A sign by the bins at yesterday's campsite said 'All rubbish is sorted at the depot,' meaning consumers had to do nothing but throw all their waste in the same big bin. I cannot imagine the machinery that would sort *all* the rubbish and I cannot imagine anyone doing it by hand. I think, like many other recycling claims, that this is a con.

The sun came up directly in front of my tent and didn't make any secret of its intention to make it another very hot day.

Having read two chapters of my book I suspect '*The Lie*' does not refer to the reason the war was fought, but to the fact that the protagonist is not who he thinks he is, but the illegitimate son of the bad man and half-brother to the woman he pursues [I was wrong about this, my plot was far more complicated than the author's. The book is simply about a young man fucked up by war].

I was off even before the dog walkers were out and hoping to find my way by the sun through Ramsden and Witney, lighter than I've been all the way with only a few sandwiches and one bottle of water. Unfortunately it went behind some dense clouds as I set off.

There was a big hare idly patrolling one of the big empty camping fields. I have never seen one so close or relaxed.

The long entrance to the site is flanked by dozens of stone troughs that look genuinely old, as well as a few bits of cylindrical carved column. A pen contains two hairy 'Kune Kune' pigs. One of them scratching itself on the gate like it was going to knock it down.

I thought about staying on the A road to Witney and not bothering with Ramsden, but within seconds I was being passed by revving engines and dangerous overtaking – it can't have been seven o'clock. The only problem was that the B road via Ramsden was just the same, and it was quite a long way round. There's nothing there, I've been before – I picked the A road.

257

It was truly awful, dusty and bumpy and busy – an endless roaring procession of human stupidity. There were plenty of other cyclists all fighting the same battle. There were people on sit up bikes, men in ties on Brompton folders – risking their lives for health reasons; risking their lives so that we all might live. Pompous – it's only what Christians say – and I think it really is that serious. And there were lots of people walking beside it too – in summer clothes, breathing in the shit. Yet there were houses (*new* houses at that) and pubs facing onto it like it was some quiet lane, and we all tolerate this apparent normality. And everywhere the yellow signs pointing to new housing developments – one road sign had three attached to it. Anyone can see the south is overheating – it's where the money is and where the money's spent.

A new posh estate (in fake yellow stone of course) sold itself on being ten minutes from Oxford by train. At Hanborough a roadside cycle path started. The *George and Dragon* (with a similar image to the war memorial yesterday on its sign) advertised beautiful homemade food and bar and kitchen jobs. If I pretended I served beautiful homemade food I wouldn't advertise outside that I couldn't keep the staff that are trusted to cook it.

At home, cycling is a novelty and cyclists all exchange greetings. Here it's normal and they all ignore each other – that and the fact that northern people are friendlier (straight after I'd written this a bloke went out of his way to say good morning to me – and so did the next few cyclists).

But the most incredible thing; the thing that strikes you most; the thing you cannot ignore; is the number of posh housing developments, always of 3, 4, and 5 bedroom houses. It's one, after the other, after the other – 'Shepherd's Walk,' 'Woodland Grange,' 'Orchard Park,' all names implying rural peace in an obvious giant rat cage.

One pub was clearly desperate to attract overnight guests. Had it been four o'clock I might have done them a favour. I'm about due to stay inside, but the sun was hardly up and I was having a leisurely ride on a roadside cycle path, marvelling at the madness of it all.

On a narrow path (the cycle path just ended), in a rare bit of countryside, with the cars hammering past, I bumped into Reece from Anglesey walking with his wheeled suitcase. All it took was a 'going anywhere nice?' He'd been in Oxford on a course to do with his work and was as dismayed as I was about it all. He wanted to talk because he was Welsh, not a too-busy southerner, and he mostly talked about how unfriendly people were here and how mad they drive. The only cycling he does is on his exercise bike 'and that's boring.' Really? He'd just missed a bus and thought nothing of walking another two miles to the station.

The cycle route signs turned me into New Leigh. Fifty yards away from the main road it's a different world. Even though I'd barely done ten miles I sat on a bench to brew up and read a few pages. Every few minutes a tipper went past full of top soil, the empty ones bouncing back, then a truck full of building mortar. I had wondered further back why the verge was all destroyed on a corner. Now I knew why.

A man went past on the other side with a dog. I didn't bait him – he was also swinging a little bag of dog shit. Another walked briskly past on my side and said of my stuff all spread out and my little stove, 'That looks very civilised sir.' And there was me thinking it was the opposite of civilised, and that cars and cafés and careers were civilised. It seemed a funny way of talking to people – sort of distant and insincere, but I may be imposing that on people.

The cycle route sign was a typical trick and it brought me back onto the main road half a mile further on, just like I knew it would. Why waste money on a bit of tarmac when you can send cyclists all over the place? The assumption is if you're on a bicycle you can't possibly be in a hurry. The result is that people going to work continue to ride on the road because they want to get there. The other thing is that many of the old pavements you are consigned to, in order to get you out of the way of the more important traffic, are as bumpy as fuck and reduce your speed by half.

Actually, generally speaking, if they're not interested in my bike they're not interested in me.

For some reason 'Canis,' 'The finest dog grooming,' found it necessary to fly above its car park a 'lest we forget' flag depicting silhouetted troops stupidly making themselves targets by walking on the skyline. This is what I mean about the pervasive military mind-set. Twenty years ago no one would have dreamed of flying a flag like that – they didn't give soldiers, past or present, a second thought.

Right beside the road at the Witney turnoff a 'traveller' was living in two traditional wooden caravans. There were horses tethered all around and wooden carvings for sale – what is referred to as 'chainsaw art.' Really I should have spoken to him. He was at the back faffing with his chainsaw.

By following the road signs I avoided the worst of Witney and came upon a Lidl that was mobbed out. In my excitement I forgot what I'd gone in for, which was tea bags and fruit and came out with only water, crisps and chewing gum. So I had to go in a small Tesco's, but I refused to pay what they were asking for fruit tea bags.

One of the papers says 'The day you voted for Brexit again.' We can safely assume that the deluded remainers in the Liberal Democrat and other parties didn't make any headway with their boss supporting agenda.

The lovely road through Ducklington almost made me swear no more main roads, but as such a thing is impossible I didn't.

Within seconds I was shot back out onto the busy A415 with no pavement for a while until the traffic light turn off, where a bloke in a jaguar with a personalised registration overtook me and stole my bit of road simply because he could. From there it was tiny back roads through Yelford.

A bloke passed me on a K registered Honda CB175 – 1970 or so – once everywhere in its candy orange paint. Asparagus and sweet Williams were for sale outside houses. Once more I saw crows harassing a bird of prey. It was bliss. The countryside was level and there was no one on the road but me. I stopped on the bridge over a lazy river where ducks were swimming. An old bloke came by with his basic bicycle and told me it was twenty to twelve. He'd just pushed up the rise to the bridge. I could hear birds singing, flies buzzing, rubber on tarmac, the breeze in my ears and nothing else (apart from the occasional plane).

I stopped to sit on a wooden footbridge for my lunch. My tomatoes were from Morocco and my oranges from Spain.

'Once I was in camp, I knew almost at once… what the distance was between an officer and a man. They were creatures from another world.' 'I was pig ignorant, green as grass… what I knew after the first week's training was to keep my head down and my nose clean… I'd see faces go blank, because they couldn't take in any more, and what they couldn't take in might be the one thing they needed to know.'

There were tall reeds in the river, lily pads and black butterflies and if it wasn't the Thames it was a river that soon becomes it.

But an unclassified road is no guarantee that my four wheeled fellow citizens won't be arseholing along it, and for the next bit I was back in the danger zone, including from RAY in his lowered and blacked out BMW, MOM in her little pink Fiat and SHIRLEY in her 2CV, although Shirley had just put a big sticker across her boot rather than waste money on a pretentious number plate.

It was better after I crossed the A420. I can hear planes and helicopters all the time, which isn't surprising because I'm near Brize Norton, and must be fairly near Wooton Bassett, that had to be prefixed 'Royal' after it became fashionable to clap corpses. I once worked out how many construction workers had died while British soldiers were serving their country fighting futile and illegal wars in Iraq and Afghanistan. Needless to say it was considerably more than the number of soldiers killed. But bricklayers and scaffolders, tunnellers, bridge builders and steel erectors, though they do a job for money, just like soldiers, are not heroes. No one throws a union flag over a scaffolder and claps his coffin through the streets when most of us wouldn't dream of such menial employment as hanging off the outside of tall buildings. I was a soldier. I was sent to Northern

Ireland. If I had been shot and killed there the responsibility would have been mine and my parent's for being ignorant of our history and the history of Ireland and the British government's for creating and prolonging a situation that was intolerable to half the population. If you put on a green uniform and occupy people's communities you are asking to be shot at or blown up. It happened to the Germans when they occupied France, but somehow that was just.

There was a man on a horse. 'You know you're in a posh area when you see men on horses,' says Oades.

By this method – picking my way through hamlets and villages, stopping to study every finger post sign, of which thankfully there were many, I wound myself south to Grove, enjoying it more, but covering half as much distance on the map and twice as much on the ground.

On the edge of Grove a green field site is earmarked for hundreds more houses. All that is required is that the DoE is satisfied there are no reptiles involved. Coming out hundreds more were already under construction by Persimmon, a firm that is currently coining it in.

I impeded for a brief moment at a junction a blacked out BMW just like RAY's, but with the registration 666. When the driver could get past he brayed the tits off his car completely unnecessarily, just to show me.

At one point as far as the eye could see land had been designated for housing and on its periphery work was ongoing. I have never seen as big a housing development site in my life.

At the entrance to Wantage a big fighter plane was suspended in mid-air for us to celebrate.

Wantage wasn't funny for obvious reasons that there's no need to repeat (it was cars) and I exited without really entering on the B4494 for Newbury, which wound its way up and down through big fields of standing crops over the Lambourn Downs. Someone had written in big letters 'Oh what a world' on a big tank in a field. What on earth could they mean? It is a fast road (for cars, not for me) but it wasn't at all busy. At the top the road crosses the Ridgeway, which

262

apparently people walk in their retirement, and at other times, as some sort of pointless challenge.

A bit further on I left Oxfordshire without any sadness and entered Berkshire without any joy. I didn't expect to have much joy finding a campsite either, but then I usually don't.

A car passed me with a big poppy sticker in the back window and a big silhouette of the downcast soldier that has become de rigueur on the boot. This is bizarre behaviour reflective of a growing mindless jingoism and a can do no wrong attitude with respect to 'our' soldiers. Coming into Newbury it was 'Liberal Democrats - Demand better,' but there was no campsite.

So at five o'clock I went straight to the first pub I came to, which was the *Bacon Arms* and got a room for £70. The landlady had a soft Irish brogue and was interested in my trip. She asked where I'd come from today and as usual I couldn't remember. For the most part I couldn't remember where I'd been if my life depended upon it. My bike is safe and I'm in what might once have been a stable or store in the yard. The room is OK, as it should be for £70, but a bit faded. The bathroom floor is clearly rotten under the lino. Rather than compound the expense by eating and drinking out I walked into town and bought a few bits to eat in the room with my last two day old sandwich.

Newbury has one of those big shopping centres that you like, but you don't know why, and an apparently pedestrianised main street that people still drive down.

Theresa May has broken down outside number 10 Downing Street while announcing her resignation – and not before time. Whoever becomes prime minister next will want to renegotiate the Brexit deal. EU leaders have said categorically they will not reopen negotiations. The pundits favour Boris Johnson as the next Tory leader. The BBC is busy telling us that the Tory Party membership will choose the new leader for the first time. This isn't true. All the candidates, and there may be a dozen, will be whittled down by parliamentarians until there are only two left. The membership will chose between two people the hierarchy approves of, exactly as the

Labour Party does (unless of course the Labour Party makes the grave once in a lifetime mistake of letting a left winger onto the ballot paper in order to humiliate him and prove to the world that the left is dead).

Labour is calling for a general election. Labour has been calling for a general election for months. John McDonnell is a remainer and in an interview he fudged all over the shop.

Donald Trump's visit to the UK will coincide with the last days of Theresa May's reign.

I also discovered that Steve Bannon is funding the rent on a disused monastery in Italy and has installed a British fruitcake in it. Their plan is to defend Judeo-Christian Europe. The fruitcake says Britain 'is bending the knee to Sharia Law.' These people are mad, but they are very dangerous.

Day 36 – Newbury to Salisbury (via Faccombe)
(Berkshire and Wiltshire)
Out like a light last night and awake before six to prolonged speculation about the Tory leadership contest and the news that Donald Trump is sending more troops to the Gulf to threaten Iran. At the same time he's actively bolstering the relationship with the brutal, warmongering dictatorship of Saudi Arabia. In the past he's bragged about the value of the weapons the US sells to the Saudis, as if weapons have no consequences.

I keep getting my maps out and looking at them expecting some sensation. But there is no sensation in looking at the maps – I just get them out one at a time, use them up and throw them away. The individual maps actually mean nothing, only the big overall map tells the story – or rather hints at the possibility of a story.

In the early stages of World War One the whole of British industry was effectively nationalised. The previous dogmatic adherence to *laissez faire* and free trade was unceremoniously dumped. That they might keep their members in order the trade unions were effectively bribed and bosses were brought into government. This was the beginning of the corporate state – what would later be referred to as 'Britain PLC.'

The war also necessitated much social reform, firstly because the government realised that it ruled a population great numbers of which were even too unfit to die in the trenches, and secondly because it made promises to the population that in some part it was obliged to keep. It is the social advances forced by the war, which seemed at the time like enlightenment, and led to the modern welfare state, which are being squandered now by businessmen and politicians who would return to the ruthless priorities of the nineteenth century.

Paradoxically, while the dead of World War One are being systematically canonised, the better world for which they thought they were fighting is being systematically destroyed. Perhaps it isn't a paradox at all – perhaps it is as simple as this – that the government needs cover of past glories from which to mount its ideological economic offensive.

Men like Robert Tressell's painters fought the First World War and they came back to the same squalor. It is a mark of great shame that men like Robert Tressell's painters exist today, in large number, and their families live almost the same futile, impoverished, hopeless existence.

Some older people can't see this because they benefitted from the good years. But Harry Leslie Smith (*Harry's Last Stand*, 2014), as a spokesman for the informed octogenarian, died disgusted, and disgusted is what we all should be.

The BBC weather woman talked about her dog climbing on the bed for a cuddle and the viewer's weather picture featured another dog. I despair at this obsession and am endlessly reminded of George Orwell's prediction that dogs (and horses) would die out on the grounds of hygiene. He might have seen the modern surveillance state coming, but he fucked up big-style over Britain's fetish for pets. Having said that he died in the fifties, when it looked like we might begin to care about each other, rather than lavish ridiculous attention on dogs, fooling ourselves that they are something other than dirty, scrounging pack animals.

The BBC is under attack for 'sneering' at Nigel Farage getting covered in milkshake. 'Would it have been as happy to broadcast endlessly the footage if it had been a female left wing politician? Asked one viewer. He forgot to include 'black' in his question and entirely blow his cover.

At breakfast the main news featured a thatcher who got on air by pretending his dog liked being on the roof, and other dog-related stories. I ate all before me – two glasses of orange juice, two mugs of coffee, two individual boxes of fruit and fibre, I full breakfast, six slices of toast with jam or marmite. There were eight people at breakfast besides me. Four of them were very overweight. As most of them ate less than me I can only assume they are inactive.

Outside Tesco's was someone's rolled up sleeping bag, together with an uneaten box of fried onion rings and a pre-packed sandwich – the peace of mind offerings of the privileged.

It wasn't easy getting out of Newbury – just one more city designed entirely to cater for cars. All the signs wanted to take me on four lane speedways with no refuge from Mr Petrol Head. New barriers were being constructed to corral local pedestrians hundreds of yards out of their way to get through their own town, while through traffic speeds through unimpeded. At many junctions, underground tunnels kept human moles out of the way of the metal god.

I kept the sun on my left ear until I found a just bearable road south. It even paid lip service to cyclists here and there – though one always wonders what to do when fifty yards of gutter path finishes abruptly with 'cycle route ends,' which might as well says 'cyclists disappear up own arse.' It is under trees where I am most afraid, where anyone tuning their radio or texting would have a ready-made excuse, and sadly, one that most magistrates would accept. 'Cyclist killed by car driver.' 'I'd just come out of bright sunlight into the shade your worship.' Fair enough, derisory fine, off you go.

A house with a Liberal democrat placard was called *The Haven* – from reality one suspects – stop Brexit, demand better, winning here, not supporting tuition fees. Given the downward looks and nods you see on street corners it appears that people meet each other with the words 'why don't you bore me with banalities about your dog.'

I passed 'a landmark development of contemporary detached houses,' but I couldn't detect anything particularly special about them.

The endless roar of traffic is wearing. It destroys the therapeutic exercise and quiet contemplation that cycling can be. Cycling is a peaceful self-effacing form of transport. Motoring is a noisy aggressive macho one. Cycling goes with semi pastoral living at one with the world, motoring with the dog eat dog rape of the planet and each other representative of capitalism itself. Cars are the face of the system, the profit in their production, their reliance on oil, their intrinsic individuality. Cars are capitalism. When there are no cars its rule will be over and we can turn to each other like Christians do in church, shake hands and say 'peace be upon you.'

It was obvious as soon as I turned off the main road that it was going to be a big climb to Faccombe. A dog walker said, 'It's a hell of a hill to ride up.'

An older man and a young woman were coming down the verge on horses. Urging it to step off the verge the man said to his horse, 'Go on you bitch,' and then, 'You cow,' when it faltered. Then he said 'Good morning' to me while I was still recovering from his outburst. As I passed the young woman's horse it let out an almighty fart. I said, 'Lovely.' She said, 'When you've got to go...'

The geology is chalk with flint.

Ashmansworth looked like nothing had happened since the 1930s (if you ignore the cars). The war memorial was modest. The preparations for a wedding in one big garden weren't.

There are now tiny lilac coloured flowers in the verge and little white ones with a yellow centre.

It was down from there and up another big hill towards Faccombe. Any turn off the main road away from the flat lands means extreme climbs and descents.

Four lightweight lads overtook while I was walking and one of them said, 'You know you want to.' I had no idea what self-justifying desire he was attempting to impose upon me. The sky suddenly became very ominous, the atmosphere heavy and still. I kept finding ants on me.

Faccombe, my fourteenth destination, belies its name by being on top of a hill. Its pub is called the *Jack Russell* inn. There is a heavy gated but anonymous mansion, a flint built church, and it is the centre of Faccombe Estates, the corporate descendent of the feudal lord.

I sat in the churchyard to reorder my maps and decide my route south.

It was hot, hotter than it's been so far, but the forecast is for a change. Faccombe Estate's managed deciduous woodland went on for miles – much of it with a deer fence around it.

I rode past an encampment in the woods and a bloke with a beard fixing a car, with a cylinder head in his hands, responded to my wave. I stopped, thought about it, and went back. It was the home and property of Becky and Jake, mother and son. Becky works in mental health in a big hospital, Jake is studying motor sport engineering at college. The older bloke clearly wasn't keen to talk and made himself scarce.

Over the gate Becky told me that Faccombe Estates were owned by Arthur Langdon, who a decade ago was the fifth richest man in Britain. She said his father led the military coup in Sudan and he was rewarded with an oil well. Faccombe Estates has another estate in Northumberland, which is the premier shooting estate outside Scotland. The royal princes regularly shoot on the Faccombe Estate in secret. We talked about how disgusting it all was – the senseless blowing away of life for the amusement of otherwise bored aristocrats and they liked my assertion that they only did it because they couldn't shoot working class people. They'd kept pigs, but decided it wasn't right, and hens, but the Doberman killed them all. The sloes that grow round here are the best around she said.

Becky asked me if I was wild camping – almost assumed that I was wild camping. I said I'd planned to, but hadn't done it because you never feel really secure. She said I was welcome to stay there, but it was early and I couldn't have stood the dogs. She also commented on my bike. Jake said he wanted to learn fabrication, but didn't want a generator shattering the peace where they lived. It's impossible to escape the modern world. They had a truck. Becky needs the internet for work, Jake for his studies. They were a lovely pair, salt of the earth, worth ten toffs any day of the week, partly doing their own thing, but at the same time intrinsically linked with the best and worst aspects of modern society – motor racing and a desperate mental health crisis.

Otherwise the whole area stank of money.

After three miles of downhill it was back to the main road. I haven't the energy for the endless climbs on the unclassified ones.

Yesterday I saw black butterflies, today bright yellow ones.

I was in the Bourne Valley. There were big motors with personalised registrations parked in bespoke oak sheds. A rat ran across the road. It made me laugh. The rat is no respecter of wealth, like we are.

I bought chutney and bread. I have learned to carry only what I will need to eat over the next few hours and to make meals from what I've got.

The next two things I saw in the gutter were a dead badger and a bloody great chrome plated spanner. The spanner probably had some value, the badger none.

The A road wasn't too bad – smooth with light traffic. I didn't stop to find out how the village of Enham Alamein got its name, but its crest is a poppy with a crown above.

Then I was in Andover, which is in Hampshire (and so might Faccombe Estates be). Or rather I was in the retail part that precedes Andover, and every other place. There was a bloke carrying a bundle of rods, but I don't think he was a lictor.

I rode into the centre and asked a postie if there was a Holland and Barrett. I'd been reading about cheese in my novel and fancied some vegan substitute for my lunch. To get to it I had to ride through the open market, where I heard all sorts of languages and accents. It was in the massive shopping centre, where thousands of people were at their Saturday entertainment – shopping.

It wasn't too difficult to get out of town, though one sign was obscured by overhanging trees, and a car full of Neanderthals were shouting at people randomly. I was soon on the road for Salisbury.

It was worth going out of my way for the cheese and I enjoyed a relaxing lunch in a field gate just beyond the A302 – see, our lives are governed by major roads.

The A343 to Salisbury was busy, fast and toxic, but it was just about tolerable. As always there were the cautious, the considerate, the brave and the downright bastards, today the latter class seemed to be towing caravans.

I watch drivers looking in their mirror after they've overtaken me dangerously to see if they've knocked me off and I'm lying broken in the road.

I rode through RAF (Middle) Wallop, which had plenty of hardware on display, and the Museum of Army Flying, which had a 'fun for all the family' WWII Day advertised. War – fun for all the family. That wasn't how it seemed to be in Croatia and Rwanda. Ironically a man was putting up signs for disabled parking.

When people overtake me too close with Help for Heroes stickers in the back I wonder if there's any conflict – they care so passionately about hoodwinked mercenaries, but not about ordinary people going about their business. I think the same when people with 'Child on Board' stickers cut me up.

It seems to me that the average Help for Heroes supporter is a bloke with a beer belly, tattoos and right wing opinions who'd also wear T shirts that say things like 'These colours don't run,' and 'Kill 'em all, let God sort 'em out,' and have a Staffordshire Bull terrier with a studded collar, or the female equivalent. The kind of person that thinks Tommy Robinson speaks for the white working class.

The working class don't have a colour or a culture. Class is precisely about seeing beyond the divisions our rulers exploit to what is in the collective interest, and what is in the collective interest is not killing foreign workers for oil and other resources.

I entered Wiltshire. The Ministry of Defence owns massive parts of Wiltshire. It's one of the bits of the empire the army has managed to hold on to – but it wouldn't be a surprise if it was flogged cheap to Capita and leased back in perpetuity. It uses the land to train young impressionable men how to kill foreign young men.

The Chalk Valley History Festival poster featured the same three fake WAAF dolly birds I'd seen in Lytham St Anne's. If the government wanted to inspire mindless jingoism in the nation it couldn't do better than encourage these sanitised celebrations of WWII.

There was most of a dead deer in the road. The cars just went round it, like they would if it was a cyclist. Nothing must stop the flow of traffic – it's the money in our veins.

I passed the turn off for Porton Down, which is euphemistically categorised under Public Health England, but as everyone knows is a chemical weapons research centre.

I suddenly realised I was enjoying myself. I stopped in a layby beside acres and acres of so-called free-range pigs. The whole site was dry, bare chalk. They were about as free range as the average French poodle. They really are horrible creatures, and they do put their feet in the trough. If they were really free range they'd be in an oak wood, rotated before they turned it into a desert. Keeping them like this is as cruel as if they were in pens because, given the choice, even pigs would not stay in this dust bowl.

Some other pigs had filled the layby with rubbish.

Approaching an Equine Therapy Centre drivers are asked to slow down in case there are horses. Horses deserve respect.

Years ago the obsession was with vehicle noise pollution. This was before it was realised (as if) that traffic posed many more serious dangers. Nowadays it is possible to buy a posh, fake 4x4 that comes out of the factory with a throaty roar that says 'I am.' The driver of one of these used his window washer as he went past me at low speed, when the water is obviously going to go right over the car. I couldn't possibly suggest he tried to wet me on purpose.

Salisbury is one more place ringed by four lanes of tarmac designed not to let anyone who isn't in a car find their way through. Fortunately, like the travellers of old, I could see the cathedral spire, which got me into the centre. Again there were accents and languages from all over – though this time some of them were visitors ogling Britain's glorious heritage.

My map showed a campsite at the racecourse and I headed south by the sun and then asked. A woman gave me good directions, but it was a long way, all up hill, and I was worn out.

There was an evening race meeting on, but the thousands of people attending had all arrived before me and I only had to make my way through the periphery to the campsite, which has nothing to do with the racecourse a sign says. It was £14.50. The man said he bet I'd been charged £50 and was surprised when I said my highest was £20 and my lowest five. He also said he bet I hadn't seen sitting rooms, coffee machines and microwaves on campsites before. I have, but I didn't say so. I suspect many of the campers and caravanners are at the races – and it's a bank holiday – because it's reasonably full, but there's no one about.

Some reactionary opposite is flying the Red Hand of Ulster up a big pole. Being an Ulster protestant is an accident of birth – flying the Red Hand is a political statement. It is to sanction and justify centuries of Catholic oppression and support the continuance of the sectarian Orange State.

On inspection it's a very nice site, with polite notices, plants and paintings in the facilities. I took my food to the kitchen dining room and used their on-tap hot water for my tea. It was luxury to sit on a comfortable chair to eat and read, instead of being propped up on my elbow.

From there I saw three 4x4 off-roaders come in and prayed they wouldn't be pitched next to me. They may of course be OK. On the other hand they may be drinking and talking all night.

I didn't have anything to cook – unless I cook porridge, so I ate the rest of my sweaty cheese with pittas and pickle and great handfuls of raisins for pudding, and all the tea I wanted without using my gas.

In the kitchen I met Rob from Bournmouth who came here to do a park run this morning with his girlfriend and stayed for the horse racing. He's doing another big run in the morning. While we were talking the after-racing music event started up. It wouldn't have been so bad if it was just music. But every song had that ridiculous booming bass even the old classics have to be redone to. You can feel it reverberating even though it's two fields away – and it goes on till 10.30. Call me a miserable old bastard but I think songs should sound different to each other.

Rob was about the sixth person to tell me I should write a book about my trip.

When I'd heard enough I went back to my tent. The 4x4 wallahs were next to me, about ten of them, and the music boomed on – 'We're up all night to get lucky, We're up all night to get lucky' – *ad nauseam.* Just what a person who's been listening to roaring cars all day needs. It was all very depressing – I wish I was back in the rain and snow in Scotland. The 4x4 lot are all Scots. 'I wanna dance with somebody who loves me,' sang the crowd. The ear plugs won't be enough tonight.

They're all shouting and laughing. Actually they're not Scots, they're east European and the shouting and laughing is getting louder as they drink, probably.

Day 37 – Salisbury to Bridport (via Ibberton)

(Wiltshire and Dorset)

Despite all the noise I went straight to sleep. When I woke up for a piss they were all still round their campfire like cowboys or Stone Age men. I went straight back to sleep again.

I woke at four just as the first signs of light were appearing. I thought I'd make use of the common room, but it was locked till

273

seven – I suppose to stop people having parties in it – it's one of those sites where they might.

I could still get in the foyer, but there was no access to the hot water boiler. Instead I could have paid £2.30 for any kind of coffee I wanted (i.e. with any amount of milk) from a big machine called Doozy that was clad in rustic wood to make it more attractive. There was even a choice of colours of cup that came out of three rubber sleeves. On them they said, 'I think you drank this yesterday.' 'I think you made the right decision,' and 'You're here again and it feels good.' It was marvellous piece of human ingenuity and engineering involving half a ton of materials and constantly using electricity that could have been replaced with a kettle, a jar of coffee and a few mugs.

My history book tells me that World War One was a great catalyst for female emancipation and talks as if witnessing the carnage at the front as nurses was some great privilege. The consciously upper class and often patronising Emmeline and Christabel Pankhurst are praised for acting as army recruiting sergeants (who saw no contradiction in campaigning for the emancipation of women while campaigning for the enslavement of men to the martial cause). The author cannot resist a slight on the socialist black sheep Sylvia, who did not engage with the moralising pressure on men to go and get themselves killed or maimed. The truth is that 'total war,' as the author acknowledges, required the complete ditching of all pre-existing prejudices. Afterward the government was effusive in hollow promises while trying its damndest to get the genie back in the bottle. Granting the franchise to posh women over thirty was the very least it could do to reward them for helping to send working class men to their deaths.

The weather has changed as predicted. It is decidedly cooler and windy. I am down to my last £20 note again. In no way could this be described as a cheap holiday.

At the top of the field I noticed someone is flying a Celtic flag, along with the Skull and Cross Bones, which may be St Pauli, the progressive Hamburg based football club that promotes anti-racism

Back on the road at six. It was between seventeen and twenty five pounds to get into the horse racing and picnics were only allowed in one enclosure.

In the absence of signage I headed south on the unclassified road and then struck west through the quiet villages – past the Old Malthouse and other hangovers from a functioning community with their new Range Rover residents, including BEK, with her big black one.

There is quite a breeze from the front.

The older houses are brick with split flint infill – the newer anything the heart desires. Much money has been spent on 'traditional' gates and railings.

In Broad Chalk the clear river runs beside the road through the clear consciences of the residents, just as it does in Midsomer Norton. The church is now the village store, the Old Bakehouse is a home and the *Queen's Head* offers fish Fridays and a new cider selection. The pub's sign is a new pound coin, rather than an image of the queen to which it was originally dedicated. This often happens – pub names are modified and distorted to suit the times. I think of the *Winston Churchill* in Bradford, which now celebrates the man and not the hill on which it stands, and a *Sportsman* I once saw whose sign depicted a speedway rider.

An old Triumph Herald burbled past me. There is thatch, rosemary tiles and slate – even one house in yellow stone that must have come from miles away. The roads were mostly level and where they weren't the hills were gentle. What would have once been a very big chicken farm, with dozens of ornate chicken style vents on the roof, had long since ceased to operate in favour of less ornate methods. The man at *Hillberry* styled himself a motorcycle racer on his house sign and only fifty yards further on was the entrance to today's Gurston Down Speed Hill Climb. The rolling hills were once more full of bleating sheep. There was now purple clover in the verge, along with clumps of small white and yellow flowers. Some hawthorn is still in blossom.

It was also a marked cycle route and it took me through Fifield Basant with its tiny isolated chapel and its big square stone house on the corner. Some man was flying the red ensign. The crows were numerous and raucous. The sun disappeared, the wind strengthened and high clouds massed. Hares ran full tilt across a field. A cyclist passed me and said nothing. Many have music on in their own little world. They are in training. The landscape is irrelevant.

Ebbesbourne Wake was fully moneyed, thatched and Range Rovered. There were signs for a dig – I thought it might be archaeology, and in a sense it was. I came upon Gary and Patrick doing traffic duty for a metal detectors' meeting in the field belonging to the big house. Gary is a market trader who has been selling fruit and vegetables for thirty five years. Patrick works in a car body shop and we talked about cars all being plastic and computerised, and body filler being a thing of the past. If you can't maintain and repair something you've bought yourself than you don't own it – the firm who made it does, and they own you too.

Gary looked a bit heavy, but healthy. Richard was thin with half his teeth missing. They didn't seem to have much idea about what they were looking for, but then who does? 'A bloke found some gold – it was Iron Age, no Bronze Age.' 'It's Wiltshire, there's Roman stuff and that.'

Gary and Richard asked me if I was wild camping as well, and I made my excuses why I wasn't. I'm beginning to feel soft and a bit of a fool for paying out the money, but none of those who ask have ever fly-camped.

I'd picked a hilly route they said. Hadn't I thought about an electric bike? I have, but not yet. There was a dead rat on the road, intact. It looked kind of sweet, almost smiling. 'Did you know that a rat gets finicky if he's overfed? He'll eat the eyes and liver out of a dead man and leave the rest. He'll pop out of a hole he's made in a dead man's cheek.'

Alvediston looked modest at first, but there was a stud and more mansions. The *Crown* claimed to be a seventeenth century free house with a large car park. The village notice board advertised yoga,

Buddhist meditation, open gardens, dog walking and a barn dance – no witch trials or public humiliations.

Berwick St John was bigger than the others and had two or three grand old mansions. The *Talbot* Inn advertised Morris dancing this evening. The First World War memorial was only a year old, a slate plaque on the end of the old school house – 'At the going down of the sun and in the morning we will remember them.' Churchill's words if I remember rightly, and the trendy silhouette of the slightly bowing soldier. It is a funny thing to do – suddenly think a hundred years after a war that you need to commemorate the people who died in it, and who can gain nothing from their revival.

Memorial
The warring band of brothers
Couldn't share a bed
And rather than negotiate
They had to fight instead

The baker and the cow hand
All they had to go
The turner and the weaver too
To save a world
That they would never know

Your country needs you bonny lads
This war must needs be fought
And it must be fought by men
There did not come the brave retort
'Well you go fight it then'

The great and good all sanctify
The workers blown to bits
If the dead could speak
Perhaps they'd say
Fuck off you hypocrites

The cycle route wanted to send me across the A30 into the hills on the northern side, but I was missing the taste of diesel and the roar of traffic, so headed straight for Shaftesbury.

A roadside mobility shop, selling battery powered chariots for a diseased population, flew a Union Flag. Why? No one, but no one, flew a union flag when I was young. Now it will be the last thing to stick above the waves when the country finally sinks. Unfortunately the flag won't save us, no matter how much we wave it.

The *Grove Arms* is old – it's a country inn. Aren't they all?

Charlton had a new Remembrance Hall, to go with our new sense of remembrance.

Perhaps a new level of desperate pretentiousness was reached in the *Rising Sun's* 'Coffee Tavern' serving barista coffee. Am I right in assuming that a barista is simply a worker who knows how to make coffee and that it is exactly who you would expect to be making your coffee? An empty slogan is one where the opposite could not be equally true – much like Churchill's rhetoric. 'Sheep shearer made coffee,' 'We will not fight them on the beaches, only in places of our own choosing.'

A yellow sign pointed to Chilmark Glade and someone towing a horse box overtook me on double white lines forcing a young woman coming the other way in a little Peugeot into the gutter.

I left Wiltshire and entered Dorset. The new housing development stopped fifty yards short of the border.

It was just before ten, but I bought my lunch at the big Tesco, waiting for the legal time supermarkets can sell things on a Sunday to pay, followed my nose around town and proved the featureless desert theory in fifteen minutes, ending up exactly where I'd been half an hour earlier. At the second attempt I left by the longest downhill I've seen on a main road since Scotland. A big gang of 'Bros' overtook me on ridiculous shop bought caricature choppers and it was still the wrong road. I had to weave through the hamlets to get to the B3091 for Sturminster Newton and my next destination.

When I stopped to brew up in a cut field my stove fell over on the rough ground onto my waterproof coat that I was using to sit on – leaving me sat in hot liquid for the second time.

Just after that, by Guys Marsh Prison, the first small drops of rain began to fall.

Once again it came to nothing. That's been the story of the spring and summer so far.

I came to a finger board sign that was pointing in the wrong direction – perhaps it was to confuse the Germans. Thankfully a passing cyclist put me right.

The *Plough* at Manston had shut. The grand house in brick was built in 1869. At Newton people were living in wooden houses that looked like they'd been there since the war.

Sturminster Newton traces its past to 1219, and once had the biggest calf market in Europe. They used to come and go by train – as did all the other farm produce. Today there is no market and no railway. That's progress. It has the *Poet's Corner* Café, the Friends of Blandford Community Hospital charity shop, a Brainwave charity shop, an Original Factory Shop and a Bulgarian food shop, and that was only the start.

The *White Hart* (1708), once the headquarters of the Cyclists Touring Club, was shut. The *Red Lion* was shut. There were a lot of classic cars about and the air stank of half burned hydrocarbons.

At the bottom of Glue Hill was a sign that said 'Please stick to the pavement' and it took me a while to get it. Someone had ambitiously called his new yellow fake stone town house *Rockdene*.

I was in the back of beyond again through Okeford Fitzpaine and Fifehead St Quentin. Here the blackberries were flowering.

I was hungry, but held off until Ibberton, my fifteenth destination. There was an event on at the village hall involving screaming children, so I went into the car park and announced myself to a woman called Louise. She said the village hall, a corrugated tin shed, used to be the church and that she used to live across the road. She said it was a lovely little village. I said it took some finding. She said everyone says that. But that's because half the fingerboard signs have fallen down. In other areas they have been in fully restored condition. Louise didn't ask me to stay, not when I told her she was one of the twenty six places on my itinerary, not even when I asked her where the nearest bench was, knowing full well it was across the road. If a pilgrim like me came to my village I'd give them more of a welcome than that.

Now all I had to do was find my way out of the maze I'd found my way into. The verges were full of wild garlic and my left arse bone is painful. It's not exactly my arse bone, it's some kind of carbuncle one gets.

A clock said it was a quarter to four. It can't be a quarter to four. That would mean I'd been cycling for ten hours and I didn't feel as if I'd got anywhere. I headed what I thought was west. It was walking steep and I stink. At the top I was high above the plain I'd been on all morning.

I was just thinking what a warren it was when I passed Warren Farm with no real idea where I was going – all I could do was stop at each finger post and plan anew – and then the signs for the place I'm aiming for disappear and I plan again. I know I'm riding miles further than I need to, and that's so annoying that it overrules everything else, like enjoying myself.

It was biscuit tin villages all the way, but because it was taking so long to get anywhere I decided to sack my planned trajectory and head towards the coast – you can't go wrong with the coast.

Basically there are five main roads running south and I was trying to dissect them in turn, which is bound to be difficult and involve a lot of climbing.

It still wasn't plain sailing, but straight into the centre of Dorchester. It is Thomas Hardy's birthplace, which is why the industrial estate is called *Casterbridge*, and the Victorian fair was called The Thomas Hardy Victorian Fair. A man in a big blue truck called a Barbarian overtook me more stupidly that I would have believed possible. Actually I could easily believe it possible.

Dorchester has an impressive main street (full of cars) and plenty of pubs offering accommodation, but I rode straight through, direction Bridport, on the A road, thinking it would be OK on a bank holiday Sunday tea time, and that it would be downhill all the way to the sea. I was wrong on both counts.

Dorchester used to be a barracks. Much of it still looks like one, especially the new stuff.

The A35 was actually a mad dieselfest and I could taste the stuff by Winterbourne Abbas, where the *Waggon and Horses* had closed.

The road went up and down like a rollercoaster – long hard climbs, fast descents and very fast cars. I aimed for Bridport because there were campsites shown on the map, bypassed the centre and to the first one at West Bay. It was full of a private rally. I had to ride all the way back to the busy roller-coaster at 7.45 when I'd had enough and more. The next site had a drive half a mile long with wide expanses of grass either side, but the woman on reception said it was full. She did her best to find me somewhere else without success. She said she'd tried all the other sites and they were all full. She looked for B&Bs. They were all full as well. I had to return to the A35 and was resigned to either camping out in a field or sitting in a bus shelter in Lyme Regis until it got light again. It looked like for the first time in five weeks I was going to come unstuck.

I knocked at a B&B in the village to no response. I could see the next campsite was chocka. I went to reception anyway with nothing to lose. Reception was closed. I went into the packed bar. They were rushed off their feet, but a man said if I found a bit of grass I could stay. I found a bit of grass by the road right next to the bar/entertainment centre, but I don't care. I've to pay in the morning. There's nothing to fasten my bike to, but it should be OK. There's kids everywhere but if I could sleep last night I'll sleep tonight. Immense relief all round. It was turned eight o'clock – fourteen hours after I started cycling and a mad amount of miles. This morning seems a week ago.

And then the campervan man who thought it was his pitch came back. He was stressed and angry and not at all interested in my tale of woe, or that I'd cycled from Salisbury (did I really do that?) and started going on about coming from Luton. As he was stressed and English wasn't his first language there was no point in trying to make light of the situation and all I could do was apologise profusely. He managed to squeeze in, but carried on walking about stressing in public while I was cooking and eating my tea. There are people on site speaking all sorts of languages. By the time I'd showered it was dark and I was asleep as soon as my head hit my dirty pink blow up pillow.

I wasn't impressed with West Bay, it was mobbed out with people milling around eating fish and chips. I've timed it as badly as I could possibly have done, coming to the south coast on a bank holiday when the kids are off for a week.

Day 38 – Bridport to Crediton (via Jack in the Green)

(Dorset and Devon)

Up early, before anyone else. The place is absolutely chocka. It's camping, but not as we know it.

For the first time on the trip there's a phone box that takes coins and I didn't have enough change. If I had, I would have rung Oades, not knowing if I really wanted to as it might break the spell.

The A35 is already roaring, only now there's wagons too, but from here there is a minor coast road, along which I expect to see the holidaying Briton in all his glory.

I walked to the toilet block with a young man and told him about the irate campervan man. He asked if it was a VW – 'VW campervanners are like that,' he said – and I thought VW campervans were the ultimate in chill, 'I'd rather be surfing,' etc. – so much so that there's a big market for form over substance replicas made in Brazil.

I was breakfasted, packed up and ready to roll before there was anyone in reception and could just have ridden out. But the bloke trusted me so I waited.

My honesty cost me £29, which is bare faced opportunist robbery. I've had a B&B for £35. I wish I'd fucked off, but hung about thinking they'd never trust anyone else – but who cares? I need to get done here and blow – some of the B&Bs the other receptionist looked up for me last night wanted £150. 'It should have been £36,' the receptionist said, without shame, 'but seeing as it's only a one man tent...' No wonder there was a camper van parked in a layby just down the road. And no wonder Oades and I resorted to fly-camping. It's downright robbery. How glad I am that I live in the north and not among these thieves. Being down here is a mistake in anyone's book and where the clever plan I had falls down.

Charmouth was charming – all the pubs were decked out in union flags and St George crosses, and a new one on me – the silhouetted soldier made entirely of poppies with the slogan 'There but not there.' It is absolutely sick making. Jingoism is replacing a coherent social fabric.

I got a big smile from a nurse or care assistant walking to work in the sunshine. She wasn't British, she was Johnny Foreigner, the person the loud-mouthed patriot loves to hate because he's got nothing else in his sad little life.

Lyme Regis is an ancient royal borough. Its Jurassic coast is a world heritage site. All I can say is that when I arrived at 8.45 it was fairly quiet, though there were still people with dogs on twenty foot leads who didn't have the gumption to know that not everyone thinks dogs are brilliant. One man ran like a four year old onto the beach with his pet despite numerous signs prohibiting the dirty things.

An empty shop had its windows covered with a newspaper from 1945, obviously a patriotic reproduction. On the front page was a hubristic account of Hitler's defeat. Inside a smiling Stalin who had come up trumps – Russia's so-called socialist citizens dying in their thousands to save capitalism.

Walking up the main street I met Kerry and Murray, two clearly well off Australians doing the European grand tour. Murray was a firefighter and had mates who'd come from Britain to Australia and loved it. Everyone I've talked to who's been to Australia didn't like it for its racism and unfriendliness. We were doing OK discussing where was nice and where was busy in Britain – even they were astonished at £29 for camping, saying everything is twice as much for Australians. Their next day trip is to the Minnack Theatre to see *Sister Act*. I couldn't remember which film that was. Kerry said, 'it's the one with the ni... – black actress,' stopping herself before the word came completely out, obviously being aware of their reputation abroad. They said lots of British people had gone to Australia (most of them racists I suspect) and loved the pub culture etc. Kerry said as many as wanted to come could come, 'it's better than the other bludgers.' I didn't ask what a bludger was because by then I'd had enough of their latent prejudices, but I don't expect it's complimentary – people who don't work possibly.

Murray said he liked my 'I Still Hate Thatcher' badge. He didn't really like it because if he'd have been British he'd have been a fan. 'She's dead,' he said. 'We should dig her up and cut her head off,' I said. I'm not joking, but she's not buried – her grave wouldn't have lasted a week intact, even statues of her get vandalised, as they should. It is worth restating, and reminding the working class reactionaries who grew up in the good years, who assert as if it's gospel that she 'saved the country,' that Thatcher is responsible for setting in train the sociopathic economic policies of Hayek and Friedman that began to reverse all the gains of the sixties and have led to a deliberate redirection of wealth upwards. She was a class fighter of the first order in a country where class is regularly asserted to be a thing of the past. Class will never be a thing of the past until the majority class is in charge.

In Tesco's at Bridport, which had hiked its prices accordingly, the local paper said a third of local children were living in poverty. I saw some of them yesterday playing beside the A35 where they live. When they're worn out, breathless, on inhalers and unable to work when they're thirty five, moralising lickspittle supporters of the status quo will have a special derogatory name for them.

The hill out of Lyme Regis is a grade one bastard and there'll be many more of them to come. I hate it down here. As I left on the road to Seaton the massive car parks were rapidly filling. 'Let's pick a place where everyone goes and go there.' It's elitist to say you don't want to go where there are tourists and grockles, but it's hell if you don't.

A man let his dog have a little bark at me before gently encouraging it into his gate.

At the top I left Dorset, whose motto is 'Who's afear'd' – who's afraid to overcharge presumably – and entered Devon, which I don't expect to be any better. Its motto is *Auxilio Divino*. There is a grass overspill car park I could easily have slept in and no one would have been any the wiser.

East Devon sells itself as an area of outstanding natural beauty, but doesn't mention being an area of extreme human ugliness.

In fact there were lots of places I could have slept and a much nicer 'normal' campsite that didn't look over full, but I'd done all I could do last night. I sat in just such a field entrance for an extended break – even though I'd only been going an hour and a half. From the tracks in the grass I suspect a camper van has been here too.

There was no real decision about whether to go into Seaton and Sidmouth or stay on the main road, as terrible as it was. To descend into the bays and climb out again would have taken all day and I had no particular desire to be subjected to a sea of obesity and philistinism. The main road it was. May the Lord be with me. The hordes seemed to be heading home.

Colyford claims a history going back to 1230, but like the caretaker's old broom there is nothing left of the original shaft or head. Two fully geared up touring cyclists came the other way. Clearly flustered the man hit the kerb trying to make himself heard over the traffic. The woman came alongside and an angry and impatient van driver blew his horn at them. No one thinks, 'These people are obviously on tour, I'll give them a bit of space to decide where they're going.'

The road wasn't too bad, but it only takes one of the dangerous bastards to kill you. The road signs are 'crash friendly.' I'm not. I began a poem which became;

That awareness raising thing

We all know what great clarity
Some facts and figures bring
So let's all do together
The awareness raising thing

It's almost automatic
When we have all liaised
That earth will be uplifted
On the awareness we have raised

My knowledge was abysmal
My awareness was a laugh
Now there's a giant uptick
On my awareness graph

We may just face a crisis
But until then let's sing
Cos we're happy to be doing
The awareness raising thing

So let's all raise awareness
Pile fact on dismal fact
Till we all know what the problem is
And it's become too late to act

rejected verses

So let's all raise awareness
Show how aware we are

Not go and buy a bicycle
And fasten it to our car

I've heard the planet's dying
My awareness has been raised
But by doing next to nothing
We can't hope to be praised

I've seen it on the telly
Time and time again
I know the ice cap's melting
So can I fly to Spain

I know that cotton growing
Is polluting round the globe
But I've still got fifty T shirts
In my Swedish made wardrobe

With my awareness lifted
I'll know what the problems are
I won't try to save the planet
With a new much greener car

I know that diesel's killing us
And using it isn't cool
So can I use a diesel car
To take my kids to school

If I want to save the hedgehog
Coral and impala
Can I buy those sugar snaps
That come from Guatemala

One can only assume that when three cars in procession give you plenty of room and the fourth one comes too close that the fourth one has done it on purpose.

There was a substantial roadside memorial to Thomas Gilbert-Smith MD, FRCS, who, after watching a glorious sunset on 3rd August 1904, fell dead from his bicycle on this spot. As he was a good bloke thunder and lightning immediately followed.

Shortly after that I turned off the coast road for Ottery St Mary, having survived one more dice with madness.

Dog Friendly Devon

I like the 'doggies welcome'
And little signs that say
There is no dog pooh fairy
So let's all go on holiday
To Ottery St Mary

It was a single track road and they simply cannot take their life and mine in their hands and overtake when there is something coming the other way, plus the traffic is much slower.

I stopped to recover and watched a strong wind blowing a tall cornfield.

The car park at the *Hare and Hounds* at the junction with the A375 was full. The smell of deep fried traditional home cooking filled the air. The Caravan and Motorhome Club site at Potts Corner had had to make a little extra hanger for their sign, 'Sorry no tents.' Tents are for poor people. With some exceptions caravan and campervan people are snobs engaged in a never-ending battle of hierarchical one-upmanship – they are an extension of the malaise that pervades the motor and housing markets, personified in the slogans of some manufacturers and builders that you are no one till you own their product. We are all no one and no amount of accumulated stuff can change that – that's why rich celebrities turn to Buddhism – because endless acquisition and consumption are empty.

While I was sitting on the wall outside Ottery St Mary church a big four prop military plane went lumbering over, twice. And then again. No one looked up. It must be normal to have great big war machines above everything else.

Ottery St Mary is quite big. Its inhabitants once worked in a big mill, which is now derelict. God knows what they do now – wait on holiday makers, the mentally ill and the senile, probably. There are a remarkable number of care homes, one styling itself 'Your home from home by the sea.' It must be like elephants going to Devon to die.

The Kings School doesn't look like the other posh fee-paying schools I've seen in Oxfordshire and Berkshire, but the sign says it was founded in 1545, when about 1% of the population were lucky enough to get an education of any kind.

The front pages of all the serious papers feature the fratricide at the top of the Tory Party and within the wider ruling class.

The big pub coming into Rockbeare had become an oriental restaurant, but still had a public bar. A massive housing estate was under construction – uninspiring boxes, rendered and painted garish colours.

Jack in the Green, my sixteenth destination, was just a big food pub of that name, as I suspected it would be. It celebrated twenty five years in business in 2017. Like many of these places – the *Marsh* in Cleckheaton for example, it was a fairly old building with modern extra seating extensions built on to deal with the fashion for eating out that never existed when I was young. Nowadays any pub that does not do food, either basic, like Weatherspoon's, or pretentious, like those that call themselves eateries and gastropubs, is doomed.

At the vets opposite an assistant was walking a paggered little dog round the car park attached to a saline drip. Do these people not see the TV pictures of children in Yemen? – the owners I mean – the staff are just engaged in one more pointless, socially useless job that pays the bills.

289

I very nearly came a holiday finishing cropper trying to mount a little kerb to write about it, which I've done before and hurt myself.

There was a big brand new massive chain pub at Cranbrook – the kind that will drive the smaller ones out of business, as the supermarkets have shut all small filling stations and, along with the Co-op, are proceeding to do the same to small grocers with their aggressive market domination. And why would you go into small shops and pay twice the price unless you were on a bicycle trip and panicked?

There was another enormous new housing estate at Cranbrook, built by swilling in money Persimmon. I know housing is needed, but where's it all going to end? (Probably in the collapse of the housing market, negative equity and all that stuff).

One could get the impression that house building is keeping the whole economy afloat – along with gambling, speculation and money laundering in the city. As it's all on green field sites miles away from any work it just means more and more traffic (which also stimulates the economy).

A Lada went past. There aren't many of them left. Earlier today I heard the unmistakable sound of a Russian flat twin and a Ural outfit came round the corner.

An RAF helicopter flew over.

A bit further on a great big business park was under construction. It's all completely insane.

Some fantastic cycle paths had been incorporated into all the construction work, some of them even told me where I was going. I pissed in a ploughed field. It looked like the most water it had had in months.

I stopped to talk to three youths before crossing the M5 on a high bridge on the cycle route. The spectacle is breath-taking. Looking south it's like the Champs Elysee without the artefacts. One of the lads said 'nice bike,' so I went back. Then he said he bet he could wheelie it.

The cycle route led me a merry dance so I followed the sun and was spot on. Out past the jail, do not pass campsite, and an equestrian statue of some imperialist, 'He saved Natal' – from what? It was ten to five – at least an hour after I should have stopped. The Weatherspoon's in the student area was called *The Imperial*. It had rooms, but I rode out for Crediton, tired.

A steam engine went the other way on a Foden low-loader. It rained a bit and that smell came off the hot road which I have been told is made by microbes.

Three vehicles passed in ten minutes belching black smoke that hung over the road. All the exposure to traffic fumes is giving me a sore throat.

There are no campsites between Exeter and Crediton.

Crediton associates itself with St Boniface. The first thing you see is a big brand new housing estate, the second a big Tesco, the third a big food pub. Different town, same shit. A family had their French windows open two feet from the A377. The Holy Cross church is red stone and ornate. It needs £1.5 million to repair the roof. It was six o'clock.

There was nowhere to stay and the whole place was covered in traffic filth, it is a dirty nothing place.

A mile or two beyond I'd just about abandoned all hope when there was a sign for farmhouse B&B half a mile off the main road. I've never stayed on a farm before because I've always thought them to be mucky and full of animals, but David and Angela Searle's farmhouse B&B at North Hollocombe was immaculate.

David is 68 and Angela 61, which is about the average age for farmers in the UK. Angela asked if I'd eaten. I lied because I don't want a fuss – I've stuff to nibble on. David only showed his face and Angela is the proprietor on the back of the door info.

Asked about breakfast, and being on a farm, I ashamedly said I was vegan, but Angela was used to it. She said she thought she had some Stella McCartney sausages and went through the other possible ingredients (Stella McCartney is of course the living millionaire fashion designer daughter of Paul 'Beatle' McCartney, whereas Linda McCartney, nee Eastman, is the long dead first wife of Sir Paul, heir to the Kodak fortune and founder of a range of vegetarian foods that still bear her name).

With the EU election results now in, the media are calling it the most shocking election result ever. On only a 37% turnout Nigel Farage's Brexit Party, which wants a no deal exit now, got just under 40%, and the Lib Dems, who want to stop Brexit by any means, got just over 40%. Labour and the Tories had their worst result in any national election ever. It might be assumed that the election shows the country to be fundamentally divided, but what it actually shows is that over 60% of people have lost all faith in the process and have more important things on their plates.

Nigel Farage is now one of the most important politicians in the country, along with whoever is in charge of the LibDems. In an interview Farage did very well in portraying his two month old party as one with a coherent political program. Vince Cable said there are now two choices regarding Brexit – leave with no deal or annul the referendum result altogether.

Helen Dunmore devotes several pages to the camaraderie soldiers have for each other – it's the 'no greater love...' thing put into the horse's mouth – the kind of solidarity the bosses hate when it's shown in any other line of work.

The forecast is for twenty seven degrees in the south east over the next couple of days, but I'm not there yet.

'The Vet' Angela mentioned turned out to be an Australian guest and I wished I was part of the conversation I could hear bits of rather than skulking in my room.

I soon put the TV off, finding nothing worth watching, but messed about with my maps for too long, poring over possible routes that might provide some pleasure but not get me lost and take all day to get nowhere. If I am to finish the ride in the two months I set myself I have less than three weeks left and it will take the rest of this week to reach my furthest point south and get back here.

My heart was pounding when I settled down, like when I've had coffee or I'm excited, but I soon fell asleep.

I was awake in the night though and a dog had several barking episodes.

For the second time my scabby earlobe made blood marks on the pillowcase. It's still very sore from overexposure to the sun in the first couple of weeks.

I read *The Lie* when I should have been sleeping. I would have been sleeping if I was in my tent, where I can't put the light on at the slightest provocation.

'"Ignorant armies..."' he said. That's very good isn't it?'

'"The guns cut across the lines rather don't they," as if where the firing came from was the only place that was real.'

'It was what happens when nothing mattered, or everything mattered in the same dull, ugly, pointless way, day after day after day.'

There was a heavy shower that beat against the window.

The response from Labour is likely to be that they should back a second referendum. Brexit has fucked the Tories, but it's fucked Corbyn too – he may as well have gone with his conscience and tried to win the argument for leaving the EU bosses' club.

I eventually went to sleep again, worried I'd got cancer of the earlobe or a flesh-eating disease.

Day 39 – Crediton to Lydford (via Zeal Monachorum)

(Devon)

Rain against the window woke me at 6.30. Eleven people have been killed trying to climb Mount Everest this year. The TV news has made great play of queues of climbers on their way to the summit.

At breakfast 'The Vet,' curly wet look, longhaired, denim shirted Travis, wasn't interested in talking. He was only interested in his mobile phone. I got the impression he was working on the farm – perhaps in some sort of exchange. It was clear neither he nor his parents believed in stereotypes because they'd chosen to call him Travis and he'd decided to wear his hair in long wet-look ringlets.

Angela was a bit Dawn French. The breakfast was filling and well presented, but a bit deep fried. The décor was classical in a 1960s way, with glass, silver and family pictures.

When I put my dog tag on the string was still wet with yesterday's sweat. I thought about apologising for my obvious odour, but didn't.

Even the farmer's wife asked did I 'just pop under a hedge' with my tent, which makes you feel like a bloody fool for paying rip off prices. She has, of course, never 'popped under a hedge' in her life, because she is like Annie Sugden, whose job it is to look after men who work hard on the farm.

Angela said to come again on the way back, and I might have done, but the plan is to go south of Dartmoor on the return leg. She sent me off through Coleford, a thatched and whitewashed hamlet, with five pounds in loose change, which, along with the fried breakfast, made the climb out of the other side all the more interesting.

The chances of not getting wet today are slim, and tomorrow even slimmer.

My crow flew from pole to pole ahead of me, leaving off its breakfast of squashed squirrel when it saw me coming.

There was a good shower half an hour in and it's always a debate about whether to don waterproofs. My clothes dry easily, but it can take ten dry miles if I get a good soaking and there aren't going to be ten dry miles this morning. At least the trees have leaves on for some shelter. This wasn't the case when I set off. Any more than five minutes though and the rain begins to drip through them.

From there it was through the village of Bow, across the main road and, it being Devon, up and down some big hills to Zeal Monachorum – 'cell of the monks' – my seventeenth destination.

The village is a rendered, whitewashed and tiled one-streeter on a steep hill, with a gated mansion at the top by the church. The rich are always by the church. I sat on a carved bench that replaces one made by Frank Howard in 1977 to mark the Queen's Jubilee, the present one being made by his son Roy in 2012. On it is inscribed, 'If all the world were paper and all the sea were inke if all the trees were bread and cheese how should we do for drink?'

A woman came out of the posh house and looked down the hill because the electricity had gone off. There was nothing going on down the street. I was right at the top looking down like one of the kings of Bohemia.

A woman came by with two Labradors on long leads so they could piss on everyone's gate post. Three more dog walkers were at the same job. No one offered to speak to me and I don't want their dogs near me anyway.

It was comfortable – so I sat for an hour drinking fruit tea and watching the blossom fall from an ancient tree. Lots of people saw me but none spoke. Zeal Monachorum has lots of high walls and closed gates. St Peter's church is small, but has fluted pillars, a vaulted side aisle and a rood screen. The pulpit is dedicated to those who died in World War One and there is a picture of a Merlin helicopter on the wall that was given to the church by 820 Naval Air Squadron, HMS *Culdrose*. Whether a church is the right home for pictures of military hardware it is not my place to say. The names of rectors went back to 1276. They were all men until 2010. There was a book on display – 'The Servant Queen' – about how Her Majesty has a big cross to bear.

In the absence of anyone to tell about my achievement I wrote about it in the visitor's book. I should have put 'disappointed no one spoke to me.'

On the way back down I could see Dartmoor in the distance and a bird of prey soared on the wind, but this is normal. An old building had a window glazed in a way I wouldn't have considered – small panes all lapped over each other in vertical strips.

I crossed the preserved Dartmoor Railway and a campsite at about noon, before climbing the massive hill two miles before Okehampton. The first sight was of a town that looked as if it had been built last week – about two hundred stark new houses resembled a Lego village as much as anything could. Another two hundred were under construction across the way and a new primary school had been built among. On the hillside opposite, more of the same. It would be interesting to discover by what percentage Okehampton, or many other such places, have grown in the last decade, population, land area etc.

I had my lunch on the site of the town's first prison, which has a chain and a plaque on the wall and some bars to amuse the kids. Afterward I met cycle tourers Josh and Ria from Holland, who were cycling from Harwich to Plymouth and then back along the coast. They were looking for a bike shop to get their chains oiled. I said I had some oil and an old toothbrush with which to apply it – it's in a little holder fastened to my frame – but Josh wasn't interested in that – he wanted to do it easy, in other words to pay someone else to do it. It's a two minute job that a five year old could do. They said it was hilly. It is. But then anything is hilly beside Holland. They were disgusted that I'd been turned away from a campsite at seven o'clock in the evening, saying they should never turn away cyclists, and so they shouldn't. Perhaps they have rules in Holland that make sense and are to do with people's needs, rather than rules for their own sake and jobsworths who apply them.

The marked cycle route rises steeply out of the centre and I decided to take it, rather than the main road, in the hope that it would take me to Tavistock, where two campsites are shown on my map.

For the first few miles it runs alongside the preserved railway line, just like one could do beside every railway line in the land. The track is still on the same oak sleepers it was on when it was closed decades ago by short-sighted money grubbing fools. Way down below runs the mad A30 speedway, with all the little individuals in their little cars exercising free will and freedom of choice in this great consumerist democracy.

It was flat and level up on the high ground. There were rail tracks going everywhere and a big overgrown siding. It was one more case of criminal neglect of what it had destroyed men and resources to build – and these people are in charge of the NHS. Not everything was going in the right direction in the sixties and the destruction of the railways in favour of individual transport would have suited Thatcher down to the ground. The proof of the argument that the railways should never have been destroyed is in the environmental destruction we see today – and in the belated reopening of stations on some of the remaining lines.

When the preserved stretch of track stops the cycle path crosses Meldon Viaduct – a giant feat of engineering in itself – and there were thousands of them on the network, most of them now pulled down and sold for salvage because we are stupid wasteful creatures.

From there we are on the old track bed and colour pictures along the way show us, me, lots of other groups of cyclists, groups of walking boy scouts, the railway that could still be if we weren't governed by people interested only in profit.

I spoke to two groups of touring cyclists on various trips, but didn't record their names. There was a clown cycling with a dog on a long lead which is dangerous for them and everyone else, and another with a dog in a trailer.

And then it all stopped at Lydford, where The Granite Way ends – for lack of funds and permission I suppose. I was all set to ride on to Tavistock, which is off my proposed trajectory, but has campsites, when a brown sign for one at Lydford appeared like a miracle. Bollocks I thought – I deserve an early finish. So before three there I was pitched and sitting on a bench dedicated to the founders, Noreen Calcott and Peter Waldergrave-Stokes, who 'spent many happy years together establishing this campsite.' You don't think of people struggling to establish a campsite as a kind of mission when you're being ripped off at the coast, but it's clear some of them do. At Salisbury racecourse site pictures were proudly displayed in the recreation area of the campsite under construction. This is a beautiful site with a clear view over to what I suppose are Great Knesset, Lynch Tor, Cocks Hill and Great Mis Tor, but I could be wrong.

Peter Waldergarve-Stokes was 'an independent traveller, adventurous to the end.' And fair play to him, which is what the groundsman, who may also be the proprietor, said about me when he discussed my homemade bike – and he was an engineer by trade. He said my bike was like an army bike. It isn't, it's just green. He said army bikes had forks like mine because they chucked them out of planes. Army bikes didn't have forks like mine and the ones they chucked out of planes were folders nothing like mine. It's the green paint that gets them going – they don't want to believe anything that's army green isn't army. But he was a nice man and so was the old lass on reception, who's got my cider in her fridge – my first drink since Lytham St Annes.

At £8.50, nearly a quarter of what I paid two nights ago, I thought I was entitled to two tins of Strongbow, a bag of nuts and a packet of biscuits from the shop. It still only came to £12.50.

The First World War destroyed the once great Liberal Party due to its ambiguity over conscription and hesitancy in joining a Grand National Coalition. I'd like to bet it wasn't the war that destroyed it, but the jingoistic pro-war press – just as they attempt to do with any anti-war activist today. The Liberals' place in British politics was taken by the Labour Party, which also contains pro and anti-war factions. But on the whole they'll back any war and they'd back conscription again should it become necessary.

The real beneficiaries of the war were the Tories, the party of war, national war and class war.

Britain won the imperialist war and in doing so extended its empire into the Middle East, just as it was becoming obvious that it couldn't hold on to it. Ireland led the way in the war to boot Britain out.

The Dutch couple, Josh and Ria, turned up and bought themselves a can of Stella each. They're on to a winner selling beer in the little shop. Serious drinkers wouldn't pay the inflated prices, but cyclists only want the odd can.

The cider made me sleepy. I lay on my back on my air bed with my legs out of my tent and fell immediately asleep, which won't do me any harm. It was luxury

I loved the slightly intoxicated, warm, half awake and half asleep feeling and I thought this was the best possible thing I could be doing with my life. Oades is far away in another world. I cannot miss her, or home, because they have ceased to have any reality. Reality now is waking up. Packing my few things and cycling. Tomorrow I will have been out for forty days and I could carry on like this forever.

In the trenches Billy Ranson goes off for sticks to boil a dixie for tea. For some reason coming along the trench he lifts his head. 'At that very same moment a rattle of machine gun fire crosses the spot where Billy Ranson's forehead rises above the rim of the earth. Earth and stuff out of Billy flies around like a blizzard. He folds up backwards without a sound. There he is: dead, his face, thank Christ, turned the other way. In an instant, in the blinking of an eye, he's not Billy Ranson anymore. His little fire is still going. And what I feel isn't shock or anger or even pity for him: it's annoyance. It sounds a simple enough thing: a wet grey morning and Billy Ranson here one minute and gone the next, but I can't get past it, and no one who wasn't out there can get anywhere near it.'

And a century later people like David Cameron, the millionaire son of a millionaire son, and Tony Blair, who sent young British men into futile wars in Iraq and Afghanistan against the wishes of the British people put on their black coats and stand at the cenotaph as if they know what war is about. It's about the fucked up men who'll never be right again because they were stupid enough to do what they were told, thinking they were doing right because their betters said they were. Men who drink or hang themselves to make the nightmares stop. It's nothing to do with being heroic. And treating them as heroes is guilty conscience because we know we shouldn't have let them go. It's in all of us to say no to our sons and brothers being sent off to war. 'We didn't volunteer, they came to get us.'

The sky is the classic one painted on chapel ceilings by famous artists, mostly blue with bulky, white, slow moving clouds.

Josh and Ria made an attempt to communicate. They had a big tent, folding chairs and smart clothes and went off to the pub to eat.

The sun has gone off my tent and the breeze is cool. I made my meal – porridge with baked beans and an Oxo. I planned to wash my pan, fill my water bottles and go to sleep, but as I was walking to the facilities a man who looked like an overgrown boy scout was walking up with three lads and a dog. The dog barked at me on my way back to my tent. I hate dogs. The periphery of the site, ten yards from where I'm pitched, is the official dog toilet circuit and the evening parade began.

I went out like a light – after deciding that if it was raining early in the morning I'd set off later and if it kept raining I'd stay where I was.

Day 40 – Lydford – rest day
(Devon)
I slept soundly all night. It was properly light when I woke and raining. I fell back asleep and dreamed I was pushing my bike through a town. Even though it was warm a copper in a big black coat was leading a woman he had in handcuffs. There were paratroopers on the streets with weapons. A woman with an Irish accent locked the royal family in a room and threw away the key. I said I was in Ireland when I was nineteen and had no idea what I was doing there, but now knew a lot about the situation. She said I knew nothing about it, walked off, turned a somersault and went into a house. Then I was walking with Oades. We had a disagreement and she walked off. Then she came back and accused me of saying there were soldiers with guns, but they wouldn't kill you and I had to make up my mind which side I was on. I woke up and it was still raining.

Once I'd pissed in my pan and tipped it out under the fly sheet I was comfortable for as long as it took, with enough food to last all day. The only problem is my small tent does not really allow for boiling water inside without risking a spillage or setting it on fire. I don't want to get wet. I've no dry knickers or socks until I get to a big Asda or Sports Direct and there isn't going to be one of those for a while.

'Officers and men selected to take part in the operation should, where possible, be volunteers. The men should be quartered together in a comfortable billet for the week preceding the operation.'

On night-time trench raids soldiers weren't expected to shoot the enemy. That was too noisy. They were expected to stab or beat them to death with army issue knives and truncheons. In other words they were expected to kill other young men at close quarters with their bare hands. This is what Special Forces are trained to do today. It was what the paratroopers did to young Argentines in the Falklands War. It's messy and it can be wasteful of your own human collateral if your enemy is properly trained and not just hastily conscripted schoolboys.

Nowadays our heroes mostly kill the enemy cleanly from 30,000 feet or they get the Americans to do it from screens is Nevada, like it's a computer game, played by young men who still play computer games.

'Ignorant armies clash by night.'

'They ought to have put the graveyards of all the dead over here... miles and miles of them, going from town to town. Hasty wooden crosses like the ones we make, all leaning different ways from shell blast. Bodies blown out of their graves.'

For better or worse

Much too young men married
Before heading off to France
It was a new beginning
But alas they'd had their chance

The many men, so beautiful
And they all dead did lie
And a thousand thousand slimy things
Lived on: and so did I

And God saw all that he had made
And marked 'good' on his card
But if he thought that all was good
He looked not very hard

It didn't seem dull. I didn't look out but it was bright in my tent. The wind blew fine rain against it and I could hear other couples huddled up and talking.

There were brothels organised for the men in France. That's how much they thought of the men who were fighting for the country – so much cattle with animal passions to be satisfied – just another problem of logistics – degrading the heroes by providing it and degrading the women even more. That's how much they care for the working class in the trade of war or sex – these suited Oxbridge millionaires who turn out at the cenotaph each November and for the rest of the year make hypocritical pronouncements about the military pact, the duty of care for the fucked up youths the tabloids call heroes.

When I looked out it was horrible fine rain blowing at you and a full grey sky. I'm staying here. The Dutch couple haven't moved either.

'They say the war's over, but they're wrong. It went too deep for that. It opened a crack in time, a crater maybe.'

The other was a softer voice,
As soft as honeydew
Quoth he, 'The man hath penance done,
And penance more to do.'

I finished my novel. The war hero is driven to his death, possessed by nightmares, by people who didn't go and can never understand.

I've no idea what time it is. I'd guess mid-morning. The air is still full of miserable drizzle.

If you wanted a trip
Without hectoring sessions
Stick to the road
And avoid the digressions

A dog barked in the distance. The dog belonging to Baden Powel and his boys barked in response. He said, 'Be quiet Sally.' Sally carried on, shattering the peace.

My Tesco note book is made in India.

The Daily Mail's a mouthpiece
And jingoism's free
Take who you want for heroes
So long as it's not me.

One of the most annoying things, even on the nicest campsite, apart from dogs, is the tendency of the staff to go everywhere on small tractors. And for some reason one had to be twice up my end of the field, even though it was persistently raining. From inside a thin tent at ground level it sounds like an armoured vehicle is about to flatten you – and this is beside the terrible smell and noise they make. There is no reason why the bins can't be emptied with a handcart and the use of these toys is a sign of the lazy and gadget obsessed society we've become.

And as for that great get out
That God made all men free
Which of those poor conscripts
Did any free will see?

And then a third time came he back
His tractor loud and roaring
I thought that he had work to do
But he was just exploring

No more is greed the cause of war
Than nations are a fact
It's for the profit motive
The band of robbers act

The arms trade is a gold mine
Peace would its rights deny
As long as that's a fact of life
Young men will have to die

But the barking dog annoyed me most. It made me grind my teeth. I could have driven my pen into its heart.

But God is not the cause of war
Or yet the cause of peace
And nor are human nature
Or testosterone release

Or taken its head off in one swing with a big sword.

I walked down to see if they'd got a book exchange and got talking to the campsite man in reception. He asked more questions about my bike. He used to have a car repair business and then a holiday coach firm. Now he's got a campsite and an electric bicycle and tried to convince me I needed one. He told me how simple the engines were on various coaches and about their cylinder configurations – and moaned, like all practical men do, about how electronics had ruined everything. We talked about different sorts of welding, MIG and TIG. He was old school and liked brazing because you could do cast iron and everything. I told him I'd been to Mongolia welding on Russian motorcycles and he said, 'It's funny what you do.' It was a quarter past twelve.

His wife was in the laundry, which also held the modest book exchange, mostly trashy love stories and murders. I don't read about murder (unless it's state murder). She is a big reader, saying her dad taught her when she was two, especially of historical fiction and we went through all the stuff we'd read, from Ken Follett to Dean Koontz. She surprised me by saying she thought Andy McNabb was brilliant with his stories about the doings of the SAS. He's been ridiculed and parodied, but someone must read them. It's funny that I've read loads of novels and biographies of WWI, but next to nothing about later wars – except for the one about a British sniper in Iraq that Steve recommended, which I found hard to put down. Perhaps it's because the First World War seems clean and between soldiers, whereas later wars are messy and involve everyone. I've read a lot about Vietnam and that was anything but clean.

She said she had an electric bicycle but didn't like cycling because she didn't understand gears. I told her how gears work and what they do. She said she understood all that, but didn't know what they *did* and when to change gear. She had decided she didn't understand gears and nothing was going to shift her from that position.

And she said she loved maps and told me about a coach driver who worked for them who drove the same school run every day, and every day used his sat nav because he didn't know the way. This is what internet technology does – makes us into mindless dependant fools. In this sense it might be called addictive and the attachment to it an illness.

I came away with *Preparation for the Next Life* by Atticus Lish, an ex-Marine who 'served a brief stretch in the Marine Corps in the war free period between Gulf One and 9/11.' The book is what would be called a gritty love story, and is written in a difficult vernacular (and it's heavy) but it drew me in as I sat in the laundry out of the drizzle. I also took *The Battersea Park road to Enlightenment* by Isabel Losada, which I thought might be funny. I can always put one of them back in the morning.

And I paid for another night. It only came to just over ten pounds with some overpriced biscuits and beans.

When I got back to my tent I had to zip up because it rained some more, but the forecast is good for tomorrow.

In the first paragraph Isabel Losada dismisses people who say they are contented. I've said I am contented because I don't want to say I'm happy when there's so much in the world to make one unhappy. But actually I can't be contented either, or I wouldn't be always building new bikes or want all the time to go away. I must be one of the Not Contents personally as well as politically. Where that leaves me I've no idea – except for holed up in a wet field in Devon eating marmalade sandwiches and ginger nuts and drinking camomile tea. But it's a self-help book and I don't need that kind of help – book rejected.

Atticus Lish, whose name reminds me of Atticus Finch, begins with an illegal Chinese immigrant to the US who works a series of shit illegal jobs before being arrested in a migrant sweep and put in a detention centre where she is deprived of anything that might keep her sane. If you get into the US 'under the radar' you're not allowed bail – that's The Patriot Act. You don't have to have done anything wrong in the Land of the Free – just being there is enough. It seems that migrants innocent of any crime are put in big shared cells with hardened criminals. If they are lucky, after being sent half mad with nothing to do, they might get deported. If they are unlucky they might be abused or raped by a member of staff.

It poured it down. It was the middle of the afternoon and all the ginger nuts were gone. Biscuits are one of my weaknesses.

She's a Uighur Muslim. That's why she's left China. She doesn't get much better treatment in America.

The Dutch bloke is hammering at something. I don't know what. There is a tendency for the materially incompetent to hammer their tent pegs in – and when I look out that's exactly what he's doing in a cack-handed way. I haven't been on a site these last forty days where I couldn't push the tent pegs in with my hand – in fact only in Spain have I ever needed a hammer and had to use a stone.

My property is getting increasingly dirty from doing everything in the tent. My light coloured air bed is full of stains, my blow up pillow the same. My coat has food spilled on it from being used as a picnic blanket. My luminous yellow waterproofs are covered in grease from my chain, though I've only worn them three times. The only clean clothes I've got are my thin fleece, my Ron Hills and a T shirt which I'm saving in case I get wet. The tent, which cost the same as the night before last's B&B, is bearing up well. We've had flimsy lightweight aluminium poles snap before, but these ones are steel.

Now we're back in the China that Paul Theroux saw, which doesn't even pretend, as the west does, to have any regard for the individual. They're all working for the people – 'the people' being amorphous and abstract. That's why it's Stalinism, which is authoritarian and blind to people's hopes and desires, and not communism, whose motto is 'from each according to their ability, to each according to their needs.'

I had another go at the self-help book – at the section on colonic irrigation – to be informed that things can get 'wedged' inside us that need washing out; 'They have found parts of sausages inside people who have been vegetarian for ten years. And people who take lots of vitamin tablets in little plastic containers – sometimes literally hundreds of bits of plastic can be flushed out of the gut.'

> And if they wed before they go
> His wife must bolt the door
> Cos when a man returns from war
> He is that man no more

Possible title - *Strange bedfellows*
And then it's another fucked up soldier like it's some kind of theme.

In relation to the General Strike, which was sold out by the union leaders – like they all are in the end, Kenneth O Morgan says; 'Britain's class war had been a brief, bloodless skirmish,' as if it was a one-off. The class war is always there, sometimes open, sometimes hidden. If it appears not to exist it is because their side is winning. It is an imposed peace on their terms. Morgan goes on to say that the General Strike, though it was 'defeated,' led to deep suspicion 'about the alleged neutrality of the police or the civil service, even perhaps of the newly formed BBC.' And that after it 'the unions and the Labour Party were no more accommodating towards a social system so manifestly distorted in its rewards and opportunities... which made such a mockery of the supposed social unity of the war years.' Thank goodness a century later all that's behind us, thanks to the unions and the Labour Party who never accommodated to the manifestly distorted system.

It must have been later than I thought because the Dutch bloke said goodnight in the ablution block.

When I'd had my shower I filled my little hotel soap bottle from their hand wash dispenser. It's much easier than carrying soap, which turns into a sticky mess.

My meal was porridge and beans again. In the self-help book, which I took back, the writer says her ex-husband was a Yorkshire man who wanted something dead on his plate at every meal. Not me. I'm perfectly happy with simple food at home or away, as long as there's plenty of it.

Atticus Lish was a good choice. It contains a devastating account of what the war in Iraq did to the Americans who fought it, how they survived on dope, energy drinks and anti-depressants. How they were sent back out after being injured when they were clearly mad as hell and expected to die any day. The account of Skinner's service reminds me a lot of *Catch 22*.

People were watching game shows in their caravans while I was reading this stuff, which is possibly why I despise the whole rotten stinking system and they don't.

And that was day forty. The trip feels like a week and it feels like a year.

Day 41 – Lydford to Nr Mevagissey
(Devon)
One minute there was a hint of light, the next it was fully light. Up and breakfast on oats, dried fruit and cold water as usual. Broken sky

with mist on the hills. I was off as the sun came up over the tors, but it looked far from certain we wouldn't get more rain.

Lydford has a castle, an old church, a gorge and a waterfall and it is clear it is sustained entirely by tourism. Consequently there was virtually no other traffic on the way out at 5 am. The sun was behind me and in the verges the bluebells were being replaced by shocks of tall pink flowers and buttercups.

There was a castle on a big hill to my left, but I couldn't identify it on the map and I wasn't sure where I was heading, but anything vaguely south-west would do. It was actually the thirteenth century hilltop St Michael de Rupe parish church of Brentor and it had been built by some zealot (or rather had been paid for by some zealot and built by others) right on top of a rocky outcrop.

I was three days early for Tavistock Steam Fair, which was a pity because I may have hung around – even possibly got a night's free camping. I don't think I'll get back up in time for it on Sunday.

I arrived in Tavistock at 7.30. It is a world heritage site so they are building a big new housing estate on the outskirts so all the people with money from the shit holes up north that are world disgrace sites can come to live where it's nice, leaving the rest to rot in their own juices.

A big stone viaduct strides over the northern end of town, but no trains have gone over it for fifty years because the line that once ran to Oakhampton and beyond now stops at Albaston, five miles to the south.

As far as Britain is concerned a world heritage site is a place that used to have things but doesn't anymore – only the empty shells and the sterile and sentimental re-enactments.

The Tavistock Heritage Trust runs the Tavistock Heritage Centre, which is funded by The Heritage Lottery Fund, which is a tax on poor people, who already paid for it with their sweat and muscles when they built it. Perhaps we should tax the use of the word heritage.

The town's main claim to fame are its Guild Hall and the town hall 'built' by the Duke of Bedford in 1860. How the Duke of Bedford came by his wealth and estate is not mentioned, but as the town is built on the site of an abbey we can assume he was given church lands as a bribe by the king, like the rest of them.

I could have gone to Weatherspoon's for breakfast, but instead found the Co-op and bought things that were good for me after surviving for three days on porridge, beans and biscuits. One of the papers has provoked the liberal reactionary John Cleese into claiming vindication for saying London was being taken over by foreigners (and he didn't mean Russian oligarchs and Saudi sheiks), with 'I was right – London is no longer an English city.' Go on John you Oxbridge toff, feed the fascists what they want. We've known for some time you despised the lower orders.

I took the A390 out at the wrong time of day. It didn't seem too bad, but is still got several good lungful's of diesel on the steep winding climb a couple of miles out. On the outskirts that way another big green field was earmarked for a housing estate.

After a long descent I crossed the Tamar into Cornwall at Gunnislake, which is also a world heritage site due to defunct tin mining. People were flying all sorts of flags, which is what happens when a country is falling apart. There were sarcastic notices on domestic bins asking visitors not to trash their property by putting rubbish in them. It was very close and I was sweating like a pig as big tippers started rumbling past me.

At Calstock a monument commemorates the coronation of George V in 1911 and 'the alteration of the gradient of Sandhill during the great distress in this parish' 1808-9. I can only assume that men were put to public works for their dole. And this 'distress,' which did not just affect Cornwall, goes some way to explaining why men were willing to volunteer for a short foreign campaign rather than starve at home (It'll be over by Christmas).

It wasn't long before the tippers started coming back full of tarmac for more roads. The primary school was part of a privatised multi-academy trust. Cornwall's not that independently minded that it wants to keep big business out of its schools. Which only shows that you can elect who you want, nationalists or otherwise, in the principalities, the provinces or the regions, but the neoliberal agenda is bigger than any of them.

Tamar Meadows was the housing development here, but it has to be said that the houses seem to be two, three and four bedroomed, rather than the unashamed mansions of Oxfordshire.

A pub was called the *Rifle Volunteer* and its sign depicted a rifleman in nineteenth century uniform, such as they wear in *Zulu*. A teenage girl walked past in urban camouflage because militarism is mainstream.

Over to my left I could see the Tamar estuary, which I hope to cross by ferry on the way back.

Fifteen German and Belgian motorcycles passed me, the first group I've seen down here and the biggest of the trip, most of them BMWs.

St Ive, on top of a hill, seemed a nice, unspoiled place, so I sat in the churchyard to eat my grapes and read for half an hour.

Having been discharged straight after a tour of Iraq Skinner goes to New York alone, 'holding to the idea that if he parties hard enough he will eventually succeed in having a good time and would start wanting to live again.' He takes his medicine with beer, gets out of his face on drink and dope and has nightmares in a hotel.

An old bloke said it couldn't be fun cycling on these roads. I didn't think it was too bad. It was a lovely bright day, cool with a headwind, but I was having a good time.

At Merrymeet the Methodist church was in private hands, but all the good Methodists were still buried out back. Liskeard, which has been a chartered town since 1240, is having a stunning selection of two, three and four bedroom houses built at *Trevethan Meadows* and *Liskerett Vale*, in addition to the other ones already completed.

I bought my postcards and was told off by a man for leaning my bike on a big flower pot while I was writing them. They spend a lot of time on the displays he said. A bit further on a lazy bastard blew his car horn at me because he wanted to stop at the side of the road where I was stopped – so I had to move. Fuck Liskeard.

311

I rode out cringing in the concrete gutter of the A38 dual carriageway to the St Austel road. Two German blokes on Royal Enfields were in as much danger, if not more danger, than I was.

A cycle path crossed the road. It wasn't going my way, but there was a bench, so I had my lunch. Most of the traffic seemed to be staying on the A38 towards Bodmin. It wasn't too bad, but a big wagon, followed by a German coach overtook me dangerously close. And the wind picked up. It's in my face and making it much harder. Yesterday I had to stop myself thinking I was on the last lap – there's a long way to go yet and I want to be home for Oades' birthday on the 20th June. That will be exactly two months as I planned.

A four by four driver overtaking me when there wasn't room gets a wanker sign from van man coming the other way.

Climbing the long hill out of Lostwithiel Grisly Adams came out of a field and said I'd soon be going downhill. I said 'and then up again,' when I should have cheered. He probably thinks I'm a glass half empty kind of person.

At St Blazey everything stopped for ten minutes while a great long goods train went through the level crossing.

There were campsites coming into St Austel, but I didn't have enough food and I knew there were sites out towards Truro, so I resupplied at Tesco (I could have chosen Asda or Aldi) and stayed on the A390. There were no signs for sites, which was ominous and had me worried, because I'd had enough, so at Polgooth I doubled back to Tregorick and through London Apprentice, asking an effusive old gardener for directions on the way. I had, as he said I would, a choice of three sites on either side of the road. I chose *The Meadows*, which is adults only and has little individual pitches mown among the long grass all linked together by mowed paths. Barrows are provided for the car drivers to transport their gear. The young man was an ex-bagpipe player and asked where I'd been. I told him if I'd my time again I'd be a drummer in a pipe band and that my favourite tune was *Highland Cathedral*. He asked me which pitch I wanted and I chose one with a table and chairs. I've never got to choose my own pitch before and all this was £13.50. A lovely spot and not a bad ride at all today – even though most of it was on main roads (I've already forgotten the first three hours of it that weren't). But where do the days go? One minute it was very early, then it was noon, and when I got here it was five o'clock. Tomorrow morning I will reach my most southerly destination and turn round. I should leave my tent here and do it naked. (And he said it was only the 30th, so I've gone wrong somewhere).

I ate my meal at the table with my bike leaning against it and my little tent up and thought, once more, 'this is the life' – though a cushion would have been nice.

I washed up and read a bit more. It wasn't getting dark, but I'd had enough for today. Other people were cooking on barbeques because that's what you do on campsites when you haven't tired yourself out and need something to do.

Day 42 – Day ride to Mabe Burnthouse
(Devon)
Even though I went to sleep early it was fully light when I woke. I have reached a new level of smelliness and must do something about washing or purchasing clothes. I am tempted to head out today with nothing, tools, pump, spares or anything, for Mabe Burnthouse.

I was ready to go at 7.15. Reception didn't open till nine and I'd already suggested I might want to stay another night so I set off with just my waterproof coat, four pitta breads with jam and a bottle of water.

The B road to Mevagssey is twisting and hilly. Within minutes I was subject to the usual dangerous and aggressive driving. The view to the left was over a wide expanse of flat sea as far as the horizon.

There were plenty more campsites and some of them looked nice. I also kept crossing a cycle path, but it weaved all over with no clear signage for the long distance rider. Like all cycle routes it will use existing tracks and lanes that, if they went anywhere important, would have become main roads a century ago. Britain's cycle paths are not a network at all, not in the sense that you could plan a long ride from A to B on them. They are routes designed for people to park their cars and have a jolly toddle round in a circle. And as long as this continues cycling will never be regarded as a serious form of transport.

On the back road to Grampound a distinguished looking man came out of an isolated cottage. When he overtook me a few minutes later his 4x4 was registered RAF. I speculated he might be a retired bomber pilot living in isolation with his conscience doing the garden to forget, turning over the earth with a fork, rather than with thousands of pounds of explosives.

It was a rather cloudy and humid day – or at least it felt humid to me, cycling the roller-coaster roads. I look forward to having the breeze behind me for a while.

A stinking half decomposed deer lay partly in the road. I had to slow down while a car passed me or ride over its legs. The main public entertainment round here seems to be gardens. There's no need to visit gardens, the whole country is a garden that has its flower beds and shit heaps.

The clock on the commemorative tower was striking nine as I rode into the ancient borough of Tregony, where I could have bought food – at a price. There was a nice seventeenth century house with a full-length first floor balcony. I asked a delivery man if the ferry would be running. He assured me it would and I turned onto the A3078 for St Mawes. He called it the King Herod Ferry.

There are all sorts of little businesses out in the countryside. There was one called Bloody Mary Metals, so I pulled in to see what it was. It made jewellery for would be alternative people and 'bike babes' (their claim not mine). A woman with lots of tattoos was outside unloading chemicals from a car. I asked if she was Bloody Mary. She said she was. I told her I made my bicycle, thinking that there might be some affinity between us metal workers. She just laughed at me like I was an old idiot, turned her back and went in the shop. Not as much as a, 'Did you? That's nice.'

Phileigh had its converted chapel and its mansion, but as yet no Persimmon-built new estate.

I don't think it's just the tattooed jeweller, there are lots of people about and generally they deliberately ignore you. Perhaps its nationalism that makes people bitter and selfish.

The ferry is actually called the King Harry Floating Bridge. It's a flat chain ferry with its bridge high on one side. It's a pound to cross with a bicycle and a charity donation for a pedestrian. Maximum charges for other vehicles are £15 return.

I was asked to wait to the side during loading and assumed it was health and safety. The captain said they'd 'had cyclists flattened' before, which doesn't surprise me at all given the selfish way they drive on the road. There was a bloody great ship anchored fifty yards away mid-stream.

The conductor, who had a big purple nose, told me it was a five year old Russian cargo ship that was 'under arrest' because it owed five million to the Royal Bank of Scotland. The ship had been anchored where it was for six months with four crew on board.

It was steep climb from the ferry, but nearly everywhere is a steep climb or a steep descent here. There's a round tower just up the hill that someone is living in and then another National Trust posh house and garden to visit, this time with the added attraction of a *Wind in the Willows* event. It turned into a nice day with scattered cloud and sunny spells.

Cars went by containing occupants with dogs on their knees and blank stares, like trapped goldfish going round in circles. I bet they've not smelled rape seed, wild garlic or a dead deer.

Even though I was worried about getting back to the campsite in time to pay I tried to avoid doing the last leg on the A39, at the cost of a long, steep climb I had to walk even without my luggage. When I looked over a bridge at the roaring dual carriageway I knew I'd made the right decision.

As soon as I saw a Spar shop I went in and bought nice things for my lunch, with not a thought for how I was going to carry it all. So I had to sit on the verge by the road and eat it. An Asian man came back with his shopping and said I was sitting outside his house, and there was a Chinese woman serving in the shop – so John Cleese

315

probably wouldn't think Cornwall is English any more either – which would please some Cornish people because they don't think it is either.

The old road seemed as if it would take me there. At Perranwell the bus shelter had big silhouettes of First World War soldiers in it.

The last bit was on a busy main road, only single carriageway and windy. A car coming down a slip road politely slowed down to let me pass, rather than cutting me up. The van driver behind repeatedly blew his horn at the driver. Two minutes later the driver of a car coming the other way blew his horn at me and gesticulated that I should be wearing a helmet. It's not the law and it's none of his business. It's him and people like him that are the problem, not my choice of apparel.

I forgot to mention that last night a bloke leaned right across his passenger seat and shouted at me to 'get a car' because he'd had to wait two seconds to pass me, before putting his foot down and leaving me in a cloud of stinking diesel fumes – so I can be like him presumably.

Now very conscious of the time and the distance between me and my belongings I rode to Mabe Burnthouse post office and out again. And that's the furthest south I go. Actually what was really bothering me was the irrational fear that I'd be in bother at the campsite because I said I'd pay for another night's camping this morning and hadn't.

From the vantage point of Mabe Burnthouse (my eighteenth destination) I could see picturesque low cloud hanging over the sea in the Helford Passage and nowhere else. Then I steeled myself for the A39. For the first time in days I had a following wind, but it was fucking dangerous. I wasn't on it for long, turning off to follow a different route on unclassified roads back to the ferry. With a bit of local knowledge, not least from the Chinese woman out of the Spar shop, whose house I just happened to stop outside, and the strategic use of a footpath I would never have known was there I got back to the ferry in no time.

There were only three cars in the queue, but the woman in the front one was singing at the top of her voice to some pop song with no shame. I have to have six pints of cider before I'll do that.

The ferry was founded in 1888 and looked like a floating shed. There's a statue on it of a bloke leaning on the railings and one of an old bloke slumped in a deck chair on the shore.

It was three o'clock and it had already been a hard day. A bloke overtook me on an old Yamaha. Those were the days of innocence – when I thought I could just tootle round back roads on a little two stroke for ever.

On the way back I saw a young women in a beat up car with a 'Keep Hunting' sticker in the back

> Wherever there's a rich man
> There'll be a sycophant
> To lick his pampered arse

I saw a mirage. It looked like there was water right across the road. Coming over the top and down onto the Mevagissey road miles of beautiful shore line and cliffs lie ahead.

It was five o'clock when I got back to the campsite and paid my £13.50 for another night. I'd had enough cycling but I was OK for anything else. I sat in the little mown circle surrounded by tall grass with butterflies and purple flowers in it.

Camped near me is Herman, a 71 year old Dutch bloke touring for the first time on an electric bicycle, having decided that pedalling was no fun anymore. I asked him about charging his battery. He said at most sites they asked if he wanted electricity, meaning a hook up like caravans and, unbelievably, some campers have. When he said he needed only to charge his battery they said they didn't charge for that and he could do it in the amenities block – until the other day when a site wanted to charge him £8. He refused to pay it and went somewhere else. Having got wise he asked at the site over the road how much they wanted. They asked for £4, and he wouldn't pay that either, saying it only cost about 35p to fully charge

317

it. This site charged him £1. I told him about the rip off campsites on the south coast, which I'm probably going to have to experience again.

I could see across into the tent of a motorised couple. They've got proper beds at proper bed height. Another couple took half an hour to wheel all their gear to their pitch in the campsite barrows.

A woman from Leeds came to talk to me. She was interested in me because I've got a little tent and am obviously touring on a bicycle. They've got a big tent and all the trimmings. She asked me where I'd been so she could tell me where they'd been. I do that. I'd forgotten where I'd been and had to unfold my map I'd just folded for tomorrow. When I told her where I'd been she said I must have done some of it on the train.

I was making porridge with chickpeas, peanuts, curry powder and an Oxo for my tea. She asked 'do you eat that every night – high protein stuff?' I said it was porridge.

Skinner came from Shayler near West Virginia. The people in his town were patriotic, racist and poor. 'He would have signed up even if the recruiters hadn't come right to his high school. 9/11 was the big reason, but he would have gone anyway, just to do something.'

'What makes the world go round?' asks his Uighur Chinese girlfriend.

'To be honest, war.'

'War?'

'Actually I'd say first money, then war. Everybody's all like, patriotism, the flag, all this horseshit.'

And then there's the Afghan kids with deformed joints from the depleted uranium. Where next will the children suffer for this system? Iran? Dorset, Burnley?

Donald Trump says he thinks Boris is a good guy. That should help his campaign to be prime minister.

When I got showered I washed my T shirt, top shirt and socks. The top shirt dried enough to bring it in when I retired. The T shirt and socks didn't. I haven't any other socks, so they'll be going on wet. For the first time in a week I didn't stink and I'm not sticky. The shower ran red with the dye from Mike Ashley's cheap T shirt.

'His episodes of weeping had not started yet. But they would. The not sleeping and the irritability were already there, were familiar... he looked around for something or someone to blame. His mind did not have a safety catch and there was no way to shut it off.'

Day 43 – Nr Mevagissey to Modbury
(Devon)
It got light but I couldn't make myself stay awake. Being Saturday the road to the site is quiet and I can hear a woodpecker. I've promised myself I'll go right along the coast, but it will be hard and take ages. The woman from Leeds mentioned a ferry from Mevagissey, but when I open my map out properly the land's nothing like I thought it was and that's going south. The last campsite I can see marked before the mess of Plymouth is at Hooe, near the monkey sanctuary – which should be a nice short day's ride. I've no idea why monkeys should seek sanctuary in Cornwall. Herman said he had taken a ferry from St Mawes to Falmouth that isn't marked on my map. Then there's a campsite by Dartmouth and Paignton. If I plan my riding according to campsites it will be less stressful and I shouldn't end up doing ten hour days – but it's not far enough between them to get me home in twenty days. I can revert to longer days when I get to flatter terrain. From today maps of the south coast start following Scottish and Welsh ones into the bin.

When I emerged the sky was blue, the sun was nearly up and my socks were still soaking, there was mist in the valley.

The dog walkers were out – 'Women in sagging sweat pants walked their pit bulls talking to the men... in rasping voices, smoking while they talked. He's rednose, half red nose, half American pit. They're twins. The other one is Lucky, this is flash. He wants his mommy. Be careful, he's a sweetie, but he bites.' It's not like that on this site – though one couple have a big St Bernard and another dog – but it is on some of them. Here only one person is flying the union flag, pit bulls and patriotism going together. Although there is a bloke in joggers walking round talking to someone that isn't here – all wired up with earpiece etc.

I put my wet shirt and socks on. That solved that problem instantly.

As I left another man was having a bollocks conversation on his phone, via multi-million pound satellites in space.

The campsite over the road offered ice-cream for dogs. The world is truly mad.

Caravans and camper vans trying to beat the rush north overtook me in processions.

At London Apprentice there is a retail leisure warehouse, just in case those on holiday needed to satisfy their addiction.

One house had a silhouette of a man ploughing with horses – as if ploughing with horses was something the owner, his parents or his grandparents might ever have indulged in. Then there was the Cornwall Health Spa and Estate with its Laura Ashley tea rooms that looked like a load of overgrown ski chalets.

When I hit the A road I realised I'd been there before – stayed in the Travelodge among B&Q and Macca D's on some trip to see Oades' family.

There was a nice wide pavement all the way to the Fowey turn off. Caravans passed me called Affinity, Odyssey and Avante. That took me out through the retail parks, past derelict industrial areas and several very big current ones and past the Dog Spa.

Two skinny females overtook me on racing bikes. It said 'live to ride - ride to live' on the back of one of their shirts.

As far as Par it was flat and then some knob heads shouted at me out of a car.

Whenever there's a rich man
In town or sleepy hollow
He'll always have his entourage
Of sycophants that follow

There were two big climbs and a steep descent to the Bodinnich Ferry.

Fowey is an 'ancient village' that is now merely picturesque, requiring acres of car parks. The ferry is a free-floating one that can take a dozen cars and was £2.50 as opposed to yesterday's £1 charity donation. And I'd done half my proposed ride already.

There was no viewing point on the way up from the ferry because it was all owned by someone with too much money and a Porsche 911 Targa 45 and a speedboat. But I watched the ferry from the roadside above his swanky property. I hope he's happy. Actually I hope he isn't. I believe there was actually a turntable in the drive to turn the car round. I couldn't help thinking that if I pushed on I might get through Plymouth today – there's always the Travelodge.

A couple came up and asked me about my bike. The man asked me if I was an engineer. I said, 'I'm a bricklayer, that's why it looks like that,' and then I wondered if self-deprecation was more attractive in a person.

Other mansions were available. A Jaguar and two top of the range Range Rovers came down. For the time being capitalism has got over the tendency towards progressive politics by creating a very big, well-off, greedy and selfish, ultra-aspirational middle class, a minority of whom might just vote Labour, out of conscience, but they won't vote for Corbyn.

I started riding harder, like a man on a mission, and 'getting through Plymouth' coalesced into a fact. I feel like I'm on the downhill run, the last fortnight, like a tumble drier that does the last five minutes cold so you don't burn your fingers on the buttons.

Some places are 'proud to sell Cornish coffee' like I might be proud to use Anusol. Coffee only grows in a narrow strip around the equator.

The wind wasn't helping and by the way the grass stalks were bending it didn't look like it was going to. I found 2p in the road. I have a policy of always picking coins up. It's surprising how many you can find.

I entered Pelyntrad, Trelawny's Parish, where modest new homes were for sale through shared ownership. A driving instructor allowed a learner to drive inches behind me up a hill in an intimidating way.

I arrived in Looe at 11.20. The resort is centred on a seven arch stone bridge, which is looked down on by ascending tiers of white and off-white houses, many of which are hotels. As it was Saturday hordes of already overweight people were arriving to consume ice cream and fish and chips. A train load of them came past at once like an invading army. Naturally there were union flags flying – what could go better with such excess than patriotism?

I refuelled by the river and made my escape. Torpoint was signposted. That's where I was going, sixteen miles. The first bit up a very big hill. The traffic was queuing on the other side to get in.

Barrett's had been at it big style at the top and buses ferried in the Chinese cotton clad from outlying holiday camps.

The next village was called No Man's Land – the killing zone – and the next farm *Cleese Farm*. It was hot and hilly. An older cyclist coming the other way said it was only another 200 miles to London. A pair of touring cyclists came the other way. They had at least three times as much gear as me, each.

Signs on the A374 to Torpoint say that 23 motorcyclists have been injured in the last five years and three killed. I watched them with their silly nylon knee sliders screaming into bends on the wrong side of the road hanging off their seats. And a new Luton hire van was smashed up in a field after leaving the road down a drop. If I hadn't stopped to record this I wouldn't have noticed the majestic twelve arch viaduct over the inlet at St Germans.

I passed *HMS Raleigh* and could hear shouting. Walter Raleigh was a pirate licensed by the British monarchy, as was Drake – they did what Somali pirates do today and their descendants were moored at Devonport. When I came over the hill and saw the metropolis I didn't like the look of it. I hadn't seen one for a while. The Torpoint ferry is another chain one, but bigger – perhaps a hundred cars – and a double deck bus looked small on it. There are three of them going backwards and forwards non-stop. No one asked me for money.

Getting through Plymouth wasn't remotely amusing and it took an hour of messing with buses and cars. Eventually by guesswork and asking I got onto the A739 for Kingsbridge. The further I got out the quieter it got because anyone with any sense is at home having a barbeque or watching *Come Dancing*.

I passed a campsite at 3.30 but didn't stop because I didn't have anything other than porridge to eat. I should have stopped. Instead I paid over the odds for a few bits at the next garage. People were buying cases of cider and barbeque stuff. A young woman had 'Dirty Diesel' on the back of her car as if it was something to be proud of. This amoral, 'fuck you', I'll do what I want attitude is the obverse of the arrogant self-entitled middle class and they're both products of Thatcherite individuality and the deliberate undermining of working class solidarity.

Modbury is 'a heritage market town,' the 'heritage' being entirely superfluous. It's also Britain's first plastic shopping bag free town and is having a fantastic collection of two, three and four bedroom homes built by Bloor. We are invited to 'discover the Bloor difference.'

At just five o'clock and a couple of miles further on I rode onto a campsite, £12, which was deceitfully a mile off the main road – fine if you're in a car of course.

It's a good job I stopped because when I opened my map out I've no need to go anywhere near Kingsbridge, which is where I was heading. I need to head across to Torquay, where I believe Fawlty Towers was set, the third Cleese connection.

The toilet block was full of screaming kids and banging doors and I couldn't shit. Thankfully it calmed down. Some people packed up, others ate a lot of meat and no vegetables.

Then, while I was reading, the pole just snapped in the back of my tent, like I knew it would one day, but I thought it would be the front one. I've used it too many times. You're supposed to buy one of these Chinese tents, use it once, then decide you don't like camping and throw it away – the same as you're supposed to do with a Chinese bicycle. I used the repair sleeve they provide. We'll see how long that lasts.

I was in my tent reading when something else twanged. I thought the pole had broken again so I went out. It hadn't. After the noise I heard running feet, it could have been a coincidence or it could have been some kid who hasn't been told to keep out of other people's space tripping over a guy rope. There's a world of difference between an adults only site like the one I was on last night and a noisy playground like this one. Roll on the morning.

'So much of the military, including its most outstanding soldiers, came from the lower end of civilian society.'

And then the thudding of footballs started. It must have been nine o'clock. For fuck's sake, what am I paying for? And then they started singing.

'At the next table, he saw a little girl in a nun-like habit screaming at her mother's headless body.'

And on that note...

But first a final piss.

There were two notices in the washing up room. One advised campers not to set fire to their tents. The other was about dogs dying in hot cars and advised anyone who saw a dog in distress in a car to dial 999. There was no advice for anyone who saw a human being in distress.

Day 44 – Modbury to Otterton (via Babbacombe)

(Devon)

I was awake well before dawn, waiting – if it's going to rain, as the woman on reception said was forecast – I wanted to be off before it started. Also I can feel the trip descending into a sprint for the finish line.

I headed east on the back roads – there was a weathervane on the site, I haven't needed to use my compass as yet, and followed the signs for Totness through California Cross – hitting rain within half an hour. It was far too warm and hilly to put my coat on, so I just got wet, hoping it would fine up later and I'd dry out.

At Avon Bridge a deer ran across the road and then crashed back out of the hedge and along the road in front of me.

The rain was only sporadic, it was a good fast road and once I got my legs on I caned it all the way to Totness and was there even before the dog walkers were out. It's probably a nice place.

I'm bored with reporting that every place has a massive new housing estate under construction, but here the names amused me – 'Camomile Lawn,' 'King's Orchard' and 'Great Court Farm.' Do not pass go. No one seems to want to name a street Helmand or Abu Graib, like they named them after Inkerman and Balaclava, or after politicians like they did Peel and Gladstone – only after symbols of a long-lost rural past. It's an A road and a rare Sunday tipper bounced past.

The river Dart looked nice with no one around. Someone had put posters up saying 'NO5G.' It's a long climb out of Totness.

I rode into Paignton, 'a great place to be beside the sea,' at 8.30. A sign said welcome to the English Riviera, birthplace of Agatha Christie and a global geopark.' Hercule Poirot was lifting his hat in welcome. Campsites, caravan sites and holiday parks abounded. There were also signs of decay, with one big place at the top of the hill shut and falling down.

Coming into the centre a woman wearing headphones and oblivious to her surroundings pressed the button to stop the traffic to cross the road. There was no one on it but me.

The Toyota garage said it was time to move on. 'Moving on' involved buying the new Corolla. There were two Animals in Distress shops. I've been to places before and been pleasantly surprised at two shops raising money for desperate asylum seekers. Paignton isn't one of those places. There was a Cecil Road. I've forgotten what injustice Cecil was famous for, but I was brought up on a street also named after him. Today is the second day of the Torbay Air Show and the Red Arrows are coming. I'm surprised I didn't see them yesterday. Aren't jet fighters brilliant?

A nice couple quizzed me outside Sainsbury's. He was white, she was Asian. He didn't tell me my bike was an army bike like a lot of them do. He knew It was home made. Then they let their dog piss all over the sale signs outside Wickes. Paignton struck me as a bit of a dump.

Ten minutes later I was riding into Torquay. I can see why they play on the Riviera thing. The bit of the coast that sticks out does look like it could be somewhere exotic. Unfortunately it's attached to the rest of Britain.

I rode along the prom, which is something I always think I want to do, and looked at the luxury yachts in the harbour, by which time the sun was coming out.

At nine o'clock two rough sleepers were still in their bags in a doorway.

Babacombe, my 19th destination, is virtually a suburb, and the main road out north is called Babacombe Road.

One fairly ordinary looking establishment offered 'boutique B&B accommodation. 'I need to look up boutique when I get home ['a small shop or department of a store selling clothes or accessories.' So a boutique B&B must double up as a shop].Two stupid little dogs yapped at me as I was riding up the hill.

When I got there I discovered that Babacombe is 'the home of the cliff railway.' There was a big mobility centre, selling electric chariots, self-ejecting sofas and walk in baths because these seaside places are full of people who go there to die in increasingly comfortable trousers.

It also has a model village, a place called Bygones and a main street full of takeaways. Somebody crashed their car last night but tape said the police were aware. Overweight people walked dogs wearing humane harnesses.

One of the papers reports Nigel Farage saying he'll smash the system just like Donald Trump. He'll do no such thing and neither has Trump. Trump is a wheeler dealer shyster son of the system and as a former merchant banker so is Farage. Anyone who trusts him to do anything for ordinary people is a fool. Trump says he's going to make America great again. American 'greatness' has depended upon military might, union busting and the suppression of the left.

Actually that wasn't the main street, only the road in. Babacombe is quite big and has everything, including an Animals in Distress shop. Three morbidly obese people went into the Co-op. There are clearly some problems in this area. The downcast and the respectable citizen alike patrolled round letting their dogs piss on everything. I ate two samosas and a full bag of Doritos because I fancied something like that.

The road got twisty, busy and dangerous, not least because by then it was pissing it down and car drivers have no concept of how rain affects other road users. One impatient woman drove only a few feet behind me all the way down a steep hill. I missed Daccombe somewhere along the way. It too was part of Torquay and I decided I was near enough. Riding into Teignmouth at 10.45 it brightened up again.

I'll be glad when leaving every place doesn't involve a massive climb. There was plenty of close overtaking and a dog barked at me out of a car, where's my revolver when I need it. During the Penny Farthing period cyclists were offered a small revolver called a velopistol, with which to shoot dogs that chased them (dogs didn't enjoy their current elevated and bizarre status then). An acquaintance researched and wrote an article on these understandable firearms for a cycle magazine. It was turned down by the dog owning editor on the grounds that it was inappropriate – which in my opinion constitutes the thin end of the wedge of historical revisionism which also includes the attempt to reinvent the First World War as a glorious crusade for democracy against despotism.

In Dawlish the new developments were 'Warren Grove' and 'The Copse' and a Chinook helicopter flew over on its way to impress the gullible celebrants of militarism in Torquay.

Cycling up the hill out of Dawlish a man had a little dog in his front basket – twat. And Dawlish, not willing to be left out of the epidemic of militarism, is having an Armed Forces Day at the end of June, when all the fucked up veterans will be remembered for twenty four hours, then forgotten till next time they need to be wheeled out for an opportunist commemoration.

There's a lot to Dawlish as well. I could probably spend a morning in the charity shops looking at the books, but I'm a man on a mission – home by Oades' birthday. I shall tell her so.

A lovely cycle route took me along the banks of the Exe estuary past Powderham Castle, the historic home of the Earl of Devon. We are invited to ogle (for a fee) at treasures he amassed on the backs of workers. There was another pillock on there with a dog in a basket and, off the other end, when I was crossing the Exe, one in a trailer.

I wasted the best part of two hours trying to find a way east that wasn't the main road or didn't take me to Exmouth, going round in circles several times. Eventually I had to concede it was impossible and, on the advice of a posh bloke in a Range Rover, I got onto the cycle path to the south so I could go a dozen miles out of my way. It would have paid me to do that in the first place, but as a treat the path passed the bottom of the Royal Marines base and we could see the assault course, which was glorified on display boards.

Posh man was right – it was a nice cycleway, much of it on specially constructed 'board walks' (with dog shit), but it still didn't go east, so I came off it again and asked advice. For my pains I had to walk up a long steep hill. No wonder the cycle route goes round. The cycle route via Exmouth is fine if you're just out for a jolly ride round in a circle to put your bike back on the back of the car and home in time for tea – but it's no good to someone heading east unless they have all the time in the world.

And then I got lost again, every road I took pulling me inexorably further south and no signs for Sidmouth. It was very frustrating and it kept raining, but funnily enough I didn't lose my temper because there was no one to lose my temper with.

Having nearly been into Budleigh Salterton and out again I finally saw a sign for Sidmouth at the same time as I saw one for a campsite at Otterton. It is probably the most hideous commercialised monstrosity I have stayed on so far. I have a view of the sea over the top of rows of static caravans. The reception is like the front office of corporate enterprise.

And I'm beginning to think the staying on the coast idea wasn't such a good one. There is no road on the coast as such, and the ones that do exist are quite often major ones I don't want to be on, otherwise they're small and weave about all over. Anyone who tells you they've cycled round the coast of Britain is having you on – you can't.

I'll have several more big cities to negotiate and I don't want to do it. I hate it down here. I may go north and head across via Salisbury way and east from there. And I'm bored with this diary as well, which I've written in such a slipshod way it needs typing. What's it for anyway? I thought I'd make a book of it, but it's pure vanity. I'd make better time if I didn't have to keep stopping to make notes about stuff anyone can see for themselves. And if I'm honest I'm only doing the bloody trip so I could write about it – because that's what I do – do things so I can write about them.

This isn't a campsite, it's a holiday village and it's shite. The pitch isn't even level and the toilets are miles away. It's depressing that I've sunk to this level. There's diesel people carriers chugging past and dogs barking. I want to go home.

'Skinner watched videos uploaded by disaffected soldiers, in which his comrades in arms gave testimony about the folly and evil of what they'd been part of.' There follows descriptions of the self-destruction, rape, abuse and murder US soldiers have carried out because they can't live with themselves or anyone else.

The weather has been shit today, I got lost and I didn't sleep last night. Tomorrow will be better. I'm fed up of my beard, fed up of smelling, fed up of corporate campsites and riding on busy roads. But I felt a bit better after a shower. The shower had an electronic control panel because a simple mechanical push button that has sufficed for decades wasn't good enough.

One woman reported that an army psychiatrist had told her they couldn't treat her husband for his nightmares. She rang her husband's commanding officer, to be told that the army doesn't give out hugs to cry babies.

'When Skinner thought he was going to die in Iraq the idea of never having a woman to love him summed up all his pain. Now he'd got a girlfriend [but] when he was low he thought she was just like any other female – she had certain functions. And he had seen those functions turned inside out by high explosive, he knew what was inside people, and there was nothing there. It was gross. It was boring. It was sickening and that was all.' This thought hit him hard. It took his hope away.

The campsite is on Ladram Bay and it has won platinum awards for five years in a row. The people who give out the awards must know what the people want. The woman on reception told me the fish and chip wagon was coming tonight and about some other holiday camp stuff I don't care about.

When I'd washed my bowl and was ready to settle down a lad ran past and shouted at the top of his voice, 'Daddy, why's there a tiny tent.' It seems that children have no idea what camping actually is.

Then I had to listen to a nearby conversation about why glamping is so much better than camping, between two people staying in fake pre-erected tents. Then the man started bragging about the company he works for and within five minutes I knew his entire family history. He was a good Polish Catholic boy. His mum was a nurse, his dad was a chef who fought in the war. Then they started on about the rip-off prices to keep a static caravan here. And then he mentioned he was a good Catholic again. He sounded to me like an empty headed braggart who only thinks about making money. He droned on and on about what they were having for tea and only his voice was audible. What a boring bastard.

The coast is too clogged with cars, too expensive and too difficult to negotiate.

Day 45 – Otterton to Salisbury
(Devon, Dorset and Wiltshire)

Woke as it was getting light. From the toilet block this holiday park looks like some mad Brazilian favela.

I was breakfasted, packed and ready to go before the sun came up. There was a man in the toilets who looked like he'd been doing drugs and not gone to bed yet. At Mevagissey you had to sign a form to say you wouldn't take drugs on site. The warden said he'd had people refuse to sign it and leave. Perhaps camping isn't the wholesome pursuit I imagined it in my naivety to be.

'Thankyou for your visit, we hope to see you soon' said the sign on the way out. Not if I can help it.

Otterton itself pleaded 'Please drive carefully through our beautiful village. ' It was all thatched and roadside streams with plenty of 'keep out' signs.

The road to Sidmouth is narrow – no wonder they don't advertise it. But people come here in droves. The farmhouse B&B, 'en suite, colour TV,' had no vacancies.

There are split flint faced buildings again and fuchsias are coming out, as well as that creeping pest with its big white trumpet flowers.

It was a long, steep climb. Looking back from the top I could see the whole peninsula, over Budleigh Salterton and across to Plymouth, the land lifting off at the end like the take-off ramp on an aircraft carrier. The roadside bench outside the hill top car park was dedicated to Anthony Brice Hill Litten (tony) 1931- 2009.

The descent into Sidmouth was like a helter-skelter – leaving me in no doubt about what was to come – another steep climb. I was on the cycle route I'd have been on all the time if I'd done as I was told yesterday. I'd no need to be on it at all, but it was nice to hear the waves lapping below.

The Victorian hotel in Sidmouth was built in 1902 by Colonel Balfour, Sidmouth's Lord of the Manor. It was immediately popular because it had en suite rooms and garages for cars (and thus began the madness). Various celebrities have stayed in it.

The Bedford Hotel was built in 1813 as a grand library, billiard rooms etc. It was virtually destroyed in the 1824 great gale, when the family who ran it had to escape by boat.

The place retained, as far as I could see, its Victorian or early twentieth century demeanour, if you ignored all the cars and the acres of car parks, which you can't, and it looked as if it would be very expensive to stay here. The first house on the front was built in 1776 and restored 'as a Gothic confection' after the great gale.

Unusually signs prohibited cycling on the promenade. It was only seven o'clock and the promenade contained only the odd dog walker and a few smoking coach drivers in white shirts and waistcoats, so I ignored the rule. The main shopping street was done up in bunting and union flags like the war had just ended.

I bought the day's rations at the Co-op. One of the papers says delaying Brexit will hand Number 10 to Corbyn, another that May must confront Trump on the climate, presumably during his visit, which people should make as uncomfortable for him as possible, preferably covering him in red paint and chasing him back to the airport. Unfortunately it is the police's job to protect visiting bigots and warmongers from those who elect them. On Corbyn I think the Tories delude themselves and it is possible that the writing is on the wall for both the major parties as the country splits into two increasingly hostile camps over Europe, possibly represented by Farage and the LibDems. How far we are off civil war is anyone's guess, but it's always possible, given what's happened in other countries. In the disintegration of the major parties Britain lags behind the rest of Europe. The cause is neoliberal destruction and increasing authoritarianism. Brexit is a symptom, but like religion it has become a banner to fight under.

Sidmouth too has a pub called *The Volunteer* – they mean hoodwinked or economically conscripted cannon fodder, but that's too long for a pub sign.

I took pot luck on the way out and was straight onto the Seaton/Lyme Regis road, not knowing what to expect and still undecided about whether to go further inland. It doesn't really matter because it's sunny, I've slept well and I'm up for the ride.

I had my second breakfast on the bridge over the River Sid before tackling the inevitable big hill. The sun is shining into a tree covered tunnel on the climb and I can see the diesel fug I have to ride through. It's always there, but now I can see it.

The *Blue Ball* Inn claims a history dating back to 1385. Heritage is everything it seems.

Keep on Trucking

I'm trucking for the skinny
And so the fat can gorge
I'm trucking for my family
I'm trucking for St George

I'm just another trucker
Trucking cos he must
We've got to keep on trucking
We're trucking till we're bust

I'm trucking into Europe
I'm trucking everywhere
You think of a country
I'll be trucking there

If you live in London
I'll truck the stuff you sup
I'll truck down the stuff you eat
Until I truck things up

333

I turned off the main road for Colyton. The decision is made. Peace descended as the roar of the main road receded behind me. I didn't have to ride in the gutter, through the grates, be intimidated, keep stopping, be in fear of my life – and it was much more enjoyable.

The tide was in at Sidmouth and that'll be the last sight of the sea I get. The seaside offers so much and delivers so little. But then that's life, small pleasures etc.

Colyton claimed to be Devon's most rebellious town but it looked nice enough. There was a no-frills Caravan and Camping Club site with only two camper vans on it, but it was only 9am. In fact it was very scenic. I left between the abutments of an old railway bridge and began the climb to the next place, for a while riding along with an older woman on a mountain bike. We talked about how horrible the main roads were.

By the roadside in some village or other a row of trees had been planted in 1965 in honour of Winston Churchill. Honouring our oppressors is nothing new. The Brexit Party posters say 'fighting back.'

The road surface was good all the way to Axminster – which makes a big difference. Riding over an endless broken surface is very wearing.

In Axminster I posted my fourth note book home. The post office is in the hands of a Sikh family – 'All breakages must be paid for.' 'All shoplifters will be prosecuted.' It sold everything from miracle bamboo bras through shoe polish to 'L' plates, but it didn't sell toilet seats like the post office in Cleckheaton once tried. I wonder if they listen to *Fags, Mags and Bags.*

I sat in a churchyard/dog toilet. Within thirty seconds a bloke had brought two dogs in to shit while I was eating. Then a woman in combat trousers brought in an ugly bull terrier to shit right in front of me. Can it only be me that is thoroughly disgusted by this?

I chose as a shortcut east to the B road one of the steepest and longest hills I've ridden all week. When I asked a local cyclist to

334

confirm my route he said, 'There's a big hill up there.' And he was right.

And then there was a loud twang. When I looked at the back wheel a spoke had broken, and it was the second one – which explains the similar noise I heard yesterday. This is serious; especially as I've just embarked on a cross-country trajectory where there was guaranteed to be no bike shops – not that they'd be able to fix it in a hurry anyway.

I left rip-off Devon and entered rip-off Dorset.

The chances of doing another five hundred miles without any more spokes breaking are very slim – now I'm cringing at every imperfection in the road just when I needed to do some serious cycling. I've never had a broken spoke before. It is the wheel I bought on e-Bay in the German bike and had clearly been rebuilt. Fifteen days is what I have left. All speed. The show must go on.

The road took me over Pilsdon Pen, traditionally the highest point in Dorset, and the site of an Iron Age hill fort. If I weren't being sponsored I might be tempted to panic and go home by train.

Dozens of big birds were circling overhead like they probably were two thousand years ago, because they haven't advanced like us.

It was a good day, sun out, following breeze, but now I'm preoccupied with the imminently collapsing back wheel.

In a Spar shop an overweight woman bought two pasties and two tins of energy drink. It could be worse. I could be addicted to sugar-loaded caffeine drinks. One of the coffee companies that spring up everywhere calls itself 'Insomnia.' That's what it gives me.

The road to Evershot had recently had a top dressing applied over all the holes, so the descent was punishing on man and machine.

It's also come to my notice that my back brake blocks are worn out and shredding my rim, covering the back of the frame in silvery aluminium dust.

Today I feel as tall and princely on my bike as ever (pity about the spokes). I'm starting to have thoughts about getting to Salisbury – I can't see a campsite anywhere else on this route – taking advantage of the wind bowling me along. The scenery by the way is magnificent. The wind would be a complete killer if it was in the other direction.

Daft as it might have been at three o'clock I rode past a lovely Camping and Caravan Club campsite, after asking a young man fixing a van outside a commercial vehicle breakers what time it was. I asked him should I camp or carry on. He pondered, as if was really asking him to make the decision, and then said I wouldn't get to Yorkshire today. As the going was good and the wind was behind me I carried on.

On a narrow lane a big tractor towing a massive grass rotator came at speed from behind and forced me to throw myself onto the bank or be squashed. I stayed there while the five foot tyres of the following combine harvester went past inches away from me – good job there wasn't a drop or a stone wall. I put my hand out to stop myself falling over and a mile later I was still pulling the thistle barbs from my fingers.

Shaftesbury is a Saxon hill town, and it shows. The climb to it was ridiculously steep and long. There was sweat pouring out of me and I was wet through. When I had pushed my bike to the top a woman walking with her husband said, 'You should be riding up there.' This sort of wit from non-cyclists when you are struggling gets a bit wearing. I offered her my bike and said, 'Go on then – I've been cycling for sixteen hours (I hadn't of course, it just came out), you're fresh.' She just laughed and no doubt thought I was a miserable bastard.

I bought some over-priced crap to eat and was told by a man propping up the doorway of a pub smoking that it was twenty one miles to Salisbury. I said I'd be there by 8.30. Actually I rolled onto the racecourse campsite at 7.25 – making it two hours and five minutes from Shaftesbury to Salisbury, which isn't bad at all on a fully loaded bike. That made about thirteen and a half hours cycling today – but one of the best days of the trip. Plenty of top gear mile munching, the wind behind me and most of the climbs, after the initial ones first thing, short. It is both mad and fantastic that I could ride in a day from Sidmouth to Salisbury.

Campsite over £15. Shower, beans with curry powder and bread, post card home, write notes and it was getting dark.

I had the idea while I was riding of jettisoning all the stuff I'm carrying that isn't essential for life – stove, clean clothes, waterproofs etc. it doesn't seem such a good idea once I've stopped – but anything to save the back wheel.

Both broken spokes are on the same part of the wheel – so when one breaks it must put extra strain on the others. I don't think there's much chance of it getting me home.

Day 46 – Salisbury to Billingshurst
(Wiltshire and Sussex)

Up at 4.30. On the grounds that I haven't worn them for weeks I threw away my tracksuit bottoms, fleece and waterproof trousers. On the grounds that I can eat cold I threw away my bowl and mug. I also threw away two spare note books and six spare pens. My stove, penknife and compass I prepared to send home. I put my spare T shirt on and threw the dirty one away. My reading books I left in the canteen – I know what will happen to Skinner. He'll live with his nightmares, become an alcoholic, kill himself by drugs or suicide or end up in jail – like thousands of other British and American veterans have done. Living happily ever after is not an option. This isn't a man in his fifties, but a man in his twenties who has seen everything – war, drugs, prostitution and death. Armed Forces Days and the like are collective guilty conscience that we let this happen.

I kept my Charles and Diana spoon to spread jam and eat beans.

I am now down to a bare minimum – tent, air bed, sleeping bag, the clothes I have on, waterproof coat, toothbrush and toothpaste, remaining maps, spoon, earplugs, flannel to get dried on, reading glasses, lip salve, pens and notebook and a bit of food – that's it. I threw all my spare tent pegs away and put my tent on my front forks instead of on the rear carrier. I'll carry one water bottle and drink as much as I can when I get chance. All this made me very nervous and excited.

I exited Salisbury via the ring road and out on the A30 London road. It was strewn with the stinking remains of wild animals – deer, foxes, the odd badger, as well as the usual rabbits – because, like people, they come a poor second to cars.

The road was sporadically busy, as was to be expected – people have to commute to London to trade in shares and commodities – though there were short breaks of almost silence. I had to physically cringe away from several vehicles that overtook me at speed when there was clearly something coming the other way, including a big man truck and an HGV with a forty foot trailer. Had I not cringed I think the trailer would have hit me.

Rabbits scuttled about in the side terrified out of their lives. I know how they feel because that's what I am – a frightened rabbit on Britain's roads.

It was a bit better after I turned off the Andover road for Winchester. I entered Hampshire, where the road surface immediately deteriorated. Bang, bang, bang went my back wheel through sunken bits and over the broken surface and bad patching. It slowed me down and jarred my back.

It was just eight o'clock when I rode into Stockbridge – another main road with shops – to breakfast at the roadside on falafel and cold beans from the Co-op.

The papers are full of Trump's 'because he can' visit to Britain and his apparent snub of May in favour of satisfying his vanity by fraternising with the queen as an equal – though I've no doubt that her blue-blooded Britannic majesty considers him the tedious, vulgar, lying, upstart nobody he actually is. There were protests of course, but as there weren't any reports of vandalism and violence we can safely assume they were ineffective. Everybody agrees with the right to protest peacefully, but the moment any protest is likely to cause any actual disruption, and the police wade in to manhandle people, it is denounced by all and sundry as 'violent.' This blindness is usually accompanied by allegations that the protests has been hijacked by politically motivated outsiders, as opposed to those with a genuine grievance, whose only ever intent was to appeal to the consciences

338

of people who don't have a conscience – or they wouldn't have allowed the injustice in the first place.

The sun had come out, so I pointed myself towards it through Winchester, posting my camping stove and knife home on the way, and headed out on the Petersfield road. Winchester was a snarling traffic jam, but has a lovely clear river running through it, which goes under a preserved mill. That's all I can say, but I'm sure it's got a Tesco, a Topshop and a Marks and Spencer's if you need to shop there. It was ten o'clock as I rode out.

After crossing the M5 that rings the city like a horseshoe river round a medieval town I passed a posh school and the regional freemasonry centre, conveniently opposite each other.

There seemed to be a lot of police vans heading east and I wondered if the Leader of the Free World was still in town. I stopped in a layby at Cheriton, where on 29th March 1642 a major battle in the English Civil War took place. The royalists were beaten, but not soundly enough that they couldn't come back for more.

For mile after mile the road had a deep sunken crack across the inside four feet every ten or twenty feet. Some were left, some were badly filled. Every one banged my back wheel. Where I could I went round them, but that wasn't possible when there were cars and trucks speeding past me. Aside from being bad for my back wheel the endless banging makes you irritable. D-duff, d-duff, d-duff, d-duff. By the end of the morning the wind was dead against me and I was pedalling downhill.

Leaving Petersfield for Midhurst it was still big arable fields, trucks, and the wind against me. I entered West Sussex. There is a campsite on my map at Billinghurst and the next one isn't till after Crawley. I'd like to make the latter, but my wheel might give up the ghost anytime.

A tipper driver had on his tailgate 'I slow down for ponies.' He didn't slow down for me. There are some nice places along the way, no doubt with meaningful histories, but which are now just part of the seamless thread of tarmac that runs through them all to who knows where.

Then it started raining like it meant it, so after sheltering for ten minutes under a tree I put my coat on and carried on. I quite enjoyed it. It made the driving even more bizarre.

Midhurst was gridlocked due to road works, so I took to the pavement and straight out – direction Billinghurst. I saw articulated trucks full of teams of polo horses, not something you see that often in West Yorkshire. I really am now in the money belt of Britain.

Approaching Billinghurst there was a campsite sign, so I followed it a mile up the road to the *Bat and Ball* pub, which has a basic site attached (basic usually includes showers nowadays). A woman was sat in a little shed for a reception and told me it was £25 a night to camp. There was no one else on the site. As I was wet through I asked about the few 'pods' they had. They were £95. I told her that I was never coming down south again, that I'd been out forty-four days and they were the second dearest campsite in the country. She acknowledged that there was 'a bit of a price differential.' She was also quite delighted to see that I was 'doing it old school' (no doubt spelled with a 'k'), i.e. using a map. Anyone that isn't permanently attached to a load of electronic gadgetry these days is some sort of exotic throwback – the equivalent of a caveman dressed in a leopard skin and carrying a wooden club. I might have had a pint, but they'll get no more out of me.

It stopped raining and the sun came out, so I was able to spread my coat and top shirt out to dry. My shorts and T shirt will have to dry on me because I've now nothing to get changed into. I don't know what time it is, but it's only early and I've got nothing to read and nothing to do but pore over my maps, but it doesn't matter because I've survived another day and the mission is still on. I've barely enough food to see me through the night, but I'll manage. As I've nothing else to do but sleep I'll be ready to go as soon as it's light – and won't be able to get any food till the shops open, so need to save something for breakfast.

There's nothing in my tent now apart from me, my sleeping bag, my bit of food and my maps.

If I can be on the road at five I can get some of the A road done before the commuters get on it.

When I got here, after I'd put my tent up, I walked up the road to see if there's a shop. There isn't, just about a dozen industrial premises. The people who work there must bring sandwiches.

I shouldn't have stopped. If I'd carried on I could have cleared the outskirts of London and crossed the Thames tomorrow – now I'll be stuck among it all, always assuming my wheel holds up.

The sun is still high in the sky and I'm bored. I wish I was still riding. I'm going to have to get something else to read. If I was a normal person I could fuck about with my mobile phone – it seems to occupy them for hours.

And I'm down to my last twenty pound note – that's over a thousand pounds I've had in cash, besides hotels I've paid for by card.

There are planes going over all the time. I expect that goes on all night.

I was reduced to reading the labels on my peanut butter and pittas – only to discover that I can't even eat Spar pitta breads because they've got milk in them. Why the fuck have pitta breads got milk in them?

When I lay down to sleep I thought I could smell garlic. When the sun shone through the tent it reminded me of lying on the bed at home with the sun shining through the back window and I thought 'what am I doing here?' When I fell briefly asleep I dreamed I was at a motorcycle racing meeting and someone was killed.

When I woke up – it could have been ten minutes later, or two hours later – I was cold, but my shorts were nearly dry.

People were laughing and talking outside the pub. I imagined they were laughing at me. A plane went over every ten minutes. Who in their right mind would think that was normal?

There'll be no campsite tomorrow and I'll be stinking.

The woman said there were two big washing up sinks at the back. I haven't got anything to wash up. This isn't camping either. There is a sign saying no boots or shoes in the shower block. What else can you wear? I haven't got anything else but my boots. The window over the urinals looks out into the garden. It's probably the best view from a toilet I've ever seen. It was the longest afternoon of my life.

I didn't mind the cycling today, even though I've spent every bit of it on main roads. But it's not exactly a holiday. The only fun is in seeing how far I can cycle in a day. It's turned into a mad pointless dash. There's no point in stopping because I can't make tea and I've nothing to read.

When I thought it was time I ate my two pathetic pitta breads with peanut butter and some tomato based party dip, saving the last one for morning. When I next have such a clever idea I need to remember how utterly miserable this is. I reckon I've got six or eight more days of it to do. I haven't had a conversation with anyone for days and I'm not likely to.

I was wrong about the planes. It's every minute. Never was a species more comfortable about its own destruction.

I couldn't go into a pub stinking like I do and I certainly couldn't go into a posh one. There's nothing to stop me buying clean clothes, but I'd have to go into a city.

I thought I'd had a good day, but there was nothing good about it – standing at the side of a busy road eating, eating cold beans in the street, being driven into the gutter, overcharged and patronised.

Very high proportion of sports cars today – Porsches and the like.

Day 47 Billingshurst to Chatham (via Oad Street)

(Sussex and Kent)

Not a very good night's sleep. Got up at the first sign of light, even before the birds started, and packed my few things. Big black clouds moved slowly over. The occasional car went past on the B road and I thought 'only one of those needs to hit me and it's all over.' I have my eye on getting around London today, but I think it's impossible.

I got a good two hours cycling in before the mayhem started. Naturally a big housing development was underway on the outskirts of Billinghurst, but rabbits were leaping in the long grass, crows and magpies were feasting on the remains of last night's MacDonald's meals chucked out of car windows and slugs had left it too late to cross the road. The *Selsey Arms* was covered in RAF flags.

And when it did start it started with a vengeance. Like fighter pilots going down the runway but never achieving lift off, all in their own Top Gun world – cars, vans and trucks all overtaking me too close all the time. One false move, say if I try to avoid a pothole at the wrong time, and one of them will hit me. What I am doing is recklessly dangerous and it doesn't have to be like this.

If there's a footpath I ride on it, but it's often so overgrown it's hardly possible. At one point a great bramble got hold of my clothing and nearly pulled me off – as well as making me look even more like a tramp.

I got to Hayward's Heath unscathed just after seven and overdosed on sugar with coffee and doughnuts in Greggs. I would have preferred Wetherspoon's, but the road sweeper said there wasn't one. And then back into the fray. Towards Ukfield children with lovely hair waited patiently for a gap in the traffic so they could cross the road on their way to school. We're doing this to our own kids.

The road passes Piltdown, east Sussex, where I expect they found Piltdown man. I kept going for Heathfield and two Belgian Blokes on Royal Enfields overtook me. I wonder what they make of it all.

A man voluntarily picking up the rubbish other people throw out of their cars outside Mayfield said I was taking my life in my hands cycling on this road (A267). Actually I'm placing it in other people's hands, which is worse, and it had quietened down a bit by then.

I think generally coach drivers are the worst for overtaking too close – it's happened all over, but one passed me this morning so close I could have polished it as it went past. Posties and bus drivers are the best. Tanker drivers and scaffolding truck drivers are suicidal.

Taxi drivers vary. [After I returned home my friend reminded me that two brothers of his colleague were killed instantly together by a coach driver while cycling in the Lake District.]

On a badly potholed part of the road to Wadhurst someone had painted 'fix me' across the carriageway. The traffic was so light it was almost civilised.

The B road to Wadhurst was very quiet and I paid over the odds for my lunch from the convenience store to eat it by the war memorial (it was only eleven o'clock), only to discover there was a Co-op just round the corner, like there always is. Around the war memorial it says; 'Let those who come after see to it that they are not forgotten.' And so they are not, every time there's need to rally the population round the flag. For the most part the men who fought in the First World War did not volunteer – they were compelled to go and die for the empire, only for it to be rightfully surrendered in subsequent years. It was stupid and futile war and the commemoration of its victims is empty unless we learn the lesson. The lesson being that blind faith in your leaders will get you killed, and we never have.

The papers say Trump has demanded access to the NHS as part of any trade deal. By access he means US companies being able to bid for bits of it, which is the essence of neoliberalism. One of the tabloids squeals that he must keep his hands of 'our' NHS, but it has said nothing about the creeping privatisation that's been going on for years. It doesn't mind the NHS being stolen from us as long as it's stolen by British companies.

At Lamberhurst I rode into Kent and, going north, I now had the breeze behind me again.

The big *White Hart* at Horsmonden was closed and boarded up – along with dozens of other pubs I've seen along the way. In Marden there were big banners; 'We say no to 2,000 more homes in Marden.' A Battle of Britain air show was advertised – displays of military hardware yes, new homes no. There was a big sticker on the sign for the village of Collier Street; 'Honk of you want a blow job.'

There are a few 'Tudor' timber framed houses round here and several converted oast houses. The roads are quiet and the villages pleasant. In Yalding a campaign had failed to keep the post office open.

People along the B2163 demand a relief road (and a road to relieve that, *ad infinitum*). Over the M20, through Hollingbourne. The *Dirty Habit* said it was a thirteenth century country pub. It was no more thirteenth century than my house is. These heritage claims get ever more ridiculous.

There was a massive climb from there onto a plateau, from which I think I would have been able to see across the Thames Estuary but for the habit of erecting very tall hedges round all the fruit orchards.

There was a detour on the descent down a very narrow lane and everything came to a standstill for ten minutes, so I had a jam sandwich in a farm gate while motorists got irate. A bloke in a car asked me if my bike was carbon and told me there was a big bike shop in Canterbury where I could get it fixed. My home-made bike is so obviously not carbon that only a complete ignoramus could imagine it was.

When I eventually got to the bottom it was a warren of little lanes I could easily have got lost in, but a nice woman told me the way to Oad Street, my 21st destination. I rode right through, past another big traffic hold up, by sneaking down the side of a wagon lifting a new telegraph pole into place.

Another old woman stopped her car to give me directions while I was studying my map at a junction and I was soon on the A2 heading for the Medway towns and some crossing of the Thames – I had no idea which one I could use – past the house of some patriot flying his union flag upside down, the first one I've seen on the trip, and I've been paying close attention as I always do.

As I rode into Rainham loads of military planes flew across in the middle distance. People seemed quite excited by this and stood in the street taking pictures with their mobile phones. Men with beer bellies and fags in their mouths came out of pubs to celebrate the glory reflected on Britain's entire manhood.

I knew I'd be staying inside tonight and looked for a Travelodge or a Premier Inn and came across the latter first, expecting to have to pay a lot of money. The receptionist said they had a room (pause while I waited) but it was £98. I said I'd have to pay it. She said they had thirty rooms left and it was too much – did I want her to look on the internet and see what else there was in the area?

She found a room for me at the *King Charles* Hotel, with breakfast, for £55, whereas at the Premier Inn breakfast is an extra £9.50, which she also said was too much. I asked her if it was Charles I or Charles II, but she didn't know. I asked her if she was pissing about at the back of the class when they did it at school. She said she generally was. To be honest I'd rather have stuck with what I knew, but she gave me directions and no choice. It took some finding and I asked four different people, including one who wouldn't take his earphones out to speak to me.

The *King Charles* Hotel was big and modern and looked a bit of a dump, not least because half of it appeared to be derelict, but was actually undergoing refurbishment. I put my bike in the meeting room and two intoxicated Polish blokes in the lift said I looked like Chuck Norris. I don't know who Chuck Norris is, but it will be my Tilley hat, it usually is.

It turns out that the planes flying over were Dakotas and it is part of a big commemoration of D Day and the Normandy landings – there's always some war to celebrate.

I ate jam sandwiches and watched crap on the TV all evening.

It's been a good day's cycling today and I've enjoyed it. I never thought I would get this far. I thought Kent might offer some relief from all the hills of Devon and Dorset, but there's been some very big climbs. I've survived another day and the back wheel seems to be holding up.

It even looks nice out back, which is very rare in a hotel. Lots of decaf coffee, big kettle, nice big mugs, fan, telly, hot shower.

Day 48 – Chatham to Tattingstone

(Kent, Essex and Suffolk)

Slept well and awake before five.

Donald Trump has intervened in the Brexit 'debate' by saying 'a wall could be good for Ireland.'

And it is suggested that food ordering apps are making us lazy, with people ordering cups of tea and slices of toast to be delivered. No kidding.

Denmark has elected its youngest ever premier. She ran on environmental issues and has Greta Thunberg to thank for her victory. It was mentioned in parliament yesterday that several of the figures in the Tory leadership contest have links to organisations engaged in climate change denial.

The news on every channel was of old men assembling on the beaches of Normandy to commemorate as teenagers charging up them into machine gun fire and surviving. How many of them are driven by survivor's guilt one wonders.

I was surprised to discover that my underpants and socks I washed last night were almost dry. I should have washed my T shirt as well.

Yesterday I plotted the whole day's ride by putting arrows on my map so I didn't have to make decisions at every junction. It worked well, but today's route depends on where I can cross the Thames. It will no doubt be easy, but as yet it is a mystery. It was a beautiful morning, but the forecast is for rain later.

A good breakfast served by friendly staff in a very pleasant dining room. There were people from all over, including those on the coach trips one always gets in these big hotels. Some of the hotels are actually owned by the coach companies it seems.

When I left at 7.30 I discovered I was right next to the Royal School of Military Engineering, where I did my bricklayer's course in 1974. I didn't recognise a thing. And yet the hotel must have been here at the time. There was also a signposted cycle path which wouldn't have existed in the seventies. While I was at Chatham I experienced some mild bullying and will remember till I die buying a

347

copy of *I'm not in Love* by 10cc for someone else on my course. He played it so much that I have hated the song ever since. Even thinking about it now fills me with distaste.

It was quite fun negotiating Chatham and Rochester out towards Gravesend – and parts of it were much quieter than I expected. There were good cycle paths. Though they weren't all in the best condition – some of those marked by a white line on the road were unrideable due to the broken surface. It was by no means flat and the hills were hard on my full breakfast.

The *Sir John Falstaff* at Higham is 'a traditional Kentish pub.' Whatever can that mean? Nothing probably.

Riding towards Gravesend I saw and caught up with David and Elspeth, who were on the second day of their ride to Shetland – they slept in the woods last night – again making me feel inferior for my resort to the luxury of hotels and official campsites. They had four panniers each, a big holdall each, bar bags and folding chairs. David did all the talking, one of those who does a running commentary on everything, and said they were playing a game called pub cricket, where you got 'runs' for the number of legs in a pub's name, and in which Elspeth did not seem remotely interested. But he knew there was a ferry to Tilbury and they led me there. It was four pounds each – like everything else four times what it costs anywhere else. It was a proper boat, not a flat calm pontoon like the others I've been on, and the first time I believe I've been on the Thames.

We parted company at the other side. David seemed keen that I did not tag along with them – something I had no intention of doing. After using the same pen for weeks, until it ran out, I got a new one out of my bag and immediately lost it.

Tilbury is like any other port – cranes, containers, wagons thundering in every direction and road signs designed to get them away by the quickest possible means. There were some good cycle lanes and signing, but everything was dirty and dusty. All the signs wanted to send me west and I had to go by the sun for a while, eventually finding my way out north. During a brief spell among countryside the verges were strewn with rubbish, but also there, and on wasteland, were lots of poppies, since they are the only thing that will grow on a wasteland, which is fitting on the anniversary of D Day isn't it?

I had to buy some index cards to use as postcards. They don't do postcards for Chatham and Tilbury. Had there been no cards I was going to buy a box of cereals and cut the box up for cards. In fact I already had a box of Fruit and Fibre in my hands when I saw the index cards. While I was waiting for the Southend train to cross the level crossing at Stanford-le-Hope a man beside me was telling a fellow worker how 'market conditions' had led to a big loss for a client who didn't really know what he was doing.

It was very slow going picking my way about using a combination of road and cycle route signs, but it suddenly dawned on me how pleasant and relaxing it was, and how it might be a good idea if I enjoyed the last few days of the trip, rather than hammering along A roads like I have been for the last week as if I was in some mad race. Although if I hadn't done I wouldn't now be in a position where there's plenty of time.

What surprises you most in Tilbury, after being in the Caucasian enclaves of Hampshire, Oxfordshire, Devon and Cornwall, is the incredible number of black people there are.

I dropped off an overgrown shared path to let a young couple pass. She was pushing a pram. He was wearing a fleece tracksuit and walking a big ugly dog. They both thanked me, though there was no need. Old people generally don't thank you because they haven't got used to it being OK for cyclists to be on the pavement rather than get killed on the road – and they fought two world wars to preserve their right to have the pavement all to themselves.

A sign entering Thurrock said a police number plate recognition system was in operation – not just for a car park, but for a whole town. Big brother or what?

I called in at one of the biggest Tesco stores I've ever seen for a few bits. I could have had anything I wanted, but I didn't buy anything that was any good for me. There was a woman begging outside. In Bradford people beg sat cross-legged on traffic islands at major road junctions with labels round their necks. You can find people that say not all beggars are poor and that begging is just a way to make a living – an attitude redolent of Elizabethan England, where the poor were beaten out of town and strung up if they returned. They say this because they don't want to acknowledge they give tacit support to a society that degrades people so. If begging is a profession it is no less noble than that of scab, mercenary, arms dealer or exploiter. Begging is more honest than overcharging for a service. No beggar is ever going to ask me for £25 to put my tent on their grass when it's only worth a fiver.

Tesco even run a hand car wash in competition with illegal immigrants enslaved by ruthless gang masters. An overweight young woman had 'I just can't' on her shirt, a play on Nike's 'Just do it.' Lots of other people clearly couldn't either.

Eventually, when I'd hardly cleared Basildon by lunch time, it became very wearing being funnelled round and round in circles on bumpy cycle paths whose main purpose is to make it easier for car drivers, following signs that eventually disappear and paths that come to a sudden stop with the word 'end' written on the road, and I had to take to the main road. In any case many of the cycle routes utilise long neglected pavements, and an overgrown and broken footpath that was laid in 1960 does not constitute a reasonable cycle path.

At Woodham Ferrers someone had erected in front of some bungalows replica wooden tank trap star things with the names of all the Normandy beaches on them. The school house and chapel had two big bowing silhouettes of WWI soldiers. It seems everyone has caught the convenient remembrance bug.

I was back in the villages for a while – 'Brutus had rather be a villager than to repute himself a son of Rome under these hard conditions as this time is like to lay upon us.'

A big low-loader driver drove six feet behind me for several hundred yards revving his engine trying to intimidate me, which he did, when there was nowhere for me to go. When I was able to pull in to let him pass he had a sticker on the back warning cyclists about the danger zones around the vehicle.

In fact at 3.30, having been deafened and intimidated all day, I'd come to the conclusion that Essex is blighted with the same disease as everywhere else – too many cars and a stupid freight transport policy.

Car

The car is the symbol of freedom
The car is the mark of success
The car's any flavour you want it to be
The man in the showroom say yes

The car's any colour you want it to be
As long as the oil is black
The car is driving the human race
And we're all strapped in in the back

The car's any colour you want it to be
As long as the dollar is green
We all hot foot to the showroom
Like lemmings at a ravine

The lungs of the planet are wheezing
There's tarmac right up to the door
There's tarmac and cars in the lobby
And businessmen baying for more

The car's any colour you want it to be
It's cars that keep us afloat
The car's the colour of congressmen
Who need the cash and the vote

The car has its place in culture

Its place in the national song
The car's any shit that you want it to be
And six billion flies can't be wrong

Humanity has reached an impasse
With the driver the king of the road
The car is as black as it's painted
We all need a different mode

Humanity is at a crossroads
The future needs to be read
But it's no use pretending we're Lenin
When we're Jeremy Clarkson instead

The car's any colour you want it to be
Says the spiv in the motor trade
Take the bourgeois symbol of freedom
And drive down to the barricade

The car's any colour you want it to be
And conscience is deeper than paint
But I need a car to get to my work
I'm a school teacher not just a saint

With oily tongue and greasy palm
And lips that never speak
The car's any colour you want it to be
As long as the future is bleak

I forgot to mention that one of the rhetorical questions on the news headlines last night was; 'After sixteen more migrants attempt to cross the channel by boat: Is our asylum system in danger of killing people with kindness?' This is the asylum system that Theresa May instructed to create a hostile environment for migrants and which keeps innocent people in concentration camps where they are mistreated and abused by privatised guards.

Colchester calls itself Britain's oldest recorded town and as you enter a big sign says there's no excuse for poor driving. There's always an excuse, the question is whether it is valid.

As I rode into town the bin men were leaving the council depot on bicycles. I asked one of them if he'd done enough for today. He said, 'More than enough.'

I kept the sun behind me going through and asked several people for directions, but they all wanted to send me on the big main road to Ipswich. So I kept my shadow in front and carried on for an hour. When there was eventually someone to ask – a nurse unloading her car at a lone house in the countryside – I wasn't far off and she told me about a little lane that would take me to the right road. I didn't know where I was, but several big banners were opposing the building of 7,500 new homes.

I didn't see anywhere I could stay so I didn't stop.

Once on the right road I was bowled along by the wind, past the house of another patriot that doesn't know which way up to fly the flag he is so proud of. (I suppose it is always possible that these people are aware that flying the flag upside down is a sign of distress and actually believe Britain is in distress.) It was a lovely evening and the road was quiet, the sun was quite high, why not keep going?

At Manningtree the commuters were streaming out of the railways station. I entered Suffolk and a big banner read; 'No building on Greenfield.'

I can't express here how peace shattering it is when you are riding along a fairly quiet country road in the evening and all of a sudden there's a series of bumps – d-duff, d-duff, d-duff – every one of them jars your back and makes you think your back wheel is going to explode. It makes me call out 'fucking roads' at the top of my voice to no one. And then at 7.15, on the basis that something will turn up, something turned up, I spotted half hidden by the trees, a tiny brown campsite sign. It took me along a narrow lane to a very basic but nice and flat campsite at the back of the *White Horse* at Tattingstone. At

£3.50 per person per night I felt I could give them the price of a pint of cider. At the bar I told the landlady and the young chef, who was leaving on Sunday and sitting at the bar working out instructions for his successor, the extent of my travels and discovered nothing about them apart from that they were both on Facebook.

I am in clover. I kid myself each day that I am going to keep riding because I want to, but what I really want to do is stop. I don't care if it's nine o'clock as long as I stop and I'm comfortable somewhere.

It's been as good riding today as any day and I've survived to carry on – though I feel every bump in the road and dread the total collapse. Can I really complete the trip so damaged?

I had my hummus and pittas, drank my blue pop and got my head down for an early start. I was content in my tent listening to the evening chorus and I thought I'd done rather well getting from Chatham nearly to Ipswich in a day, given that it took me most of the morning to get across the Thames and clear Tilbury and a hotel always means a late start.

Day 49 – Ipswich to Mildenhall (via Ubbeston Green)
(Suffolk)

Even one pint of cider ensured that I wouldn't sleep properly. I was awake hours before dawn, willing it to get light, and kept putting my head out and looking for signs of light. I was up as soon as I could see and availed myself of the Spartan facilities – the old outside toilets of the pub complete with traditional full length piss stones and a single washbasin. The sky was heavy and red – red sky in the morning etc.

On the way back down the lane to the main road the sun appeared on the horizon a big red ball.

Ipswich is 'East Anglia's Waterfront Town.' It is one more port managed by Associated British Ports. Containers were already rolling out. It was just 5.30 as I passed through the centre. Orwell seems to be a common name in Suffolk.

There are some big old houses in Ipswich and there must have been money made – the road grates for example were cast in the town by C. Mills and Co. (Ipswich). There's a pub called *Case is altered*, a Khartoum Road, a Gordon Road and a Nelson Road – a massacre and two imperialists.

On the back of the buses, which are run by First Group, it says, 'Make a difference, become a police officer.' Becoming a police officer is not making a difference, it is the opposite of making a difference. It is upholding and reinforcing the status quo.

Just before I crossed the A12 toward Woodbridge a crow was stood on a dead squirrel in the gutter. It stood its ground with both feet on the squirrel as I passed. Crows never stand their ground like that. In fact generally the blacker a bird is the more cowardly it is.

In Martlesham some pudding had called his house *Endeavour* and it had it in foot high letters across his gate. His neighbours preferred *The Coppice* and *The Brambles*.

Woodbridge is a historic market town. It has a street called California and a big pub called the *Duke of York*, the second I've seen this morning. An advert for father's day designed to inspire guilt in sons and daughters features random spanners and hammers, because that's what fathers do – fix things, with tools, all of them.

John Grose Motors is selling a car called an Eco-Sport. It's telling consumers they can have a new car and be environmentally friendly at the same time. They can't.

Melton Chapel (1860) uses the classic picture of Kitchener pointing to say, 'You are the reason Jesus came.' Can there be a more crass misappropriation?

Wickham Market has got a big church for a small place and a tattooist called The Ink Spot who is a 'black eye' specialist.

Coming into another village a concrete wagon went to overtake me round a blind bend and had to jam his brakes on when a woman came the other way in a car. I rode into the kerb, thinking he was going to flatten me. They all have these lecturing yellow stickers on the back telling cyclists how to ride.

When I stopped for an emergency piss there was nothing to lean my bike on and I had to lay it down in the grass. The chain came off and got trapped between the back sprocket and the axle plates. I had to remove all my luggage and fully slacken the wheel to free it and ended up sweating and with my hands covered in two months' worth of accumulated black grease.

At Shawsgate Vineyard (there are several vineyards about) a marquee was erected in the garden for some event. It was done up in George crosses and looked like an EDL rally was about to take place.

I arrived at Ubbeston Green, my twenty third destination, mid-morning. There was no one to speak to, so I spoke to no one, turned my map over, had a jam sandwich and headed west, which just happened to be the direction the wind was blowing in.

There was a nice campsite at Ubbeston, with picnic tables set out under a shelter, but it wasn't time to camp.

I made good time to Eye. It has got a massive church – almost a cathedral. There was a big banner outside 'Stop Brexit – any deal is a bad deal – contact your local Liberal Democrats.' Can we assume the Church is against Brexit and that it is now the Liberal Democrats, rather than the Tories, at prayer? In the Co-op there was a notice saying that money laundering funds terrorism and that the Co-op had an active policy against money laundering. A woman wanted to see the manageress, and then asked if we could still call her the manageress with all this political correctness stuff. I notice on the TV that they've started referring to 'men's cricket' instead of just 'cricket' now it's been noticed that women play too.

Among the nauseating coverage of the D Day celebrations (for every man who wants to remember there'll be ten who have spent seventy five years trying to forget) the tabloids find the space to say only Boris can stop Farage. That's because they both believe the same thing, one of them just happens to be in the Tory party. It was trying to stop Farage and UKIP that got them into this mess in the first place.

I had my lunch sat on the wall outside the Eye poultry factory. It had a better security fence than some barracks. All the workers I saw were dark skinned and foreign. I thought I heard Arabic being spoken, but it could have been Kurdish or Farsi. British people don't want to work in a poultry factory, they just want to eat chicken with a clear conscience. It looked as if it was the major local employer – so that's OK. Anything that creates jobs is OK – nuclear weapons, arms sales – OK.

The church of St Mary the Virgin at Gisingham had two big modern plastic camouflage nets spread over its wall with hundreds of knitted poppies sewn to it – again I would suggest inappropriate – a glorification of the military, rather than a sombre demonstration of remembrance and regret.

The local paper says gangs are shipping stolen cars through the port – perhaps before spending the money on tortilla chips and chocolate digestives at the Co-op like I did.

On an unclassified road west a woman was walking three dogs wearing a T shirt that said, 'If I can't bring my dog I'm not coming.' Actually the boot is on the other foot. 'If you insist on bringing your dog then don't bother coming, because your dog will not be entering my premises.' How dare they try to impose their dirty animals on other people with threats?

The Anglian reports 'Public meeting over youth problems.' Bring back National Service, that's what I say. 'What we need is another war,' you can hear the *Daily Mail* readers saying. There was no vandalism and hanging about on corners then.

I popped into the cemetery at Walsham and found the grave of 47107 S.A. Cracknell of the Kings Royal Rifle Corps, who died on 16th December 1918, a youth who didn't cause any problems.

The Young

The young, the young
I'm sick of hearing the young
Send them off to fight the foe
That'll silence their tongue

357

A bit of military discipline
That's what young people need
A dose of a Sergeant major
He'll put a stop to their greed

Get them lined up and marching
Forget the job seeking farce
That'll stop them slouching about
With their trousers half round their arse

The young today are shiftless
They just don't want to work
Make them work for their benefits
That'll teach them to shirk

They think we owe them a living
Well let them work on a farm
Up to their knees in shit all day
It never did me any harm

They go and get educated
And think they should have careers
When I was their age I was out in France
With mud right up to my ears

They think some jobs are below them
What's wrong with washing plates?
When I was their age I didn't complain
I was in Ireland losing my mates

The young today are bone idle
They won't get out of their beds
When I was their age I didn't lie in
I was in Korea stopping the Reds

They think they should be respected
But to pamper them just isn't right
When I was eighteen I didn't sign on
I was in Flanders losing my sight

The young today they are feckless
They think they can steal and beg
When I was nineteen I didn't do that
I was in Normandy losing my leg

The young today they're always doped up
We've got to be cruel to be kind
When I was their age I didn't take drugs
I was in Bosnia losing my mind

The young of today I'll tell you
Have never had it so good
When I was their age I didn't complain
I was overseas shedding my blood

Preening themselves like strutting cocks
And lathering gel on their hair
We'd no need to worry about what to put on
When we were over there

The young, the young
They'll never be satisfied
They'll never realise how well off they are
Until a few of their mates have died

When I was young I was always abroad
Fighting the country's foes
And just like them and all them to come
I couldn't see past the end of my nose

I once sent this poem in to a competition. The judge said the problem was that young people received conflicting messages – they do – 'Patriotism is good racism is wrong.' Actually patriotism and racism are the same thing, and both lead to war. The message young people need is the one I've mentioned before – Blind faith in your leaders will get you killed.

Then it started raining and clearly wasn't going to stop for some time. I passed a pub that was dog friendly and three doors away a house that offered 'short breaks for dogs.'

Wet through before Mildenhall I went in the Travelodge. The nice young man said they had a room, it wasn't too expensive, £44, all fine and dandy – till he said I needed photo I.D. to book a room, which I've never been asked for before. Despite my please there was no way he was shifting – no photo I.D. no room. This means that in my own country I have to carry my passport – I have no other photo I.D. He was adamant and I was gobsmacked. I was going to be turned away. When he'd let me sweat he said there was one way – I could phone central bookings on his phone and book a room that way. So I did and it was cheaper, £41.50, not only is the system authoritarian, it is illogical. The receptionist said he'd had a disciplinary for letting someone stay without photo I.D. 'and I've been here seven years.'

Unfortunately when I got in the room with my bike I discovered that I now have three broken spokes in the back wheel. I put that problem to one side, turned up the radiator, washed all my clothes and then myself.

I worked out a route and there's a campsite about ten miles from Peterborough. I could go there and pitch and ride my bike unloaded into the city, but what would happen there I don't know. (I was thinking of getting the wheel repaired).

Incidentally Labour has kept its seat in the Peterborough bi-election on a reduced majority. The Tories lost a lot of votes and the Lib Dems gained. Nigel Farage's Brexit Party did well, but not well enough.

Obviously it stopped raining and I could have made it to the campsite today, that's if my wheel didn't collapse on the way and I hadn't noticed there were now three spokes missing.

I reckon I could have been home in three or four days if it wasn't for the wheel problem and I don't know if a bike shop will be able to offer a solution – there's only some new spokes and re-truing and they probably won't have the right length spokes in stock, or be able to do it straight away – or a different wheel, which would only be single speed, which doesn't exist in most shops, or in 26", or a hub gear, which would cost a fortune.

I watched an antiques program and a house finding program. They make towns and villages out to be traditional and appealing. They all ignore the fact that everywhere is clogged with cars and every architectural attraction is surrounded and obscured by cars. It's like we've all got some great big blind spot and we simply pretend they're not there.

After watching crap on TV all evening I must admit I'm quite worried about what I'm going to do, even though I shouldn't be. I put the light out, but couldn't sleep for worrying about my problem. Eventually it dawned on me what I have to do – rather than embark on a wild goose chase expecting someone else to get me out of my predicament. I have to get the train home, get a different bike, come back and take up the trip where I left off. It's not ideal and it will be expensive, but it's the best solution. It will mean I haven't done it in one go as I intended, but if my wheel collapses I might not complete it at all. The question now is which station to head for – it's got to be the one I come back to to resume. At least I shouldn't stink on the train.

Day 50 – Mildenhall to Home
(Suffolk to Yorkshire)
Up early. It was reported that the new political party made up mostly of pro-EU, anti-Corbyn splitters from the Labour Party with a few Tories, calling itself 'Change' and fronted by right-wing Blairite Chukka Umuna, has fallen apart after only two months in existence.

361

Cycle to Kennett unmanned station. Buy ticket for Peterborough from a machine – nearly £23 for a ten minute journey. No wonder people drive. We're fucked. My reading of the timetable said there'd be a train just after eight – but it wasn't on the digital display and there are engineering works the other way requiring a bus replacement. I have no faith that the plan will work – and if it works it will be eye-wateringly expensive. I feel demeaned by the ticket price because I am being fleeced by train operators who pay themselves massive salaries and their shareholders big dividends, while milking what should be a public service and is actually a cash cow – which is exactly what Donald Trump and the most rabid of the neoliberals want to do to the health service.

The night man at the Travelodge, who had a speech impediment and bad teeth full of food and plaque, said I'd to go to Bury St Edmunds. It wouldn't have made any difference, but then he didn't know where I wanted to go. I knew no train was going to come. [Actually it would have made a great deal of difference due to the engineering works and the bus replacement that can't carry bicycles].

Somebody came into the car park and it looked good. And then a cyclist came in and locked her bike up.

A train did come, but it was going to Cambridge and I had to change for Peterborough. As we went past Newmarket it was raining. I could have probably got a train home from Cambridge, but there's definitely a train to Leeds from Peterborough.

I think I've had my fill of mammoth trips. I wish this was over. I wish I hadn't said I'd do a talk about it at club camp and I wish I didn't have to type it all up.

On the train I met Jill – a nurse at Addenbrooks Hospital and we talked about the ridiculous price of train travel. I wish this was over.

Change onto Birmingham train at Cambridge for Peterborough. I wish I wasn't being sponsored and then I could just pack this in.

A man got on with a modern lightweight bike. My bike is ridiculous beside his. Why do I endlessly make life difficult for myself?

I am having a get rid of all my bikes except two moment. Stop doing big marathons. Stop writing everything down. I've been here umpteen times before.

First things first at Peterborough – I bought enough rations for the day at the Waitrose outside the station. When I went to buy a ticket the next two trains to Leeds had no bicycle spaces available. Not till the 12.51 train was there space available, but at least there was a reasonable comfortable waiting room to spend two and a half hours in. At the last minute I decided not to resume the trip immediately, like tomorrow, as I had planned, but to buy an open ticket and regroup at home, especially as the weather is to be bad next week. I thought my ticket to Bradford would cost a fortune, but it was 'only' £74.00, which bears no comparison to the £22 I paid to get from Kennett to Peterborough.

I went to the right place on the platform in plenty of time to put my bike in the 'guard's van' part of the propulsion unit, but when the train arrived the platform attendant couldn't open the door, though she pulled and tugged at it. She got the driver, only a young man, out of his cab, which I'm sure he's not supposed to do, and he went inside and pushed and shoved, but it wouldn't open. Because they are on such a tight turnaround and a late train makes ten others late, for which train operating companies get penalised, the stationmaster made it go. I had to wait for the next train to Grantham, on which neither my bike or I were booked, and change at Grantham – all of which meant I could have got on a train three hours earlier but for bureaucratic rules.

On the Grantham train I spoke with another cyclist called Darren, a man clearly not in possession of the full range of faculties, and who, though probably in his thirties still lived at home with his mother. He had tattoos all over him, mostly of skulls, and said he'd only been to Leeds once and it was a rough place. He was on his way to see his dad in Boston, which is also a rough place. Darren thought I looked about seventy. No one ever guesses I'm older than I am. It must be the full grey beard that does it. None of this mattered because I've got an open ticket – and the bicycle reservation business is a farce, there's plenty of room in the guard's van.

On the next train I met George, a Zimbabwean, who teaches African Studies at the University of Edinburgh. He was very interested in my trip, especially in what I ate. He understood the technical side of my bicycle because his father had a business making security gates and railings – my bike is essentially a gate with wheels. He was also quite negative about the asylum system, his own mother-in-law being refused a visa for some family event, saying the Home Office was the inhuman face of Britain. He knew Glasgow as well, as his wife was studying there when they were courting.

Only fifteen minutes to wait for the train to Leeds – again one where bikes have to go in the guard's van three coaches away from where a standard class passenger sits. But all went well and I got a seat to stare blankly at the passing countryside from.

Not long to wait either in Leeds for a train to Bradford. The guard wasn't checking tickets properly so I stayed on till Low Moor and cycled home down the Spen dog toilet greenway.

Oades was in, cooking and glad to see me – though she said she hasn't been sad in my absence. She's been to see her brother and his wife, who spent the whole of her visit lamenting about Brexit. They have put their house up for sale and intend moving to their other house in France before Britain actually leaves the EU. It amazes me that people ignored or celebrated forty years of neoliberal destruction, but imagine Brexit to be the end of the world as we know it. Perhaps they think it will hamper their travelling to and fro, their childrens' study abroad etc. – though her brother has for a long time run his own business and has much to say on the possible economic consequences.

Apparently Donald Trump while he was here said that Sadiq Khan, Mayor of London, was 'a stone cold loser.' Khan didn't have to do anything to incur the president's wisdom – just be Muslim, allegedly left wing and have criticised The Donald for being the dangerous idiot he is. Khan isn't left wing of course – he's New Labour.

While I have been away a friend has been diagnosed with throat cancer, and another has had stoma fitted after having half his bowel removed. There is pathos in the throat cancer because the victim is an educator and public speaker. Could it have anything to do with his going running among the traffic in Leeds? Oades thinks he used to smoke roll-ups.

A freind, who initially refused to sponsor me, but came to the send-off with energy bars for me, says he'd like to sponsor me personally – i.e. specifically not giving anything to asylum seekers – because he appreciates what I'm doing, even though he doesn't support the cause.

She made a nice curry and afterward I reviewed my maps in readiness for getting the train back to Cambridge on Tuesday. But first I'm going to change the handlebars on my Thorn for a more leisurely sat up style.

Incidentally about ten bikes have been delivered for me – the surplus from a friend's collection after his move from Norfolk to live with his partner in Northumberland. Some of them look nice, but there'll be time to look properly later.

All this took us to well past ten o'clock, much later than I have been awake these last few weeks.

Day 1 of Hiatus – At Home

While we were having our tea and toast in bed Oades let me into a secret – she has booked a venue for me to do a little talk for my supporters and others when I get back – which I was going to arrange myself. When she invited one of our friends they said they wouldn't come to something about cycling – as if I'd do a talk just about cycling – it would be shit boring. And they should know I wouldn't do something that was empty of political and social comment.

I didn't get up until 8.30. Oades had gone for a run. I changed the handlebars on my Thorn, fitted a new chain and extra water bottle carrier and a container to put my oil bottle and chain oiling toothbrush in.

We went into Bradford on the bus, got me a train ticket back to Cambridge, booked bicycle places on both trains and bought gas cylinders for my stove.

Looking for a book to take away I re-read Hugh Trevor-Roper's account of the invention of the Scottish Highland tradition in Hobsbawm and Ranger *The Invention of Tradition*. The kilt was invented by an English Quaker industrialist in the eighteenth century. He bought the rights to a forest for its charcoal and moved his iron smelting business north. The men he employed found the single piece of material they wrapped round themselves cumbersome for forest and factory work and the kilt was designed to give more freedom of movement *for workers* – as such the wealthy would not have been seen dead in it.

When the kilt had become widely worn by all classes the rich wore coloured kilts and the poor brown ones. The members of one family might all wear different patterns and as late as the mid eighteenth century specific clan tartans were completely unknown. It all had to be deliberately invented – just like all the other timeless traditions we honour as natural.

When I picked up Peter Ustinov's autobiography he mentions on page five the seriousness with which American tourists take researches into the origins of the kilt. They are as likely to discover the truth as the rest of us are to discover the truth about all the other pseudo archaic traditions we are surrounded by. It can be taken for granted that anything described as traditional will be a patchwork of contrivances in which the past has been repeatedly used to bolster contemporary social relations, political expediencies or profits. The very fact that something needs to be referred to as traditional means it probably isn't.

Ustinov tells us that when Russia was industrialising 'an imperial decree had compelled those of high birth to relinquish their titles should they stoop to commercial activity.' Later this humiliation was compounded by a rule that the nature of a family's business be included on their crest. With the passage of time these emblems became proofs of relative antiquity, to be displayed with pride.

Institutions are adapted to suit the times and 'tradition' is fickle and flexible. We should no more accept that our law is administered by out of touch pompous public school toffs than we should that an out of town Barratt house gains anything from the misapplication of a dubious adjective.

Day 2 of Hiatus – At Home

Boris Johnson has promised tax cuts to people earning over £50,000 p.a. – about one in ten very well off people – if his is elected Tory leader. This is described by the BBC as 'red meat' to his potential electors. One of the other contenders, Michael Gove, is all over the media due to his admission that he took cocaine on several occasions. This has given his opponents the opportunity for wholesale hypocrisy, with one of them, Sajid Javed, making ridiculous comments about people taking drugs while pretending to have healthy 'green' lifestyles. Eight of the eleven Tory leadership candidates have admitted to using drugs – which, while providing much entertainment at their squirming, reveals nothing about their suitability to lead the Tory Party, let alone the country. In fact the country would undoubtedly be run more fairly if it were in the hands of a government of reformed drug addicts (even current drug addicts) than it is in the hands of these calculating, business obsessed hypocrites.

Protests continue in Birmingham against the teaching about lesbian and gay relationships in schools – centred mainly around one school. The opposition is led by Muslim parents.

Peter Ustinov suggests that one of his overweight ancestors lived to a hundred and eight because there were no doctors competent to warn him of the dangers of obesity. He was writing in 1977, long before the current epidemic (and anti-smoking campaigns), but his thinking is entirely in line with the view that every personal attempt at healthy living is a fad, every pronouncement by doctors is bound to be contradicted later and the opinion that a head in the sand 'it never did me any harm' attitude is the best philosophy.

Ustinov is clearly fond of an axiom and points to the inevitable coming together of 'the affairs of the heart and the affairs of the mind.' I think of all the couples I know who share their opinions about the world and can't think of one that doesn't.

Swapping between books as I do – The Scottish highland 'tradition,' particularly in its outward appearances, is a highly formalised cult built on very dubious foundations. It is not a tradition in any real sense of the word. It is an artificial contrivance with no more basis in history that the modish apparel of skinheads, punks, mods or teddy boys – the only difference being that it was promoted by people with influence and adopted by the aristocracy to the extent that the current heir to the throne now parades in a garment deliberately designed for those who make a living through manual labour. It is as if those at court today took to wearing Dickies work wear, steel toe-capped boots and fluorescent jackets. Highland dress is a modish fad elevated to a national dress, recognised and replicated the world over.

The kilt was taken up by the well-to-do, it was reinforced by the founding of the Scottish regiments in imperial service and it became the national dress of a whole nation with an apparent history from time immemorial. All its advocates ignored a wealth of evidence disproving its antiquity. The past was effectively rewritten to suit the fashion and upon it a whole history was founded.

Peter Ustinov's autobiography was a good charity shop choice – at least it seems so after a dozen pages. He details in delightful language the history of his family in Germany, Russia and Jerusalem. I can feel a critique of the Russian Revolution coming, but that is normal in any work by an author who sees the world as a series of events rather than as a series of possibilities, most of which are wasted or defeated.

Ustinov describes how one ancestor on his mother's side could not decide how to spell his own name, remarking that he is in the good company of Shakespeare in this foible. 'The insistence on accurate spelling at modern schools,' he says, 'is an effort to invest a living language with rigor mortis, and to prepare a rhapsodic means of self-expression for the glacial corridors of computerdom.' He could not have known that the internet, and even more the mobile phone, would have quite the opposite effect.

Another antecedent he describes as having the rare ability to assess his own talents accurately, 'which is an advantage in some circumstances, and a drawback in others.'

I am in danger of placing these two delightful (and heavy) books in my panniers tomorrow to take them for a two hundred mile ride in the certain knowledge that the time I have to read them will be limited.

Last night the teenage girl from over the road, brought Oades a big expensive plant from Marks and Spencer's to thank her for taking up her expensive prom dress. High school proms are a tradition that have crept in over the last decade or so and previously did not exist. Oades was shitting herself working on the expensive garment containing many voluminous yards of material, but all seems to have turned out well. While I have been away she has made me another shirt and a dress for an upcoming wedding. In the evening she made a handbag to complete her outfit.

On counting I discover that there are now thirteen non-roadworthy bicycles on the premises – most donated by one person, but a couple from elsewhere. At least three of them are ladies' bikes and two of them are children's. None have a frame really big enough for me – a fact which I can rectify only if Oades agrees to do my welding. They are all at the same time perfectly good bikes, projects I don't need and so much scrap. Piled up in the cellar they currently have no value whatsoever and stand as testament to our misplaced values and throwaway society. On the one hand I know I need only two bicycles, on the other I can't see perfectly good ones go to scrap. At the same time I am torn between pointless bicycle projects and pointless writing projects.

Half of me wants now, on a day dedicated to rest, either to pull one of the bikes out and start fettling it or start typing this diary – neither of which I need to do. The only question is of which is the most pointless.

With that I idled away an hour looking at some of my diaries from earlier this year. Personally I think they make interesting reading.

When I return to Ustinov he's on about his great uncle, who painted melancholy sunsets, and says, 'As with many casually talented people, he was accused of overriding facilities, but critics often fail to recognise that no amount of fretful application would have improved those particular sunsets, and to heed criticism to the extent of refraining to paint sunsets when sunsets are your particular forte is to go the way of many facile people who scandalously betray their facility in order to work hard and masochistically at things they are no good at, while the critic who is not much good at anything himself breathes down their necks with the sterile satisfaction of a sadistic schoolmaster.'

I take this as a licence to carry on writing and building bicycles, because we always use what we read to reinforce what we already believe.

Peter Ustinov also reports his aged aunts telling him there were lots of pretty girls in Russia before the Bolsheviks spoiled it all. His attitude to the Russian Revolution seems to be that everything changed and yet nothing changed, which again ignores its potential. It also contradicts his earlier sentiment, suggesting that if one bakes a cake that sinks one should refrain from any further attempts at cake baking.

After lunch I tried to read some more but fell asleep. To be honest I am bored. I went in the cellar to look at all the bikes again. They are a pile of crap I don't need. My friend gave them to me because he couldn't stand to see them go for scrap, by agreeing to take them I've made my life more complicated again. After spending six weeks living out of two panniers I've come home to a cellar full of problems. The best thing I could do is give them all to the scrap man to weigh in, but I'm as sentimental about them as he is, and he thinks by giving them to me he's saved them from destruction. The fact that all of them could be made useable is irrelevant. Asking someone to ride one would be like asking them to watch a black and white telly or pay their bills by cheque.

Apparently Cecil Rhodes once advised a nervous young officer about to go off to police a bit of the empire, 'Remember that you are an Englishman, and have consequently won first prize in the lottery of life.' Sadly some people still believe this and among the candidates in the Tory leadership contest there is a whiff of the delusion that Britain is still a world player, and short of that, the tacit admission that Britain is shit in the empty promise to make it great again.

Peter Ustinov recalls in his classroom a large print entitled *The Boy Scout's Oath*, depicting a boy scout being led by Jesus, 'who with his other hand indicated a map of the world on which the empire was lit by a strange unearthly radiance.' The empire is no more, and, only temporarily and artificially propped up by the gambling and speculation in the city, even with the help of God and his only begotten son, Britain is slowly sinking down the rankings.

Besides Boris's promise of tax cuts for the rich, other Tory hopefuls have made equally rash but slightly more progressive promises. Why they should be doing this is anyone's guess, since the pair selected for the final duel will be chosen by Tory MPs and the final victor only by about one hundred thousand Tory Party members. One may as well invite the public to give an opinion on the contestants at Crufts. Nevertheless *World at One* entered the world of radio phone-ins by subjecting one of the candidates to the public. The first question was quite predictable, to the effect – 'Isn't Brexit the greatest disaster ever to befall this great nation and should it not immediately be stopped?' I put it off before the second question – 'Have not the people voted and should not their decision to leave the EU be immediately implemented, deal or no deal?' There is little point after three years in continuing to listen to this sterile debate because, save for a few who want to leave at all costs and the few who want to remain at all costs (about which the latter are rarely honest), there isn't a politician in the land who likes either option and their endless evasions and prevarications are boring.

The young Peter Ustinov was sent to Westminster School on the eve of World War Two, where they were 'forced to dress like undertakers' and soon witnessed 'the premature signs of that nervous affectation which passes for breeding.' Like many posh boys at the time he was cajoled into the schools officer training corps section.

Yesterday the Sunday morning Radio 4 magazine program on the anniversary of D Day trailed an interview with 'a man who refused to fight.' I didn't hear the interview, but have decided, rather than either of the books I have begun, to take Peter Laufer's *The Soldiers Who Say No – True stories of soldiers who refuse to fight in Iraq.*

It is revealed that parts of the new Liverpool hospital, which was being built by Carillion before it went bust two years ago are substandard and will have to be pulled down and redone. The same outsourcing PFI system is being used to build nuclear power stations.

Day 51 – Cleckheaton to Cambridge by train

Boris Johnson is accused of allowing the Conservative Party to be portrayed as the party of privilege with his promise of tax cuts for the rich. Fancy that.

I was almost as stressed setting off the second time as I was the first. Gentle ride to Leeds, mostly on the pavement beside the traffic queues. Tea in Wetherspoon's and train to Peterborough. The earlier train had been cancelled, which is par for the course, so it was full and the seat reservations were all void, which always causes tension as people unreasonably expect to get what they have paid for.

The BBC has decided it will no longer grant free TV licences to pensioners unless they are on supplementary benefits. The government used to cover the cost, but a few years ago transferred the responsibility to the corporation. This is how they pay for tax cuts for the rich.

Other candidates for the Tory leadership, being just as opportunistic as he is, have condemned Boris Johnson's tax cuts for the rich promise. It might sound suicidal to promise tax cuts for the rich after nearly a decade of a government that has systematically transferred wealth upwards, but then Boris isn't appealing to the population at large, he's appealing to the greedy, selfish Tory faithful.

The train was late arriving in Peterborough and I missed the direct connection to Cambridge on which my bike was booked, but it didn't matter, I just had to change at Ely.

I'd had enough by Cambridge North and got off, finding my way into and out of the city to the west without too much trouble. There are thousands of people cycling in Cambridge, and half of them are on what one might call Dutch or town style bicycles, it being a flat place with miles of cycle paths and marked routes. But being a still, damp day, it was one of the worst places for diesel fumes I've been to. I could taste it in my mouth within half an hour.

Highfield Farm campsite at Comberton was easy to find in light drizzle. On the way I passed a big American cemetery, which I assume contains World War Two dead. The woman on reception said she wouldn't charge me full price as I was on my own. It was £10. I was there soon after two, which left me seven hours to kill in the rain, so I started my book.

The Soldiers Who Say No was published in 2008. On the fly leaf Howard Zinn says he hopes it will be read 'by young people who may be enticed, by false promises or deceptive patriotic exhortations, to go to war.' Michael Ratner, author of *Guantanamo: What the World Should Know* says; 'When this country gives [soldiers who refused to fight in Iraq] medals of honour I will know we live in a just society.' Ann Wright, a retired colonel in the US Army Reserve and former US diplomat says; 'In the military real courage is taking a stand against orders one believes are unlawful and accepting the consequences. Moral cowardice is taking the easy way by accepting unlawful orders and committing illegal actions. Ultimately one must live with oneself. These women and men have chosen the hard short path to freedom from the long-term emotional, spiritual and physical consequences of conducting state sponsored murder in a conflict that has nothing to do with our nation's security.' All powerful stuff – but if it were true no army could function and most wars would not have been fought. There are people, soldiers and civilians, who resist every war – they are usually punished and silenced.

In her introduction Clare Short speaks of how hard it is for the parents of soldiers to lose their children in a war in which there is no honour because lies had been used to justify it. She is right, but lies are used to justify all wars and there is no honour in any of them. Most wars are fought over resources – and the Iraq war was one of them. Thousands of soldiers and hundreds of thousands of civilians died because America wanted the oil. Full stop.

Searching for a word that covers the various people in Iraq who resisted the US led invasion Peter Laufer rejects 'terrorists' because 'it could just as accurately be used to describe American personnel in Iraq.' 'Given the US tactics, from the initial threat of a "shock and awe" attack to the assaults on cities whose populations rejected the US occupation, American actions could accurately be termed terrorism.'

Laufer decides upon 'enemy'. And then he quotes Pogo (I don't know who Pogo is, perhaps it's the nickname of a soldier), 'We have met the enemy and he is us.'

When the war started the French national newspaper *Le Monde* said 'We are all Americans.' The British press took the same line. Decency, morality, belief in the rule of law, fairness and justice should have made any right thinking person say 'We are all Iraqis.' The US was wrong and Britain was wrong to back it. When something is wrong honest people say so. If you lie to yourself about the reasons for war you'll have to keep lying to yourself all the way through the inevitable atrocities 'your' side commits and you'll be as guilty as the naïve, brainwashed and impressionable young men who do the killing. If you don't know what the war's about find out, ignorance is no excuse. If you think the war's about what the government and the mainstream media says it's about, think again, because it never is.

I'm not comfortable on my trip yet, and probably won't have enough of it left to get comfortable. If I hadn't had to break off I'd have finished by now. I wish I was at home. It's raining and it's forecast to keep raining. I'm just finishing this off because I have to finish it off.

When I went for a piss the rain was coming down in sheets. This is going to be a sad finale.

'...that's the problem with war,' says one AWOL soldier holed up in Canada, 'Your president, your generals, and all the way down to your commanding officers, they don't go out there with you. They send you out there to fight and do the crazy shit and do the dirty stuff. You're the one who has to live with the nightmares from it. You come back, you're nothing you know? Guys are living on the streets that fought in Iraq just as well as I did. I mean it's horrific... I had to do things for the wealth of other people. I blame them because they made me do it. You can lie to the world, you can't lie to a person who's seen it. They made me have to do things that a man should never have to do, for the purpose of their gain, not the people's - their financial gain. George W Bush should be the one to go to prison – but that ain't never going to happen.'

Another soldier says, 'In October of 2004 they said there's no WMD, and I just sat down and cried. That was the last straw. It was for absolutely nothing. I felt totally worthless. I sacrificed part of my humanity ...for what? For what? I can't point to a single thing. We're going to liberate the Iraqi people by killing them?

'I'm a veteran of Operation Iraqi Plunder,' he tells a conference. 'I think it is important to tell it like it is. I refuse to call it Operation Iraqi Freedom. There was no freedom over there. It was not a war to liberate Iraq. It was a war to make it safe for US business interests. It was a war of aggression and occupation. To call it Operation Iraqi Freedom is an insult to the Iraqi people and it is an insult to humanity.'

'People were saying "I'm proud of what you did over there," and I'm saying, "God I'm not. Why are you telling me you're proud of me? You don't even know what I did."' And this goes for all those who think British troops are heroes – you don't know what they did. You don't want to know what they did – because if you did know you'd either be horrified or certifiably incapable of human feeling. Given the above, the random wholesale murder of civilians, the impunity with which it was done, the destruction of whole towns and the resulting 'Islamic' reaction it might seem incredible that there are American and British people who only think western troops shouldn't be there because the Iraqis are ungrateful, but there are people who subscribe to that perverse and twisted logic. These people are ignorant and they are dangerous because they are driven by racism.

The mother of one US soldier, not entirely sympathetic to his desertion, encapsulates the attitude; 'You know these people want to get rid of us. It's another Hitler situation. They want to exterminate the white race. We've got to preserve ourselves here... I don't believe we should be over there dying for these people.' There's getting it wrong, and then there's getting it spectacularly wrong. They're the kind of people who wrote 'English' in the campsite register book above me. I always hesitate when I'm asked to write down my nationality because I don't subscribe to nationalism and I don't believe in nations. And then I write 'British' because it's not worth the argument. Next time I promise I'll write 'global citizen' or something.

One deserter turned activist says he's only fighting for the things the United States was founded on; 'The United States wasn't founded on oil. It wasn't founded on the fact that everyone has a right to lay a pipeline in Afghanistan. It wasn't founded on the fact that some guy can make money from Haliburton building things in Iraq.' Unfortunately he's incorrect. The countries and the companies might be different, but these are exactly the principles on which the US was founded. It was built on genocide and slavery under a political system deliberately designed to prevent real democracy. The US in the last seventy years has invaded over fifty countries and it has helped destabilise and topple numerous progressive regimes. Like the much vaunted principles on which Britain is founded those of the US are a mythology that can't bear the slightest exposure to the facts.

It rained all afternoon and evening and all I could do was lay in my tent and read. It's cold and I haven't brought enough clothes because it's June.

Day 52 – Cambridge to Greetham, near Stamford

(Cambridgeshire and Lincolnshire)

It rained steadily all night but I slept like a log, even falling back asleep after waking as it was getting light.

Pigeons were prominent, crows distant and the smaller birds the backdrop. There was still wetness in the air when I emerged to make coffee, having reintroduced my stove now I've got a solid back wheel. Only two other people are camping – an 'adventure' motorcyclist and a drop-handlebar cyclist with front pannier racks who is carrying his bike on a car. There are plenty of caravans, but they are on a different field.

I was only two minutes from the B1046, which I followed all the way to St Neots in light rain wearing full waterproofs, and consequently was wet through with sweat inside. Thankfully the terrain is flat or it would have been much worse. Plenty of mansions along the way, some of them thatched, some wood panelled – and the occasional oak car port or man shed.

In one village the old reading room, rather than the chapel was now a house, enlightenment no less subject to private capital than obscuritanism.

The Chequers in another village had attached to its traditional pub sign an even bigger portrait of Her Majesty in front of a big flag of St George. Such overt displays do not come without a truck load of reaction and bile and I suspect some of these backbone of England Tory village dwellers would as soon put on a fascist uniform as a suit and tie, though they would no doubt consider themselves liberals.

The next pub was called the *Crown and Cushion*, so the area has probably always been a stronghold of lickspittle, hierarchical monarchism and backwardness.

To confirm it the *Eight Bells* at Abbotsley was flying the union flag in its car park and a builder's truck advertised 'English building and restoration.' It is just possible that the builder's name was English. It is equally likely that he considers it profitable to pander to

377

the local moneyed population's prejudices – as in 'traditional fish and chips', which is code for fish and chips cooked by white people.

The road got busier towards St Neots, though not dangerous as most of the traffic was going in the opposite direction. It fined up and I was able to take my waterproofs off and began to enjoy myself again.

Cycle paths are the norm in St Neots and young people were cycling to school on them – though one lazy young man was sat between the feet of his obese parent on her electric chariot messing about with his mobile phone.

I still had the coffee stop I promised myself while it was raining, in the market place café, plus beans on toast overpriced at £4.95, which I think was run by Turkish people, the old man sitting at the top table looking on like they do. The waiter called all the male customers boss at the end of every sentence – I later discovered that this was normal for the area. The big pub on the square was shut and boarded up. There were plenty of charity shops and a very disturbed woman with her belongings in a bicycle trailer was having an episode outside Café Nero.

A woman in the café said they'd had two months rain in two days. As I crossed the bridge over the river big areas of the park and the car park next to it were under water.

I headed out on the B645 over the flat landscape with fields full of crops surprised that more of them hadn't been flattened by the rain. The hedges now full of pink flowers, possibly wild roses.

There were more mansions at Stonely and Kimbolton (a historic market town), the Bellamy Brothers were coming to play at the castle and car transporters were specifically not permitted through the village, which, as I've never seen such a sign before, suggests there's a car manufacturing plant nearby.

Kimbolton is overflowing with an exaggerated sense of its own history – with conservation spilling over into caricature. It also has a posh school and a place that quite possibly once belonged to the bloke who owned all and everything. A chapel on the outskirts now belonged to a wealth management company – a non-socially useful 'industry' that seemed to employ several people sucking up to the rich.

I took the B660 out over the long-ago closed railway. Rich people don't need railways – unless they form part of their shares portfolio or they make their money as asset strippers.

The road was practically deserted. There were by the side of it the remains of strip fields and, if outward appearances were anything to go by, the mentality that went with them. It could be argued that we are living under a new phase of feudalism.

Catford looked more modest, but pretentiousness was creeping in in its black Range Rover coupe, stealth edition, all the same identifying itself by its personalised registration plates.

In fact the strip fields were remarkable, a sloping one at *Fox Farm* in particular.

By Old Weston the sun was nearly out and a cottage was dated 1622. The community centre advertised yoga, a knit and natter and a barbeque lunch involving 'fun and games'.

Many of the pubs around here look like ordinary houses. The only thing that identifies them as pubs is one single sign up a post – there are no big names of pub or brewery on the buildings themselves. The *Swan* at Old Weston was one such.

Towards The Giddings hills began to reappear and every small village had a big church.

While I was having a rest a woman told a horse she was leading that I was just a man on a bench. Actually I'm just a man on a bicycle. There was no shortage of women who didn't have to go to work about on big shiny horses.

In Steeple Gidding the chapel belonged to a firm specialising in corporate identity – bullshit designed to fool the public. Another firm specialised in in equestrian and designer country clothing. The pub was called the *Fox and Hounds*. Average Britain it isn't.

After that I picked my way on empty unclassified roads towards Elton, safe in the knowledge that they wouldn't plunge me into a deep valley or take me over a big hill. Out there in the backwoods some of the road signs had bullet holes in them.

A pair of big white owls flew over a crop field, with one of them landing first on a road sign and then in a tree as I passed. All over, where subsidies have been earned for grubbing up hedges, subsidies are being earned for putting them back. Someone had changed the sign for Bullock Road to Bollock Road – such things always make me laugh – along with the big penises young men draw in bus shelters, which in the past would have been regarded as harmless fertility symbols.

The warm damp weather is bringing out the midges, which we don't want. One of the reasons for setting off in April was to avoid them. The other was to avoid reality.

I am informed by a roadside board that 'the picturesque Huntingdonshire village of Elton, with its pretty stone and thatched cottages and romantic stately home is well worth a visit.' I fail to see anything remotely romantic in an ostentatious mansion built on the backs of people living in shit – although the popularity of celebrity worshipping magazines today suggest that some people do.

For all its quaintness Elton is at the centre of a big estate, the answerable to no one lord having merely been replaced by an answerable to no one corporation – actually answerable to its shareholders, to whom it is legally obliged by the Companies Act to provide the best dividend possible.

Coming out of Elton on an empty road a 4x4 driver put his boot down unnecessarily to overtake me and issued fumes so noxious and acrid into the still air that I had to stop and cover my mouth and nose – this is from one vehicle. There wasn't any visible smoke, as if the engine was worn out or running badly – the normal allowable emissions just got right on the back of my throat.

Sibson Aerodrome is home to Peterborough Aero Club. In this twisted amoral society it's fine for some people to have aeroplanes while other people sleep in the street.

Wansford, once on the Great North Road and with a grand old bridge, is yellow stone, twee and definitely up-market, though one pub was called the *Paper Mill*, so there may have once been industry.

Having come up against the A1 I asked an old lad for guidance. He told me a way under it by the river, through a disused picnic area, along a wide empty stretch of the old A47 and past some kind of encampment with scrap wagons and barking dogs. He used to be a cyclist and a caravaner, but was now on a stick and said I'd still have to do a bit on the A47, which was dangerous, and he was right. But it wasn't even half a mile, giving only about six wagons time to frighten the life out of me. There was nothing wrong with the way he told me to go – it was just overgrown and neglected. It needs tidying up and extending for others who want to follow the same route without getting killed.

It's very close – jungle weather – and every time I stop I can feel midges on me [I was imagining this – I never got bitten].

A couple of mansions were under construction on the edge of Southorpe. By the memorial bench and the phone box that now houses a defibrillator were two big stones; 'Examples of Barnack rag limestone which fell from carts during transportation to the River Nene before 1450 AD for building Peterborough and Ely cathedrals.' More recently the stones were a meeting place for young people. 'More recently' gives quite a bit of scope, but it was presumably before the bungalow with the twitching curtains opposite was built.

The notice board contained an invitation to locals to get more involved with their police force by receiving regular updates on crimes, witness appeals and police events – so they could act like vigilantes. Perhaps we should bring back the armed squirarchy to police the people and do away with any pretence of neutrality – the kind of armed citizenry that gets black people gunned down in the street in the US for straying into the wrong neighbourhood.

Between Southorpe and Barnack I was riding beside what was once clearly a major railway line that probably joined the mainline a mile or two to the east, and possibly the preserved Nene Valley Railway to the south.

A yellow stone predominates and many of the buildings seem to have been built towards the end of the nineteenth century.

Barnack 'Hills and Holes' is a national nature reserve. It consists of mounds of limestone rubble from quarrying, which took place between Roman and mediaeval times.

I went round Stamford to the east via Uffington and saw potato fields full of potato-sized round pebbles, which must have been glacial and made it a bastard to harvest them. They'll need some east European people for that kind of work.

Uffington still has a manned level crossing. There can't be many of those left (when I look at my map there are six level crossings in a row on a mile of track).

Uffington Manor is still occupied by money. Whether its old money or new money is anyone's guess.

I entered Rutland, motto *'Multum in Parvo'* – much money in a small place that is. You wouldn't think it possible that there could be entire sizeable places with almost nothing but half million pound and over houses, but there are in Rutland.

It started raining again about half an hour from Rutland Caravan and Camping Park, where I intended to spend two nights, leaving my tent here to visit two places to the west, which was a bit of a pisser, but not the worst thing. Not the worst thing by far. The worst thing was being charged twenty five pounds to put my already soaking wet tent up on a deserted camping themed amusement park in the rain. This makes the site equal second in the blatant robbery table – and it's like a prisoner of war camp with a barrier that doesn't open till 7.30 unless you pay a deposit for a card, which you can't surrender till 7.30 if you want to leave.

By the time I got my tent up and got inside it was nearly six o'clock and pissing it down. I'm miles away from the toilet and shower block and I haven't got enough food, but I wasn't going to give another penny to the thieves who own this site.

There was no sign of the rain stopping and I wasn't going out to get wet again once I'd got inside only damp – so my big pan had to fulfil its secondary function – closely followed by its primary one. Cooking inside a tent is a bit of a risk, but I didn't have much choice – noodles and a bit of bread, a few oats and nuts left for breakfast.

After that there was nothing to do but get in my bag and read. So that's what I did – at probably seven o'clock.

One US soldier who fled to Canada, rather than be sent to Iraq, gives his reasons; 'I object to the Iraq War because it is an act of aggression with no defensive basis'. It has been supported by pretences that cannot stand even elementary scrutiny. First, before the US dropped the first bomb, it was quite evident the Iraq had no weapons of mass destruction. Second, the Bush administration had the gall to exploit the American people's fear of terrorists by making the absurd assertion that a secular Baathist government was working with a fundamentalist terrorist group. There was never any evidence to substantiate this. Third, the notion that the US wants to export democracy is laughable. Democracy is by the people, not an appointed puppet theatre.' All this is true. What is also true is that there is little point looking for logic in the arguments for the war. The US had decided to attack Iraq years previously, long before 9/11 (and there is a good chance the British government knew this), all it needed was some flimsy excuse.

The soldiers' barrister says, 'If you had an actual government based on people who learned something from the Vietnam War, you'd be in a better position. But the government is those who didn't serve and didn't learn.' This suggests that governments are like individuals who learn from their mistakes. Governments aren't like that. They act out of economic and political expediency. The Vietnam War wasn't 'a mistake' – it used up lots of armaments, helped develop new technologies and made some people lots of money – just like all wars do. It would have been better if the US hadn't been humiliated by a peasant army using bicycles and bamboo, but hey-ho, you can't win 'em all. The Iraq war wasn't a mistake either, and though the US lost militarily it's debateable whether they lost economically, considering they're getting the oil and rebuilding the country they destroyed. The Iraq war cost trillions of dollars – that's all grist to the mill of US capitalism. What's a few fucked up, dead and crippled working class men beside that?

Day 53 – Greetham to Ashby-de-la-Zouch

(Cambridgeshire and Lincolnshire)

With my ear plugs in I slept well. It rained all night and it's still raining. It's also windy and blowing the fly-sheet against the inner tent. I've now been inside this tent for at least twelve hours, reduced to pissing in my pan. I didn't get washed or clean my teeth last night because it would have meant bringing my wet coat and over trousers into the tent.

It would be madness to set off in this weather, but it's £25 a night to stay here and I haven't got any food, save a bit for breakfast. Even to tell them I want to stay and buy something from their shop would mean getting wet, which nature demands I'll have to do at some stage. On a global scale this is only a small disaster, but it's a disaster all the same. It rarely rains for this long in winter, let along in summer, and we're already heading for the wettest June ever. If this is to be the pattern it makes camping, even long-distance cycling, a bit of a non-starter. I suspect we may have fucked the planet up - taken beside the twenty eight degrees some places had in February. Maybe even cycling itself will become unviable. Maybe the sensible options are no longer possible and a tipping point has really been reached.

The church clock chimed, but I couldn't count the strikes for the rain lashing on the tent. It could be six or nine. From inside the tent I keep convincing myself it's brightening up, but if anything it's getting worse, the rain heavier and the wind blowing the sides of the tent in. What am I doing here? Why did I take this on? I have no need to do anything but stay at home – take day trips by bus every day if I want, even eat out. It would be cheaper than this mess – and I could sleep in my own bed every night. This is worse than the snow in Scotland and the wind on Skye.

And then for a brief moment it almost stopped and I could hear the birds and the traffic on the A1. If I set off in the rain I'll be soaked to the skin in half an hour. The clock struck eight. It's still relatively early, but I've been prostrate in this tent for fifteen hours.

I took three dextrose tablets someone had given Oades and began packing up. What's the worst thing that can happen? Whatever it is it won't kill me, and if it does so what? The rain got heavier as I was doing it.

When I went to hand in my gate key I felt like asking if they wanted to take any more money off me because I still had some left. Instead I just said thank you and was told it was their pleasure, 'boss'.

Back on the road, even though it was raining, I felt like I'd escaped – like I do when I've camped out for free, but instead because I'd escaped their clutches, with their security gates and signs everywhere for people who really should already know what they can and cannot do.

I made myself celebrate a long straight road that stretched out in front of me and once I got away from the death zone round the A1 it was quiet on the back roads, until I got to the B road for Melton Mowbray – also not too busy.

On the way there were numerous well-preserved strip fields that clearly hadn't been cultivated since the peasants were driven off, to be replaced with the animals that still occupy them. As if to symbolise how the rich ride roughshod over the people, then and now, a point to point course crossed some of them.

Some might say the peasants had to be driven off the land in order for civilisation to progress, but that depends on whether you judge civilisation by superficial criteria, by art, buildings, parliaments and organised religion, or by how people live and coexist with each other. On the latter criteria we are hardly beyond barbarians.

Otherwise there was standing water and running rivers all over the road and streams, and rivers that were almost dry when I set off are fit to burst their banks.

On entering Melton I sought out a café to recover from about fifteen miles – over two hours – of exposure to the elements. My hands were numb, my map was wet and so was I – in fact I was thoroughly soaked.

The old blokes in the café were talking about the operations they'd had. 'Think how much that must have cost,' said one, 'if you'd had to pay for it you wouldn't get it.' Indeed, and the next generation of working people won't – it'll be like in the US where the Red Cross is providing health care and people die for the lack of funds for treatment. There wasn't a thought for all the money they'd paid in.

Then the women who work there got on about the idiots on the roads in the bad weather – still driving like maniacs. They don't know the half of it.

When I got my wallet out to pay my wad of twenty pound notes had turned into a solid wet mass. In Morrison's, where I went to resupply, not wanting to get caught out with insufficient food again, my wet note wouldn't go through the new machines that check for forgeries and a supervisor had to be called.

Deprived of danger I planned to take the A606 towards Nottingham for Ab Kettleby, but on the way through town came upon a Premier Inn. I went in to see if they had a room, but it was a computerised check in desk, and though I pressed the button for assistance three times no-one came.

It was a good job really because my plan to cycle to Ab Kettleby and then to Ashby-de-la-Zouch and ride back tonight was mad. Twenty minutes later I rode through Ab Kettleby, my 24th destination, but it took the rest of the day to ride to Ashby. It was hard, and when I got there I could hardly function. It stopped raining non-stop, but there were a couple of heavy showers and I was wet through again after drying a bit in the café in Melton.

And then I had to search for accommodation, trying one place at the other side of town that was full before being directed back to the Premier Inn just off the road I'd come in on.

They had a room, but the receptionist primed me for it being expensive, 'because we're quite full and there's an event in town.' It was £98, but to be honest I didn't care. I just wanted to get my soaking wet clothes off and get a warm drink. The more people wanting a room, the more expensive they are. There's no such thing as a fixed price any more. It's supply and demand, but it used to be called profiteering.

I spread my clothes all over the room and hung my tent in the bathroom, before reviewing my maps and watching shit on TV.

After the first ballot Boris Johnson is favourite for the Tory leadership, a possibility that seemed ridiculous only a few months ago due to his bigotry and racism.

On the way here I saw a Cemex wagon pulling out of its depot emblazoned with a union flag and 'Building a Greater Britain.' Not only is cement a very environmentally damaging product, but Britain is not going to regain the greatness it obtained in raping the world by building endless yuppie houses. Britain's inexorable decline cannot be arrested by the pouring of ever more concrete any more than can the wider problems of humanity be solved by it. And any artificial boom the Tories do manage to create by giving carte blanche to their millionaire donors in the construction industry to build what they like, where they like, will not only consume thousands of acres of wildlife habitat and food production land but it will lead to an eventual and inevitable slump for which ordinary people will pay the price. I'm not entirely convinced by the 'there aren't enough homes' argument which has now become the orthodoxy. There'd be a lot more if we took one off all the people that have two – without compensation as they bought them with money they clearly didn't need. Then we could kick all the lords and ladies, and all the would-be lords and ladies, out of their multi-room mansions and make them into social housing. Whether there's a shortage of homes or not it's not going to be solved by building modern day palaces in the Cotswolds – that's a homes for votes scandal Shirley Porter could only dream of. Several other trucks had union flags as part of their logo and Lidl has joined in with big flags in its window. It seems the shitter Britain gets the more people resort to empty patriotism.

One of the main responses of US soldiers who refused to serve in Iraq, when it was pointed out that they were volunteers and knew what they were letting themselves in for, was that they were lied to by recruiters, who are no doubt on bonuses. They were promised cash hand-outs to get them out of financial straits (which they usually did not receive), that they would be given noncombatant roles, or that they wouldn't be sent to Iraq at all. These promises were hollow.

Their advocates in Canada dismiss the notion that there's any such thing as an army volunteer – '…young Americans are compelled to join the army because of an "economic draft" and a "poverty draft."' The US also operates a "stop loss" system, whereby soldiers whose contracted period of service is nearing its end are prevented from leaving if they are needed for a war. 'The net effect is not much different than conscription.'

One of them goes further; 'Iraq is where the US has to be defeated – categorically defeated. We have to impose the kind of limit on the US ability to conduct mayhem around the world that was imposed by the Vietnam defeat. There's only a few ways that can happen. There has to be a refusal within the military to participate, and obviously there has to be a refusal around the world to support it. [As I type this British ministers are pledging their blanket support for any aggression the US may mete out to Iran].

Lenin advocated 'Revolutionary Defeatism'. If your country is involved in an aggressive war it needs to lose. If it wins it strengthens the warmongering politicians who started it. If it loses it weakens them. Blair could have been brought down by a popular refusal to support the war in Iraq by soldiers and civilians. The same goes for George W Bush.

I could pretend I've enjoyed the riding today, but I'd be lying to myself. No one enjoys riding on major roads in the rain soaked to the skin. And besides the bad weather this week generally I've been driven off the road, shouted at, ripped off, stinking and exhausted. And I have endlessly been affronted by the blatant disparities that exist under this so-called democracy. If Britain was really a democracy this situation could not and would not pertain. Only by subverting democracy can the rich maintain power.

A lesser man, perhaps one who wasn't combat trained, might have given up. I may not have the sense I was born with, but I have stamina, dedication and principles. I'm never doing anything like this again. This is my last big trip.

Day 54 – Ashby-de-la-Zouch to Keadby, via Camborne and Laceby

(Leicestershire and Lincolnshire)

Got up at the first sign of light, before four, for an ambitious ride to a campsite near Lincoln I'd spotted on the map, but first I have to visit Packington to the south of Ashby.

All my belongings are perfectly dry. My tent is as dry as when it came out of the shop, but the forecast is for similar weather.

Chukka Umuna, who left the Labour Party for 'a new kind of politics' and founded the short-lived and imaginatively named 'Change', which stood for nothing but remaining in the EU, has joined the Liberal Democrats, the party that propped up the Tories in coalition. The cynicism and careerism of these people beggars belief. Liberalism is the last bastion of a scoundrel. Dr Johnson says patriotism is the last bastion of a scoundrel, but many Labour politicians have descended into patriotism long before it becomes apparent they are nothing more than liberals. In any case liberalism and patriotism are bedfellows since liberalism means only free trade – 'free trade' being a euphemism for a situation in which the weak are forced to trade with the strong at a disadvantage – witness Trump's insistence that the NHS is opened up to US capital as the price of a new trade deal.

While I was getting ready there was an extended interview with a retired professional cricketer who'd gone off the rails with drink and philandery. It was a salutary lesson, and was perhaps meant to be. I wondered if he had a book out. He had.

I was back out in the rain at five o'clock and fifteen minutes later riding up the main street of Packington, the twenty third place on my list I have condemned myself to visit. From there I retraced my steps to Melton Mowbray in sporadic downpours, looking forward to the same café I was in yesterday.

On the way I saw a truck belonging to a company which makes bedding. Its motif was a bulldog wearing a union jack waistcoat. We've really entered a danger zone when sad little patriots feel they can use their businesses as a vehicle for their right wing views. Any progressive and organised workforce would tell the boss to get the jingoistic shit off the wagons or they weren't going anywhere.

It was too early for the nice cafe and I had to make do with Greggs, but any half hour out of the rain was welcome. I indulged myself with two of their famous vegan sausage rolls and a jam doughnut and went back for another doughnut and a second cup of coffee.

The end is in sight – I'm on my next to last map sheet.

Not long after Melton the passenger in a car shouted at me 'Get off the fucking road.'

I could have made the campsite near Lincoln, but a road diversion sent me away from it. It was then I decided to attempt the last two destinations today and to get to our Eddie's for bedtime.

By Woodhall Spa I had a blood sugar crisis and had to take two dextrose tablets. That's what it's come to – a quiet ride through back roads stopping at country pubs, to a mad dash on main roads eating sugar lumps so I don't faint.

Horncastle Garden Centre is part of the British Garden Centre Group. Their symbol is a poppy, because they too are poncing on the symbolism of cynical remembrance.

I hammered north by B roads to the A46 and then east to Camborne and Laceby, my last two destinations. Then I retraced my steps to Caistor and took the B road west till I hit the Trent, following it north to Keadby and found Eddie and Shirley's house straight away. Having condensed this visiting of my last two destinations into one short paragraph I've made it sound easy. But it wasn't – it was desperate.

My nearest sibling, Gordon, is staying with Eddie and Shirley. I haven't seen him for over twenty five years, but we still didn't seem to have anything to say to each other. After spending years in Greece and Germany he starts a job in the Golden Wonder factory five miles away at five tomorrow morning and went to bed soon after I arrived.

Shirley looked it up and reckons I've cycled 130 miles today, which is mad. The whole trip has been mad, the expense, the stupid mileages, the pointlessness of just riding hard all day, grabbing something to eat at the side of the road without sitting down. Shirley said, 'But you'll be glad you did it.' I said I didn't know.

While I ate a big bowl of pasta and Eddie went to the cashpoint for my sponsorship money, Shirley, a career foster carer, told me about her battle with cancer. Their adopted son, David was killed in Iraq after leaving the army once and re-enlisting. He was ignominiously drowned when the vehicle he was in plunged into a canal during the night. He had been in trouble with the police and when he was thinking of joining up Shirley wouldn't let me talk to him, having possibly come to the conclusion that the army was his only option. When I was fifteen in 1972 the army wasn't my only option and I have my bastard of a stepmother to thank for the fact that the army robbed me of my formative years and made me the man I am. Unlike most of the population I *have* held a loaded rifle in my hands and been taught how to kill someone with it. Fortunately for me I never did. Though I went to Northern Ireland twice I was spared first-hand the trauma of that awful conflict.

I have never spoken to Eddie and Shirley about the Iraq War or David's death. I suspect they would like to believe he was doing something useful at least – perhaps even that he was a hero. Actually his life was wasted in a senseless, futile and illegal war fuelled by greed and vanity and the people who launched it should be in jail for crimes against humanity. The chasm that has opened up between Muslims and non-Muslims around the world and the drift to the right across Europe is entirely their doing.

With regard to heroes, I suspect that most parents know that their sons were nothing of the kind. 'Hero' is a label assigned by opportunist politicians and overweight wasters who only seek to bathe in the reflected glory of someone else's war. There was nothing heroic about the Iraq War and no one comes out of with any glory. It was also the latest in a litany of imperialist adventures perpetrated by a country that has somehow managed to obtain a reputation as the world's policeman. If the US is the world's policemen it is the biggest bent cop ever and Britain has perjured itself in backing up its lies.

Shirley said Gordon had decided to come back to Britain because of Brexit (?), because of his pension and because he's getting older. He's sixty. I have no idea what Gordon has been doing for the last twenty five years. When he left school in about 1974 he went straight into engineering and served his time as a metal turner. This was before all the big engineering firms in Bradford closed. They once employed thousands of people.

So that's all twenty six places visited. I don't need maps anymore. I know my way home from here.

One of the reasons I carried on today was because I couldn't bear to arrive at a campsite at two o'clock. I'd be bored for six hours. When I'm in a hotel I put the TV on to stop myself getting bored, just like everyone else does. One of the things about the trip has been its intensity – you don't have to do anything else, just cycle. There's no time to get bored. The trip filled some time.

Darrel Anderson joined the US Army just before the invasion of Iraq. He joined because he needed healthcare, money to go to college and money to take care of his daughter. Joining the army was the only way he was going to get these things.

He also swallowed the bullshit about protecting his country and he wanted to be a hero. It didn't take him long to realise that the Iraqis didn't want their liberators there, or to hear other soldiers bragging about kicking Iraqi prisoners to death. He deserted rather than go back, saying that if he was an Iraqi faced with an invading force that destroyed everyday life, threw people in prison for no reason and killed people with impunity he'd do exactly what the insurgents did. He didn't want to have to live with having murdered innocent people.

Day 55 – Keadby to Cleckheaton

(Lincolnshire and Yorkshire)

I left *The Soldiers who say no* on the bedside table last night before Shirley made up the bed. I knew she would see it, but it never occurred to me the connection it would make. She possibly now thinks I left it there on purpose.

I left Eddie and Shirley at 7.30 and followed the Trent north through the villages with the breeze behind me. Who knows what once went on in these riverside places?

In Garthorpe some shallow patriot was flying his flag upside-down – making it a hat-trick for the trip. The pub was shut and the railway long gone. There was another upside-down flag to spoil the neat set – the ignorance regarding the flag a symbol of the profound ignorance regarding the nation and its history.

Then it was Whitgift, with its *Falcon Mews*, *Sheldon Lodge* and *The Old Smithy* and the stump of a lighthouse on the river. It's exclusive enough that you need your name on your car and a car to get anywhere (though to be honest it did see a couple of buses). And more importantly it's white – a piece of old England with old England's prejudices and twenty-first century trappings. In fact there are flags all over, including St George and the Three Lions – and none of it has anything to do with football. I wonder what Eddie and Shirley think of Muslims. Do they think it was they and not Tony Blair who got their son killed?

At Swinefleet someone had fixed a notice to his fence in this community, to the effect 'Want to do yoga? – Start by bending over and picking up your dog shit.'

A westerly wind picked up. It's going to be a hard ride home.

Goole's sign says it's a Haven of Opportunity. I'm not convinced. There'd been a ram-raid at the Co-op in Old Goole. Two police cars were in attendance and it was surrounded by incident tape.

There'd certainly been an opportunity for Tim Martin to make the old bank into a big pub so I fortified myself with one of his vegan breakfasts before turning into the wind.

393

The couple on the next table were discussing her weight – she was massive and looking for low-calorie recipes. Then she put a load of sugar in her coffee and said it was hard to go to the gym what with work and cleaning the house. The bloke was on thin ice. Then they discussed the merits of a book written by a gay woman they both knew (I think the woman was some kind of agent), but not a book about being gay. It was a very in depth conversation in which the big bearded man expressed a rare understanding of relationships. It went on throughout my breakfast.

It was nine o'clock when I left Wetherspoon's and headed through Goole centre.

After the Boothferry Bridge I turned left for Barmby on the Marsh on the marked cycle route. To be honest I was worn out and the last thing I needed was to have to cycle into the wind.

Asselby has a new war memorial for a war that's still being fought over – as if sacrificing millions of men to retain an ill-gotten empire was our finest hour. There are scarlet poppies everywhere in the fields.

Home via Selby, Hillam, Burton Salmon, Fairburn, Allerton Bywater, Wakefield and Osset.

In Allerton Bywater, an ex-mining town, there was an 'English and Proud' leaflet in the window of a shitty little terrace. There was a George Cross flying over someone's garage. These people are racists pure and simple – whatever the reason. It was open day at the big dragline left over from the open cast pit that is now a nature reserve.

I'd no sooner got on the greenway/dog toilet at Ossett when a man with two dogs, who I was sure had seen me from a distance coming up behind, walked diagonally across the path in front of me. I was riding slowly and said gently 'Coming past mate.' He said 'Couldn't you ring your bell? I could have walked into you,' and as I passed, 'You haven't got a bell, you should have a bell, come back here I'm a police officer.' I didn't stop. If he was a police officer he should have known that you are not legally obliged to have a bell on a bicycle at all. I fail to see the difference between warning someone verbally that you intend to pass and ringing a bell at them, which I have always considered impolite. Perhaps I should say 'ring ring,' but that wouldn't satisfy those anti-bicycle dog owners who are determined to complain about something. In my experience dog owners are mostly miserable bastards who hate everybody. I must have come almost to a stop for a dozen unrestrained dogs between Ossett and Cleckheaton. I hate dogs.

When I wasn't thinking about dogs I was thinking how tired I am of the roar of cars, of bumpy roads and cycle paths, of fumes, of being soaked wet through. Tired of being in my tent, of being ripped off, of eating rubbish, of watching crap on TV in hotel rooms. But mostly I was just tired, dog tired.

I thought of things I could do instead, the things I like doing – reading, making things, cooking, eating, writing. My plan is to type up this diary, possibly make it into a book, and I fancy making a dummy engine for a bicycle to represent the early motorcycles – the kind of motorcycle I'd have built if I hadn't given up building motorcycles. But that's another story.

Even though the wind wasn't really in front of me most of the way home it was a real struggle. Yesterday's mammoth sixteen hours riding and 130 miles really finished me off. I was so tired I was seeing things – mostly things moving that weren't there and blocks of bright colours.

There were good parts of the ride early on, but since Devon it's been full on all day, and the last five days have been the worst of the lot. I've raised money for my charity, but I could have just given them my own money and read a big book.

I was in the house on the point of collapse at half past three. In my post ride despondency I said to Oades that I might have instead gone on numerous day trips on the bus for the cost of the two months I'd been away. She said bus trips were something you might do at sixty five, whereas my cycle adventure was the endeavour of a younger man. It's the same 'old before your time' discussion we've had before.

Two cabinet members have criticised Jeremy Corbyn for suggesting there's insufficient evidence to blame Iran for an attack on two oil tankers in the Gulf of Oman during the week – with one of them asking why he never supports the country he says he wants to lead – in other words suggesting he is unpatriotic. Naturally the BBC repeated this slur gleefully as it always does. All Corbyn has said is that the incident should not lead to an escalation of violence – a reasonable sentiment one might expect, and one also expressed by an ex-defence minister. Britain has a record of going to war on bad evidence (i.e. Lies) and Corbyn, the traitor, was right last time. The situation is currently complicated by Donald Trump's sabre rattling against Iran and a war with the country is far from an impossibility.

By the time I'd had a bath and a few cups of tea I was already starting to look back on the trip fondly. Oades told me that immediately she had posted her last bulletin saying I had finished the ride an old friend donated £150. I tried to read, but couldn't stay awake and went to bed at eight o'clock.

Looking back the high points were when my bicycle gained me an introduction and I got talking to people, the old soldiers, both ex-military and otherwise. I have no doubt that I could find people as interesting and diverse in my own city and that I had no need to traverse the country. This reinforced my idea that I might go around Bradford with my brass bike and record the conversations it got me into. The bicycle always was, and remains, a social tool – at its best it's the clergyman visiting his flock and the matron doing her rounds, the rides with friends chatting side by side on quiet roads.

I pretended to myself that I was torn between bringing my computer out of the loft, where it had been parcelled up since I decided I would live my life rather than endlessly writing about it, or just putting all my note books in a box and forgetting about them with the hundreds of others. I decided that if there is a story to be told I should tell it. In any case my notebooks are disordered and would be as unintelligible to me if I left them as they are as they would be to anyone else.

Within two days it felt like I'd never been away. The mammoth trip which had seemed to be everything while I was doing it just melted into the past. Everyone I saw told me I'd lost weight

At a bicycle show before I left a clever fellow told me to my face that the geared rear hub in my bike was worth more than the rest of the bike put together. That man is a philistine. He knows nothing about human creativity, nothing about the pride you can have in something you've made yourself, nothing about the attachment you can have to a machine, nothing about cycle touring. He knows the price of everything and the value of nothing. Actually my bike was worth more than all the other bikes in the hall put together because it's a one-off and I made it with my own hands, my own sweat and the skin of my own knuckles. I should have asked him where was the bike he'd built and how many miles had he done on it? Or said 'that depends if you measure everything in monetary terms.' Personally I don't and I've probably now done 5,000 miles on my heavy, ugly, impractical bicycle. And all that solo cycling has given me plenty of time to think...

Just Cycling

Because the world's in shit-state
I like to get out on my bike
To take my mind off the troubles
I just look at things I like
I like a bit of mud
And I like a bit of water
I like to see a father
Out cycling with his daughter
I like to see the gridlock
Caused by the petrol heads
Then turn off on the by-ways
With all their ancient threads
I like to ride in sunshine
I like to ride in rain

I like the moral high ground
And the barren plain
I like to ride in waterproofs
I like to ride in shorts
I like to ward off naysayers
And all the smug retorts
I'm cycling as a metaphor
I'm cycling for the truth
I'm cycling for the NHS
And cycling for the youth
I'm cycling for the poor and sick
And I'm cycling for the old
I'm up against the bastards
Who like their cycling cold
I'm cycling for my heart rate
I'm cycling for my blood
But most of all we're cycling
Because it does us good
I'm cycling as a simile
I'm cycling as a sign
I'm cycling to signify
That your injuries are mine
I'm cycling for the dispossessed
I'm cycling for the poor
I'm cycling for the Sabbath
As well as Yom Kippur
I cycle to Gurdwara
And ride to Friday Prayers
If Atheists had a festival
I'd ride my bike to theirs
Should I express a sentiment
You're programmed to dislike
I'm not aboard a hobby-horse
I'm just riding my bike.

The money I raised on this trip has gone to help desperate people from all over the world who have fled war, oppression and persecution, sought refuge in Britain and received assistance from DASH (Destitute Asylum Seekers Huddersfield), where I work as a volunteer. If you would like to know more about DASH's work or would like to make a donation please see www.huddsdash.org. It goes without saying that the opinions expressed in this book are my own and are not necessarily shared by the good people at DASH.

I am indebted to everyone who sponsored and supported me and helped to make the ride a success – and also to the clients, staff, volunteers and trustees at DASH for enriching my life. Many thanks also to Oades, mostly just for being there, but also for proof reading the text. Any remaining mistakes are entirely her fault.

Dave Ramsden, February 2020

Printed in Great Britain
by Amazon